Building the Black City

The publisher and the University of California Press Foundation gratefully acknowledge the generous support of the Peter Booth Wiley Endowment Fund in History.

The publisher also gratefully acknowledges the generous support of the Literati Circle of the University of California Press Foundation, whose members are Gary Kraut, Melony and Adam Lewis, Judith and Kim Maxwell, and The Dido Fund.

Building the Black City

THE TRANSFORMATION OF AMERICAN LIFE

Joe William Trotter, Jr.

UNIVERSITY OF CALIFORNIA PRESS

University of California Press
Oakland, California

© 2024 by Joe William Trotter, Jr.

Library of Congress Cataloging-in-Publication Data

Names: Trotter, Joe William, author.
Title: Building the black city : the transformation of American life /
    Joe William Trotter, Jr.
Description: Oakland, California : University of California Press, [2024] |
    Includes bibliographical references and index.
Identifiers: LCCN 2024013153 (print) | LCCN 2024013154 (ebook) |
    ISBN 9780520344419 (hardback) | ISBN 9780520975514 (ebook)
Subjects: LCSH: Cities and towns—United States—Growth—History. |
    African American neighborhoods—United States. | African Americans—
    Civil rights—United States. | Urban African Americans—United States.
Classification: LCC HT384.U6 T84 2024 (print) | LCC HT384.U6 (ebook) |
    DDC 305.896/07301732—dc23/eng/20240618
LC record available at https://lccn.loc.gov/2024013153
LC ebook record available at https://lccn.loc.gov/2024013154

Manufactured in the United States of America

33   32   31   30   29   28   27   26   25   24
10   9   8   7   6   5   4   3   2   1

To Bryan, Jeffrey, and Melvin C. Anderson, Jr.
In memory of your beloved cousin and my wife H. LaRue Trotter

CONTENTS

ILLUSTRATIONS

FIGURES

MAPS

ACKNOWLEDGMENTS

As always, it is a joy writing acknowledgments to recognize and thank a few of the many people who have helped to make my research and writing possible over the years. First and foremost, I thank Carnegie Mellon University for providing an extraordinarily supportive environment for scholarship, teaching, and public service on the African American experience. University encouragement include most notably support for the Center for Africanamerican Urban Studies and the Economy (CAUSE) and the Giant Eagle University Professorship of History and Social Justice. More specifically, I am especially grateful to Nico Slate, my Department Head; Richard Scheines, Dean of the Dietrich College of Humanities and Social Sciences; Jim Garrett, Provost; Ramayya Krishnan, Dean of the Heinz College of Information Systems and Public Policy; Wanda Heading-Grant, Vice Provost for Diversity, Equity, and Inclusion and Chief Diversity Officer; and Farnam Jahanian, President of Carnegie Mellon University.

Building the Black City is also indebted to numerous other friends, colleagues, students, and staff members within and beyond CMU. At Carnegie Mellon, for their consistent support of my work at the interface of the academy and the larger Pittsburgh metropolitan region, I wish to express my gratitude to our CAUSE Advisory Board: Eric Anderson, Edda Fields-Black, Andrew Masich, Katherine Barbera, and Evan Frazier. In addition to Department of History colleagues Joel Tarr and Wendy Goldman, special thanks to Arlie Chipps, administrative assistant and CAUSE Program Coordinator; Natalie Taylor, business manager; current and former graduate student research assistants Stacey Akines, Michael White, Arko Dasgupta, Wyatt Erchak, and Clayton Vaughn-Roberson (now PhD, and Assistant Professor in the Department of History, University of South Alabama). This book also benefited from the thoughtful input of undergraduate students Paloma Del Toro, Grady Kenix, Joshua Odunade, and Josiah Smith, and graduate student Manique Braziel Johnson, all enrolled in my team-taught course on African Americans, race, and the fight for reparations in historical and comparative perspective.

Among colleagues at other universities, I wish to thank my longtime friend and collaborator Dr. Earl Lewis, the Thomas C. Holt Distinguished Professor of History and Director, Center for Social Solutions at the University of Michigan. Under Earl's leadership, this book was also shaped by participation in the national three-year A. W. Mellon–funded "Crafting Democratic Futures Project" on reparations. Writing and research partners for the Pittsburgh component of the CDF project greatly enhanced work on this book. These scholars, activists, and community leaders included historians Laurence Glasco, Rob Ruck, and Benjamin Houston; sociologist Waverly Duck; journalist Tony Norman; past president and CEO of the Urban League of Greater Pittsburgh Esther Bush; and educators, cultural consultants, and community fellows Patricia Pugh Mitchell and Carla Young, among others.

Building the Black City also owes a huge debt to my colleagues and co-editors—Leslie M. Harris, Northwestern University; Clarence Lang, Pennsylvania State University; and Rhonda Y. Williams, Wayne State University—for the book *Black Urban History at the Crossroads: Race and Place in the American City* (University of Pittsburgh Press, 2024), a collection of essays based on two CAUSE state of the field conferences. I also extend thanks to the Urban History Association (UHA) (Andrew Sandoval-Strausz, president), and David Goldfield, editor of the *Journal of Urban History*, for the opportunity to deliver and publish my recent UHA Presidential Address on the topic "Building the Black City: Expanding the Case for Reparations for Descendants of African People Enslaved in America."

Equally important, for their abiding support of my work, I am also grateful to my labor and working class history colleagues Will Jones, Liesl Orenic, Jacqueline Jones, Ron Lewis, and others. Moreover, as a work of historical synthesis, this book leans on the contributions of scholars working in the urban field over more than a century. Without their foundational research, this book would not be possible. To my colleagues, living and deceased, I extend sincere thanks and appreciation for your scholarship. To readers of this volume, please peruse the footnotes and bibliography at the end of this text for a sample of the many scholars who have made this book possible.

Finally, I am much obliged to the University of California Press, especially editor Niels Hooper, editorial assistant Nora Becker, and cartographer Bill Nelson, for their diligent work on the production of this book. In addition, special thanks to independent copyeditor Susan Whitlock, who not only provided indispensable editorial work on the book, but also offered compelling suggestions for strengthening the organization and argument of the study ahead of its submission for peer review.

As always, for their enduring love and support, I owe my deepest and most profound gratitude to my family, the Trotter-14 siblings (now the Trotter-12), and my late wife H. LaRue Trotter. They are the principal inspiration for all that I do. In accord with the centrality of family in my work, this book is dedicated with love and appreciation to my cousins-in-law, in memory of their beloved cousin and my wife H. LaRue Trotter.

Introduction

FRAMING THE BLACK CITY-BUILDING PROCESS

IN THE WAKE of the coronavirus pandemic and the escalation of deadly police violence against young Black men and women, calls for social justice not only intensified. They also resulted in a massive groundswell of demands for reparations for generations of racial injustice from the onset of the transatlantic slave trade through recent times. Over the past decade, scholarship on the destructive impact of slavery, Jim Crow, and the emerging postindustrial order offered compelling support for the development of reparative justice programs for descendants of African people enslaved in America. However, as we accent the material, psychic, and spiritual damage of racial capitalism on the lives of Black Americans and strengthen the rationale for reparations, *Building the Black City* reminds us that the case for restorative justice must include more than the debilitating impact of racial injustice on the bodies and spirits of Black folk. The case for reparations must also include a profound appreciation for the creativity and productivity of African Americans working on their own behalf. Even as their unpaid and underpaid labor enriched the nation's economic, political, and cultural elites, African Americans set about building their own Black city within the city. This was a major achievement of people living and working under ongoing duress from the advent of the transatlantic slave trade through the opening decades of the new millennium.

But how should we define the Black city? The notion of a Black city is by no means new. As early as 1945, in their classic *Black Metropolis: A Study of Negro Life in a Northern City*, sociologists St. Clair Drake and Horace R. Cayton gave substantial attention to the political and cultural aspects of Chicago's city-building process under the rubric "Bronzeville," but they also defined the Black metropolis in geographical, spatial, and physical terms as "a city within the city—a narrow tongue of land, seven miles in length and one and one-half miles in width, where more than 300,000 Negroes are packed solidly—in the heart of [the predominantly white] Midwest Metropolis."[1] Nonetheless, the meaning of the Black metropolis or Black city remains unclear or rather contested terrain. In concluding work on a recent anthology, *Black Urban History at the Crossroads: Race and Place in the American City*, the editors (Leslie M. Harris, Clarence Lang, Rhonda Y. Williams, and myself) confronted the definitional problem head on.[2] For some scholars of Black urban life, the idea of a Black city not only seems misleading, but also seems to distort the historical record. Historically, as Harris, a historian of colonial and early America, noted, Blacks in America have never fully controlled the resources and power of urban spaces. "So, what is the (singular) 'Black City'?"[3]

In addition to underscoring the ways that Black people built their own city, this book also aims to clarify the Black city-building process in historical perspective. It builds on the interdisciplinary theoretical and conceptual insights of recent twenty-first century scholarship on the subject. Research in a variety of disciplines—history, sociology, architecture, and geography—has focused increasing attention on the different ways that African Americans have influenced the built environment of American cities.[4] Together, this scholarship acknowledges the diverse physical, geographical, institutional, cultural, and political threads of the city-building process and offers a fuller and more complete portrait of the Black city—one that moves well beyond the usual emphases on its physical configuration as a racially segregated space or neighborhood. In their innovative book *Chocolate Cities: The Black Map of American Life* (2018), sociologists Marcus Hunter and Zandria Robinson connect the rise of majority-Black cities in late twentieth-century America to the long history of Black community-building before the onset of the Great Migration.[5]

According to Hunter and Robinson, "For generations these chocolate cities—Black neighborhoods, places on the other side of the tracks, the bottoms—had been the primary locations of the freedom struggles, the sights and sounds of Black art and Black oppression, and the container for the combined ingredients of pain, play, pleasure, and protest that comprise the Black experience."[6] Similarly, in their pioneering collection of essays, *"We Shall Independent Be": African American Place Making and the Struggle to Claim Space in the United States* (2008), architecture and planning historians Angel David Nieves and Leslie Alexander treat "space-making" as much

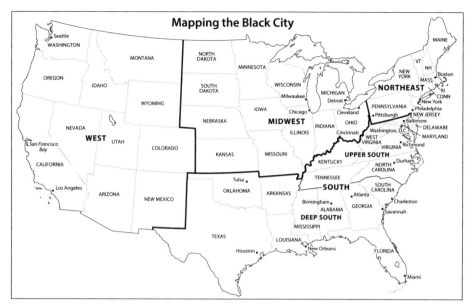

MAP I. The urban map of the United States illuminates Black city-building as a national phenomenon. It also suggests variations on the city-building theme from place to place. The cluster of regional cities—North, South, and West—identified on this map is the primary focus of this book.

more than "just documenting physical space." It also includes "intellectual and spiritual spaces of resistance and self-definition."[7] Likewise, architecture historian Brian Goldstein recently explained that late twentieth-century changes in Harlem "did not arise solely through the actions of opportunistic speculators or middle-class outsiders.... Residents themselves, through the social movements they joined and organizations they shaped, helped to produce the Harlem that we find today."[8]

Informed by these compelling definitional and conceptual insights, I define the Black city and city-building process in cross-cutting socioeconomic, spiritual, political, and spatial terms as a mode of self-emancipation for Black people. Based on a broad range of existing historical studies—local, regional, urban, labor, social, political, elite, middle- and working-class—this book explores the development of Black urban communities from their late colonial and early national beginnings through recent times. It shows how African Americans repeatedly built and rebuilt their communities across all regions of the country—the urban North, South, and West—against the violent backdrop of recurring state and civilian assaults on their civil and human rights, including the right to the city.

In 1825, Andrew Williams, a twenty-five-year-old African American boot-black, purchased three plots of farmland from John Whitehead, a New York City landowner.[9] Located between what later would become West Eighty-Third and West Eighty-Eighth Streets and Seventh and Eighth Avenues, the area became Seneca Village, New York's largest early nineteenth-century African American community. In 1853, however, the municipality condemned Seneca Village, destroyed African American homes and institutions, and made way for the building of New York City's famous Central Park. African American residents scattered across the landscape in search of new space to reestablish their homes, families, and communities. The institutional infrastructure—religious, fraternal, entrepreneurial, and political—that they built not only serviced the needs of Black residents and eased their dependence on the racialized capitalist market. It also left an indelible mark on the landscape and built environment of the many cities in which African Americans lived and worked. At the same time, against extraordinary odds, African Americans used their urban spaces to organize social movements against the institution of slavery during the nineteenth century; the Jim Crow system during the twentieth century; and the postindustrial age of "color blind" inequality during the late twentieth and early twenty-first century.[10] We do not yet know how successful grassroots activism will be in demolishing today's system of racial injustice. Even so, *Building the Black City* illuminates how the organized Black metropolis helped to eclipse manifestations of white supremacy in the past (namely slavery and Jim Crow) and can inspire movements for social justice in the present.[11]

The book is divided into two straightforward but overlapping chronological and geographical sections. Part I (chapters 1–4) charts the development of Black life in the urban South from its origins during the colonial and revolutionary years through the early twentieth century. It illustrates how African American urbanization was more pronounced in the early Lower South than it was in the Northeast. By the turn of the nineteenth century, chapter 1 shows how Charleston, New Orleans, and Savannah had emerged as majority or near-majority Black cities in the Deep South. By the late antebellum years distinctive African American communities, with their own institutional infrastructure, slowly took shape in New Orleans and Charleston in areas called "Congo Square" and the "Neck," respectively. In Savannah, however, leading Black institutions, most notably the First and Second African Baptist churches, developed in the white-majority Franklin and Green wards of the city. These different forms of community led to liberation politics that varied somewhat from city to city.

Chapter 2 examines how the post-revolutionary rise of the urban Upper South framed the African American fight for freedom and space on the middle ground of Washington, Baltimore, and Richmond. In significant ways, the road to liberty, independence, and community development was much more difficult in the urban Upper South than it was in the Northeast or even the urban Deep South. Slaveholding Maryland, Virginia, and the District of Columbia rejected the gradual manumission legislation that fueled the abolition of slavery in New York, Boston, and Philadelphia during the early nineteenth century. Upper South states and the District of Columbia also emancipated fewer women and children of mixed-race relationships, including by means of bequests of land, money, and property, than their counterparts in Charleston, Savannah, and New Orleans.

Limited access to emancipation notwithstanding, enslaved Black men and women in the urban Upper South used a variety of overlapping economic, political, and institutional events to press their claims for emancipation, access to property, citizenship rights, and opportunities to build their own families and communities. The confluence of growing revolutionary ideology, egalitarian religious sentiment, regional economic transformation, and the rise of a vigorous antislavery movement strengthened the African American quest for liberation. Black people harnessed these diverse historical developments to their own self-interests and negotiated agreements to hire and live out on their own, purchase their freedom, and embark upon a new life as free people of color. By the onset of the Civil War, most enslaved Blacks had obtained their freedom in the urban Upper South, where they fashioned their own preindustrial communities.

Following the devastation of the Civil War and the emancipation of some four million enslaved people, the African American quest for land, freedom, and their own metropolis took on special significance in the expanding "new" urban-industrial South. Chapter 3 documents the rise of Birmingham's central city Black Business District (BBD); Atlanta's Auburn Avenue and Decatur Street district, which adjoined the city elite's downtown Peachtree Street neighborhood; and Durham's "Hayti," an outlying African American community incorporated into the city limits in 1901.

Postbellum southern economic and political elites articulated a clear vision of urban capitalist development; attracted rising levels of northern economic and infrastructure investments; and declared a firm commitment to improve class and race relations. But New South rhetoric about class and race relations quickly gave way to the rise of the post-emancipation racist system. Increasing racial restrictions on wages, the franchise, entrepreneurship, and educational opportunities undermined African American access to resources for building their own metropolis. Nonetheless, against the lengthening shadow of Jim Crow and the spread of industrial capitalism, African Americans forged a variety of new communities across the postbellum urban landscape. By the early twentieth century, escalating Black labor migration had enabled Birmingham, Durham, and Atlanta to rebuild dynamic industrial cities in the wake of economic collapse during and after the Civil War; at the same time, these New South Black urban centers also provided the institutional and political foundation for challenging the emerging Jim Crow order.

The Deep South, Upper South, and urban New South did not exhaust the range of southern sites of the Black city-building process. African Americans also occupied and transformed space on the edges of the Deep South—in the urban Southwest and Southeast. Chapter 4 uncovers the unique experiences of Black city-builders in Tulsa, Houston, and Miami. Black southeasterners and southwesterners built communities in cities that were more racially and ethnically diverse than elsewhere in the urban South. Miami's turn of the century "Colored Town" gave way to Overtown in the central city and two suburban locations (Liberty City and Brownsville) in outlying areas as the twentieth century unfolded, while Houston's Fourth and Fifth Ward communities rapidly supplanted the earlier "Freeman Town." For its part, Tulsa's Greenwood community jumped from just under 2,000 residents in 1910 to nearly 10,000 in 1921, when white mobs aided by law enforcement officers launched one of the most violent attacks on a Black community in the nation's history.

In documenting the history of Blacks in the urban Southeast and Southwest, chapter 5 also underscores how racial and ethnic diversity affected the emergence of a complicated politics that defied usual characterizations of racial unity and fragmentation. Southern-born Black migrants and substantial Latinx and Asian American communities shaped the history of Houston, while in Miami, the Caribbean's contribution of migrants to Miami's Black population led to substantial friction. This internal Black ethnic divide challenged African American unity and the fight against racial inequality. Still, the urban Southeast and Southwest developed forms of solidarity that reinforced the modern Black Freedom Movement against the segregationist edifice nationwide. As such, *Building the Black City* demonstrates how the rise of the Black metropolis fueled both national and transnational Black liberation movements.

Part II (chapters 5–7) examines the city-building process in the urban North and West from the colonial and early American roots through the onset of the industrial age and the rise of the modern Black Freedom Movement. Focusing on the northeastern cities of New York, Philadelphia, and Boston, chapter 5 shows how African people gradually built their own urban settlements on Philadelphia's North and South Sides; in Boston's West End; and on the east side of Manhattan Island, in "Fresh Water Pond," and later Seneca Village. Chapter 5 also illustrates how early Black neighborhoods would help to frame African American responses to the challenges of slavery, class, and racial inequality in the post-revolutionary, antebellum, and Civil War–era Northeast.

The rise of the Black Midwest metropolis is the subject of chapter 6. African Americans forged new communities on the South, West, and North sides of Chicago; the North Side of Milwaukee; and Detroit's East Side, supplemented by smaller settlements elsewhere across these different midwestern cities. New areas of African American residence, institution-building, and political mobilization strengthened the Black metropolis and spawned fresh assaults on the white supremacist system.

Chapter 6 also examines Black communities that developed in Cincinnati, Cleveland, and Pittsburgh—cities that emerged in the unique geography and environment of the Ohio Valley on the one hand and the northern Ohio Great Lakes Western Reserve on the other. Similar to developments in Chicago, Detroit, and Milwaukee, these cities became dynamic centers of social justice movements against class and racial inequality. But Cincinnati's Black city-builders repeatedly struggled with the city's dual border-city heritage. Henry Louis Taylor, one of the city's leading scholars, invokes W. E. B. Du Bois's famous notion of "double consciousness" to explain Cincinnati's special place on the urban landscape. It "was not simply a northern city looking South." It was a northern city and a southern city, "two warring ideals [freedom and unfreedom] in a single city."[12]

Whereas the city-building process took place against the backdrop of mainly Black-white relations in the North and most of the South, African Americans carved out distinctive neighborhoods within a larger multiracial context in the urban West. Chapter 7 explores the emergence of San Francisco's Western Addition, a narrow strip of land "along Fillmore Street from McAllister to Sutter, bordered by Divisadero Street and Webster Street"; Los Angeles's "Central [Avenue] all the way to Jefferson Boulevard (or 35th Street), about twenty blocks south of Washington"; and Seattle's Jackson–Yesler Street district, where Asian Americans accounted for 68 percent of all residents during the early industrial era.[13] As elsewhere, the Black city of the Pacific coast strengthened the larger struggle to dismantle Jim Crow nationwide.

The concluding chapter focuses attention on the current postindustrial moment in the Black city-building process.[14] Specifically, it reflects on the transformation of Black urban life under the impact of deindustrialization, mass incarceration, worldwide epidemics and pandemics (namely HIV/AIDS and COVID-19), and the emergence of the New Jim Crow.[15] Accordingly, this chapter moves beyond the different cities and regions to explore these momentous postindustrial changes within the context of the nation as a whole. Perhaps most important, the final chapter discusses how a new twenty-first-century Black metropolis is slowly taking shape around the renovation of old central city neighborhoods; the demolition of large-scale public housing projects; and the creation of new communities on the city's periphery and in its heretofore all-white suburban neighborhoods. Notably, one of the most violent episodes in recent race, police, and class relations emerged in the St. Louis suburb of Ferguson, Missouri.[16]

The conclusion also returns to the question of reparations and the implications of this study for the contemporary movement for redress to compensate Black people for past patterns of class and racial inequality in American cities. It reiterates the need to integrate the creative role of African Americans as city-builders into an overall case for reparations for descendants of African people enslaved in America. If some of the most violent episodes in contemporary Black urban life occurred on the suburban periphery, so did some of the most forceful grassroots demands for redress. In the spring of 2021, the city of Evanston, Illinois, approved a pioneering reparations program to compensate the city's Black residents for years of racial discrimination in the housing market. Nonetheless, even as African Americans reframe the city-building process for the class and racial politics of the new age, they are not breaking entirely new ground. They are building upon their long history as city-builders dating back to the first generation of African people on American soil.

PART ONE

South, Southeast, and Southwest

ONE

Majority and Near-Majority Black Cities

BLACK CITY-BUILDING HAD ITS DEEPEST and most profound beginnings in the majority and near-majority Black cities of the Lower South.
From the outset of the new nation, southern Blacks developed their own
sense of entitlement to land, property, freedom, and human rights in
Charleston, Savannah, and New Orleans. Until the outbreak of the Civil
War, however, the preponderance of enslaved people among Blacks in these
areas complicated the Deep South city-building process. While this process
was by no means uniform over time or from place to place, a small but influential slaveholding, propertied, and mixed-race elite emerged across the
Lower South and undercut movements to build cohesive multiclass and
mixed-race communities. In January 1811, when slaves on the Andry plantation some forty miles north of New Orleans rebelled, killed whites, and
marched toward the city, free Blacks joined the local militia in putting down
what turned out to be the "largest slave revolt in United States history." Free
people of color defined their interests narrowly. They firmly believed that
they had to protect their interests against encroachments from any source,
including the desperate needs and pleas of their suffering kinsmen on nearby
sugar plantations.[1]

Despite unique features of Black life in the region, the Deep South story
connects with the nationwide African American quest for urban space, city-
building, and freedom. As such, it also reveals in no uncertain terms that the
urban exploitation of Black labor had deep roots at the beginning of the
nation's history. Hence, it is misleading to construe the contemporary quest
for reparations within the context of an almost exclusively rural understanding until the onset of the Civil War, emancipation, and the rise of the Jim
Crow order during the late nineteenth and early twentieth century. Still, the

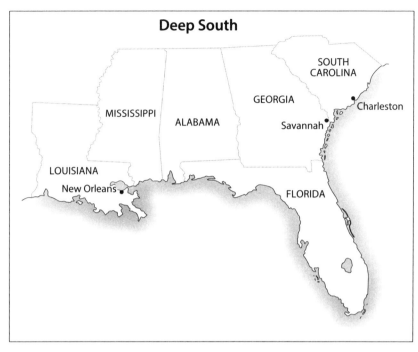

Deep South

SOUTH CAROLINA

GEORGIA

MISSISSIPPI

ALABAMA

Charleston

Savannah

LOUISIANA

New Orleans

FLORIDA

MAP 2. Charleston, New Orleans, and Savannah emerged as the principal urban centers of the late colonial and early American Deep South. There were important differences among them, but each of these cities soon became the site of majority or near-majority Black populations. These huge concentrations of Black people would have a profound impact on the African American quest for their own independent space.

creation of the early Black city was not only a product of their labor exploitation. It was also a consequence of their resolve to construct their own place on the urban landscape. As we will see, this was a long and arduous process of double-taxing their own labor in the interest of their own self-defined community, which in turn influenced the culture, politics, and shape of the larger built environment of early Lower South cities.[2]

CLAIMING SPACE

Sugar, rice, and indigo-producing slaveholding regimes spurred the growth and development of the majority and near-majority Black cities of the Deep South. Profitable staple production demanded what economists describe as "forward linkages in the transportation, manufacturing, and service sectors, which could most conveniently be made available in a central urban place" like Charleston. Founded in 1663, Charles Town soon emerged as the principal port of arrival for enslaved African workers who supplied the labor needs of commercial rice and indigo production. It also became a predominantly Black city by the early eighteenth century.[3]

Nearly two decades after South Carolina proprietors established Charles Town under the British Crown, the French claimed possession of the Louisiana Territory. But only during the 1720s did France initiate an aggressive drive to transform Louisiana into a tobacco, indigo, and finally sugar-growing colony centered on New Orleans and enslaved African labor.[4] Established in 1718, the total population of the "Crescent City," nicknamed for its location on the "outer arc of a great bend" in the Mississippi River, was substantially altered by successive waves of colonizers: French (1721–1790), Spanish (1790–1803), and American, mainly people of British descent (after the Louisiana Purchase of 1803). But as early as 1763, New Orleans had emerged as a majority-Black city of about 4,000 people.[5]

Whereas legally enslaved Blacks buoyed urban as well as rural growth from the outset in colonial South Carolina and Louisiana, Georgia prohibited slavery and the slave trade from the beginning of its settlement in 1732. Nonetheless, even before imperial authorities relented and authorized the importation and use of enslaved African labor, Georgians had already imported some 400 enslaved people to augment the colony's workforce. The number of Blacks in the colony rapidly increased to an estimated 16,000 as the American Revolution got underway. Some 2,800 of these enslaved workers entered Savannah between 1767 and 1771. By the turn of the nineteenth century, nearly a majority of all Savannah's residents were Blacks. But there were also a few free people of color.[6]

Despite extraordinary limitations on their freedom and economic self-sufficiency in the predominantly slave-driven urban political economy, Deep South urban Blacks (especially skilled craftsmen and women) gradually gained access to their own land, housing, and neighborhoods.[7] As a foundation for their city-building efforts, African Americans sought access to their own land and homes, primarily as owners but also as renters. However, the legal act of ownership, as historian Tara A. Dudley suggests, was often "the first step" in a complicated city-building process by which many free people of color "established their place" in the urban landscape.[8]

By the onset of the American Revolution, free people of color (and to some extent enslaved people as well) purchased, rented, and maintained land, buildings, and residential properties in both the city and countryside. During the 1760s, the "carpenter and planter" John Williams, one of Charleston's earliest Black landowners, purchased 400 acres of plantation land on the Santee River in Craven County. A decade earlier, the free Black butcher Matthew Webb laid claim to property on King Street. At about the same time, John Gough (also spelled Goff and Goffe) held 227 acres of land in Christ Church Parish along with "several buildings" in Charleston. During the American Revolution, Gough "leased a mercantile building" to the Jewish merchant Emanuel Abrahams, for 350 pounds "current money of Great Britain." James Mitchell, another Black Charlestonian, lived above his own carpenter's shop; Mitchell also advertised in the *City-Gazette and Daily Advertiser* "to rent a six-room house with stables and outbuildings."[9]

Following the American Revolution and the rise of the new republic, Black property ownership fluctuated but gradually increased during the early nineteenth century. In New Orleans, for example, the first generation of two prominent free families of color, the Dolliole and Soulié, each acquired an estimated thirty-five different properties. Many of these properties served as rental units that reinforced and broadened the families' impact on the city-building activities of both free people of color and those who were enslaved, but "living out."[10] At about the same time, the Crescent City tailor Francois Lacroix, a creole of color, and his tailoring partner Etienne Cordeviolle had emerged as two of the most successful real estate owners of their time. According to historian and American studies scholar Shirley E. Thompson, "Lacroix and Cordeviolle bought, sold, and collected large sums in rents on large parcels of property throughout the 1830s and 1840s. . . . In the middle of the nineteenth century, it would have seemed virtually impossible to trace a route through New Orleans without traversing at least one Lacroix property." Furthermore, Lacroix took an abiding hands-on approach to his property holdings. He "very literally marked his territory, staking claim to his various properties in person." By 1850, the city's free people of color owned an estimated $2.2 million in real estate. Much of this was located in the Central Business District. When urban developers and capitalists moved to widen Bourbon Street and "transform that winding alley into a busy thoroughfare" to enhance trade and commerce, they were dismayed to discover that "the choicest lots were owned by free Negroes."[11]

Between 1850 and 1860, Charleston's successful free Black property holders of color increased by 227 percent, from only 37 in 1850 to 121 in 1860. The average value of holdings also increased, despite a slight decline in the free

Black population in the city, from nearly $4,550 to $5,115. When Savannah outlawed the purchase of real estate among free people of color, African Americans not only maintained control of the property that they had secured before this restrictive legislation took effect and passed it on to their heirs, but also continued to increase their ownership of land through subterfuge. Black men and women obtained estates in the name of white guardians or bought buildings on land owned by white realtors and landowners. Thus, seamstress "Poly Baptiste owned a building on lot number five in Greene Ward; street vendor Nelly Dolly held the 'improvement' on half a lot in number thirteen in Washington Ward; [and] cooper Benjamin Reizne owned buildings on one-fourth of a lot in Yamacraw."[12] Some of these free women of color also protected their property through "prenuptial arrangements" to ensure their ownership of real estate remained intact following marriage.[13]

While most slaveowners placed few resources at the disposal of newly emancipated people of color, some enhanced the Black city-building process. They occasionally took a keen interest in the welfare of their own mixed-race kin and assisted their acquisition of personal property, skills, and sometimes land to support families and self-sufficiency as free people. The Savannah slaveowner William Gibbons took an ongoing day-to-day interest in the welfare of Salley and their children, and, upon his death, bequeathed to them valuable property, including land. According to historian Feay S. Coleman, Gibbons "left real estate comprising town lots and farm acreage, as well as slaves, in trust for each of the children. As the first-born male, John Charles received a valuable interest in a lot and building on the Savannah River, and he would have the right to manage his own property when he turned twenty-one." In another case, following his emancipation of Tabatha Singleton, a Charleston slaveowner paid the rent for her tenement and eventually "conveyed a house, lot, and two slaves to her." Similarly, the convert to abolitionism William Turpin emancipated all his slaves, but he made special provisions for "Jenny" to receive "a lot and two story brick house on Society Street."[14] Such exceptional cases of material support for liberated relatives notwithstanding, Deep South slaveowners offered enslaved people few opportunities to gain freedom, land, or resources to build their own families and communities in eighteenth- and nineteenth-century Charleston, Savannah, and New Orleans.

As the number of free Black property holders increased, many other Black families, enslaved and free, moved into widely dispersed rental properties. In Charleston, as elsewhere in the urban Deep South, enslaved and free Blacks occupied homes "on virtually every road in the city." According to historian Bernard Powers, the "intermingling of different classes and races" persisted well into the Civil War and early postbellum era. On Church Street in Charleston's First Ward, "by the Battery at its southern end, house number one was occupied by Bruce Philips, a Black laborer. Whites occupied the next several residences on both sides of the street along with either the Black or immigrant domestics in their employ."[15] In the meantime, growing numbers of antebellum poor and working-class Blacks, free and enslaved, moved into an area called the "Neck," but they were joined by "newly arrived white immigrants" and "temporary [American-born] white residents" who shared the "little shacks, back-alley rooms, and windowless garrets."[16]

By the mid-1820s, African Americans made up a majority of the population in eleven of Savannah's eighteen wards. Two decades later, when the city expanded to twenty-two wards and three smaller administrative districts, enslaved and free people of color outnumbered whites in eight of twenty-five subdivisions. None of the city's wards was exclusively Black or white. Instead, enslaved Blacks "lived in the same dwellings with their owners, or in shanties at the back of the lots on which their masters' premises were located," while some free people of color worked as "live-in servants" in the homes of their employers. African Americans also rented homes from whites and from some Black property owners as well. Similarly, in New Orleans, in 1805, a street-by-street survey of the city showed Blacks residing on forty of the city's forty-three main streets, and the report stated, they were "usually dispersed widely among them."[17]

Although African American neighborhoods remained scattered across the urban landscape of the eighteenth and early nineteenth centuries, the rise of the Black city in the urban Deep South was closely intertwined with the gradual emergence of distinct clusters of Black residence within the changing urban political economy of slavery. Most African Americans would remain under tight residential controls, engineered by architectural decisions designed to maximize surveillance of their movement and social and political activities,[18] but such controls proved insufficient to fully stamp out African American access to their own urban spaces. Against the backdrop of restrictive legislation, enslaved and free people of color gradually carved out their own spaces within the larger residential, commercial, and administrative structures of the city.[19]

In Charleston, the heart of the Black community emerged midway through the city around Coming Street, where Meeting Street increasingly converged on an area of sturdy wooden and brick homes of Black and white artisans and merchants. By 1861, some 273 free Blacks lived on Coming Street, "more than any other street in the city." They made up 18 percent of the street's total population and occupied 23 percent of its homes. Coming Street also housed some of the leading members of the free Black community: "Jeanette Bonneau, property owner, slaveholder, and widow of free Black school teacher Thomas Bonneau, lived here, as did several individuals from the wealthy Weston and Dereef families. And further up Meeting, near Boundary Street, smaller yet still respectable wooden homes were inhabited by white laborers, enslaved persons, and free Blacks of more modest means. Among the latter was Martha Evans, a free woman of color and greengrocer who owned a home near Reid Street."

Sprinkled in among Charleston's racially diverse neighborhoods were enclaves of predominantly enslaved Black workers. These working-class enclaves were especially prominent in Clifford's Alley, located west from King Street, between Queen and Clifford; Grove Street, just above the Washington Race Course, near the city's northern boundary; and Hester Street, north of Grove. Because white faces were rarely seen in these areas, they became important "havens" for enslaved and poorer free people of color "away from the prying eyes, and control, of whites." These neighborhoods also presented

> a seemingly endless line of groceries and grog shops filled with enslaved laborers, free Blacks, and working-class whites, all drinking, playing cards, gambling at dice, and gossiping. Although it was illegal for enslaved or free Black persons to gamble, buy alcohol, or enter the premises of an establishment that sold liquor, some such businesses were actually owned by free people of color like Sophia Cochran and Sarah Blank. Others were run by working-class whites who turned a blind eye to the law. Such open disdain for the master class's municipal directives, as well as the social familiarity across race lines evidenced in grog shops, made many a visitor shudder.[20]

In New Orleans, as early as the 1740s, people of African descent started to carve out a space on Rampart Street, located behind the present day French Quarter, for "Sunday gatherings." Known as "Congo Square," or Plaza de Armes during the Spanish era, this space became the cultural centerpiece in the development of Black New Orleans. French governors had built the city around "the Place d'Armes," the parade ground facing the Mississippi River. During the late antebellum years, the city's Black population showed additional evidence of clustering "in the fifth and seventh wards at the north end of the first municipality and in the contiguous first ward of the third municipality." Together, these three areas of concentration "housed more than one half of the free people of color and roughly one-seventh of the city's white residents." Put another way, as historian Leonard Curry sums up, "the entire second municipality (the 'American' sector) contained only one-ninth of the city's free Blacks and over one-half of the whites."[21]

The rise of residential clusters of owner-occupied and rental properties provided the geographical context for the development of the African American institutional infrastructure. Late colonial and early national African American neighborhoods provided the spatial context for the rise of the first generation of formal community-based Black institutions. Fraternal, religious, business, and educational institutions proliferated during the late eighteenth and early nineteenth centuries. Each of these institutional developments left their own indelible mark on the urban landscape, as African Americans relentlessly pursued the purchase or rental of their own buildings for business, education, worship, and fellowship beyond the gaze of their enslavers.

BUILDING INFRASTRUCTURE

The independent Black church movement emerged at the organizing core of the first wave of formal Black community-building activities. In both the North and South, the journey to Afro-Christianity had deep roots in both the promise and limits of the Great Awakenings of the seventeenth and early eighteenth centuries. Under the powerful influence of the evangelical movement which spread from England to North America during the 1730s and again following the American Revolution, southern Blacks moved into a closer relationship with the Anglican church and the spread of Methodism across the South. In August 1738, when the influential evangelical minister George Whitefield visited Charleston for the first time, he reported a welcome reception from Rev. Alexander Garden and the Anglican church. Whitefield took a keen interest in the "souls" of Black folk, but he neglected their bodies and eventually became a slaveowner himself.[22]

As the Great Awakening, Anglicanism, and Methodism accommodated the demands of human bondage and propagated a religion of subservience among the enslaved, Black people sought their own alternative route to the

"Kingdom of God." In the wake of the American Revolution, their quest for a Christianity of freedom and human and civil rights picked up steam and blossomed into the independent Black church movement. Rising numbers of southern Blacks, like their northern brothers and sisters, rejected "Negro Corners," segregated pews, exclusion from white churches, and, above all, whites' insistence on advancing a Christianity of submission and enslavement for people of African descent. The movement for an autonomous Black church gained its most forceful expression among Savannah's enslaved and free people of color. Andrew Bryan, an enslaved minister, and other African Americans, slave and free, spearheaded the founding of Savannah's First African Baptist Church. In 1788, Bryan received official ordination as a Baptist minister and immediately baptized 45 slaves. The First African Baptist Church (called by some the "Ethiopian Church" and by others the "Colored Baptist Church") gave birth to Second African Baptist Church in 1802 and Third African Baptist Church in 1841.[23] In 1859, after occupying a series of inadequate church homes, First African Baptist Church erected "an impressive new seven-hundred-seat stone church with a gallery and a basement and had it consecrated two years later in 1861." The city's founding First African Baptist Church continues to grace the landscape to this day.[24]

The independent Black church movement faced a more hostile reception in Charleston and New Orleans than it did in Savannah. Still, the church emerged at the center of Black institution-building activities in these cities as well. In 1818, under the leadership of Morris Brown, a free Black shoemaker, nearly 4,400 enslaved and free Blacks broke away from Charleston's white Methodist church. They formed a new African Methodist Episcopal church under the jurisdiction of the independent Philadelphia-based AME denomination. However, in the aftermath of Denmark Vesey's slave revolt, authorities not only destroyed Charleston's African Methodist Episcopal church, dispersed its members, and drove the minister from the city, but also banned independent Black churches in the city. Similarly, the autonomous Black church movement faced an uphill battle in New Orleans, where most Blacks belonged to the biracial Catholic Church. In 1850, Louisiana legislators banned "the establishment of Black churches, lodges, and clubs." These restrictions further undercut the city's already struggling independent Black church movement. Still, by 1860, New Orleans reported four African American Methodist churches and two Baptist churches, with a total membership and property holdings, respectively, of 1,700 and $22,000 and 1,000 and $10,600.[25]

FIGURE I. Savannah's historic First Baptist Church, founded under the leadership of the enslaved minister Andrew Bryan in 1788. First Baptist stimulated the spread of the Black Baptist faith across the South. Courtesy of Documenting the American South, UNC–Chapel Hill.

As uneven as its development may have been in the urban Deep South, the rise of the Black church reinforced the growth of mutual benefit societies, fraternal orders, and schools. In Savannah, Charleston, and New Orleans, African Americans established a variety of such organizations to address the social welfare needs of free people of color. Although they did not follow their northern counterparts in setting up chapters of the Prince Hall Masonic order, these self-help organizations "loaned money to members, cared for orphans and widows, and helped to defray burial expenses of deceased members." They also provided space for members to congregate, engage in fellowship, and place their mark on the urban landscape. In 1790, Charleston's free Black elite founded the exclusive Brown Fellowship Society to serve the needs of light-skinned Black artisans. The organization devoted the bulk of its time to assisting its own members with burial grounds, loans for business development, and aid to children of deceased members who left insufficient estates to secure the welfare of their families. Charleston's Minor's Moralist Society, formed in 1803, addressed the housing, food, clothing, health, and other social welfare needs of both orphan and "indigent colored children." In 1839, the city's free Black elite spearheaded the formation of the Christian Benevolent Society for the "aid of the sick poor of our free Colored Community in the City, by pecuniary grants, and Judicious Council." Over the next decade and a half, the organization disbursed over $1,200 to some 70 individuals and families.[26]

Perhaps most important, Black churches, mutual benefit societies, and fraternal orders encouraged the founding of schools and the spread of literacy among Blacks across the urban Deep South. The establishment of Sunday Schools early on opened the door to formal education for Black children. In the early 1800s, Andrew Bryan invited a free Black Baptist minister to the city to set up a Sunday school at the First African Baptist Church "to teach our youth to read and write." Between 1826 and 1860, in addition to Sunday Schools that taught Black children to read the Bible "to gain a better understanding of God," Savannah's free people of color established no fewer than six independent schools for the secular as well as spiritual education of Black youth. These schools defied local and state laws, passed in 1817 and 1829, respectively, banning the teaching of slaves and free Blacks to read and write. In Charleston, along with operating one of their earliest Sunday Schools at the Cumberland Street Methodist Church, the city's free people of color established a peak of about sixteen schools (four of them taught by whites) for Black children, including one sponsored by the free Black Minor's

Moralist Society in 1803 "to educate orphan or indigent colored children" and another sponsored by the Brown Fellowship Society in 1807.[27]

Established under the accomplished and popular teacher Thomas S. Bonneau, the Brown Fellowship School soon attracted an enrollment so large that Bonneau added two assistant teachers to his staff. Educated in part by Bonneau, the outstanding educator and future Bishop in the AME church, Daniel Alexander Payne, opened his own school in 1829. Five years later, when the South Carolina legislature passed a law prohibiting the teaching of enslaved and free Blacks to read and write, Payne closed his school and moved to Philadelphia. Other Charleston Blacks continued to teach in defiance of the law. In 1859, one slaveholder lamented the sight of "crowds of Black children who throng our streets every morning on their way to school, with satchel well filled with books." By 1850, in the Crescent City, some 1,000 free people of color attended private schools in Orleans parish.[28] Across the late antebellum Deep South, the school took its place alongside other institutions influencing the cityscape.

African American entrepreneurial activities reinforced the expanding institutional infrastructure of Black communities in the urban Deep South. Access to skilled crafts and property provided a basis for the emergence and expansion of business activities. Opportunities to buy and sell a broad range of products and transportation services undergirded African American entrepreneurship in Charleston, New Orleans, and Savannah. African people dominated the market in the sale of fresh meat, fish, and a variety of garden vegetable products. Southern working-class Black women, slave and free, managed the informal street trade in farm produce, pastries, and other items that they "made themselves" or "purchased wholesale" from other producers. By the late eighteenth and early nineteenth century, a mix of enslaved and free Black women had transformed garden produce and home cooked goods into thriving commercial activities across the urban Deep South.[29] Some of these women, such as Carlotta Derneville of New Orleans, also operated taverns and boarding houses on streets lining the levee. They served a large but transient population of sailors, soldiers, tourists, and business travelers. In Charleston, Mary Purvis became widely known as the city's "Oyster Woman." By 1860, Purvis had built viable business connections to the fishermen along the city's busy docks, thus securing a reliable and steady supply of oysters for her street business. Her success and that of other women food vendors underlay passage of recurring legislation to curb their "control over the city's food supply."[30]

In Charleston, the 1740 Negro Act outlawed "the hiring of rooms, houses or stores to slaves," but the practice continued in defiance of the law. Contemporary commentators frequently remarked on the renting of "many rooms, kitchens, etc.," to enslaved Charlestonians who in turn "let to others, in subdivisions" which "served as places of concealment for runaways," but also underground commercial activities, sometimes in "stolen goods." Although a Savannah city statute prohibited Blacks, enslaved or free, from selling whiskey, urban Blacks nonetheless maintained a lively underground network trading in liquor. Charleston statutes also forbid the sale of liquor to slaves, but illegal local "grog shops" proliferated through the collusion of "local authorities, merchants, and shopkeepers" with enslaved and free Blacks.[31]

Marketing activities were not confined to informal trade networks. African Americans quickly entered and even dominated the public markets, as they were constructed and opened for business in the municipality. Enslaved Blacks monopolized the butcher trade in Charleston's Lower Market, founded in 1739 as the city's primary meat vendor. By the early 1770s, local residents frequently remarked that "the butchering Business in the Lower Market of Charles-Town has for many years past been carried on by Negroes." In 1770, when the city erected a building for the fish market at the bottom of Queen Street, Black Charlestonians had already gained control of the fish trade and dominated the sale of fish at the new facility from the outset. In Charleston, the free Black Jehu Jones parlayed earnings from a successful tailoring business into the purchase of a hotel on Broad Street near the white St. Michael's Church. One observer described Jones's hotel as "unquestionably the best in the city." In addition to free Blacks, Jones employed a staff of six enslaved men and women to serve his elite clientele of governors, military officials, and European and U.S. visitors to the city.[32]

The building and construction trades occupied a special place in the development of early Black businesses. African American building and construction laborers not only worked under the supervision of white artisans and elites, but also launched their own diverse entrepreneurial activities. In the town of Bennettsville, South Carolina, the slave Thomas David, according to historian Loren Schweninger, "owned a construction business." He negotiated contracts, hired his own day laborers (including slaves), and supervised "the erection of numerous houses as well as several larger buildings." In 1750, another South Carolina free Black home owner and builder advertised his business in the local press. He offered all kinds of "carpenter's or joiner's work" or any buildings "thought proper" to offer him. Moreover, as a free man, he declared, whoever employed him would "find not only their work well done and handsomely finished, but [done] with great fidelity, justice and dispatch."[33]

In early nineteenth-century Charleston, Black household servants played an important role in expanding employment opportunities for enslaved and free Blacks in the construction trades. They were the "intrapreneurs," as described by business historian Juliet E. K. Walker. During the summer months, planters traveled north for long periods of time and left their household slaves in charge of arranging repair and building contracts on large slaveholding estates. Enslaved African American managerial servants established a firm pattern of hiring "virtually free slaves and free Blacks as carpenters, builders, and masons." These contractors in turn employed their own "small work gangs of nearly free bondsmen to erect out-buildings and construct houses." Closely intertwined with the building and construction industry, Charleston also saw the rise of small wood supply businesses, which accounted for an estimated 50 percent of the city's free Black enterprises. Some of the most lucrative of these wood suppliers owned and employed enslaved along with free Blacks. Between 1841 and 1865, free men of color Robert Howard and the brothers Richard and Joseph Dereef hired large numbers of enslaved Blacks and, according to Martin Delany, they effectively supplied "the citizens, steamers, vessels and factories of Charleston with fuel."[34] Like their male counterparts, the most successful southern Black businesswomen also owned and employed slave labor. Dressmaker Leah Simpson, one of Savannah's leading Black businesswomen, owned four slaves in 1819 and purchased another in 1820. During the 1820s and 1830s, Catherine Deveaux owned property in three different wards of Savannah. On one of these properties, she built a "Negro house" to accommodate her own enslaved workers as well as other enslaved and free Blacks.[35]

The virtually free bondsman Anthony Weston became perhaps South Carolina's most successful enslaved entrepreneur and skilled mechanic. Weston "built rice mills for various slave owners at the edge of the inland river systems." Plowden Weston, Anthony's owner, praised the skill and quality of his work. Weston also decreed, in 1826, that Anthony should receive his full freedom six years after his owner's death. However, as Schweninger notes, Anthony Weston "was neither emancipated nor did he leave the state." Instead, he used his earnings "as a builder" to invest in "real estate and slaves."

FIGURE 2. New Orleans's free people of color created a unique architectural style—a blend of European and non-European building traditions—as suggested by this structure located at 1436 Pauger Street. Jean-Louis Dolliole, 1820. Photo by Tara Dudley, 2011.

Between 1833 and 1845, he purchased (in the name of his free Negro wife Marie) large amounts of real property and twenty Blacks, including skilled artisans who assisted him in constructing rice mills. In 1856, one planter described a Weston-built mill as 'better than any on the river.' By 1860, Anthony Weston owned just over $40,000 worth of real estate in his wife's name. He had also become one of the most affluent Blacks in South Carolina.

Legally enslaved Blacks like Weston, in some cases, "moved out on their own and established businesses." They could lead relatively autonomous lives; they built families, acquired property, and influenced the built environment.[36]

In New Orleans, free people of color emerged at the center of the city's colonial and early U.S. national architectural styles. According to Dudley, the city's need for architecture and infrastructure provided an unusual opportunity for "Black building artisans, developers, and patrons" to shape the urban landscape. A unique blend of "Western European and non-European building traditions"—creole architecture, as it came to be known—represented a dominant influence on the city's landscape and persisted through the antebellum years and beyond. Although the new republic sought to marginalize or even eliminate their sway over the city's built environment, the influence of free people of color lived on through numerous buildings with "galleries or verandas; a broad, spreading roofline; gallery roofs supported by lightweight wooden collonettes (posts); placement of main rooms above ground level; timber-frame construction infilled with bricks."[37]

Such exceptional African American influences on the urban landscape notwithstanding, across late eighteenth- and early nineteenth-century urban America, Blacks in the urban Deep South acquired property and influenced the built environment against extraordinary odds. After the American Revolution and the rise of the new republic, the free Black population gradually increased across the urban Deep South, but constraints on the emancipation of enslaved Blacks persisted and even intensified during the antebellum years. African Americans would have to fight for a free city against numerous barriers.

ENCOUNTERING OBSTACLES AND FIGHTING FOR A FREE CITY

An expanding series of state and local laws prohibited the freeing of enslaved people. In Charleston, as early as 1801, lawmakers limited manumission of enslaved people to those approved by "the state legislature." In 1822, the South Carolina legislature abolished the practice of "self-hiring," a major avenue to emancipation, and imposed a penalty on violators, including the possible "forfeiture of the slave" involved.[38] In the meantime, the Georgia legislature passed the Guardianship Law of 1808, requiring all free persons of color to select a guardian to oversee their affairs. In 1835, another state statute barred "any Black person except slaves and court-registered free Blacks from remaining in the state."[39] In Louisiana and New Orleans, too, lawmakers moved to strip free people of color of rights and privileges that they had enjoyed under French and Spanish rule, including access to the "Free negro militia." As historian Ira Berlin notes, "After only five years of American rule, the Louisiana free Negroes' legal status had dropped dramatically.... In addition to laws restricting free Negro immigration, Louisiana lawmakers prohibited masters from freeing slaves under thirty years of age except with special legislative permission."[40]

The military demands of the War of 1812 enabled the free Black militia to fight with the U.S. Army, but military service was not enough to secure rights

in the war's aftermath. In 1830, Louisiana enacted "a slew of new laws to further regulate the activities of free people of color and restrict their growth."
State and local legislation required free people of color who had migrated into
the state since 1825 to depart within sixty days; any Blacks emancipated
following passage of the new laws had only thirty days to leave or face re-
enslavement; and any free persons of color who had voluntarily left the state
for a foreign country were prohibited "from ever returning" to Louisiana. In
1857, the Louisiana legislature passed a law prohibiting "all future manumissions" of enslaved people. In the meantime, in New Orleans, the free Black
population declined from an antebellum peak of about 15,000 in 1840 to just
under 10,000 in 1850. Charleston's free people of color had also declined earlier from an estimated 2,100 in 1830 to approximately 1,550 in 1840, while the
number of free Blacks in Savannah never reached a thousand.[41]

During the lead-up to the Civil War, the enslaved population continued
to outnumber free Blacks by large margins. Enslaved people made up over 80
percent of the African American population in Charleston and Savannah,
and nearly 56 percent in New Orleans. Nonetheless, following the American
Revolution, the number of free people of color had gradually increased across
the landscape of the urban Deep South. Charleston's free Black population
rose from nearly 1,500 in 1840 to over 3,400 in 1850. While the number of
Savannah's free people of color peaked at 700 in 1860, free Blacks dramatically increased from about 1,800 when Louisiana entered the Union in 1803
to over 6,200 in 1820 and to about 10,700 in 1860.[42]

Small as their numbers may have been in colonial and early America, the
rise of the free Black population underscored the determination of enslaved
people to open diverse passageways to their own emancipation in the urban
political economy of slavery. Although narrow, these passageways included
the manumission of women and children of interracial sexual relations; the
hiring-out and self-purchase system; running away; and a variety of other
strategies. African American women and their kin pressed slaveholders to
free both the children of their sexual involvement with enslaved women and
the women themselves. While most slaveholders ignored such appeals for
emancipation, some gradually relented and freed both mothers and children
of these relationships. In 1754, low country slaveowner John Williams manumitted two of his enslaved children—claiming a "natural love and affection"
for "my own proper children & issue of my body."[43]

Following the outbreak of the Haitian Revolution in 1791 and for a
dozen years thereafter, waves of Caribbean émigrés reinforced the mixed-race

composition of the free Black population in Savannah, Charleston, and New Orleans, among other U.S. cities. French-speaking people of color from Haiti and later Spain (when Spanish authorities expelled them from Cuba in anger over the French occupation of Spain in 1809) flooded into New Orleans and swelled the ranks of the city's free Black population. The family of Lewis (Louis) Mirault, one of Savannah's most prominent free families of color, arrived in the city during the first great wave of émigrés from Haiti. A tailor by trade, Mirault later married Theresa, another Haitian émigré of mixed-race background. Following Theresa's early death, Louis married Nicole, a free woman of color from Saint Domingue.[44] The couple became the parents of two children, Josephine and Simon. Mirault later purchased a female slave for $800 in 1818. People of French-African descent made up the largest fraction of the free Black population in both Savannah and New Orleans during the 1790s and early 1800s. While authorities in both cities feared the potential revolutionary impact of the émigrés on the enslaved population and took steps to curtail their numbers, officials in Charleston were perhaps even more alarmed by the arrival of large numbers of new people of color from the Caribbean. According to one contemporary South Carolinian, the émigrés "gave new ideas to our slaves which . . . could not fail to ripen into . . . hope of their countrymen to be free." Indeed, Haitian immigrants, as historian Ira Berlin notes, "were completely conversant with events on Saint Domingue." Despite such fears, as elsewhere, the émigrés augmented Charleston's free Black population, the city-building process, and the ongoing struggle for a free city.[45]

CITY AS POLITICAL LEVER

Deep South urban Blacks not only defied the odds and built their own communities. They also used their churches, fraternal orders, and schools to meet a variety of needs within their communities. In addition, they employed cities to strengthen their ongoing struggle to emancipate enslaved people; end second class citizenship for free people of color; and resist racist movements to repatriate people of African descent on African soil. In other words, the vast majority of Black urbanites hoped to secure a permanent place for themselves as fully enfranchised citizens of the city, state, and nation.

Few southern Blacks embraced the American Colonization Society's Liberia relocation program. In Savannah, New Orleans, and Charleston, most free people of color used their community-based institutions to expand the fugitive slave network, consider the efficacy of emigration on their own terms, and debate the pros and cons of violence as a weapon in their fight for freedom. The American Revolution, Denmark Vesey's revolt of 1822, and the Civil War each illustrated how African Americans strategically embraced armed struggle as a path toward freedom, independence, and citizenship. Even so, it was a variety of day-to-day forms of resistance that undermined and weakened the system of human bondage and helped to emancipate enslaved and disenfranchised free people of color across the preindustrial urban South.[46]

Like their northern counterparts, southern Blacks resisted efforts to remove free people of color from American soil. In New Orleans, for example, despite an aggressive ACS chapter and support from leading newspapers and legislators, free people of color successfully prevailed upon some of the city's slaveholding elites to openly endorse the fight against African repatriation. During a legislative hearing designed to gain federal and state legislative support for the removal of Louisiana's free Blacks, the minority subcommittee chairman, Charles-Étienne Gayarré, opposed the effort, declaring, "Your Committee cannot conceive the expectation that a colored man, born in Louisiana, will break so many ties . . . to cross the ocean and settle among men whose origins, whose language, and whose manners are so different from his own. A colored man of French origin, born in Louisiana would not voluntarily go to Liberia even if it had pleased the Almighty to transform that favored spot into a paradise."[47] While Gayarré misrepresented the African American perspective on Africa, he fully captured the commitment of American-born Blacks to resist African repatriation because of family and community connections in the United States. He also underlined, in another passage, that some southern white elites, including Thomas Jefferson, acting in their own vested economic and personal interest, enabled free Blacks to stay put.[48]

During its peak years, the American Colonization Society chose Savannah as the port of embarkation for Liberia-bound Black recruits from other areas of the South. The Liberia exodus reached its zenith between 1848 and 1856, when sixteen ships took 297 free African Americans and 529 enslaved Blacks from Savannah to Liberia. Memorable farewell events marked the departures of 1848 and 1849. When the 1849 group set sail, "a large number of relatives and friends of the emigrants, two church choirs, and a band were aboard the steamer which accompanied the *Huma* until it got to Tybee Island, which is just off the Georgia coast." Black Savannahians represented only a small fraction of those departing; the city council levied a $200 tax on all free people of color and slaves who traveled to Savannah for the purpose of "sailing to Liberia, or any other African port." As in New Orleans, here it was not only African Americans who resisted repatriation to Africa, but also whites with vested interests in retaining the Black population. As historian Whittington Johnson notes, Savannah's elites showed "greater hostility toward African Colonization efforts than toward any of the slave conspiracies and revolts of the nineteenth century. Even Nat Turner's Revolt failed to produce the diatribes from the press and grand jury the *Huma* incident spawned."[49] While some free people of color left Charleston for Liberia, Canada, and other places during the period, most chose to stay put; they found some help from influential white allies, including notably Christopher Memminger, the state legislator from the Charleston district. When Black Charlestonians launched a petition drive to defeat a plethora of new bills designed to speed the removal of free people of color from the city, Memminger took up their cause and "derailed the hostile bills," arguing that white workers "were a greater threat" to the "tranquility" of the city and state than free people of color.[50]

Despite Memminger's intervention, most whites envisioned free people of color and slaves alike as threats to the peace of the community. In forging their liberation strategies and politics, African Americans carefully navigated these opposing perspectives on the role of Blacks in the urban political economy. On the one hand, Deep South urban whites envisioned Blacks as dangerous "incendiaries" who threatened the life of the city and white people through use of arson and other forms of violence as political tools. In 1796, Savannah authorities accused slaves of starting a fire that destroyed three hundred homes. The following year, Charleston officials reported a slave plot to burn the city, and, in 1825–26, accused and convicted several slaves for a fire on King Street that resulted in the destruction of $100,000 worth of property. On the other hand, even as whites defined Blacks as a destructive force in the life of the city, they also acknowledged Blacks as highly "valued fire-fighters" who repeatedly helped to save the city from destructive fires in the heyday of wood rather than brick building and construction materials.[51]

Enslaved and free Blacks were an integral part of the firefighting force in Charleston, Savannah, and New Orleans.[52] In Charleston, when one enslaved Black saved the city's elite St. Michael's Church from burning to the ground in a fire that threatened to engulf the entire city, the mayor emancipated the heroic man on the spot. In Savannah, Black firemen marched in the "annual firemen's parade," outfitted in their uniforms and manually pulling "engines, trucks, and hose carriages" in the absence of "horse-drawn" fire engines. Similarly, though whites feared armed Blacks, they repeatedly entrusted them with the care of firearms. In the conflict leading up to the American Revolution in Charleston, two enslaved men and one white man worked for twelve days "fixing bayonets to 6,600 guns" and installing "flints in about 1,000 muskets." In 1772, the city's grand jury complained that numbers of "Negroes" were "allowed to keep horses and carry fire-Arms." Nearly two decades earlier, in 1754, on one military muster day for free white male citizens, some slaveowners gave their firearms "to Negroes to carry home." The enslaved men "charged and discharged" the firearms several times as they went along the streets of the city).[53]

Understandably, given the complicated and conflicting currents in class and race relations, late eighteenth- and early nineteenth-century African Americans considered the deployment of violent as well as nonviolent strategies for social change. During the Revolutionary War, the Vesey revolt, and the Civil War, armed struggle moved to the forefront of the African American quest for freedom. As the American Revolution got underway, hundreds of enslaved people left the rice, indigo, and sugar fields to join the British forces. The imperial army deemed the southern colonies, particularly Charleston, South Carolina, "the life-blood" of the American rebellion. The crown's primary campaign against the South aimed to capture Charleston. Indeed, Sir Henry Clinton, commander of British forces in North America, declared his belief that enslaved people would rally to the British flag. As he put it, "we have flattering hopes of assistance from the inhabitants held forth to us." In his autobiography, penned nearly a decade after the war, the ex-slave Boston King recalled that he left the plantation and delivered himself "into the hands of the English" in British-occupied Charleston. King further stated, "They received me readily, and I began to feel the happiness of liberty, of which I knew nothing before." In June 1780, some 500 Black men, women, and children departed South Carolina for New York with General Henry Clinton's thirty-ship fleet. Three years later, according to King, a rumor spread among the city's Black population that the British forces planned to return enslaved Blacks to their southern owners. "This dreadful rumour," King said, "filled us with inexpressible anguish and terror, especially when we saw our masters coming from Virginia, North Carolina, and other ports, and seizing upon their slaves in the streets of New York, or even dragging them out of their beds." Two years later, in 1782, over 7,000 Blacks departed from Charleston with the British military when it vacated the city.[54]

In 1779, the British occupied Savannah with the aid of "a Confidential Slave," who guided royal forces "down a path through a swamp, enabling them to surprise and rout the rebel force." Several months later, the city's Black population helped the British repel what one officer in the Royalist Regiment called "as hard Sege as Ever has been sense the Rebelion began [*sic*]." Between September 11 and October 19, French and American troops, augmented by Black soldiers from Haiti, waged a bloody but unsuccessful attempt to take the city. In addition to providing labor battalions behind British lines, two companies of Black volunteers played a significant role in the fighting. In a report to the London government, Governor James Wright declared that Blacks "contributed greatly to our defense and safety." Likewise, in its assessment of rebel defeat at Savannah, the *Virginia Gazette* also called attention to the role of "armed Blacks" among British sailors, marines, and militia. During the British invasion and occupation of Georgia, between November 1778 and January 1779, an estimated 5,000 enslaved Blacks escaped from bondage, about a third of the state's entire Black population. As historian Sylvia Frey persuasively argues, "Because of the scale and nature of the resistance, slave flight during the war in the South might be characterized as a type of slave revolt."[55] When the British evacuated Savannah in July 1782, around 5,000–6,000 enslaved people joined the departing imperial forces. The exodus from Savannah included the slave preacher David George, who had baptized Andrew Bryan and several other slaves before his departure, ensuring that the struggle to create a Black Baptist faith would continue despite his absence.[56]

In 1822, the AME church played a key role in radicalizing Charleston's Black community and inspiring Denmark Vesey's revolt. The free Black carpenter and his enslaved countrymen devised a plan to capture and demolish the city of Charleston and leave the region for the independent republic of Haiti. Upon discovering the plot, authorities soon captured, tried, and executed Vesey and some 35 other Blacks for conspiring to destroy the city and liberate slaves. As part of the revolt, African Americans had boldly challenged Charleston's system of slave patrols, a city guard of 100 men, and another 60 state guardsmen at the Citadel. But it was the onset of the Civil War that opened fresh new opportunities for enslaved and free people of color to take up arms in their own behalf. The African American journey toward armed struggle was closely intertwined with their historic fugitive slave networks. While northern Blacks provided labor and later troops for the Union army, their southern counterparts swelled the ranks of the Union forces as fugitives, refugees, labor "contraband," and eventually soldiers.[57]

Having first been compelled to support the Confederate war effort with their labor, southern Blacks soon took advantage of the advancing Union army to desert southern plantations, encampments, and cities in rising numbers. They built upon historic patterns of resistance to slave labor and staged what W. E. B. Du Bois later described as labor's largest "general strike" in the nation's history. "Arrest that hoe in the hands of the negro," he said, "and you smite the [Confederate rebellion] in the very seat of its life." Robert and John Smalls of South Carolina became the most renowned Black naval heroes when they delivered the Confederate vessel the *Planter* to Union forces in May 1862. As Confederate officers slept ashore, the Smalls and seven other enslaved men, along with their wives and children, steered the craft out of Charleston harbor into waters patrolled by the Union Navy. It was a daring feat. The crew had to fly the Confederate flag to navigate past enemy guns as they left the city, but then had to quickly lower the Confederate colors and hoist a white flag of surrender before the Union Navy could fire upon and sink the craft. For this accomplishment, Robert Smalls received an appointment in the Union Navy.[58]

Later, in Charleston, when Confederate troops deserted the city near war's end, the *Charleston Daily Courier* reported, "the [Union] recruiting officers in Charleston are head over heels in business. The Colored men are flocking to the United States flag by the dozens and the score." In Savannah, following the Union army's capture of Fort Pulaski in April 1862, the slave stevedore and river pilot March Haynes smuggled fugitive slaves into the Union camp in a boat that he concealed "in a creek among the marshes below the city." Indeed, Savannah city officials stepped up their surveillance of Black churches and religious gatherings for possible signs of "sedition" or support for the Union cause in the interest of Black liberation. When African Americans convened at one church and sang a hymn with the refrain, "Yes we shall all be free," Savannah police stormed the church and arrested congregants for "planning freedom."[59]

New Orleans Blacks also prepared to strike a blow for their own liberty when the Union Navy captured the city in 1862. Initially, the Louisiana Native Guard, comprised of the city's free people of color, had offered their services to the Confederacy, but they were rebuffed and denied access to weapons and supplies. Thus, according to historian Rebecca Scott, long before the Union occupation of the city, "the free population of color in New Orleans was waiting in the wings, its most vocal members armed with a resolute French inflected ideology of immediate abolition and universal manhood suffrage."[60] In the meantime, on the edges of the New Orleans war zone, the number of Black refugees from the sugar plantations escalated. They greatly enhanced Union recruitment of African Americans for the new Black regiments. They also helped to forge "a pattern of collaboration and communications between the city and countryside" that would persist through the postbellum years.[61]

Despite building extraordinary forms of community, political, and cultural unity, Deep South African Americans were more deeply fragmented internally. As alluded to elsewhere, some free people of color, men and women, justified the enslavement of Black people in exchange for an opportunity to manumit their own kinsmen and women. These free Blacks also insisted that their freedom included the right to purchase, own, and employ slave labor on equal terms with their white counterparts. By 1830, in the Charleston district, free people of color reported ownership of nearly 2,200 enslaved people. Prominent slaveholders of color included John Williams, James Pendarvis, and Richard Holloway. In 1773, John Williams, apparently the grandson of early Black landowner Nathaniel Williams, was listed in the court records as both a "carpenter and planter." A decade and a half earlier, Williams had purchased four hundred acres of land on the Santee River. For his part, by the 1780s, James Pendarvis, son of a slave woman and white planter father, owned a 3,250-acre plantation and 113 enslaved people in St. Paul's Parish. He married a white woman and gave "his daughter's hand in marriage to a white man." The Pendarvis family was largely accepted by their white neighbors "as persons of wealth and prestige." Born in 1776 of mixed-race parentage, Richard Holloway became a skilled carpenter and builder, and, as early as 1806, embarked upon the purchase small amounts of real estate as well as enslaved workers. By the time of his death in 1845, Holloway had accumulated an estate worth over $20,000. His last will and testament was drawn up in 1842: "To his wife, he bequeathed two slaves (Cato and Betty), their home on Beaufain Street, and two rental houses; to his daughter-in-law, the widow of his son James, he gave a small house; to his son Richard he bequeathed a townhouse, a workshop, and several rental properties; and to each of his other sons—Charles, Edward, Isaac, John, and Samuel—he presented a house or rental property."[62]

Savannah's and New Orleans's free people of color also invested heavily in slave ownership. By 1830, the Crescent City's free Blacks owned 2,351 slaves.

Twenty-three of these Black masters owned from 10 to 20 enslaved people, while over 150 owned 5 or more bondsmen and women. But the vast majority of Black slaveholders owned only 1 or 2 enslaved persons, most often family members whom they eventually manumitted. Although the number of Black slaveholders in Savannah remained smaller than New Orleans and Charleston, the number nonetheless increased from no more than about 16 in 1810 to a peak of nearly 50 among about 22 slaveholders, with only 7 owning 5 slaves or more. While most of Savannah's Black slaveholders worked as artisans, the city's leading slaveholder was Anthony Odingsells, a fisherman and farmer; he owned 10 enslaved people. As elsewhere, Savannah's small Black slaveholding class bequeathed their enslaved property to their loved ones: "Jack Harris, a free African American, left his wife three slaves. Jack Gibbons left his wife five slaves; Prince Candy left his wife seven slaves; and Maria Cohen left her daughter a slave butcher and a forty-three-year-old female slave."[63]

With significant African American owners of enslaved people, New Orleans and Charleston exhibited elements of what some scholars refer to as a "three-tier" or "three-caste" society; mixed-race free people of color stood between the vast majority of enslaved Blacks and their white owners. The most well-to-do members of this class allied with slaveowners and distanced themselves from their darker-skinned brothers and sisters, enslaved and free. At the beginning of hostilities during the Civil War, some free people of color made emotional pleas for acceptance into the Confederate war effort based upon their biological kinship with southern whites. In Charleston, entrepreneurs and property owners Robert Howard, Anthony Watson, and the Dereef brothers petitioned the governor, proclaiming that "in our veins flows the blood of the white race, in some half, in others much more than half white blood. . . . Our allegiance is due to South Carolina and in her defense, we will offer up our lives, and all that is dear to us." Until near war's end, however, like northern white Unionists, the Confederacy spurned such offers of loyalty and service to the cause of the slavocracy.[64]

At the same time, southern officials enlisted Blacks in building fortifications and servicing the Confederate war effort in myriad other ways. Indeed, some free people of color conducted a booming business based on contracts with the Confederate war department. In Savannah these included, most notably, the butcher Jackson B. Sheftall and seafood and meat merchant Anthony Odingsells. An investigator for the federal Southern Claims Commission later reported that Sheftall was a nearly white butcher who "made money by his service" to the Confederacy and "rendered as much aid and comfort" to the rebel cause "as a white man under similar circumstances." Odingsells similarly profited from business with the Confederacy until the Union military forced the rebels to evacuate the city. At that time, Odingsells shipped his enslaved Black work force to Fort McAllister to help build fortifications against Sherman's advancing army. When the Confederates surrendered the fort in December 1864, Odingsells's enslaved Blacks secured their freedom, to the slaveholder's chagrin. Similarly, in Charleston, free Black Charles C. Leslie conducted a "lucrative gun-running operation" for the Confederacy and the butcher Francis Sasportas increased his fortunes by supplying cattle to feed the Confederate forces.[65]

As discussed above, Charleston's Brown Fellowship Society (formed in 1790) served the social welfare and educational needs of free, mainly light-skinned, people of color. The organization repeatedly professed its loyalty to the slave regime, including prohibiting debates on "political and church-related issues" in society meetings. At the outset of the war, the Brown Fellowship Society contributed $450 "to sustain the cause of the South." A year later the organization provided $50 to Charleston's white Ladies Relief Association charged with "the care of injured and sick Confederate soldiers." On one occasion, the Savannah minister Henry Cunningham apparently "turned over to the mayor anti-slavery literature he had received through the mail." In exchange for their loyalty, free people of color expected authorities to intervene to protect them and their institutions from mob violence and other forms of injury. In specific cases, Black elites prevailed: for instance, in July 1849, when a Charleston mob threatened to demolish a newly constructed African American Episcopal Church at the corner of Beaufain and Wilson Streets, Charleston officials prevented the planned attack.[66]

In 1835, a mob of several hundred whites planned an attack on New Orleans's Black community. According to *The Niles Weekly Register*, police arrested "the drunken spokesman of the assembly" and dispersed the crowd. Unlike in Charleston, New Orleans Blacks had a viable coterie of military-trained and tried free people of color who also helped to deflect white mob rule. Alliances between elite free people of color and whites allowed some free women of color to win contentious battles with their white female counterparts. In August 1782, when a quarrel broke out between free Black woman Mary Edy and Ann Fowler, a white woman who lived on Queen Street, the dispute escalated into a fight that spread out into the street, with each woman "striking the other, until passerby finally separated them." Precipitating the dispute was a debt that Edy owed Fowler. In order to speed up the collection of her loan, Fowler "apparently detained" Edy's oldest daughter to satisfy the debt. When Ann Fowler brought assault charges against Mary Edy in a local court, the judge dropped the charges.[67]

Following the establishment of the racially exclusionary Brown Fellowship Society, Black men formed their own Society of Free Dark Men and sought to improve their position as a distinct group within the African American community. As early as the revolutionary years, these color and class distinctions undercut African American solidarity. In the trial that resulted in the execution of Thomas Jeremiah, two enslaved Blacks buoyed the rebels' case against the free Black ship pilot and wealthy businessman. One enslaved witness testified that Jeremiah had instructed him: "There is a great War coming soon. . . . Set the Schooner on fire, Jump on Shore, and Join the Soldiers—that the War was come to help the Poor Negroes."[68] Unlike Jeremiah, whether men or women, light- or dark-skinned, educated Black elites energetically advanced their notions of "respectability," public decorum, and forms of worship as models for poor and working-class Blacks. The AME church urged free Blacks to contain the emotional outcry that characterized tent meetings, where "shouting, ring-dancing, and groaning" gained free expression in Methodist revival services. Elites also condemned working-class music, dance, drinking, gaming, and leisure time activities, particularly the illegal "cookshops" and "groggeries," as dens of sin.[69]

In subtle and not so subtle ways, internal shades of color also complicated ideological and gender divisions within the Black urban community. Free women of color pushed for equal rights across the gender divide. They also sided with free men of color in supporting privileges for the group over their enslaved brothers and sisters. In the winter of 1811, as noted at the outset of this chapter, when free people of color took up arms and helped to put down the largest slave revolt on U.S. soil, free Black women concurred in defining their interest narrowly. For their loyalty, according to historian Amrita Meyers, they hoped to secure for themselves the rights of slaveholding citizens of the republic, "to buy and sell other Black people for profit, use forced labor to grow their businesses, ally themselves with white persons of stature, and distance themselves from people who could jeopardize their position in society."[70]

. . .

By the onset of the Civil War, majority and near-majority Black communities had emerged in Charleston, New Orleans, and Savannah. Independent Black churches, schools, fraternal orders, businesses, and mutual benefit societies influenced the shape of the region's built environment. African Americans also employed their urban infrastructure to launch movements to emancipate enslaved Blacks, resist the African colonization campaign, and fully enfranchise free people of color. When restrictions on free Blacks intensified during the late antebellum years, some emigrated on their own terms, as well as within the context of the ACS Liberia relocation program, to Canada, the Caribbean, and Africa. Nonetheless, the emergence of a small slaveholding, propertied, and entrepreneurial free Black elite fragmented the African American urban community along class, color, and status lines. A tiny cohort of free people of color sided with slaveholders and helped to put down slave revolts and plots to revolt. As we will see in subsequent chapters, this sharp social division within the Black community created a distinctive city-building process in the urban Deep South compared to elsewhere across late colonial and early America.

TWO

City-Building on the Middle Ground

THE SOUTHERN BLACK CITY-BUILDING MOVEMENT was by no means uniform from place to place or over time. The postrevolutionary rise of the urban Upper South framed the African American fight for freedom and space on the middle ground of Washington, DC, Baltimore, and Richmond. In some significant ways, the road to liberty, independence, and community development was more difficult in the urban Upper South than it was in the Deep South. Upper South states and the District of Columbia emancipated fewer women and children of mixed-race relationships, and these received fewer bequests of land, money, and property, than their counterparts in Charleston, Savannah, and New Orleans. Even so, as compared to the Deep South larger numbers of enslaved people in Washington, DC, Baltimore, and Richmond negotiated agreements to hire and live out on their own, purchase their freedom, and embark upon a new life as free people of color. As such, by the onset of the Civil War, most enslaved Blacks in the urban Upper South had not only obtained their freedom and access to their own space (mainly as renters but also gradually as property owners). They had also forged an extensive institutional infrastructure and helped to shape the larger cityscape in their own interests. Although the rise of free Black urban communities played out somewhat differently from city to city, the Upper South Black city unfolded in a complicated geopolitical space between enslavement and liberty in the young democratic, but still slaveholding, republic.[1]

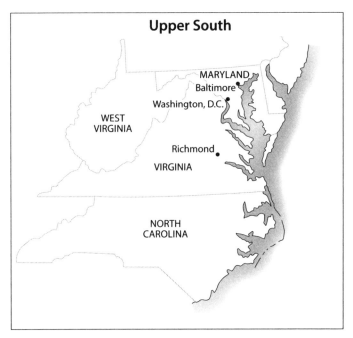

MAP 3. In Washington, DC, Richmond, and Baltimore, African Americans claimed homes and a margin of freedom on the precarious transitional space between enslavement and freedom during the late antebellum years. This process gained its sharpest expression in Washington and Baltimore, while Richmond's Black population confronted the most daunting obstacles to emancipation before the Civil War and the abolition of slavery.

ESTABLISHING HOMES

Baltimore had its beginnings in 1729 when a group of planters received a charter from the Maryland General Assembly "to erect a town" on the north side of the Patapsco River. But only in the wake of the American Revolution did Baltimore rise to prominence as the principal marketing center for the expanding wheat-producing rural hinterlands of the region. Baltimore also played an important role in the transformation of the region from a slave-labor-driven rural tobacco economy to a diversified commercial, manufacturing, and wheat-producing economy focused on the increasing employment of free wage workers, Black and white, over enslaved African American labor. The Monumental City, as it was dubbed during this period of explosive growth, also became the earliest and most prolific site of the domestic slave trade, dominated by the firm of Austin Woolfolk, that resulted in huge profits during the forced migration of some 1.5 million enslaved people from the Upper South to the Deep South.[2]

At about the same time that Baltimore started its ascent as a diversified urban center, an Act of Congress established Washington, DC, as the nation's capital in 1790. Defining the capital as a "district" rather than a "state," federal authorities sited the capital on the banks of the Potomac River. Situating the nation's capital within the larger context of a rural slave-labor-based tobacco-growing economy, boosters expressed hope that the proposed city itself, its "wide boulevards and imposing public architecture," would become "a commercial hub and a civic beacon." Although Washington failed to realize its ambitions to become the monumental capital, commercial center, and "gateway to the West" as supporters had hoped, the District's population, infrastructure, and building and construction projects nonetheless significantly expanded during the early nineteenth century. Municipal and federal authorities approved the construction of a plethora of public, commercial, and residential buildings, largely constructed by slave labor, to serve the expanding administrative functions of the federal government.

Washington increasingly overtook Baltimore as the principal city in the rapidly expanding domestic slave trade. As northern and foreign visitors, journalists, congressmen, and others arrived in the District of Columbia in rising numbers, they invariably called attention to the "horrors" of the slave trade and slavery in the heart of the nation's new capital. In December 1830, even the slaveholding editor of the *American Spectator*, a Washington literary magazine, expressed his concern that enslaved "human beings, handcuffed in pairs, and driven along" the streets of the capital contradicted the "city's pretensions as the capital of a liberty-loving nation." It was during the 1820s and 1830s that Washington, DC, Alexandria, and the ruthless slave-trading firm of Isaac Franklin and John Armfield displaced Baltimore and Austin Woolfolk as the nerve center for the buying and selling of human bodies.[3]

For its part, Richmond had its origins as a small port town with no more than a thousand inhabitants during the American Revolution, but the city's population and economic development escalated when Virginia's revolutionary authorities moved the state's capital from Williamsburg to Richmond as a wartime expedient to stave off British attacks. Equally important, its location on the James River gave Richmond access to the ocean, the interior of the state, and abundant manufacturing and commercial opportunities to market slave produced tobacco and iron products. By the antebellum years, Richmond claimed a reputation as not only "the manufacturing heart of

Dixie," but also the principal employer of nineteenth-century Black industrial workers. More so than in Washington and Baltimore, enslaved and free people of color in Richmond would encounter obstacles on their journey to freedom and in their efforts to build their own free and independent Black city. As a result, free people of color made up only 18 percent of Richmond's total Black population before the Civil War got underway.[4] Nonetheless, across most of the urban Upper South, freedom rather than enslavement increasingly defined the Black city-building process.

As African Americans became a predominantly free people in the urban Upper South, they intensified their struggle for property, business opportunities, and space to build their own homes, institutions, and communities that impacted the city's built environment. They also developed strong ideas about the role of property in their quest for freedom, independence, and rights. These ideas, like those of their counterparts in the urban Deep South, were deeply rooted in their experiences as enslaved people in rural Virginia and Maryland, where they worked small plots of land on their own behalf during their off times. As early as 1656, the Virginia colonist John Hammond declared, "There is no master almost [who] will [not] allow his servant a parcel of clear ground to plant some Tobacco for himself . . . which he may husband at those idle times he hath allowed him." As in the Deep South, enslaved Upper South Blacks came to see this land as their own—as an entitlement that would enable them to build independent lives.[5]

By the 1650s, a substantial landowning rural free Black population had emerged in the region. Anthony Johnson, perhaps the most renowned of these early Black property holders, also laid claim to one African servant, John Casor, "for life." When Casor disputed Johnson's claim in court, the court "seriously" considered and "maturely" weighed the premises in the case and ordered Casor "to return into the service of his master, Anthony Johnson." But these early free Black property owners had declined in numbers by century's end, when the Virginia state legislature passed a law prohibiting the manumission of slaves in 1691. No "Negro or Mulatto," the law declared, could be set free by anyone unless the emancipator arranged for the transport of the emancipated out of the colony within six months. It was not until 1782, nearly a century later, that the state legislature repealed the ban on slave manumissions—a liberalization of the law that coincided with the cresting of ideological and political support for the abolition of slavery. As the new republic got underway and the number of free people of color gradually increased, the number of Black property holders also slowly expanded.

In Baltimore, Washington, and Richmond, the number of free Black property holders rose from under 60 in each city at the turn of the nineteenth century to 169 in Baltimore, 497 in Washington, and 211 in Richmond a decade later. Between 1850 and 1860, the value of the real estate holdings of the most prosperous free Black property holders rose from $120,200 to $530,500 in Baltimore, from $261,000 to $1.7 million in the District of Columbia, and from $74,000 to $229,200 in Richmond.[6]

No more than about 2 to 3 percent of African Americans owned their own homes in the urban Upper South. But their small numbers included a mix of skilled artisans, entrepreneurs, barbers, general laborers, and household workers: Thomas Green, Henry Jakes, Henrietta Gun, and Francis M. Turner in Baltimore;[7] Charles King, William Costin, Francis Datcher, and William and James Wormley in Washington, DC; and a plethora of men and women entrepreneurs including Richard Taylor, James Robinson, Joseph Dailey, Virginia Cunningham, Elizabeth Beatty, Mary Sullivan, Mary Hope, and Rhoda King in Richmond.[8] In addition to real estate holdings, Black property ownership included a few bondsmen and women. In the 1830s, however, free people of color who were slaveowners peaked at about 85 in Baltimore and 75 in the District of Columbia. Richmond reported a high of no more than 13 enslaved people among free Black households. Black women made up 22 percent of these slaveholders in Baltimore, 42 percent in the District of Columbia, and were 4 of the 13 Black slaveholders in Richmond. Because state laws required newly emancipated slaves to leave the state or face re-enslavement, most Upper South Black slaveholders were those who "purchased and retained ownership of their slave families so that they might stay together" rather than face transport out of the state or resale into slavery as required by law.[9]

African American property ownership and rental space unfolded within a broad range of racially mixed but increasingly separate residential areas in or near the homes and workplaces of their employers. In Baltimore, at the outset of the nineteenth century, over 40 percent of free people of color and the vast majority of enslaved people lived in the central core of the city, near leading banks, insurance companies, "fashionable shops," and homes of the city's wealthiest white families. This area stretched "from Jones' Falls on the east to Howard Street on the west and running north from the basin to Saratoga Street." Between about 1815 and 1830, however, affluent white families moved increasingly into the center city and pushed poor and working-class residents out to the periphery. The percentage of free people of color living in the central city dropped from nearly 50 percent in 1810 to under 10 percent by 1830.

Most Blacks displaced from the central city moved to the western part of the city where developers laid out new streets and erected low rent tenement houses. The remainder of displaced free Black residents relocated to the east of the commercial core of the city—"either across from Jones' Falls in Old Town (an area of the city where most residents worked as craftspeople and laborers) or into the narrow streets and alleys in and around Fells Point, where older, cheaper housing was merging with new row-house construction." Baltimore's changing physical layout included extensive "alley ways and courtyards" where most free people of color lived. By the late antebellum years, nearly "ten times as many Blacks as whites" lived in the city's alleys. Alley housing was increasingly home to predominantly Black populations, enslaved and free. Slaves, free Blacks, and white laborers remained intermixed in the residential neighborhoods of the city as a whole, but they slowly carved out their own distinctive neighborhood spaces by the 1850s.[10]

African Americans also moved into increasingly Black residential areas in Washington and Richmond. By 1860, the District of Columbia's central city had moved toward majority white, while the surrounding periphery became increasingly Black. On the city's north side, according to one scholar, K Street emerged as "such a formidable line that one might speak of a 'K Street rule' which dictated that, with few exceptions, Blacks lived to the north of the street, whites to the south." To the south and west sides of the white central urban core, African Americans concentrated in the "low-lying lands of Tiber Island (Southwest, between the Mall and the Potomac), and Foggy Bottom (west of the Mall)." Still, despite evidence of increasing residential segregation along the color line, well into the Civil War years and beyond, free people of color owned or rented homes across the entire city. Even within racially mixed areas, however, there was substantial clustering of Black residents in particular blocks or sections of blocks. Moreover, the District of Columbia developed an extensive system of alleyways that effectively separated hundreds of Black families from white residents. The alleyways of Washington, as well as the peripheral areas, housed predominantly working-class and poor families, while the integrated portions of the urban core housed the free Black middle class and elites.[11]

Richmond developed the most extensive pattern of racially segregated neighborhoods in the antebellum South. Whereas enslaved and free, Black and white, workers had lived intermixed in the geography of the city during the opening three decades of the nineteenth century, this multiracial and multiethnic pattern of urban residence broke down during the 1840s and 1850s. By 1860, the city's Black population was concentrated in just two neighborhoods. The largest of these emerged "in the extreme northwest corner of the city between Fourth and Belvidere streets from Broad to Leigh (later established as Jackson Ward in 1871)." Enslaved and free Black workers shared this space, with the former often renting from the latter. The second largest area of predominantly Black residence developed near Shockoe Creek. Located near the docks, the train depot, and the city's diverse manufacturing establishments, this area had housed a broad range of racial and ethnic group workers during the opening years of the nineteenth century. Gradually, however, American-born whites of English descent and immigrant Irish and German workers moved into better housing on Union Hill and Oregon Hill, "the hillside just beyond the canal and ironworks," located in the western suburb above the Tredegar Iron Works. But African American residents of the Shockoe Creek area, as historian Midori Takagi documents, continued to inhabit poorly constructed and unhealthy "shacks and tenements located in alleyways that were unpaved, filled with open sewers and garbage, and considered 'breeding grounds of disease.'"[12]

Within the larger context of dilapidated housing and unsafe and unhealthy living environments, African Americans faced an uphill fight to build the Black city on the middle ground. Virulent proslavery ideology and social practices accompanied the spread of Black communities across the urban Upper South. Municipalities strengthened slave patrols, added new and more restrictive registration and curfew laws on free Blacks, and worked vigorously to control the movement, public deportment, and politics of free and enslaved urbanites alike. In 1810, Maryland disfranchised free people of color. Baltimore's free men of color had voted in municipal and state elections, and sometimes ran for public office during the early days of the republic. In 1792 Thomas Brown, the Black Revolutionary War veteran and property holder, announced his candidacy for a seat in the Maryland House of Delegates. Brown forcefully argued that Black people should be represented in the state's major lawmaking body. Although he failed in his bid for public office, Brown's candidacy underscored the early push of free people of color for full citizenship rights in the urban Upper South. When the state formally disfranchised Black citizens, one free Black office seeker vehemently protested the state's exclusion of Blacks from full citizenship rights. Before a crowd of white onlookers and voters, he roundly condemned the profound and deepening chasm between the rights of white citizens and the inequality that greeted free people of color. Disfranchisement became part of a large package of injustices that African Americans struggled to address across the early nineteenth century. In 1853, Black Baltimoreans organized a special convention to take up the disfranchisement of Black voters and to secure "civil rights for all, regardless of color."[13]

In Washington, DC, to take another prominent example, the municipal Act of 1836 required that free people of color not only register with authorities, but also post a mandatory $1,000 cash bond to presumably ensure their "good behavior." More important, however, were the day-to-day acts of intimidation, mob violence, and movements to expel Blacks from the urban environment, which both anticipated and reinforced the heavy hand of the law and slave patrols. In June 1812, after demolishing the offices of Federal Republicans and damaging ships in the Baltimore harbor, a white mob turned on local Blacks, destroying several houses owned by John Brisco, a free Black man of color who rented out a one-and-a-half-story brick house in back of his main residence at 134 N. Howard Street. "In the wantonness of their cruelty," a contemporary observer reported, the mob turned on "the unfortunate Blacks." In August 1835, in Washington, DC, a mob of 500 white men and boys destroyed two Black schools, a church, and the restaurant of Beverly Snow, a free Black who served a predominantly elite clientele near Capitol Hill.

The "Snow Riot" or "Snow Storm Riot," as it was called, underscored the ways that whites employed a variety of formal and informal mechanisms for reinforcing legal and extralegal restrictions against urban slaves and free people of color alike. Beverly Snow was violently forced out of business, presumably because he made derogatory remarks about the wives of white mechanics. The largest livery stable in the city, operated by the free Black William Wormley, was also destroyed in the Snow Riot. The following year, the municipality of Washington, DC, struck a sharp blow at Black business activities. An Act of 1836 denied licenses to Black people except for "driving carts, drays, hackneys, carriages, and wagons." The statute also prohibited "any kind of tavern, ordinary, shop, porter-cellar, refectory, or eating house to Negro businessmen."[14]

At the same time, elite white urbanites of the Upper South joined the powerful national campaign for the resettlement of free Blacks on African soil. This campaign, spearheaded by the American Colonization Society, established headquarters in Washington, DC and energetically advanced its "plan, for colonizing (with their consent) the free people of color residing in our country, in Africa, or such other places as Congress shall deem most expedient." The ACS helped to establish Liberia with a $100,000 appropriation from the U.S. Congress. The ACS soon spread outward to Maryland and Virginia and eventually across the nation. In 1817, Robert Goodloe Harper, a white Baltimorean, originally from South Carolina, published a public letter urging support for the ACS. He declared free Blacks permanently scarred by their own "habits of thoughtless improvidence," which they presumably "contracted" while slaves, and exhorted white Baltimoreans to halt this "idle, worthless race." In 1832, the state legislature appropriated $200,000 to help fund the African repatriation program of the Maryland State Colonization Society.[15]

In Richmond, the Virginia Colonization Society often met in the city and built support among white elites for the repatriation of free people of color. By the onset of the Civil War, massive immigration from Germany and Ireland, the Fugitive Slave law, kidnappings, and the re-enslavement of fugitives and free people of color had undercut the proportion of Blacks to whites in the urban Upper South as elsewhere in preindustrial urban America. In 1830, in Baltimore and Washington, respectively, the African American population had peaked at 23 and 29 percent. By contrast, Richmond's Black population, both enslaved and free, rose steadily throughout the early nineteenth century. But the population of enslaved Blacks increased much more rapidly than that of free Blacks. Between 1810 and 1860, the slave population increased from just under 4,400 to nearly 11,700, while free Blacks only slowly increased from 1,235 to 2,576. Enslaved Blacks continued to make up nearly 80 percent of Richmond's total Black population.[16]

While some free people of color fled to Canada and others left for Africa in the wake of increasing racial conflict, as elsewhere, most stayed and fought for full emancipation from human bondage and second-class citizenship in the urban Upper South. Their quest to build their own Black city within the city fueled the struggle for emancipation and full citizenship rights. Even more so than their Deep South brothers and sisters, they organized a broad range of religious, fraternal, mutual benefit, social service, educational, and entrepreneurial associations. Black churches, schools, lodge halls, and business establishments dotted the landscape. As elsewhere, however, the independent Black church movement led the struggle to resist repatriation, build the institutional infrastructure, and fight for liberation on the middle ground of the new republic.

Like their counterparts across early national America, African Americans in Baltimore, Washington, DC, and Richmond abandoned "Negro Corners" and segregated pews in white congregations and established their own churches. In Washington, DC, they reported fourteen Black churches by the beginning of the Civil War. The District's independent Black churches included most notably the Asbury African Methodist Church, located on Eleventh and K Streets on the northwest side of the city and boasting six hundred members; the Little Ark church (later renamed Mount Zion United Methodist Church); the Israel Bethel Colored Methodist Episcopal Church, located on First Street at the bottom of Capitol Hill, and affiliated with the Philadelphia-based African Methodist Episcopal Church (AME); the Wesleyan Metropolitan African Methodist Episcopal Zion Church (also known as the African Wesleyan Society), located on D Street in south Washington; and Fifteenth Street Presbyterian Church.[17] For their part, the District's Black Catholics continued to worship in white churches until the Civil War, when they formed their own independent St. Augustine Catholic Church.[18]

In Richmond, after two decades of struggle, African Americans established their own independent First African Baptist Church in 1841. They not only broke away from the white congregation, but purchased the building that had housed the original biracial Baptist church. Although they were assisted by contributions from supportive whites, enslaved and free Blacks raised the lion's share of the funds needed to purchase the building. In 1858, membership in the First African Baptist Church became so large that it exceeded the capacity of the church. Consequently, the church sponsored the establishment of new churches, including most notably Third African Baptist Church. In the meantime, a group of Black members of the biracial Second Baptist Church departed ways with the congregation and formed their own Second African Baptist Church. The Black Baptist faith and their modest but imposing edifices provided space for aspiring Black ministers to hone their oratorical skills, including most notably the Rev. John Jasper, widely known for his sermon, "De Sun Do Move," which challenged the prevailing scientific view of the solar system.[19] But the steeples of the Afro-Baptist and other churches also served notice on white Richmonders that the city's African American community was determined to etch their mark on the built environment.

The region's independent Black church movement gained perhaps its most profound expression in Baltimore. By 1850, Baltimore claimed "the greatest denominational variety of Black churches of any city in the nation." Just before the Civil War, one Baltimorean declared in New York City's *Weekly Anglo-American* newspaper that "no city where I have been can boast of better churches among our people. Baltimore churches are not a whit behind, either in beauty or attendance, for our people are a church going people."[20] Initially, the white Methodist church took a firm antislavery stand, but it soon caved to increasing pressure from proslavery forces and instituted discriminatory practices, including restrictions on interracial burial grounds, delayed communions for Black congregants in deference to white communicants, separate pews for Blacks and whites, and close surveillance and suppression of the worship behavior of Black members. Following the formation of Mother Bethel in Philadelphia in 1791, Black Baltimoreans intensified their movement toward independence. In 1810, the break finally came under the leadership of Rev. Daniel Coker, a young mixed-race minister. Referring to himself as "Minister of the African Methodist Episcopal Church in Baltimore," Coker was also the teacher in the Colored Methodist Society's school. He regularly corresponded with Richard Allen, and, in 1815, he led several hundred Blacks, enslaved and free, from the Sharp Street Methodist Church to form the new independent Black African Methodist Episcopal Church. It broke ties with the white Baltimore General Conference and affiliated instead with Philadelphia's Mother Bethel. The organization rented a lot and building that had previously housed the local Zion Lutheran Church.

Baltimore's Black Methodist congregation gained distinction as "the first independent Black church in the slave states." White Methodists tried to retain control over its property and affairs, but in 1816, the Pennsylvania Supreme Court ruled in favor of Bethel AME and severed its ties to the white body. In the same year, free Black church leaders from Maryland, Pennsylvania, Delaware, and New Jersey met in Philadelphia and formed the independent African Methodist Episcopal Church conference, with authority to establish AME bodies across the country. The Baltimore church became its first certified affiliate. Membership rapidly increased to over 600 in 1817. The organization moved into new and larger facilities—a three-story brick building on the south side of Fish Street with "the inside finished in a convenient manner with Pulpit, Pews & Galleries." The church took out an insurance policy on the building worth $4,000. Bethel emerged as Baltimore's "largest and most influential Black congregation," with over 1,200 members in 1848.[21]

The growth of Black fraternal orders and mutual benefit societies reinforced the spread of Black churches and the rise of independent Black institutions. In 1787, after the U.S. Masons denied African Americans a charter, the British Masonic Order approved the establishment of an African Masonic Lodge, with jurisdiction in "North America and Dominions and Territories there unto belonging." Under the leadership of Prince Hall, a Boston resident, soapmaker, minister, and Revolutionary War veteran, the Prince Hall Masonic order soon spread from the urban Northeast to Baltimore, Washington, DC, and Richmond. In Baltimore, African Americans formed the Friendship Lodge of Free Masons in 1825; the Zion Lodge No. 4, a Prince Hall Lodge of Free and Accepted Masons in 1848; the Baltimore Bethel Benevolent Society of Young Men of Color (1821); the African Friendship Society for Social Relief (1844); the African Civilization Society; and the Royal Arch Masons, Good Samaritans, and the Order of Odd Fellows during the 1850s. In 1835, a group of Black ministers reported some thirty-five active Black fraternal societies in Baltimore, each with up to 150 members or more. Free people of color in the nation's capital also formed a plethora of benevolent societies, including most notably the Resolute Beneficial Society in 1818.[22]

Key to the financial resources and social activities of the fraternal orders, mutual benefit societies, and even the churches were a variety of female auxiliaries and independent orders. In his address to the founding meeting of the masonic order, Prince Hall had underlined its plan to combat sexism against Black women along with racism against Black men and women. "[M]uch more on public days of recreation," he said, "How are you shamefully abus'd." He went on, "the arrows of death are flying about your heads; helpless old women have their clothes torn off their backs, even to the exposing of their nakedness." In 1835, in Baltimore, nearly a dozen Black women's organizations served the needs of the community under such names as the Star in the East Association; the Female Ebenezer Association; and the Daughters of Jerusalem. By the beginning of the Civil War, some forty-four different African American religious, civic, labor, mutual aid, and fraternal organizations reported accounts at Baltimore's Eutaw Savings Bank. Black women's work, along with that of Black men, not only fueled these bank accounts. Black women's organizations also played a pivotal role in the rise of a wide range of buildings servicing the African American population while also influencing the city's built environment.[23]

In addition to building projects focused on the specific mission of their diverse organizations, African Americans launched numerous school building campaigns to advance the education of Black youth. As early as 1807 in Washington, DC, three Black workers, two of them employed at the Navy Yard and who could not read or write, built "a small frame schoolhouse in northwest Washington" and hired a white man to teach their children. Over the ensuing four years, African Americans and their white supporters in the District of Columbia opened three additional schools for Black youth. When the Resolute Society's school faltered after a few years of service, Henry Smothers, a free man of color, built a schoolhouse for Black children on New York Avenue and soon enrolled as many as 100 students. When Smothers ceased teaching, the popular teacher John Prout succeeded him, though unlike Smothers he charged a fee. Aletha Tanner, who had enrolled her nephew John Cook in Prout's school, called the "Columbia Institute," succeeded Prout in 1834 and renamed the school Union Seminary. Established under the leadership and teaching of Myrtilla Miner, a New Yorker with strong support from the Quaker community, Harriet Beecher Stowe, and other antislavery northerners, the school opened in 1851. Before closing its doors in 1861, Miner's school had gained widespread credit as a well-endowed, organized, and successful high school for Black students. According to historian Constance M. Green, "The colored girls enrolled there received a better education than that available to most white children." By the end of the Civil War, an estimated 1,100 Black children attended private schools in the District of Columbia and over 42 percent could read, write, and figure.[24]

In 1847, when the Black Baptist minister Noah Davis moved to Baltimore from Virginia, he marveled that Baltimore's Black population was so "advanced in education." Like their counterparts in Washington, DC, Baltimoreans had started to build schools to teach Black youth from the beginning of the postrevolutionary years. In 1801–02, along the way to building an independent Black church, African Americans purchased Baltimore's African Institute, a combined church and school originally established by the Maryland Abolition Society and later known as the African Academy. However, until the community hired the educator Daniel Coker as teacher in 1809, the school made little impact on the education of Black children. Under Coker's tutelage, beginning with 17 students, the school soon emerged as a highly accomplished model of Black education in the early nineteenth-century Upper South. Coker not only taught "classical literature and history," but also African and African American history, to call attention to the achievements of Black people on a global scale. By 1860, by one contemporary estimate, over a dozen African schools taught some 2,665 Black children in Baltimore, about 10 percent of the city's total free Black population. The literacy rate for all the city's free Blacks rose from 42 percent in 1850 to 55 percent in 1860.[25]

Alongside schools, churches, and lodge halls, free people of color creatively used their property holdings to launch businesses serving both Black and white clients. They not only regularly rented out basements, attics, or rear houses to free Blacks and slaves alike, but also opened their own shops, oyster houses, cook shops, restaurants, and diverse retail establishments. Even enslaved men and women were enterprising; in an unusual case, in 1805, one slave gained permission from the Baltimore mayor's office to open "an academy school for dancing," primarily to serve "free people of color."[26] In Washington, DC, in 1814, Nicholas Warner, described in the city directory as a shoe cleaner, advertised the movement of his business to a new location, "in the cellar of the house next door to McLeod's Tavern, but was raising his prices one dollar a month thereafter." Jesse Garner, an oyster seller, informed his customers that he had ample supplies of oysters. Located in the back of the Washington Hotel and almost directly across from the Methodist Meeting House, Garner's oyster house promised oysters "prepared in any manner, at any time gentlemen may think proper to call." An exceedingly enterprising businessman, Garner soon announced the opening of a boot-and shoe-blacking business, just a door west of the Washington Hotel. He offered to clean shoes by the "month, week, or pair; and pickup could be arranged." Moreover, his ad also called attention to a shoe-shining product for sale. "Imperial Liquid Blacking," he wrote, had distinctive qualities (brilliant shine, leather conditioning, and simple to use) that "could not be surpassed by any in America."[27]

African American entrepreneurs not only provided important commercial services to their communities, but also deepened the impact of the Black city-building process on the larger landscape and built environment of Upper South cities. Such business activities also generated resources that reinforced the struggle against human bondage. Aletha Tanner, Elizabeth Keckly, and the Wormley family, among others, established lucrative businesses in the District of Columbia. As an enslaved woman, Tanner initiated a market garden near the White House at the turn of the nineteenth century. With Thomas Jefferson and other members of Washington's white elite among her customers, her lucrative marketing activities enabled her to save enough money to buy her freedom by 1810. Over the next two decades and a half, she also purchased the freedom of another 22 relatives and friends. Born on a Virginia plantation to a Black mother and white slave-owning father, Keckly became a skilled dressmaker and later served as the principal seamstress for both first lady Mary Todd Lincoln and the wives of Confederate figures Jefferson Davis and Robert E. Lee.[28] The Wormley family, meanwhile, developed lucrative transport, catering, and hotel businesses that served Washington's white elite. The Wormley Hotel and catering business emerged as the premiere establishment of its kind in the antebellum city. Wormley's hotel included a restaurant that also became popular with Radical Republicans who arrived in the nation's capital in rising numbers during and following the Civil War.[29]

In the cellars and back alleys of the cities' landscape, participation in a thriving informal economy of "grogshops and tippling houses" supplemented and reinforced the entrepreneurial activities of the African American community and deepened their impact on the cityscape. Gambling, prostitution, and the sale of alcoholic beverages punctuated this underground commercial terrain. Municipal police regularly raided and closed illegal businesses operated by enslaved and free Blacks in the cities, but they quickly reopened clandestinely in "new locations," often built with hidden passageways and doors so their patrons could escape in the event of another raid. In Richmond, free Blacks Clinton James, Richard Taylor, and Joseph Dailey operated, respectively, a multipurpose business (including a grocer and restaurant); the Taylor House, an underground hotel that offered gambling, liquor, and prostitution; and "a five-acre fishery." James Robinson established a successful dray business with ten horses and several wagons in his possession; Christopher McPherson was an outstanding example of what historian Juliet E. K. Walker describes as a late eighteenth-century slave "intrapreneur." Born in bondage, McPherson had learned to read, write, and figure as a young man. Before his emancipation in 1792, he became the "chief operating officer" of his owner's Elk Horn Store in Peterburg, Virginia. He also supervised his owner's "ironworks, mills, coal mines, and shipping concerns," all before gaining his freedom, moving to Richmond, and establishing "a prosperous carriage and drayage business."[30]

By the beginning of the Civil War, African Americans in the urban Upper South had purchased and rented property, established their own homes, and built their own community infrastructure of business enterprises, churches, schools, and a plethora of fraternal orders and social welfare organizations to meet their own needs. While the most lucrative of these Black businesses served an elite clientele, far more legal and illegal underground and informal businesses served the masses of enslaved and free people of color. At the same time, both enslaved and free Blacks broke ranks with discriminatory biracial churches and built their own independent Black churches, which in turn helped to fuel the creation and expansion of other institutions, including most notably mutual aid, burial, and benefit societies.

While African Americans occupied neighborhoods throughout the urban Upper South, these energetic city-building activities transpired within the spatial context of increasingly Black residential areas. As free and enslaved people of color encountered growing racial and ethnic hostility and efforts to dislodge them from the landscape of the city, region, and nation, African Americans would use their emerging Black city to launch equally energetic social movements to defeat the American Colonization Society, demolish the institution of slavery, and remove restrictions on free people of color.

STRUGGLE FOR FREEDOM

The proliferation of Black institutions, mutual assistance networks, and predominantly Black living spaces all fueled the emergence of stronger and more militant movements for freedom, citizenship, and equal rights in the city. Revolutionary ideology, evangelical Protestantism, and the Haitian Revolution also played key roles in the escalating political mobilization of the Black community as the early nineteenth century got underway. During the summer of 1800, under the leadership of Gabriel Prosser, an accomplished blacksmith, a large number of Black artisans tested the revolutionary potential of the Black city. They used their access to the hiring-out system to build an extensive underground army of resistance in Richmond, Virginia. Black smiths, coopers, weavers, carpenters, and shoemakers, among others, carried word of the planned revolt to and from the various plantations and from town to country.

At the height of mass mobilization for the revolt, Prosser claimed a following of some 10,000 Blacks; even conservative officials placed the number at 1,000–3,000 recruits. Inspired by the Bible, "where God Says, if we worship him, we should have peace in all our land . . . [and] five of you shall conquer an hundred & a hundred a thousand of our enemies," the plan called for an armed attack on slaveholders under the banner of "Death or Liberty."

The men pledged, "by God," to fight for their freedom as long as they had breath in their bodies. The revolt collapsed in late August when an informer alerted authorities to the plan and a severe thunderstorm destroyed roads leading into Richmond from a central gathering place for rebels on the city's edge. Law officers soon arrested, tried, and hanged Prosser and 27 of his comrades for their part in the plot. But Gabriel's Rebellion would reverberate in the minds and consciousness of Blacks and whites across the late antebellum years and beyond.[31]

In the wake of Prosser's foiled revolt, African Americans did not relent in their struggle for equal rights. Nearly two decades later, Baltimore's AME minister Daniel Coker published his antislavery tract, *A Dialogue between a Virginian and an African Minister.* Considered one of the earliest antislavery publications by a Black man, *A Dialogue* employed both biblical scriptures and enlightenment philosophy regarding the rights of man to demolish the southern defense of slavery as ordained by God and nature. In concluding his argument against human bondage, Coker used a widely cited New Testament verse: "But Ye are a chosen generation, a royal priesthood, and an holy nation, a peculiar people; that ye should shew forth the praise of him who hath called you out of darkness into his marvelous light; which in time past were not a people, but are now the people of God" (1 Peter 2:9–10). Fifteen years later, at a celebration of Haitian independence, free Black Baltimorean William Watkins lauded the Haitian Revolution for demonstrating in no uncertain terms that the peoples of Africa "never were designed by their Creator to sustain an inferiority, or even a mediocrity, in the chain of being." In his words, the independent Black republic of Haiti was "irrefutable proof" that African people were not inferior to "Europeans or people of any other nation upon the face of the earth."[32]

As the work of the American Colonization Society picked up steam and the nation strengthened the place of slavery in the economy, politics, and culture of the republic, Upper South urban Blacks developed vigorous anticolonization, antislavery, and equal rights movements for people of African descent. Although the ACS maintained headquarters in Washington, DC, the organization made little headway among the District's Black population, most of whom vehemently opposed colonization. They spoke out against the idea in public forums and wrote against it in the Black and white press. Although he at first embraced colonization, the ex-slave Thomas Smallwood soon changed his mind and became one of the strongest free Black opponents of the ACS and its efforts to recruit Blacks to the Liberia project. On one occasion, he declared that "not one in a hundred" Black Washingtonians "could be induced to go to Africa." In a conversation with one journalist, an enslaved Washingtonian dubbed colonization a "great injury" to Black people "by lessening the little interest that was before felt for them, and increasing the wish to get rid of them." In 1831, under the leadership of teacher and minister John W. Prout, a group of Black Washingtonians gathered at the AME church and declared their opposition to colonization. "The soil that gave us birth," they said, "is our only true and veritable home."[33]

Richmond's free Black population also resisted colonization, quietly but firmly. Just seven members of the First African Baptist Church departed for Liberia in the 1840s and only six left in the 1850s. But Baltimoreans waged perhaps the most militant fight against the ACS. They published numerous anticolonization essays, held indignation meetings denouncing repatriation, and confronted agents of the ACS in public forums, helping to stymie its recruitment efforts among free people of color. In *Freedom's Journal*, the Baltimore teacher and correspondent William Watkins forcefully argued that the ACS "had no right to meddle with the free men of color." Free Blacks, he said, were as "truly Americans as the President of the United States, and as much entitled to the protection, rights and privileges of the country as he." In 1825, using the handle "A Colored Baltimorean," Watkins also opposed colonization in the columns of Benjamin Lundy's *Genius of Universal Emancipation*. "Why should we abandon our friends and everything associated with the dear name of *home* . . . for the enjoyment of liberty divested of its usual accompaniments?" Watkins asked. He argued that vacating Baltimore and Maryland would strengthen, not weaken, the institution of slavery at a time that increasing numbers of enslaved people were obtaining their freedom in the city and state.

Reminiscent of the historic anticolonization meeting held at Mother Bethel in Philadelphia, Baltimoreans repeatedly denounced the ACS and pledged to stay put and fight for emancipation and full citizenship rights on U.S. soil. As early as 1817, white colonizationists Robert Finley and William McKenny reported a somewhat positive reaction among rural free people of color on the Eastern Shore, but much opposition in Baltimore and the Western Shore. White colonizationists often reported that Black Baltimoreans "left no stone unturned to put obstacles" in the way of their efforts to recruit Blacks to the cause of Liberian emigration. Free people of color interrupted ACS speeches, urging them to abandon their misguided ideas about African repatriation and devote their energy to movements to educate the Black population. They also organized numerous small working groups for the express purpose of identifying, visiting, and persuading prospective emigrants against leaving the city under the auspices of the ACS.[34]

Colonizationists and their agents frequently complained that prospective emigrants often changed their minds following these visitations. As one ACS agent put it, "In a day or two after . . . someone had been after him, filling the mind of the emigrant . . . with alarming & false statements, changing him from his purpose." In 1831, a group of free Black Baltimoreans boarded a ship headed to Africa in a last-ditch effort to prevent local Blacks from leaving the city. As a result of their efforts, the number of Blacks departing on that voyage dropped by about 50 percent. Again, in the 1850s, when some African Americans from around the state and region expressed support for emigration at a meeting in the city's Washington Hall, Black Baltimoreans rose in a chorus "with deafening opposition."[35]

Opponents of colonization sometimes described Black supporters of the ACS as "traitors to their race." In private homes and public places, ACS supporters faced vehement resistance from Baltimore's free people of color. Under the force of such relentless opposition, the Maryland branch of the American Colonization Society abandoned its recruitment drive in Baltimore by the late 1830s. Fewer than 8 percent of all African Americans leaving the state under sponsorship of the Maryland ACS departed from Baltimore. Even as early as 1832, an exasperated Maryland colonizationist remarked that "the prejudices of the coloured people of Baltimore and other large Towns, against African Colonization, are so strong that distributing literature among them would be to throw it away."[36]

African Americans were, however, by no means uniformly hostile to the notion of leaving the United States to secure economic and political independence for themselves and their families. A few Blacks departed for Liberia under the auspices of the American Colonization Society. Early on, a small group of free Black Washingtonians supported the program of the ACS. They also endorsed "a memorial of the free people of color," crafted by white colonizationists extolling the virtues of movement to West Africa. In Baltimore, Rev. Daniel Coker cast his lot with the ACS and led a group of some 88 free Blacks to West Africa in 1820. And, in December 1826, several members of Bethel and the Sharp Street Methodist churches left Baltimore for Liberia. During the years 1820 to 1835, 13 members of Bethel departed for Liberia, while another small contingent left with the lay minister and schoolteacher George R. McGill, who had received the promise of a schoolmaster position upon arriving in Africa. But most Black emigrants preferred to move on their own terms under their own leadership, and to other places in North and South America and the Caribbean as well as Africa. In 1839, following a meeting at Bethel AME Church, a group of Black Baltimoreans selected Thomas Green, Nathaniel Peck, and Thomas S. Price to spearhead the exploration of South America and the Caribbean for possible resettlement opportunities for Black workers. In April 1840, after nearly three months of exploratory visits to Guiana and Trinidad, over 250 Black Baltimoreans left the city for Trinidad.[37]

Despite a few notable examples of African Americans leaving the urban Upper South for places outside the United States, most determined to stay and work for liberation in Virginia, Washington, and Maryland. They forged alliances with small numbers of sympathetic whites and helped to build local and regional movements against the slave trade and the institution of slavery itself. In his groundbreaking study of interracial antislavery movements during this period, historian Stanley Harrold carefully documents how these Black and white activists built what he calls a "subversive community." They waged "a desperate struggle to *subvert* slavery on its own ground." In Baltimore, African Americans—most notably William Watkins, teacher and minister; Jacob Greener, housepainter and teacher; Daniel Coker, minister and teacher; George R. McGill, minister, teacher, and businessman; and Hezekiah Grice, butcher, to name a few—built alliances with such antislavery whites as Elisha Tyson, Benjamin Lundy, and, for a while, William Lloyd Garrison. A northern-born Quaker, Tyson moved to Maryland at an early age and later became a successful flour merchant in Baltimore. Lundy moved to Baltimore in the year of Tyson's death in 1824. Born in New Jersey in 1789, Lundy had published his weekly abolitionist paper, *The Genius of Universal Emancipation*, in Ohio and Tennessee before arriving in the Monumental City. For his part, William Lloyd Garrison also joined this group of white supporters of the antislavery movement when he moved to Baltimore to take the post of associate editor of Lundy's *Genius of Universal Emancipation* in 1829.[38]

The rise of interracial antislavery efforts in Baltimore had roots in the early years after the American Revolution. In 1789, Quakers and other antislavery whites in Baltimore formed a society to promote "the abolition of slavery, and for the relief of free negroes unlawfully held in bondage." Until it disbanded in 1792, in addition to aiding fugitives and pushing for the emancipation of enslaved people, the organization filed numerous individual legal petitions for freedom on behalf of free Blacks. Following the War of

1812, the antislavery activist Elisha Tyson and other concerned whites launched the Protection Society of Maryland to stop the kidnapping and re-enslavement of free people of color as the domestic slave trade from the Upper to the Lower South intensified. The group petitioned the Maryland legislature to pass stronger measures. African American churches reinforced these efforts by holding fundraising dinners and other support activities, including establishing neighborhood watch patrols that monitored the movement of slave-catchers and kidnappers. In one case, when hired hands of Baltimore's Austin Woolfolk slave-trading company dragged a Black woman through the streets toward the local jail for sale to the Deep South, Black and white antislavery activists confronted the men and freed the woman.[39]

Tyson is reported on occasion to have gone "alone and unarmed and helped to rescue six enslaved people from five pistol-wielding slavetraders." Tyson reportedly faced down the traders, declaring "shoot if thee dare . . . but thee know, that the gallows would be thy portion." For his part, Garrison spent forty-nine days in the Baltimore jail for charging one of Austin Woolfolk's ship captains as "a robber and murderer." In 1826, under the leadership of white Baltimorean abolitionist Benjamin Lundy, the city hosted a meeting of the American Convention for Promoting the Abolition of Slavery and Improving the Condition of the African Race. The convention attracted 23 delegates from both northern and southern states and pledged to advance the movement to free slaves and "protect the rights of free persons of color." Emboldened partly by such evidence of interracial support, free men of color Hezekiah Grice, William Watkins, and others intensified their assaults on slavery from the pulpits and other public places in the city. Grice and Watkins also spearheaded the formation of the National Convention of the Free People of Color, designed to create a national forum to debate pressing issues affecting the lives of both free and enslaved people of color, including slavery and the colonization movement. This organization laid the foundation for the rise of what became known as the Negro Convention Movement of the early nineteenth century, resulting in annual meetings between about 1830 and 1835.[40]

As the center of the domestic slave trade shifted from Baltimore to Washington, DC, antislavery activists focused increasing attention on efforts to outlaw the buying and selling of human beings in the nation's capital. The daily scenes of auction blocks, slave pens, and chained coffles pushed assaults on the slave trade to the forefront of a vibrant antislavery movement in the

District of Columbia. Blacks and their abolitionist white allies dubbed Washington "the great Man-Market of the nation." As early as 1802, a group of residents petitioned Congress, urging legislators to prevent outsiders coming into the District solely "for the purpose of purchasing slaves." On one occasion, Edward Coles, a young assistant to President James Madison, decried the sight of slave caravans in the nation's capital, describing one scene as "such a revolting sight," with "gangs of Negroes, some in chains, on their way to a southern [slave] market." In 1835, the northern colonizationist Ethan Allen Andrews loudly proclaimed the slave trade "an outrage upon public sentiment." He decried the U.S. capital becoming "the very seat and centre of the domestic slave trade."

Debates in the halls of Congress also reinforced the movement's focus on eradicating the slave trade in the District of Columbia. In 1828, Representative Charles Miner of Pennsylvania declared that northerners had an obligation to address the slave trade "because their tax money helped to pay for jails used as holding pens for slaves awaiting sale." Over the next decade, an escalating number of petitions calling for an end to the slave trade in the District provoked southern congressmen to impose a "gag rule," terminating the government's receipt of any more petitions against commerce in human beings. Over the next eight years northern congressmen led an ultimately successful fight to repeal the measure as a "denial of freedom of speech and petition." Enslaved African Americans later recalled the intimate details of life inside the antebellum urban slave markets of the nation's capital. Captured and enslaved in the Deep South during the 1840s and 1850s, the New York–born Solomon Northup later recalled his sojourn in a "slave pen" in Washington, DC. Northup and his fellow bondsmen and women occupied a room "about twelve feet square—the walls of solid masonry. . . . [T]here was neither bed, nor blanket, nor any other thing whatever. . . . The building . . . was two stories high. . . . [W]ithin plain sight of this same house, looking down from its commanding height upon it, was the Capitol." Still, as late as 1862, when Congress emancipated slaves in the District of Columbia ahead of the Emancipation Proclamation, Washington's city council pleaded with Congress to delay emancipation in the District which would, in the council's view, transform the city into "an asylum for free negroes, a population undesirable in every American community."[41]

Perhaps the most potent manifestation of the fight against slavery and the slave trade in Washington was the collaborative work of Thomas Smallwood and Charles T. Torrey. Born a slave in Prince George's County, Maryland,

Smallwood learned to read and write and purchased his own freedom for $500 at about age 30, around 1831. He paid for his freedom in installments while living and working with a Scottish immigrant named John McLoad, who also contributed to Smallwood's education. He developed a business buying and selling shoes, married, started his own family, became a class leader in the African Wesleyan Church, and gained employment at the Washington Navy Yard before meeting the white, Yale-educated abolitionist Charles T. Torrey. Torrey and Smallwood shared a belief that slavery as an institution "oppressed Blacks, corrupted both races, and violated Christian precepts" of the brotherhood of man and the fatherhood of God. Smallwood, his wife Elizabeth, Torrey, and Torrey's friend Mrs. Padgett, supported by a small group of white abolitionists, helped to construct "a clandestine network of safe houses" in the city that enabled 150 enslaved people to escape over a two-year period. From the outset of his collaboration with Torrey, Smallwood described their activities on behalf of enslaved people as "our new underground railroad."

The District of Columbia's resistance network included hundreds of people, stretching from Washington northward and to some extent southward. This network not only included the activities of organized white Quakers and free people of color in Delaware, Pennsylvania, and New York, but also the ongoing actions of "the escapees themselves, who frequently provided funds and logistical support for their northward journey." According to historian Stanley Harrold, the biracial underground railroad network developed by Smallwood and Torrey "remained for over twenty years a central facet of Washington's subversive community." Furthermore, according to Harrold, the subversive activists Torrey, Smallwood, and others conducted what amounted to "guerilla war against slavery in Washington and its vicinity." The two men, Harrold said, pushed resistance to the trade in human flesh to the edge of violence. After they arrested Torrey for his activities, authorities reported that he "carried pistols."[42]

In 1848, Washington was also the scene of the largest attempted escape of fugitive slaves on record. Under the leadership of the free Black carpenter Daniel Bell, a Navy Yard employee, and several other Black and white men, including the captain of the *Pearl*, 76 fugitives boarded that schooner to set sail for freedom. The escapees included men, women, and children; skilled as well as general laborers and household servants; dark- and light-skinned Blacks; educated and less educated. All in all, they were considered "representative of the *respectable* people who constituted the African American component of Washington's biracial antislavery community." As historian Stanley Harrold persuasively argues, the free Black Daniel Bell and his family were key to the *Pearl's* bold effort:

> Born a slave in Prince George's County, he worked for twenty years molding and casting iron at the Washington Navy Yard. . . . When his sale to traders disrupted his life, Bell rebounded in 1847 by purchasing his freedom for a total of $1,630, part of which a local white nonabolitionist merchant named Thomas Blagden provided. Later that same year Bell's wife, her children, and two grandchildren faced sale south. On the basis of a former master's will, they had been free for a number of years. But, despite Bell's engagement of Joseph H. Bradley as counsel in their behalf, the master's widow successfully challenged the will and prepared to sell all eleven to the highest bidder. Arranging to have them shipped aboard the *Pearl* was Daniel Bell's desperate attempt to avoid losing them.[43]

As the *Pearl* set sail, the "winds died" down and the ship lost time. In the meantime, a mob of some 30 white men, "armed to the teeth," overtook the ship and returned the captives and their white accomplices to Washington. Authorities and slaveowners swiftly "sold and scattered" the fugitives across the South, while their white collaborators received long prison terms. At the jail, where numerous bystanders, reporters, slaveowners, and officers of the law gathered to determine or witness the fate of the captives, one young domestic worker boldly refused an offer "to repent" and return to the household of her owner. When a reporter asked why, she replied, "Have I not the same right to my freedom that you have, and could you have neglected a chance of gaining it, had you been a slave." Frederick Douglass also weighed in on the significance of the *Pearl* escape attempt: "Slaves escaping from the Capital of the 'model Republic!' What an idea!—running *from* the Temple of Liberty to be free!"[44]

The aftermath of the *Pearl*, and, two years later, passage of the Congressional Compromise of 1850 changed the context of the freedom struggle in Washington, DC. This legislation outlawed the slave trade in the District of Columbia. Slave auctions, street coffles, and prison pens gradually declined, though they did not readily disappear. Slave traders moved their operations out of Washington over to Alexandria, which had broken ranks with the District of Columbia and returned to the state of Virginia in 1846, and continued buying and selling human beings. Thus, Washington's African Americans and their antislavery community continued to collaborate to foil sales, rescue victims, and inch the city, region, and nation closer to full emancipation of enslaved and free people of color alike. However, direct confrontations with slave traders and authorities gradually gave way to increasing emphasis on raising funds to lodge freedom suits and undermine the system of slavery through the courts. Indeed, Washington's antislavery community had foreshadowed the growing use of this strategy as the fate of the *Pearl* fugitives unfolded. In the "most famous and expensive" of these cases, William Chaplin helped to free Richard Edmondson and his two sisters Mary and Emily from being sold into slavery further south. Chaplin had succeeded Charles Torrey (who had died of tuberculosis in the Maryland penitentiary in 1846) as the northern newspaper correspondent in Washington, DC, and as a close ally of African Americans and the antislavery movement. Chaplin and Paul Edmondson, the three captives' father, traveled to New York, where Harriet Beecher Stowe helped to raise $2,250 to free the Edmondson children.[45]

In Richmond, too, African Americans developed a network of interracial subversives who helped to construct an elaborate fugitive slave network. Black and white antislavery activists enabled enslaved people to escape bondage through aid with shelter, disguises, transportation, and even travel guides. In 1858, for example, local authorities uncovered a complicated underground escape route that extended from Richmond to Norfolk. On the Norfolk end of this network, police arrested nine people, soon dubbed the "Norfolk Nine." The group included a mix of six Blacks and three white ship captains who helped to stow away fugitives seeking passage to freedom. But African Americans organized the escape, including raising money to pay the ship captains for their part in the escape network.[46]

Antebellum urban Blacks also waged spirited fights against racial discrimination in the newly created and expanding public school system and against recurring legislative assaults on the rights of free people of color. Washingtonians challenged the District of Columbia's discriminatory registration and bond system. Some free people of color, such as William Costin, refused to register or post the bond. When authorities fined Costin for his actions, he appealed the decision in the courts. While the court upheld the provisions of the Act of 1836 for newcomers to the city, it repealed the measure for established free people of color like Costin. In Baltimore, African Americans protested the exclusion of Black children from the city's new public schools, opened in 1829 on basis of taxes paid by free people of color as well as white citizens. In 1839, 50 free men of color (Nathaniel Peck, John Fortie, Moses Clayton, and others) sent a signed petition to the mayor and city council "Praying that Colored Persons May be Exempted from the Payment of the Public School Tax" because they received none of the benefits. But the city steadfastly refused to support the opening of Black schools with public tax dollars.[47]

On a more upbeat note, however, Baltimore's African American community mobilized their resources and defeated the "Jacobs bills," a series of destructive anti–free Black legislation sponsored by the rabidly racist Maryland legislator Curtis W. Jacobs. The Jacobs bills called for "nothing short of an ultimate extinguishment of the free negro element" from the city, region, and ultimately the nation. Specifically, the Jacobs measures asked lawmakers "to forbid all future manumissions" of enslaved Blacks and encourage the re-enslavement of "all Black people already free" to be "compulsorily hired out for renewable terms of ten years." Under the leadership of men like William Watkins and others, African Americans organized a petition to lawmakers staunchly opposing the Jacobs bills. A thousand Black people signed the petition and succeeded in rallying sympathetic white men and women to their cause.

One group of 200 white women organized their own petition against the measures. They sent the petition to the legislature, declaring their firm opposition to "the adoption of such unrighteous bills" that "trample underfoot every precept of the Gospel." In the determined African American drive to defeat the Jacobs legislation, Black barbers helped to secure signatures for the petition and Black churches organized a "day of fasting and prayer." Churches also organized special presentations/sermons in which ministers spoke out specifically against the Jacobs bills. Thanks to their efforts, the measures were roundly defeated. When the proposals reached the floor for a vote, a broad cross section of the white community and legislators rejected the bills as too "severe and oppressive" even for slaveholding Maryland, as the region and nation inched closer to war over the institution of slavery.[48]

Construction of the Black city in the urban Upper South was by no means an uncomplicated project of racial, color, gender, and class solidarity. It entailed significant intraracial conflict along each of these lines. To take one prominent example, the phenomenal growth of Baltimore's African Methodist Episcopal Church unfolded largely without Rev. Daniel Coker's pioneering leadership. Following charges brought against him in the AME Conference and the levying of subsequent sanctions and limitations on his ministry, Coker departed the city and country for Liberia. Meanwhile, in 1832, the predominantly Black Sharp Street Church (with over 1,900 Black members) was incorporated into the white Methodist Episcopal Church Conference hierarchy, which promised greater exercise of authority and opportunities for leadership among African American ministers and members. In addition, more so than Baltimore, Washington's free Black population included a substantial number of people of mixed-race or mulatto ancestry. These people had somewhat "greater access to education and employment opportunities than their darker-skinned peers."[49]

As modest as African American property ownership may have been, there were important status distinctions even among property owners themselves. In early nineteenth-century Baltimore, at one extreme, the drayman George Douglass owned "three lots of property, including a brick house, valued at nearly $2,000," while the city assessed the property of the free Black woman Harriet Berry at "just $13.75" and waived taxes on it. Few women gained access to the skilled crafts and lucrative service trades that translated into greater capacity to purchase real estate. Aggravating such status and gender cleavages, the independent Black churches restricted leadership to men and favored skilled over general laborers and free over enslaved Blacks for leadership positions. In 1852, at a national Black convention in Baltimore, most of the 18 Baltimore delegates were skilled craftspeople, ministers, or semi-skilled workers. Only one appeared in the city directory as a "laborer." Such distinctions often prevailed against the grain of more egalitarian church charters. In its articles of incorporation, the St. James Protestant Episcopal Church declared that "all the male members of the church above the age of 21 years whether bond or free, holding seats in the Church are entitled to vote."[50]

By the late antebellum years, color consciousness also intensified. Free people of color scrupulously identified themselves as "respectable families" and fostered intermarriage within the group—emphasizing the "weight that family name carried." By the 1850s, Baltimore's free Blacks had started to marry along the color line. In a sample of 360 marriages in four wards of the city in 1850, the evidence shows that "most marriages were endogamous." African Americans most often married someone of the same color. "Mulatto husbands were more than four times more likely to have mulatto wives than Black wives, while Black husbands were nine times more likely to have Black wives than mulatto wives." Unlike elsewhere, however, color consciousness in Baltimore sometimes favored dark over light-skinned Blacks. Daniel Coker, the light-skinned elite minister, failed to get his way in a religious dispute in the AME Church and decided to leave the city for Liberia as a consequence. Indeed, one historian has suggested that Frederick Douglass might have departed Baltimore in part because his mixed-race heritage secured little favor in either Black or white communities. Chesapeake society seemed reluctant to accord light-skinned people any special privileges over their Black counterparts. Douglass himself later suggested that divides among newcomers and old residents, rural and urban residents also gained some modest expression in the preindustrial urban Upper South, recalling that the children in Baltimore chased him, calling out, "Eastern Shore man."[51]

Nevertheless, such socioeconomic, political, and cultural conflicts in the urban Upper South were less pronounced than they were in the Deep South, or even the urban Northeast, partly because the propertied Black elite was smaller and more integrated by color than it was elsewhere. In Baltimore County, between 1806 and 1816, an estimated 78 percent of Blacks applying for freedom certificates were considered "African" and not "mulatto." This ratio persisted through the 1850s, when about 22 percent of Baltimore City's free Blacks were light-skinned people of color. By contrast, in New Orleans, light-skinned Blacks made up about 75 percent of the total free Black population; and in Charleston, mulattos constituted about 67 percent of all free Blacks by the late antebellum years. Moreover, compared to their counterparts elsewhere, fewer Blacks moved into the property-owning class in Baltimore, Washington, and Richmond. In 1820, for example, Baltimore's percentage of Black property holders stood at 5.3 percent, compared to 11.6 percent in Philadelphia. By 1850, the Philadelphia figure had dropped to 0.72 percent, but Baltimore plunged even further, to 0.40 percent, "not only the lowest of any major city in the slave states but also the lowest in the nation." In the urban Upper South, Charleston's Brown Fellowship Society had no significant analog.[52]

．．．

In the urban Deep South, the African American city-building process had deep roots in colonial British, Dutch, French, and Spanish America, but Black life in the urban Upper South unfolded almost exclusively within the context of the American Revolution and the creation of the new slaveholding republic. Hence, a complicated blend of slavery and freedom shaped the city-building process in the region, where most enslaved Blacks had won a hard-fought battle for their freedom before the onset of the Civil War. Unlike the urban Deep South, however, the line between slavery and freedom blurred considerably in cities of the Upper South, where far less pronounced internal class, color, and social conflicts than elsewhere encouraged racial solidarity, strengthened the city-building process, and enhanced movements to abolish slavery, fight African recolonization schemes, and secure full citizenship rights for free people of color. As the Civil War got underway, the Black urban Upper South would not only play an important role in the emancipation of some four million enslaved people of African descent. It would also help to complete the fight for formal citizenship rights for a half-million previously emancipated but disfranchised free people of color.

THREE

Forging the New South City

FOLLOWING THE DEVASTATION of the Civil War and the emancipation of some four million enslaved people, African Americans' quest for land, freedom, and their own metropolis took on special significance in the expanding urban-industrial South. By the early twentieth century, escalating Black labor migration had enabled Birmingham, Durham, and Atlanta to rebuild dynamic industrial cities in the wake of economic collapse during and after the Civil War. Postbellum southern economic and political elites articulated a clear vision of urban capitalist development; attracted rising levels of northern economic and infrastructure investments; and declared a firm commitment to improve class and race relations. But these ideas were quickly folded into the post-emancipation white supremacist system. Increasing racial restrictions on wages, the franchise, entrepreneurship, and educational opportunities undermined African Americans' access to resources for building their own metropolis.

Nonetheless, against the lengthening veil of Jim Crow and the spread of industrial capitalism, African Americans forged a variety of new communities across the postbellum urban landscape. These New South Black urban centers also provided the institutional and political foundation for challenging the emerging white supremacist Jim Crow order, even as they helped to transform the larger southern cityscape. But the descendants of African people enslaved in the urban South would now face a new form of inequality and social injustice. Whereas the urban case for redress was heretofore a minority experience for antebellum Black urbanites, it would now become a majority experience as the Great Migration picked up steam during the late nineteenth and early twentieth centuries.[1]

MAP 4. As this maps shows, Black community development in the so-called "New South City" was situated geographically in both the Upper (Durham) and Lower South (Atlanta and Birmingham). Hence, this cluster of cities is defined less by subregion than by ideological and political orientation. They were overtly and even aggressively modernizing but racist capitalist urban-industrial areas.

NEW SOUTH CITY

Although federal forces destroyed southern iron works, foundries, roads, railroads, and other components of the urban infrastructure during the Civil War, New South cities soon rebuilt from the ashes. In 1870, a British visitor described Birmingham, Alabama, as "by far the most deeply interesting material fact on the American continent." Pennsylvania's iron and steel man Andrew Carnegie later described Birmingham as his most "formidable enemy." After formation of the Pratt Coal and Coke Company in 1878, the

Birmingham district attracted increasing amounts of northern capital under a vigorous campaign for the creation of a "New South" urban-industrial economy. Three decades later, in 1907, Birmingham deepened its ties to northern capital when the region's large Tennessee Coal, Iron, and Railroad Company merged with the giant U.S. Steel Corporation headquartered in Pittsburgh.

Partly through annexation, Birmingham's Black population rose from 3,000 in 1880 to 26,000 in 1890 and to 133,000 by 1910. African Americans had increased from only 10 percent of Jefferson County before the founding and growth of the Birmingham iron and steel district to 43 percent of the total population in 1900, nearly evenly distributed between men and women. During the first decade of the twentieth century, however, Birmingham's white population expanded at a faster rate than its African American population, and even with huge leaps in overall numbers, the Black percentage of the total slipped to 39 percent in 1910. From the outset of Birmingham's rapid industrialization, it attracted increasing numbers of Black women domestic and personal service workers, but the sex ratio reached near parity in Birmingham, as employers recruited growing numbers of Black men to work in the district's expanding iron, coal, and steel industries.[2]

After its destruction by northern troops during the Civil War, Atlanta also rebuilt through a successful campaign to attract northern capital to the city and region. Atlanta's Black population rose from just over 16,300 in 1880 to about 52,000 by World War I, but as a percentage of the total population peaked at 46 percent in 1870 and steadily declined to 33 percent as World War I got underway, since the city's total population had also dramatically increased, from 37,400 in 1880 to nearly 155,000 in 1910. Emphasizing its capitalist development and values, Atlanta became a major rail center, manufacturer, and marketing center for Georgia's extensive cotton plantations.

Touting itself as a "New South" city, Atlanta staged its first International Cotton Exposition in 1881. This exhibit underscored the city's commitment to "remodeling the South in the image of Northern industrial capitalism." Atlanta's textile industry was less successful in employing Black workers than the Birmingham coal and iron industry. In 1897, when the Atlanta Fulton Bag and Cotton textile company employed Black women to fill 20 to 25 positions as "bag folders," previously a job reserved for white women, some 200 white women in the folding department walked off the job. The following day, an estimated 1,200 white men, women, and children joined the strikers. After four days of strikes, the company discharged the Black women employees.[3]

In North Carolina, the state legislature acknowledged the rapid growth of Durham Station from a mere railroad outpost before the Civil War into the state's leading city during the postbellum years by naming the nearby rural countryside Durham County. By 1910, the city's population had increased to over 18,200. Durham's Black population also mushroomed from just a handful of residents at the outset of the postbellum years to almost 7,000 by 1910, nearly 40 percent of the total, with women outnumbering men at a rate of 100 to 83. But, as in Birmingham and Atlanta, the Black population as a percentage of the total lost ground in Durham during the second decade of the twentieth century. As elsewhere in the post–Civil War years, rising capitalist investments fueled the growth of Durham as a major postbellum city. As early as 1887, the city witnessed the construction of twelve new tobacco factories.

The southern-born industrialist James Buchanan Duke utilized African American labor to transform a small tobacco firm, founded by his father, into the giant American Tobacco Company. Duke not only took advantage of Black labor, but also exploited new technological breakthroughs in cigarette production as well as the absence of significant government regulations of his business ventures. These advantages enabled Duke to squash his competition and catapult his company to the top ranks of the U.S. industrial system, along-side Standard Oil, U.S. Steel, and others. Thus, while Julian Shakespeare Carr, Jr., and other industrialists moved to Durham and set up lucrative textile and other businesses, tobacco production dominated Durham's industrial land-scape. In 1889, *Turner's Directory* enthusiastically reported, "Durham exports her bright leaf tobacco to all the principal markets of Europe, and her smoking tobacco and cigarettes to every nation under the sun." The packaging on Duke's tobacco products gave Durham its industrial era moniker, "Bull City."[4]

Alongside capitalist economic development, New South ideologists prom-ised new and improved class, race, and community relations. At its first world's fair, Atlanta described itself as a liberal "gateway city" to social change in the South. Similarly, Durham elites declared that the "*broad-gauged, Liberal Minded Gentlemen*" of the New South would usher in a "spirit of racial cooperation necessary to make the city a success." Influenced by the persistence of an Old South paternalistic and racist ideology of social rela-tions and cooperation, New South industrial elites urged northern employers to "harmonize" the interests of capital and labor, Blacks and whites.

Aware of the massive postbellum labor strikes and ethnic conflict that engulfed Pennsylvania and other northern industrial states and cities, New

South industrialists argued that southern labor relations (including the use of Black workers before and after the Civil War) were less violent and exploitive than northern industrial relations. One Alabama newspaper, the Selma *Southern Argus*, declared, "There is suffering in the manufacturing cities of New England. There are want and destitution in the coal and iron region of Pennsylvania and New York." By contrast, the *Argus* concluded, the South represented a model of "well-fed, well-clothed," and presumably "contented" workers, whites and especially "Negro laborers."

But New South class and racial rhetoric quickly faded as economic elites firmly embraced racial segregation and the socioeconomic and political subordination of Black people. Atlanta's journalist and popular leader Henry Grady invoked scripture to support white supremacy. "What God hath separated," Grady said, "let not man join together. . . . Let not man tinker with the work of the almighty." In Durham, according to historian Leslie Brown, Jim Crow was a form of "homegrown oppression and terrorism, an American apartheid sanctioned by all three branches of government."[5]

Grady and other New South spokesmen promised white workers a protected place in the pantheon of white supremacy. In Birmingham and elsewhere, as historian Henry McKiven makes clear, "Blacks would perform common labor, freeing white workers to achieve positions in society reserved for them only. Recognizing their interests in the maintenance of the racial order, white workingmen would assist [elites] in the control of the Black laboring class." Although New South industrialists assured white workers that their "superior" economic status would be protected, they recruited growing numbers of Black as well as white industrial workers and stymied the organized labor movement. During the late nineteenth and early twentieth centuries, as the United Mine Workers of America organized Black and white miners in the region, coal mine operators used subcontractors, convict prison miners, arbitrary hiring and firing decisions, and the police forces of the various states to suppress worker rights and deny demands for higher wages and better working and living conditions. In 1907, following TCI's merger with U.S. Steel, corporate resistance to the organized labor movement intensified and reinforced the "open shop."[6]

Nonetheless, against the backdrop of the expanding Jim Crow order, New South Blacks gained access to their own spaces. They purchased their own land, built homes, and rented property in a growing range of neighborhoods. Their city-building activities would also seed the early struggle against the spread of the white supremacist regime itself.

As the segregationist and class-stratified racial order took hold, African Americans intensified their quest for land and urban space to construct their own New South city. Their historic quest for their own homes intersected with larger predominantly white homeownership movements. In Birmingham, the city's real estate brokers launched an aggressive "Own Your [Own] Home" campaign that targeted potential Black and white buyers. Boosters placed ads in Black and white newspapers, extolling the virtues of homeownership under such rubrics as "Buy Now," "No Place Like Home," and "Own Your Home." The nationally circulated Black weekly *Pittsburgh Courier* reported that perhaps "no other group believed so thoroughly ... in the Philosophy of home buying and home owning" as "the American Negro." These ideas gained widespread articulation in Birmingham, where steel worker George Brown later recalled that he arrived in the city from Dallas County, just south of Selma, with "the idea of having my own house. My uncle had his own home and I liked that idea."[7]

African Americans initially shared space with white residents in the Central Business Districts of New South cities. In Birmingham, they occupied business and residential property alongside whites in the CBD along North Twentieth and Twenty-First Streets. But this tightly intertwined Black and white CBD soon declined as property values escalated, racial discrimination against Black workers and businesses intensified, and Black residents relocated to an increasingly segregated area near Fourth and Eighteenth Streets and "Sixth Avenue North." At the same time, other African Americans moved to the outlying suburb of Smithfield. Located west of Birmingham's original city limits, Smithfield was carved out of a five-hundred-acre agricultural site. At the start, it represented a haven for poor and working-class immigrants, American-born whites, and African Americans seeking better and more spacious homes in the region. But Smithfield soon became a predominantly Black community as Euro-Americans moved increasingly into outlying all-white settlements. Between 1898 and 1910, Smithfield grew from 55 percent Black to 83 percent Black and the Black population continued to rise. In 1910, the city of Birmingham annexed Smithfield along with some nine other outlying municipalities, but Smithfield retained its distinctive character as an almost exclusively African American city within the city.[8]

Atlanta's Black population also carved out its earliest living spaces in and around the Central Business District. But Black Atlanta's quest for land and housing took shape in the context of an extraordinary level of physical destruction of the urban infrastructure as a result of the Civil War. Nonetheless, by the late nineteenth and early twentieth century, Black Atlantans occupied an expanding array of neighborhoods across the urban landscape, including Summer Hill, Shermantown, and Jenningstown, among others. They built their largest settlement just north of Summer Hill at Shermantown in the city's Fourth Ward. Named after the man who led the destructive conquest of Georgia during the closing years of the Civil War, Shermantown soon emerged as the most significant postwar Black settlement in the city. Within this community, Auburn Avenue, a street originally settled by white professionals, emerged as the center of Black residence. During the 1880s and 1890s, increasing numbers of Black household and general laborers moved there alongside the city's rising Black middle class. The number of homeowners among Black barbers, shoemakers, draymen, grocers, and women household workers gradually increased. Some women reported property holdings of $1,200 and more, while several barbers reported taxable property between $1,900 and $2,400.

Smaller and more affordable "Victorian bungalows" on Auburn and surrounding streets offered African Americans much better housing than they occupied in other parts of the city. In 1902, for example, Johnsontown developed when Black wage earners Callie and Columbus Johnson bought a home in an abandoned area near the Southern Railway line. In the wake of the Johnsons' purchase, African Americans built the community with their own hands as stone masons, carpenters, and general laborers. Still, Shermantown persisted as the most significant Black settlement until the emergence of the West Side as the centerpiece in Atlanta's expanding New South Black metropolis. Located not far from Shermantown, Jenningstown provided African American home buyers access to one of only a few areas somewhat above the flood zone available to Black residents. The area soon acquired the name "Diamond Hill," although the homes sold for the lowest prices in the city's real estate market. In addition to professional and business elites, some general laborers and household workers like Elizabeth Pope, a washerwoman and cook, and her husband saved money and purchased homes there. Other concentrations of Black residence included the neighborhoods of Bedford Pine, Pittsburg, and Mechanicsville.[9]

During the Civil War and early postbellum years, Durham's African Americans moved into an area called "Hayti." According to an 1877 property deed, the earliest official document of the Black community's origins, the neighborhood took shape when John Daniels purchased a lot "near the town of Durham in the settlement of colored people near the South End of the corporation of said town known as Hayti." At the end of the Civil War, nearly 2,400 Blacks already lived in the area, compared to about 3,100 whites. As early as 1869, African Americans had gained access to land for a church and school, when the Black missionary and agent for the Methodist Church Edian Markum (Markham) arrived in Durham to establish Methodism among Black people in the area. Markum acquired land and "built a brush arbor and soon after a small cabin beside it." In 1870, he turned the land over to a small group of church members and moved on to another assignment. Black property ownership gradually picked up steam in the years following Markum's departure. In 1873, Dempsey Henderson purchased a ninety-three-acre tract of land in rural Durham County for $600.[10] While skilled Blacks like the blacksmith Lewis Pratt and others occupied and owned their own homes in the city center, not all central city Black artisans were land-owners: "Squire Bull, the shoemaker, also lived in town but owned no land."[11]

As suggested by the experience of Squire Bull, across the urban New South, most Black residents rented rather than owned their own land and homes. With the incorporation of suburbs, Birmingham's homeownership jumped to a high of 30 percent, but the rate of Black homeownership remained significantly lower than for whites. As late as 1910, only an esti-mated 10 percent of all Birmingham families owned their own homes. In Atlanta, even as Black property holdings increased during the final decades of the nineteenth century, less than 1 percent of the city's Black population (which was 40 percent of the total) reported owning their own homes.[12] African Americans also occupied more dwellings in low-amenity areas of the city as compared to their white counterparts. Large numbers of African American owned homes that were basic single-frame "shotgun houses," or, in some cases, "double shotgun" houses. Longtime Smithfield resident Alma Dickerson recalled that her extended family lived in shotgun-style houses across the city of Birmingham. Municipal zoning laws and discriminatory sewer and water services not only reinforced residential segregation, but also undermined the quality of housing for Blacks in the area. In 1909, a city ordinance mandated improvements in the city's sanitation services but speci-fied that such improvements would cover the area "south and west of the blocks dense with Black families." Atlanta not only neglected the sanita-tion needs of African American, poor, and working-class residents but permitted the dumping of garbage in and around their neighborhoods. Disproportionately larger numbers of African Americans also occupied floodplains with the highest incidence of unsanitary and unsafe housing prone to disastrous flooding from area rivers and streams. Despite Durham's renown as a city of homes and prosperity among early twentieth-century urban Blacks, as historian Leslie Brown documents, late nineteenth- and early twentieth-century Durham was also an unsanitary, disease-ridden place, where undiagnosed "'Durham fever" took a heavy toll on the health and well-being of the city's Black population.[13]

Although New South urban Blacks would build their cities primarily as tenants of rental properties rather than independent property owners, they rejected the idea that such dwellings would necessarily remain unlivable. Many tenants took as much pride in their homes and space as did homeowners. One Birmingham resident declared, "If I live in a [rental] place, I believe in keeping it clean and doing little things to keep it looking nice around the yard and house, no matter whose house it is." In Birmingham's central city, Ellen Tarry recalled a childhood home of "flowers blooming in the yard and the vines so shiny and green, it did not matter too much that the houses never were painted.... [The] houses were well-kept, since that was the fashionable section of town for our people in those days." Still others used rental properties as a stepping stone to homeownership. "You would rent," said one resident, "But you bought furniture and you fixed it up. You put up nice draperies, and things ... until you could get out of there and find somewhere you could buy."[14] One long-term Smithfield resident remembered that "if you were in Smithfield, you were an 'A Number One Black.'" Seetha Jackson, a resident of Smithfield for over sixty years, later remembered with pride how she "never lived in a rented house in my life, believe it or not." Moreover, as Lynne Feldman notes, Black elites "lived in grand homes. Often they built on multiple lots and built vertically as well as horizontally."[15]

However precarious rental or owner-occupied properties may have been, African American land, housing, and neighborhoods anchored the rise of a dynamic urban institutional life in Birmingham, Durham, and Atlanta. New South urban Blacks transformed the urban landscape, advanced the city-building process, and spurred the growth of the New South Black metropolis.

The African American metropolis took root within the expanding residential, neighborhood, and spatial context of the New South city. The independent Black church movement emerged at the center of African American community-building activities, supplemented by fraternal orders, and a variety of social service, civic, and business organizations catering to Black and white clientele. As elsewhere across the urban South, however, the proliferation of New South Black institutions not only influenced the city's built environment, but also established the organizational foundation for more effective assaults on the segregationist order.

FOUNDING NEW INSTITUTIONS

The rapid expansion of the independent Afro-Baptist Church dominated Black institution-building activities, reinforced by the founding of Methodist, Episcopal, Presbyterian, Roman Catholic, and Congregationalist bodies. By the turn of the new century, Birmingham's Black community reported over one hundred Baptist churches, compared to about thirty African Methodist Episcopal and Holiness congregations. Formed in 1873, as the First Colored Baptist Church, the city's pioneering Sixteenth Street Baptist Church became one of Birmingham's earliest and most influential Black churches, followed by a cluster of powerful and disproportionately elite Methodist Episcopal and Congregationalist churches, including St. Mark Episcopal; St. Paul's Methodist Episcopal; Metropolitan AME Zion; St. John AME; and the First Congregational Church, to name a few.[16]

As early as 1870, Atlanta's Black population had organized eight churches; it pulled together another fourteen over the next decade. By the early twentieth century, Atlanta reported some twenty Black churches serving the African American community. Baptists led Atlanta's independent Black church-building movement, followed closely in numbers by African Methodist Episcopal and Methodist Episcopal congregations. The earliest wave of Atlanta's Black church-building movement included the rise of Friendship Baptist Church in 1862 and the Wheat Street Baptist Church in 1869. During the 1880s, the establishment of Ebenezer Baptist Church stood out. Established in 1886, Ebenezer would become a centerpiece in the city's long civil rights movement. African Methodist Episcopal and Methodist Episcopal churches supplemented the roster of New South Black Baptist churches. In Atlanta, African Methodist Episcopal churches increased from four in 1880 to a dozen by the turn of the new century. Following the Civil War, Atlanta's African American Methodists had joined the AME Bethel congregation, headquartered in Philadelphia, through the South Carolina Conference of

FIGURE 3. Birmingham, Alabama's Sixteenth Street Baptist Church, designed by two African American architects, brothers Thomas C. and Benjamin L. Windham. The Windham brothers were not the only Black architects shaping the landscape of twentieth-century Birmingham. Others included C. Goodson, A. F. Jackson, and most notably Wallace A. Rayfield. Danta Delimont Creative/Alamy Stock Photo.

the AME church. Under the leadership of Rev. Joseph Wood, the city's AME body claimed some 1,600 members by 1900. In the meantime, Atlanta's Black community also founded Wood's Chapel AME in 1867 and Shiloh AME in 1872. These churches, vibrant offshoots of Bethel, "reflected population growth and community expansion rather than congregational disputes." In Durham, the White Rock Baptist Church and the Union Bethel African Methodist Episcopal Church (later renamed St. Joseph's AME Church) took center stage in the institutional and religious life of Hayti.[17]

Churches not only served the spiritual, intellectual, and cultural needs of the African American community; they also helped to build and reshape the urban landscape. Independent Black religious organizations launched spirited edifice-building campaigns and soon placed an indelible mark on the built environment. When Rev. T. W. Walker vacated the pastorship of Birmingham's Sixth Avenue Baptist Church in 1891, he spearheaded the formation of Shiloh Baptist Church. Within less than five years, the church reported over 2,000 members and a new $40,000 church home. Nearly a decade later, Sixteenth Street Baptist Church secured a mortgage to construct its own $62,000 edifice on the northern edge of the Central Business District. Formed in 1882 under the leadership of Burton and Hattie Hudson, Birmingham's First Congregational Church opened in a storefront on Seventeenth Street and Second Avenue North. Encouraged by the fruits of their own financial efforts, supplemented by support from the American Missionary Association, the congregation built its own edifice at Third Avenue and Twenty-Sixth Street North.[18]

In the summer of 1866, Atlanta's African Baptist Church broke from the white body, renamed itself Friendship Baptist Church, and opened services in a "freight boxcar." Under the leadership of Rev. Frank Quarles, formerly an enslaved minister, Friendship Baptist Church soon purchased a lot and built a new church home on the corner of Haynes and Markum Streets on the West Side. Somewhat later, Friendship Baptist also built a second new home to accommodate its expanding membership on "a few blocks away at Haynes and Mitchell" streets. Friendship also served as the first home for the Atlanta Baptist Seminary and for what would later become Atlanta University, Morehouse, and Spellman College for women. In Atlanta, as the demand for Black Baptist churches escalated, Friendship Baptist Church also helped to launch at least seven of the thirteen Baptist churches established before 1900. The Wheat Street Baptist Church, the most influential of the new churches, soon erected its own building on Wheat Street, where it slowly expanded until a fire destroyed its building during World War I. It took nearly three decades for the congregation to rebound and rebuild the edifice.

Supported partly with funds from the North Georgia Conference of the African Methodist Episcopal Church, Atlanta's Bethel AME built its "first small church on Jenkins Street" in 1869 but relocated to Wheat Street (renamed Auburn Avenue in 1893) a year later. In 1891, the church undertook an ambitious thirty-year building campaign. Thirty years later, during World War I, "Big Bethel," as the congregation became known, had "erected the largest Black-owned church in Atlanta and had avoided the debt that plagued many Black churches by raising subscriptions to pay for the new building as it was being constructed." Meanwhile, Atlanta's First Congregational Church, founded by white teachers and staff of the American Missionary Association (AMA), became a Black church in the early 1880s. Blacks continued to worship under a white pastor until 1894, when Rev. Henry Hugh Proctor took charge as the first Black leader of the congregation. All along, however, Black residents contributed their own resources to the church-building program. Moreover, as students enrolled in classes at the AMA sponsored Atlanta University, they also added their labor to the building of "a five-thousand-dollar brick church and a sixteen-hundred-dollar parsonage on ground deeded to First Congregational by the AMA."[19]

In Durham in 1866, African Americans founded White Rock Baptist Church. Initially called First Baptist Church, the congregation changed its name after purchasing a lot to build its first church, a frame structure at the corner of East Pettigrew Street and Coleman Alley. During the 1890s, White Rock Baptist built a brick edifice at the intersection of Fayetteville Street and Mobile Avenue. Following its founding in 1869, Durham's Union Bethel gradually "upbuilt" the church "from a mere log cabin into a wood frame structure" during the 1870s and 1880s. In 1891, the church moved into a "handsome building renamed St. Joseph AME Zion Church and made of Fitzgerald bricks." Indeed, Richard Fitzgerald responded to the religious demands of his workforce and built Emmanuel AME Zion Church in the city's west end. Meanwhile, Mt. Vernon Baptist Church developed as an offshoot of the White Rock congregation, and New Bethel Baptist Church emerged in the Pin Hook neighborhood to the northwest of Hayti. While Emmanuel and St. Joseph underscored the growing impact of the Methodist denomination on the cityscape, Mt. Vernon and New Bethel, both founded during the 1880s, strengthened the institutional core of the Black Baptist faith.[20]

Alongside the brisk church-building movement, fraternal orders and mutual aid organizations reinforced the city-building process. During the late nineteenth and early twentieth centuries, which some scholars call the "Golden Age of Fraternalism," New South urban Blacks joined African Americans nationwide in founding the True Reformers, Prince Hall Masons, Grand United Order of Odd Fellows, the Knights of Pythias, the Elks, and many other local, regional, and national fraternal orders and mutual benefit societies. These organizations not only served the material, social welfare, and cultural needs of members, but also deepened the impact of African Americans on the city's built environment. Initially, the fraternal orders met in churches, private homes, and commercial establishments to conduct business, but they increasingly raised money and built their own buildings. As the Great Migration got underway, the Knights of Pythias, Odd Fellows, Masons, and Elks had constructed their own "temples" or meeting halls across the urban New South. In Birmingham, the African American builder T. C. Windham built the Elks' Hall at a cost of $68,000, while both the Knights of Pythias and the Odd Fellows occupied their own offices at 1524 1/2 Second Avenue. For its part, the state-level Knights of Pythias, headquartered in Birmingham, purchased the large downtown Alabama Penny-Prudential Building for $75,000.[21]

African American women played a major role in the building of the religious and fraternal infrastructure of New South cities. They were especially prominent in the "upbuilding" of Hayti, in Durham, North Carolina. White Rock Baptist Church had taken shape under the leadership of Margaret Faucette, a widow with thirteen children. Faucette also helped to recruit the congregation's first minister, whom she later married. Similarly, missionaries Molly and Edian Markum spearheaded the founding of Hayti's Union Bethel African Methodist Episcopal Church and school. Durham's Black women also took a commanding position in the rise of the Episcopal St. Titus Chapel, spearheaded by Pauline and Sallie Fitzgerald, the daughters of Cornelia Fitzgerald, in 1903.[22]

Women's clubs and auxiliaries of all-male organizations—most notably the Court of Calanthe associated with the Knights of Pythias, the Odd Fellows' Daughters of Rebekah, and the Prince Hall Masons' Eastern Star—reinforced and often took the lead in fundraising drives to build the fraternal buildings as well as churches. In Atlanta, Friendship Baptist Church founded the benevolent Daughters of Friendship Union No. 1 in 1869. In addition to providing substantial sick and burial benefits, the organization launched an ambitious building program to expand the social work of the church. In 1884, during the pastorship of Rev. E. R. Carter, Frank Quarles's successor, the order purchased property near Friendship Baptist. A decade later, the Daughters of Friendship bought additional land south of the church and just north of Carter's home on Tatnell Avenue. The group later sold a building on the new property, but retained the land, which it rented out for $300 yearly. Further, as historian Allison Dorsey makes clear, the Daughters of Friendship enabled Rev. Carter, his congregation, and especially Black women to take the first step in a turn-of-the-century movement to build a Baptist Home for the African American aged and an orphanage for Black children—the Baptist Center for Wayward Youth. Black women's mutual aid and fraternal bodies provided multiple social services, while reinforcing infrastructure-building within Black urban communities.[23]

As fraternal orders and churches spread across the urban landscape, African American entrepreneurial activities undergirded the city-building process. African Americans developed Black Business Districts (BBDs) adjacent to the racially segregated white Central Business District (CBD). African American entrepreneurs—barbers, beauticians, blacksmiths, shoemakers, and especially building and construction workers—played a major role in the development of land and property across the urban New South. From the outset of Durham's postbellum history, for example, African Americans helped to construct the larger city as well as their own metropolis through the building and construction industry. The realtor and builder Richard Fitzgerald enabled African Americans to expand their access to land and homes through his thriving brick-making business. In 1887, the company reported "orders on hand for two million bricks" to meet the building needs of Durham's Black and white residents.[24]

Durham is considered by some scholars to have been the capital of the Black business world. In 1898, under the leadership of John Merrick, a former slave, brick mason, hod carrier, and barber, a group of seven Black business and professional men and a skilled tinsmith launched the North Carolina Mutual Life Insurance Company. Drawing upon the example of Blacks in Richmond, Virginia, the North Carolina organization aimed "to aid Negro families in distress." By 1915, Merrick and his partners, Dr. Aaron McDuffie and the grocer Charles C. Spaulding, had not only opened offices in twelve states and the District of Columbia. They had also established two drugstores, a Mechanics and Farmers Bank, and a real estate company, and were preparing to launch a textile mill employing Black workers. According to one manager of the company, the formation of North Carolina Mutual coincided with a time of political repression of African Americans, "when the Negro of North Carolina turned his attention to . . . education, business and industrial progress."[25]

By the early 1890s, the Duke family had recruited the Black architect Samuel L. Leary to build warehouses for their sprawling tobacco empire. But Leary also designed and built a variety of residential, civic, and commercial structures within and beyond the Black community. In addition to Trinity College's first building, which later collapsed due to a structural defect, his most outstanding architectural work included a new brick building for St. Joseph's AME Church (bricks provided by Richard Fitzgerald's brickyard)— a structure that stands to this day. As historian Jean Anderson concludes, the St. Joseph's church building represents "an exuberant expression in color and line of a talent that gave Durham a few prized landmarks." Leary's other work included Michael's drugstore, located at Maine and Mangum Streets; Mangum and Son Company; Morehead School; and his own imposing Shingle Style house on Cleveland Street.[26] Sociologist E. Franklin Frazier later lauded Durham for creating "a Black town" that rivaled and even exceeded Harlem in its material, entrepreneurial, and housing infrastructure. "Durham," Frazier said, "is not the place where men write and dream, but a place where Black men calculate and work [and build]."[27]

Birmingham's African American builder Notible B. Smith, proprietor of the Metropolitan Homes company, advertised on one occasion that he would purchase land and "build to your taste" on "easy monthly installments." In another ad, he appealed for clients who owned their own lots. Smith wanted to build no less than a hundred houses for such landowners. Birmingham's other Black contractors included the migrant C. L. Goodson; L. S. Gailard; A. F. Jackson; R. E. Pharoah; and, most notably, the brothers Thomas C. and Benjamin L. Windham. Originally from Louisiana, the Windhams launched their contracting business in 1897 and soon emerged as the city's most successful African American contracting firm. They constructed the Smithfield Trinity Baptist Church; Birmingham's historic Sixteenth Street Baptist Church; their own elaborate home office at 726 Eighth Avenue N. in Smithfield; and later the city's seven-story Light and Power Company building downtown.[28]

The Black architect Wallace A. Rayfield deepened the African American impact on the city-building process within and beyond the Birmingham district. A graduate of Howard University and the Brooklyn, New York, Pratt Institute, Rayfield worked for a Washington, DC, architecture firm and taught architecture at the Tuskegee Institute before moving to Birmingham in 1907. He set up his own firm a year later and soon opened offices across urban Alabama as well as in Atlanta. In Birmingham, Rayfield quickly secured contracts to design elaborate private homes for educator Arthur H. Parker, attorney E. A. Brown, and other members of the city's Black elite. Birmingham's African American building projects reached into Selma and other parts of the state and region, including Nashville, Tennessee and Sequin, Texas, home of Guadalupe College.[29] In 1890, a group of Birmingham, Alabama Blacks formed the Penny Savings and Loan Company. The chief proprietor and president of the bank, William R. Pettiford, a minister and realtor, explained that this bank aimed to serve the larger number of Black migrants who moved into the iron and coal district of Birmingham. Pettiford later described Black-owned banking institutions as "the practical means of financial self-defense." By 1907, the Alabama bank became the second largest Black bank in capital and deposits, behind the True Reformers.[30]

Meanwhile, in Atlanta, Mitchell Cargile, David T. Howard, Alonzo F. Herndon, and other Black real estate, building, and construction entrepreneurs pooled their resources, formed joint real estate firms, and advanced their city's home-building activities. Atlanta's Black real estate firms and financial institutions included most notably the South View Cemetery Association, founded in 1866; the Georgia Real Estate Loan and Trust Company, formed in 1890; and the Atlanta Loan and Trust Company, established in 1891. The latter company opened the European Hotel to serve visitors to Atlanta's 1895 cotton exposition, and three years later reported a total wealth of $7,000. Located at the corner of Bell and Auburn Avenues, the Atlanta Loan and Trust Company and other Black building and construction firms hired Black workers to construct commercial, civic, and residential properties, including the Schell Opera House and Hall, the Rucker Office Building, the Odd Fellows Hall, and the Carrie Steele Logan Orphanage for Black Children.[31]

In 1905, Herndon, a former Georgia slave, founded the Atlanta Life Insurance Company. Located on Auburn Avenue, Atlanta Life symbolized the growth of the city's Black business district. By year's end, the firm reported nearly $181,000 of insurance in force on 6,324 policyholders. In addition to hiring agents to cover territory across the state, Atlanta Mutual expanded through the acquisition of numerous small associations within and beyond the city of Atlanta. From the beginning, the company represented a merger of Herndon's Atlanta Benevolent Protective Association with the smaller Royal Mutual Insurance Association and the National Laborers' Protective Union. Over a two-year period, the organization acquired Empire Industrial Insurance Association, headed by AME churchmen; the Metropolitan Mutual Benefit Association; and the Great Southern Home Industrial Association. Emblematic of the rise of the New South Black city, in 1906, the National Negro Business League, formed in 1900 under the leadership of Tuskegee's Booker T. Washington, convened its national meeting in Atlanta and underscored the growing impact of African American entrepreneurship on the city-building process.[32]

As the Black metropolis took root in the expanding industrial cities of the New South, its citizens encountered mob violence, lynching, police brutality, and ongoing white supremacist movements to expel Black men from the body politic. Stunned by the emancipation and enfranchisement of Black men in the early postbellum years, Atlanta's white supremacist city council quickly voted to adopt citywide rather than ward elections to undercut the potential of Black voters to send their own representatives to city hall. This legislation diluted Black power and set the stage for recurring efforts to bar Black men from the ballot box and public office. Passage of the state's white primary law also undercut the participation of Blacks in the political process. In 1877, Georgia revised its 1868 poll tax law and reinforced the exclusion of Blacks from the electorate. The new law required payment of all back taxes in order to qualify to vote in state's elections. The white supremacist disfranchisement movement culminated with passage of the Felder-Williams Bill of 1908, which required Georgia voters "to be literate or propertied and of 'good character,'" further reducing the number of eligible Black voters. Although the city's Black population had doubled between 1880 and World War I, the number of registered Black voters had increased from 562 by the late 1880s to only about 700 during World War I.[33]

In 1888, Birmingham's all-white Democratic Party instituted the white primary and initiated the removal of Blacks from the city's formal political process. Until then, African American men had exercised the right to vote in municipal elections. Just over a decade later, the new Alabama constitution of 1901 completed the process of disfranchising Black men. Under the state's constitutions of 1868 and 1875, the number of registered African American voters rose from an estimated 30 percent in the 1870s to a range of 45 to nearly 50 percent during the 1880s. Less than six months following the 1901 law, the city's Black population of 18,000 could count only 30 registered voters.[34] And Durham's postbellum Democratic Party also determined to control the city and county in the interest of white supremacy and "white man rule." The textile manufacturer Julian Carr, who had moved to the city from Chapel Hill, became a leading figure in Durham's resurging white supremacist so-called "redeemer" Democratic Party. In 1874, Durham amended its city charter to require a ninety-day residency requirement in order to vote. This measure aimed to diminish the impact of the Black vote, based upon the great geographic mobility of the Black population and the difficulty for many Black families of remaining at the same residence for ninety days, given the volatile and shifting economic, social, and political conditions. North Carolina's movement to remove African Americans from the voter rolls culminated in the state's new white supremacist constitutional amendments of 1899–1900. These amendments included the disfranchisement of Blacks through "literacy tests, the poll tax, and the grandfather clause." Over the next five years, Blacks in North Carolina were virtually eliminated from the voting rolls.[35]

The Atlanta Race Riot of 1906 represented the most violent assault on the New South Black urban community. Throughout the summer leading up to the Atlanta riot, influential politicians and journalists had fomented a climate of racial hostility. Hoke Smith, the Georgia journalist and politician, repeatedly declared, "We will control the Negro peacefully if we can, but with guns if we must." In the weeks just before the outbreak of violence, whites circulated reports of four cases of Black men sexually assaulting white women. The Black man, the *Atlanta Journal* exclaimed, acts like the "barbarian" and destroys "what he cannot attain . . . [namely] the fair young girlhood of the South." Some 10,000 white people poured into the streets of Atlanta, killing over two dozen Black people and destroying homes, churches, schools, and places of business. Mobs entered one popular barbershop with "heavy clubs, canes, revolvers," and rifles; they killed two Black barbers and dragged their bodies through the streets, ultimately dumping them in an alley. When the violence spread outward to the upper-class Black suburb of Brownsville, police disarmed Black people in the area, while permitting growing numbers of white people to take up arms and assault Black people and their communities, both within and outside the city limits.[36]

A decade earlier, at Atlanta's International Cotton Exposition, Booker T. Washington had delivered his Atlanta Compromise Address. In his speech, Washington had underscored the efficacy of building independent Black institutions, prompting cooperative relations with white elites, and eschewing the political arena in the interest of racial peace during an expanding era of white supremacy. But these measures were not enough to secure the desired peace. On the eve of the riot, the city's leading white newspapers—the *Atlanta Constitution*, *Atlanta Journal*, and *Atlanta News* among others—had "kept up a steady drumbeat of stories designed to provoke fear and anger among whites and, at the same time, to sell many newspapers." Mob violence, police brutality, and the lynching of Blacks in nearby towns and cities also underscored the perennially precarious status of the Black city. The lynchings of Warren Powell at East Point, Georgia in 1899 and Sam Hose near the town of Palmetto, Georgia a decade later were cases in point. Some of Atlanta's armed white citizens and policemen traveled to both lynchings and actively engaged in the mob's activities at East Point, including invading Black homes and dragging Black men into the streets, where they were brutally beaten with "gun butts and whips." W. E. B. Du Bois later described the gruesome Sam Hose lynching as "the turning point" in his consciousness about the challenges of forging "reasoned" interracial dialogue "in the face of violent racism."

Nor did Black buildings escape damage. Ongoing city planning efforts sought to shape the built environment to meet the needs of commercial, civic, and political elites and middle classes. In the 1880s, Atlanta authorities demolished African American homes on Foster Street to clear a path for Edgewood Avenue—a street that permitted smoother passage between the suburbs and the CBD.[37]

Despite its vulnerability to mob violence, police brutality, and disfranchisement, the city-building process fueled the African American struggle against the segregationist system. The Black city strengthened the hand of Blacks in Republican Party politics; enabled the launch of vigorous media campaigns for social justice; and helped urban Black residents obtain tangible returns on their community-based movements for social and political change. These efforts built upon an extraordinary but short-lived moment of Black political mobilization following the Civil War. These early postbellum movements left a remarkable legacy of African American political activism that would shape subsequent efforts during the final decades of the nineteenth century and the opening years of the twentieth century.

NEW CITY POLITICS

From the outset of the postbellum years, African Americans used their expanding neighborhoods to advance their claims to full citizenship rights. In 1866, Blacks from across the state of Georgia convened a freedmen's convention "to discuss political rights, responsibilities, and goals" in the wake of general emancipation of enslaved Blacks across the entire South. The Georgia Equal Rights and Educational Association emerged from this meeting and soon organized chapters across the state, including in Atlanta. The organization played an important role in mobilizing Black people to participate in the Georgia Constitutional Convention the following year, sending 37 African Americans to serve. In 1868, Georgia's emancipation constitution enfranchised Black men. And two years later, Atlanta's Black community elected two African American men—William Finch and George Graham—to city council from its majority-Black Third and Fourth Wards.[38]

Atlanta's first Black councilmen, along with Fifth-Ward migrant and activist Jackson McHenry and other postbellum leaders, remained active in Republican party politics through the early twentieth century. McHenry regularly served as a delegate to Republican district conventions and, in 1888 and 1904, he gained election as a delegate to the Republican state convention. Similarly, in 1889, Charles William Thomas served as chair of the Republican state central committee. From the time that Finch and Graham departed public office through the 1890s, African Americans advanced their own candidates during three separate election cycles during the 1870s and four election years in the 1880s; most remarkably, in 1890 Atlanta Blacks organized an all-Black ticket and ran 10 African American men for seats on city council.[39]

In Alabama, African Americans organized the Colored Man's Suffrage Association and tested the constitutionality of disfranchisement legislation, but the U.S. Supreme Court quickly rejected their claims and arguments and ruled against them. In the aftermath of such disappointing denial of their rights as citizens, African American continued the fight for the franchise through the formation of Negro Suffrage Leagues in Birmingham and across the state. In Birmingham staunch African American Republicans launched the Negro Republican Party in 1901–02 and challenged the "lily-white" party movement's policies, including refusal to seat any of its 25 Black delegates to the Republican convention, meeting in Birmingham at the time. Some 200 delegates instead attended the Negro Republican Convention. The Black delegates roundly castigated the white Republicans for crafting and approving a "racist platform."[40]

As elsewhere in the urban New South, Blacks in Hayti, Durham, joined the Republican Party from the beginning of the reconstruction and emancipation era. Early on, they forged a strong alliance with Washington Duke. An ex-rebel, Duke had joined the Republican Party following the defeat of the Confederacy. In 1868, the state's new constitution enfranchised Black men and strengthened ties between the city's Blacks and the Republican Party, under Duke's supervision as registrar of voters for the city and county. The early postbellum Republican Party articulated a grassroots agenda aimed at dismantling the power of the old planter class in the region. When Duke prepared the voter rolls in 1868, African Americans made up 40 percent of Durham's electorate. Between 1868 and 1874, African Americans voted on equal terms with their white counterparts, meaning "any male twenty-one years or older could vote in the municipality where he had lived for ten days prior." Thereafter, despite dwindling access to the ballot box, as disfranchisement measures took hold during the late 1870s and 1880s, African American Durhamites continued their engagement in the political arena. John Merrick, Aaron M. Moore, Richard Fitzgerald, and William Pearson, to name a few, emerged at the forefront of city's Black politics during the late nineteenth century.[41]

Here too, however, racial violence and intimidation framed the African American quest for power in the electoral arena. In Durham's municipal election of 1888, the Republican Party nominated two African Americans, James Whitted and William Pearson, both teachers, to run for public office. The Democratic Party opposition launched a vicious campaign to drive them off the ballot, claiming their election would result in "Negro Domination" and "Social Equality," and accenting supposed threats to white womanhood as well as challenges to white manhood. In his newspaper, the *Durham Tobacco Plant*, Carr queried Democratic Party constituents: "White men of Durham, those who have any respect for the Anglo-Saxon Race, will you fail to do your duty on the 6th of November? . . . Will you allow negro rule or a white man's government?" Under the impact of escalating hostility and threats of violence, both Whitted and Pearson withdrew from the race, explaining that they could best serve their "race" in their "chosen profession—teaching."[42]

Despite their determination to remain connected to the formal electoral process in New South cities, by the late nineteenth and early twentieth centuries, African Americans intensified their use of churches, fraternal orders, clubs, newspapers, the press, and debate and literary societies to assail the premises of the Jim Crow order and advance demands for equal access to education, economic, and citizenship rights. By the early 1900s, a plethora of Black newspapers had emerged within the Black city. In Birmingham alone, between 1880 and 1890, eleven Black newspapers served the Black population. By the turn of the century, another cluster of Black newspapers opened for business. These organs included the *Blade*, the *Wide Awake*, the *Truth*, and *Hot Shots*, among others. Black newspapers represented a strong voice in the struggle for equal rights. Black journalists regularly condemned the destructive impact of the Jim Crow order on the lives of Black people. In some cases, their articles appeared in the columns of white dailies like the *Atlanta Constitution*. In one essay, published in the *Atlanta Constitution*, the *Atlanta Independent* columnist A. P. Nella criticized the state's convict leasing system and protested the predominantly Black chain gang under "the very shadow of Atlanta University," where the men labored in "chains and stripes." "It is anything but a pleasing spectacle," she wrote, "to see it done after this manner by Blacks exclusively."[43]

R. C. O. Benjamin, editor of Birmingham's *Negro American*, boldly editorialized on the need for change in the city's race relations. Benjamin had launched his newspaper after arriving in the city in 1886 from the Caribbean island of St. Kitts via a brief sojourn in the North. One of his early editorials declared, "We want to see the volcanic Southern prejudice and intolerance burst forth with sudden fury. We want the world to know just how matters stand with us in the South. It will cause the floods of indignation at such injustices and barbarity, to rise and swell, after that the deluge." Benjamin described the Jim Crow laws as enforced in Birmingham's city police court as "a tyranny upon justice [and] a disgrace to our Christian civilization. We contend only for constitutional rights and civil privileges." Another editor, Rev. T. W. Coffee, migrated to Birmingham from Memphis and "fearlessly" defended the rights of Black people in the columns of his paper. These activist journalists faced enormous reprisals from white supremacists, who forced some of them some of them to leave the city, including most notably R. C. O. Benjamin, for their fearless and forthright plea for social justice.[44]

In addition to Benjamin, Birmingham's Oscar W. Adams also emerged as one of the most influential Black newspaper editors in the New South. Adams moved to Birmingham from Mobile, Alabama, in 1906 to take a job at the Great Southern Life Insurance Company. He also launched his newspaper the *Reporter*. Although most historians consider the *Reporter* politically conservative, the paper's stand on civil rights was not so simple. It not only consistently supported Black entrepreneurial efforts, it also firmly advocated for the enfranchisement of Black voters and especially for equal access to public transportation facilities. Adams forcefully targeted the discriminatory practices of the Birmingham Railway, Light and Power Company, declaring that "the colored people are aroused and why should they not be aroused, when it is hardly possible for them to live in Birmingham without riding on the cars, and when they ride they are almost smothered to death in many instances because of the sandwich way in which they must ride? And, this not because of the lack of space in the cars, it is because a cruel and ignorant conductor refuses to move a little hickory board marked 'Colored.'" The *Reporter* regularly decried the taxation of African Americans for public institutions that they were "denied any permission to use." Adams also became president of Birmingham's Colored Citizens League, which later spearheaded the formation of the Birmingham chapter of the NAACP following World War I.[45]

Across the urban New South, Black residents assailed discrimination in a broad range of institutions, including the education and criminal justice systems, discriminatory voting laws, mob violence, and public accommodations and transportation, particularly the streetcars. Rev. William Pettiford used his Birmingham church and entrepreneurial pursuits as springboards in the fight against Jim Crow. In 1901, he led a petition to protest Alabama's constitutional convention, when no Blacks were called to participate.

Pettiford and other Black ministers also launched the Colored Convention and drafted a document calling for an end to lynch law and discrimination on the city's rail lines. In a direct action protest, Rev. T. W. Walker on one occasion refused to pay rail fare for separate and unequal accommodations. Authorities swiftly arrested Walker for refusing to pay carfare, for resisting arrest, and for disorderly conduct. But even the mayor of Birmingham acknowledged the injustice of asking Black patrons to pay equally for such blatantly "inadequate street car accommodations for colored people." Still, despite the mayor's recognition of city council's responsibility to improve facilities for Black people, the problem of racial inequality persisted.

In 1896, Black women launched a boycott of Atlanta's Traction Railroad to protest separate and unequal accommodations. Minister Henry McNeil Turner also called for a boycott of the city's streetcars following passage of a city council ordinance requiring "colored people" to take "back seats and let the white people occupy the front seats." A decade later, in the aftermath of the 1906 Race Riot, Atlanta's Black community regrouped. In a series of meetings with local authorities, including the mayor, police commissioner, and state militia, they explored solutions to violent race relations and lodged complaints against police brutality as well as discrimination and mistreatment of Black riders on the streetcars. Following these inter- and intra-racial meetings, Atlanta's Black and white elites forged a variety of new organizations designed to address racial conflict, including most notably the Christian Civic League and the Atlanta Civic League. The latter established a constituent "Colored Cooperative League." It sought to channel the grievances of poor and working-class Blacks into this body and formalize what historian Allison Dorsey describes as a "pattern of intraracial" class cooperation with the city's white power structure.[46]

New South urban Black activists placed equal access to education for their children at the top of their political agenda. In 1876, two years after the city opened its free public schools for white students only, Birmingham's Black community, under the leadership of activist Alfred Jackson and others, petitioned the city for the building of a "Free Colored School" for Black children. They also urged the city to provide for the equitable distribution of funds as "prescribed by law." A year later, the Board of Aldermen approved the establishment of a Free Colored School. The state agreed to pay teacher salaries, but required Blacks to furnish the building, desks, and supplies. In 1883, when the city established an all-white high school, it offered little hope for resources to open a Black high school. Only as Blacks escalated their demands during the late 1890s did the city relent and build Birmingham's Industrial High School for Black students in 1901, the same year the state's constitution disfranchised Black voters. As historian Lynne Feldman notes, "Appreciating the significance of their victory, members of Birmingham's Black community and the teachers and students cooperated in transforming the school into a unique community institution."[47]

During the 1880s, when the state approved local bond issues to build public schools, Durham officials soon constructed public schools for whites only. African Americans quickly launched a spirited campaign to build Black schools, but these efforts failed when the Democratic Party waged a massive opposition and killed the Black school movement. In the wake of this failure, activist Aaron Moore wrote to white Republican officials that the African American electorate was determined to take "definite action to strengthen our Educational Institutions, to keep negro schools and negro education out of the clutches of degraded [partisan] politics and politicians." During the election of 1898, according to historian Leslie Brown, it seems clear that Black community leaders successfully negotiated with city authorities, for although there is no existing record or paper trail to document meetings, "within days of the election, the city announced plans to build a Black public school, the Durham Colored Graded School. Julian Carr, the new chair of the school board, appointed William G. Pearson to be principal."[48]

From the early emancipation years, African Americans insisted on securing material benefits from their engagement in the political process. In 1882, the Black newspaper, the *Atlanta Weekly Defiance*, declared that "we must follow those who will be found giving us [tangible] recognition immediately." In Atlanta William Finch, one of the two early Black councilmen, secured funds to open schools for Black children, repair some of the streets in Black neighborhoods, and block early plans to demolish some of Atlanta University's buildings to make way for a new street extension. As the Republican Party lost ground to Democrats in the municipality of Atlanta and elsewhere, the most coveted patronage positions for Blacks were federal level posts. Jackson McHenry obtained employment as a janitor for the financial committee of the Georgia Legislature and the U.S. Customs House. Charles Thomas received an appointment as record clerk in the Atlanta-area Federal Court and later as private secretary to the U.S. Marshall; and most prestigiously during the period, Henry A. Rucker gained the position of collector of revenue during President William McKinley's administration. In the election of 1888, according to historian Clarence Bacote, Black political activists made it clear that they expected "two clerkships in the county courthouse, two detectives to handle Negro cases, two drivers day and night for the police wagon, four members on the Board of Education, a Negro fire company, one member of the City Council, [and] a school house for Negro children in the Fifth ward."[49]

INTERNAL CONFLICT

Building the Black city not only entailed work against the color line, but also involved internal divisions along lines of gender, class, and status. Although African American women comprised the principal foot soldiers in the fundraising brigades that built Black institutions, they were excluded from the top leadership positions in African American churches, fraternal orders, and business pursuits. Class divisions stratified the Black metropolis along multiple lines—geographic, economic, social, and political. Elite Black men, and to some extent Black women, reaped the lion's share of benefits from the rise of the Black metropolis. Atlanta's famous Auburn Avenue adjoined the elite white Peachtree Street area "just north of Five Points," an area of exclusive shops and cultural institutions, on its western edge. Popularly known as "Sweet Auburn" by African Americans, this street housed such institutions as the Prince Hall Masonic Temple as well as numerous churches, stores, and nightclubs. One domestic worker later recalled, "We just enjoyed Auburn Avenue. That's why you dressed up and put [on] good clothes and go to the show on Auburn Avenue and you were going places." While Auburn catered to a heavily middle-class and elite clientele, Decatur Street, located near the train station, housed a plethora of "saloons, brothels, and gambling houses." It was best known for its working-class and poor patrons. In some cases, even the readership of Black newspapers broke down by class. In Birmingham, general laborers, household, and semiskilled workers tended to read the *Truth*, while the city's Black elites preferred the *Reporter*. Both the *Truth* and the *Reporter* took strong positions on "equal rights and disfranchisement" of Black people.[50]

New South Black and white elites often joined forces to discuss ways to curtail the social and cultural behavior of the Black poor and working class, while at the same time protecting what they described as the "good" middle class and respectable "Negro" or the "better class." They practiced what some scholars call a "politics of respectability." In September 1922, ministers of the six largest Black Baptist churches reinforced these ideas in a signed "open letter" to the "fair-minded white people of Atlanta and vicinity" published in the *Atlanta Independent* newspaper. These Baptist leaders drew a sharp line between Black teachers, ministers, and journalists on the one hand, and what they called loafers and less literate members of the Black community, on the other. The latter, they asserted, were often ensnared in the criminal justice system for petty offenses. Intraracial class conflicts were especially prominent in debates over prohibition and third-party political movements like the Populist Party. In Atlanta, for example, leading members of the city's Black elite firmly supported the prohibition movement to outlaw the sale of alcoholic beverages.

Partly with votes from African Americans, Fulton County went dry in November 1885. As Dorsey notes, "morally conservative" Black voters, such as Rev. E. R. Carter, First Ward Club president and pastor of the Friendship Baptist Church, "were instrumental" in the prohibition victory. On the other hand, in recurring debates, many working-class Black men and women registered their opposition to prohibition and supported the return, three years later, of what some prohibitionists had called that "demon rum." As one Black proponent of repeal put it, the prohibition legislation and enforcement measure discriminated against Black residents, "I know the negroes . . . can't buy liquor and I know white men can. I ain't going to have my civil rights imposed on, and if there's any law in Atlanta I'm going to have my liquor as long as a white man has his. Prohibition is a put up job by the democrats and those high hat preachers." In short, while the temperance movement gained strong support from Black elites, working-class Blacks in Atlanta and elsewhere continued to frequent the city's dance halls and drinking establishments.[51]

Internal fragmentation and social conflict intensified by the early twentieth century. The Black city-building process became ensnared in a tangle of intraracial debates and disputes. Nonetheless, the ongoing cross-class African American quest for full citizenship rights and protection from mob violence mediated these conflicts and reconciled important differences. New South urban Blacks repeatedly pulled together across class, gender, and other social divisions. They fought mightily against the strictures of the Jim Crow order. As a result, in varying degrees of intensity, New South Black communities bequeathed a remarkable legacy of social struggle to the next generation. This legacy of activism would inform the city-building process, the Great Migration, and the rapid spread of the modern Black Freedom struggle in the years after World War II.

•   •   •

FIGURE 4. The Black church would fuel the politics as well as the spiritual life of African American urbanites. This interior view illuminates the church as an organizing site of the Birmingham movement, 1963; the Sixteenth Street Baptist Church became a key player in the modern Black Freedom struggle. Courtesy of Michael Ochs Archives.

Despite the destructive impact of the Civil War on the economy of New South cities, by the early twentieth century Atlanta, Birmingham, and Durham had emerged as thriving industrial cities with sizable Black populations. As elsewhere across the postbellum South, emancipation and the enfranchisement of previously enslaved Black men opened a new chapter in the African American city-building process. For a brief moment, Black people exercised the rights of citizens. They voted in municipal elections, elected their own representatives to public office, participated in the affairs of the Republican Party, and obtained patronage jobs for their activism in the formal electoral arena. But the emergence of the white supremacist system soon blocked this early path toward full citizenship and reinforced the growth of the separate Black metropolis. Across the urban New South, African Americans not only deepened their city-building activities, but also used their expanding institutional infrastructure as a major weapon in their fight for equal citizenship rights and economic democracy. Late nineteenth- and early twentieth-century New South political movements would set the stage for the Great Migration, FDR's labor-liberal New Deal coalition, and the rise of the modern Black Freedom struggle during and after World War II. Meanwhile, urban Blacks would have to navigate the more complex economic, social, political, class, ethnic, and race relations of the urban Southeast and Southwest.

FOUR

_____

On the Edges of the Deep South

THE RISE OF THE POSTBELLUM southern Black city was by no means limited to the Black-white cities of the New South or even the Old Deep South and Upper South cities discussed in chapters 1 and 2. The modern Black metropolis also developed in the racially and ethnically diverse settings of the Southeast and Southwest where the color line transcended the Black-white divide. In Houston, Miami, and Tulsa, African Americans not only created their own communities and influenced the built environment in concert and tension with people from a variety of racial, ethnic, and nationality backgrounds. They also forged new multiethnic communities, replete with unique forms of cooperation and conflict. Black migrants from the rural and small-town South clashed with people of African descent from the Caribbean islands. Ethnic diversity within the Black city challenged African American solidarity but deepened the transnational dimensions of the city-building process.

The transnational components of Black urban history hold profound implications for the role of immigrant Blacks for today's U.S.-based reparations movement. For a brief moment in Miami, for example, both immigrant and American-born Blacks defined their interests in almost exclusively ethnic rather than racial terms. However, despite deep ethnic divisions within Black communities in the urban Southeast and Southwest, African Americans gradually bridged their differences and used the city to strengthen assaults on the Jim Crow order. Hence, this chapter sheds light on the global dimensions of the fight for social justice for descendants of African people formerly enslaved in North America. Even so, large infusions of northern capital, industrial expansion, and the oil boom framed the emergence of a unique Black city-building experience in Houston, Tulsa, and Miami.

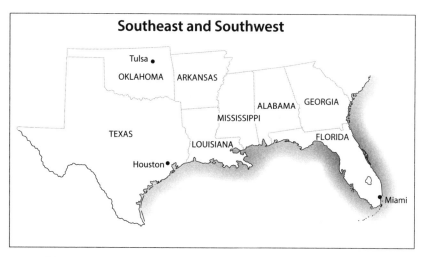

Southeast and Southwest

MAP 5. This map aims to convey a set of social determinants of the Black city on both the far eastern and western edges of the Deep South states. African American, white, and non-Euro-American ethnic group relations loomed large in the racial politics and city-building process in Tulsa, Houston, and Miami.

GAINING GROUND

During the antebellum years, New York City developers moved into the region and founded the city of Houston "on a barren edge of the Gulf Coastal Plains" in 1836. Following the Civil War, however, the Bayou City dramatically expanded as industrial capitalists connected the region to the nation's transcontinental rail network—including the Southern Pacific Railroad; the Texas and Pacific Railway; and the Atchison, Topeka, and Santa Fe.[1] By the turn of the twentieth century, the railroad industry had emerged as the city's largest employer, but it was the Texas oil boom and the rapid annexation of outlying rural and suburban communities that lay beneath the city's meteoric growth during the early 1900s. The opening of the Spindletop oil field, located east of Houston, spurred the greatest economic growth of the city. Major refineries soon sprang up in the area, including the Texas Company (later Texaco); Humble Oil and Refining; and the Gulf Oil Corporation. Moreover, in 1914, completion of the city's new ship channel (a massive federally funded project that cut through Galveston Bay and Buffalo Bayou) enabled Houston to become one of the largest port cities in the nation. The city's population exploded from about 46,000 at the outset of the oil boom to nearly 300,000 by 1930.[2]

Even more so than Houston, Tulsa owed its beginnings to the rise of Oklahoma's oil industry. As some observers and later historians put it, "Tulsa was a boom city in a boom state." The population of Oklahoma, which achieved statehood in 1907, increased "seven and a half times" between 1890 and 1920. Founded during the 1890s on land previously home to members of the Creek nation, Tulsa's population exploded after 1905, when the Ida Glenn No. 1 well, known as the Glenn Pool, gushed nearly fifteen miles away. Oklahoma soon became the nation's leading oil producer and Tulsa the city most closely aligned with its growth. Tulsa banned oil wells within the city limits and promoted the young city as "a place for both oilmen and their families." The city provided a train to take workers between the city and the surrounding oil fields. Tulsa's population increased from less than 1,400 people in 1900 to over 18,000 in 1910, and to 72,000 in 1920. Boosters soon described Tulsa as the "Oil Capital of the World."[3]

While oil spurred the growth of twentieth-century Tulsa and Houston, northern land investors buoyed the rise of Miami and the Greater Miami metropolitan region. During the 1890s, investors poured into Miami and helped to transform the city and region through this capitalist land boom. Miami also became a premier travel hub due to massive overseas immigration, technological innovations in air travel (with the launch of Pan American Airways and Eastern Airlines), and a dynamic and expanding international tourist market. Promoters repeatedly described Miami as the "Magic City," "Gateway to the Americas," and even "America's Playground."[4]

Miami's wealthy investment capitalists helped to build the city from the ground up. These investors included most notably Julia Tuttle, a widow from Cleveland, Ohio; Maine industrialist James Deering; Indiana auto-body manufacturer Carl Fisher; and Henry Flagler, a founder of the Standard Oil company and railroad magnate. Flagler played a pivotal role in the city's growth when he extended his Florida East Coast Railroad to Miami in 1896. During the first half decade of the 1920s, the city's real estate transactions climbed to twenty thousand each month, a "ten-fold" increase. Miami's total real estate value skyrocketed to $390 million before the Great Depression dragged it down to under $100 million during the early 1930s. At the same time, between 1920 and 1940 alone, Miami's population, contiguous with Dade County, jumped from 43,000 to nearly 270,000 in 1940.[5]

The African American population expanded with the meteoric rise of Houston, Tulsa, and Miami during the late nineteenth and early twentieth centuries. But the Black city-building process had deep roots in the antebellum

Southeast and Southwest. In 1836, the first people of African descent entered the Houston area with northern slaveholding investors. They worked alongside Mexican laborers in clearing the "jungle and swampy sweet gum woods" to make way for the building of a new city. By the beginning of the Civil War, over 1,000 enslaved people and nearly 200 free people of color lived and worked in Houston. The city's Black population rose to about 3,700 in 1870 and continued to grow through the remainder of the century, rising to 14,600 in 1900, then to over 63,300 as the Great Migration got underway during World War I. Migrants from different parts of Texas, Louisiana, and other Deep South states contributed the lion's share of Black migration to Houston.[6]

African Americans arrived in Tulsa as enslaved people under the control of the Cherokees and the Creeks as they moved onto Osage lands during the 1830s. In the wake of the Civil War and emancipation during the 1860s, freedmen and women remained in the area. They not only gained access to their own land under laws between the United States and the Creek, Cherokee, and other Indian nations. They also secured election to the governing council of the Coweta District of the Creek nation, the site that Tulsa would later occupy.[7] In the 1880s, some Black Tulsans supported Edward McCabe's movement to transform Oklahoma into an all-Black state for African Americans migrating from the Jim Crow South. In 1889, McCabe arrived in the Oklahoma Territory from Kansas, where he was not only active in Republican Party politics, but also the state's auditor. He purchased 320 acres of land near Guthrie, Oklahoma, and used it to launch a very popular campaign to attract Black people to the territory and transform it into an all-Black or majority-Black state.

McCabe urged southern Blacks to move to Oklahoma Territory en masse: "If you come to Oklahoma you have equal chances with the white man, free and independent. Why do southern whites always . . . try to keep the Negroes from coming here? Because they want to keep them there and live off their labor." When McCabe's program for a Black state failed under the impact of extensive white resistance, he launched a campaign to build all-Black towns across the Oklahoma Territory. Partly under his promotional activities, some twenty-eight all-Black towns developed between his arrival in the territory in 1889 and statehood in 1907.[8] African Americans from Missouri, Mississippi, Georgia, and other Deep South states swelled Tulsa's Black population from less than 2,000 in 1900 to about 11,000 by World War I. Southern Blacks soon outnumbered people of African descent born in Indian territory. By the turn of the century, "all collectively held Indian lands had been individually allotted by the federal Dawes Commission," and "many of these Indian (and Black Indian) allotments were quickly sold or ceded to white and some newer Black settlers" in the state.[9]

Miami's Black population also traced roots to the antebellum years but grew only slowly until the land boom of the 1890s and early twentieth century. In 1845, when Florida attained statehood, Miami occupied an area near Fort Dallas, an outpost of the Seminole Wars. Residents included about 500 Seminole people as well as Euro-American homesteading families; emancipated African Americans and their families; and small numbers of predominantly Black Bahamians. Over the next fifty years, Miami remained largely a remote settlement with few changes in its population. Only during the early twentieth century did the city's Black population dramatically increase from no more than 2,000 during the late 1890s to nearly 9,300 in 1920. Migrants from North Florida, Georgia, Alabama, and other parts of the Deep South as well as the Caribbean, particularly the Bahamas, fueled Miami's Black population growth. As late as 1920, Caribbean people made up about 50 percent of Miami's Black population and, as we will see, added a unique intra-racial ethnic dimension to the city-building process.[10]

Across the urban Southeast and Southwest, employers reserved the "best jobs" for whites. African American men and women faced severe limits on their efforts to move from lower-rung household service and general labor occupations into higher-paying skilled, professional, clerical, and white-collar jobs in the expanding urban economy. White migration to the cities exceeded the number of new Blacks. Hence, as dramatically as the African American population may have increased, their percentage of the total population steadily declined except for a brief incline for Tulsa in 1920. Black Houstonians declined from 40 percent during the early emancipation years to 32 percent in 1900 and to 21 percent during the interwar years. African Americans as a percent of Miami's population also dropped from about 40 percent at the turn of the century to 22 percent by 1930. Afro-Tulsans increased to a peak of 12 percent in 1920 but declined to about 10 percent in the wake of the expanding segregationist system across the urban Southeast and Southwest. Despite their declining percentage of the total, African Americans intensified rather than relaxed their ongoing quest to expand their access to land, space, housing, and neighborhoods to build their own self-sufficient city.[11]

Like their counterparts in the New South cities of Durham, Atlanta, and Birmingham, African Americans lived widely dispersed across the landscape of southeastern and southwestern cities, but they built their most prominent settlements in and around the Central Business District. In addition to such neighborhoods as Coconut Grove, Lemon City, Kebo, and Nazarene among others, Miami's African American community unfolded primarily in a near-downtown area called "Colored Town." Following the construction of his palatial Royal Palm Hotel, which employed and housed Black workers on the premises, Henry Flagler purchased and sold small "uncleared" tracts of land to African Americans to build their own homes, separate from the nearby white community. Blacks purchased 50-by-150-foot plots of uncleared land for $50 each. Located to the east of the Black district, the city's railroad tracks marked the boundary between Black and white Miami.[12]

Tulsa's Black community emerged on Greenwood Avenue after African Americans purchased property there "beginning at Archer Street." The Frisco Railway tracks represented the neighborhood's physical boundary between Black and white communities.[13] At about the same time, significant numbers of Black Houstonians lived in the city's First and Second Wards, where they made up nearly 40 percent of the total population. But it was the Third, Fourth, and Fifth Wards that emerged at the center of Afro-Houstonians' search for their own homes, neighborhoods, and community development. Houston's first substantial Black settlement emerged in the Fourth Ward following the Civil War. Newly emancipated people, mostly from plantations in the Brazas River Valley, migrated into the region and renamed the area "Freeman Town"—located to the southwest of the CBD, on the southern bank of Buffalo Creek, south to Congress Avenue, and west to Main Street.[14]

As the Black population spread across the landscape of the urban Southeast and Southwest, African Americans waged an energetic struggle to rent, purchase, and occupy homes on their own terms. After purchasing their first plot of land on Greenwood Avenue, Tulsa's African American community embarked upon its own residential building boom.[15] Early Black Tulsans built and occupied significant numbers of brick as well as wooden frame structures. Substantial numbers of Black migrants brought carpentry and brick masonry skills to the oil city. Builders not only employed Black crafts-men and general laborers. They also took full advantage of the local Acme Brickyard located just two blocks away. According to historian Henry Whitlow, "bricks were easy to secure and probably cheaper than lumber." Black business and professional people, some "rumored to have assets in excess of $100,000," contracted for the building of brick and frame houses. Sam and Lucy Mackey constructed an "elegant" frame house on their property at 356 N. Greenwood Avenue, while other Black elites like R. T. Bridgewater, the city's first Black physician, constructed imposing brick homes.[16]

After purchasing numerous small plots from Henry Flagler, Miami Blacks undertook the arduous work of clearing the land and constructing their own homes. Despite having to confront such immense odds, a small but substantial number of Black Miamians built livable and even commodious family homes and amassed significant amounts of commercial real estate. Georgia migrant Dana A. Dorsey represents an outstanding example of this phenomenon. Dorsey took full advantage of Flagler's land sales to build Colored Town, while building his own fortune. Migrating to Miami from a poor sharecropping family in Quitman County, Georgia, Dorsey brought little formal education beyond the fourth grade to the Magic City. But he had acquired carpentry skills and used his know-how on the construction of Flagler's Royal Palm Hotel. At the turn of the twentieth century, Dorsey moved into a rented room in Coconut Grove and used his income "to buy several lots in Colored Town and a few in Coconut Grove." He not only built a house for himself, but also used his carpentry skills to build "dozens of small rental homes from scrap lumber and other cheaply bought materials."[17]

Upon his death in 1940, Dorsey had amassed a million dollars in real estate holdings. His property included oil fields in Florida and Louisiana; land in Cuba and the Bahamas; stock in a copper mine in Colorado; and "properties up and down the Florida peninsula." Moreover, Dorsey's career demonstrated how Black people with money were not entirely shut out of the white market. In Miami, some members of the Colored Board of Trade purchased stock in white businesses, including insurance companies. Some African Americans like Dana Dorsey not only rented space to white entrepreneurs in Colored Town, but also owned substantial amounts of land in the white communities of North Miami, which he sold and rented to white people in the area, although he and other Blacks could not occupy property that they owned in the white community.[18]

As suggested by Dorsey's impact, the strategies that African Americans devised to secure access to urban spaces as well as the constraints that they encountered were key to the city-building movement. Poor and working-class Blacks were determined to plant their feet on urban soil, however precarious, and use it as a staging ground for their relentless search for better, healthier, and more livable quarters. In Tulsa, for example, Mabel and Pressley Little occupied a single three-room shotgun house outside the heart of the

Greenwood District. They transformed one room of the structure into a beauty parlor for Mabel and a shoeshine shop for Pressley. Mabel later recalled how business at the house "boomed so fast we were forced [to] go searching for a bigger place." The couple relocated in the downtown Black business district on 612 Archer Street. "We were glad to be on a paved street," Mabel said. Furthermore, she explained, "We had worked hard to better ourselves, for seven long years." At the end of that long investment of energy and ingenuity in the shotgun house, Mabel proudly reported ownership of "two rental houses, a new beauty salon, a comfortable home, with five rooms of brand-new furniture."[19]

Bayou City Blacks, meanwhile, transformed the Fourth Ward into a significant site of land and homeownership. The Fourth Ward's Black population had increased to over 1,300 in 1870 and to 6,400 in 1910. Soon after arriving in Houston in 1911, Clifton F. and Ruby Richardson moved into their own home on Robin Street, near the Antioch Baptist Church in the Fourth Ward: "The one-and-a-half story bungalow had two to three bedrooms, including an attic the family converted into a spare room." Two years earlier, when bartender Glenn Owen Sneed and his wife, seamstress Martha Emma Sneed, migrated to Houston from Galveston, they also moved into the Fourth Ward, where they initially occupied a house on George Street, bordering the Fifth Ward, but soon relocated to their own home on 129 W. Gray Street in the Fourth Ward.[20]

Although the size of the Fourth Ward's Black community rose steadily through the early twentieth century and African Americans occupied an expanding number of homes in the area, the Fourth Ward declined as the geographic center of Houston's Black community. African Americans moved into the Third and Fifth Wards in increasing numbers. Located near the ship channel and the large industrial district just east of downtown Houston, the Fifth Ward experienced a huge population boom during the 1880s when the Southern Pacific Railroad opened several railroad shops in the area, followed by the establishment of new manufacturing firms.[21]

The Fifth Ward's Black population increased from only about 580 people in 1870 to nearly 2,000 by 1890 and to 5,000 in 1910. In 1918, shortly after migrating to Houston from Huntsville, Texas, Joshua Houston, Jr., a blacksmith, and his wife Georgia, a schoolteacher and beautician, moved into a one-story house on Bayou Street in the Fifth Ward. After Joshua's death during the late 1920s, Georgia transformed their home into a "bed and breakfast inn" for visiting African American guests from across the region and country, including famed actors and jazz musicians Ethel Waters and Ella Fitzgerald. Survivors from the Louisiana flood of 1927 also settled mainly in a Fifth Ward community called Frenchtown, bounded by "Lelia on the south, Gregg on the east, Roland to the north, and Hogg on the west." Founded in 1922, Frenchtown included substantial land and homeowners like the carpenter Albert Chevalier who built their own homes, businesses, and community institutions in the area.[22]

It was the Third Ward that displaced the Fourth Ward as the "premier" center of Houston's African American community during the early twentieth century. The Third Ward's Black population rose from just over 1,000 in 1870 to 7,600 in 1910. Rising numbers of Black families claimed ownership of their own homes to the south along Holman, Dowling, Nagle, Rosalie, and other nearby streets and avenues. Prominent Black residents of this area included Lulu B. and Julius White; Carter and Doris Wesley; Jennie and Benjamin J. Covington; and Thelma and Ira Bryant, among others. During the Depression years, the Bryants, college graduates with advanced degrees, built a "two-bedroom, pink trimmed cottage on Holman Street and Tierwester Avenue."[23]

Despite their gradual ascent into the ranks of homeowners, most African Americans lived in rental rather than owner-occupied properties. During the early twentieth century, 17.7 percent of all Blacks owned their own homes in Miami; 31.4 percent in Houston; and 32 percent in Tulsa. In Tulsa, Houston, and Miami, increasing numbers of poor and working-class Blacks moved into "modest frame houses" as well as "shotgun" homes in the expanding metropolis. In Tulsa, one contemporary observer described the homes of Greenwood's poor Blacks as mere "shanties," sometimes constructed from the flimsy wood of "packing crates." After World War I, Miami realtors constructed over two thousand wooden tenements and shotgun houses in Colored Town. Authorities routinely confined municipal waste dumping grounds, prostitution, gambling, and other forms of "vice" to African American neighborhoods. In their quest for better living quarters, African Americans not only rented or purchased homes in different locations within the city, but often moved from one house to the next in rapid succession within the same neighborhood. Frustrated with the quest for better living conditions in Miami, one Bahamian described "Colored Town" as the "backyard of the Magic City."[24]

Residential segregation, overcrowding, and unsanitary living conditions undercut the African American quest for livable space. The legal and extralegal ideas and social practices of the emerging apartheid state seared the color line into the landscape of Houston, Tulsa, and Miami. Restrictive covenants, violence, intimidation, and a plethora of legal and extralegal measures established racially divided and unequal housing markets. In 1921, to take one prominent example, Miami's new city charter enabled councilmen to "establish and set apart . . . separate residential limits or districts for white and negro residents." It also expressly prohibited Blacks and whites from "establishing businesses in districts set aside for the other race."[25]

It was against this backdrop of racial apartheid that African Americans creatively carved out their own institutional infrastructure in the urban Southeast and Southwest. Neighborhoods with significant clusters of homeowners would provide substantial resources, material and intellectual, for building Black institutions and forging movements for liberation, but inhabitants of shotgun homes and dilapidated rental properties fueled the rise of Black churches, fraternal orders, and business enterprises. They also helped to set the stage for broader and more forceful cross-class social movements against injustice.

BUILDING INSTITUTIONS

Within the first decade of the twentieth century, Tulsa's Black community had initiated the rise of Greenwood's renowned residential, cultural, and business district, popularly known by contemporaries as "Negro Wall Street."[26] Tulsa's early Black institutions included Macedonia Baptist Church (later renamed First Baptist Church); Vernon Chapel African Methodist Episcopal Church; and Mt. Zion Baptist Church, originally known as Second Baptist Church, to name a few. In 1905, the Vernon AME church occupied a one-room house at 549 N. Detroit Street. A year later, it moved for a brief time into the Gurley Building at 114 N. Greenwood Avenue. By 1908, the church counted 71 members and moved into a frame building at Archer and Hartford Streets. By the eve of World War I, Vernon Chapel demolished its old frame building and commenced work on a new brick home on the same site.[27]

In the meantime, after occupying a succession of temporary buildings for nearly two decades, First Baptist Church, the oldest Black church in the city, founded in 1899, razed an old building and commenced work on its new $60,000 "Church on the Hill," located on Archer Street. Situated near the boundary of a white community, and mistaken for a white church, First

Baptist Church escaped the violence that destroyed Tulsa's other Black churches, including the influential Mt. Zion Baptist Church, in 1921. Under the leadership of Rev. Sandy Lyons, the original body occupied "a one-room wood frame school building" in the 300 block of N. Hartford Street. In 1913, the church purchased property to build a new edifice at 419 N. Elgin Street. But it took nearly another decade before the congregation was able to open its new $92,000 sanctuary for worship on April 4, 1921, just ahead of the angry mobs that would torch the Greenwood District and destroy the fruits of their labor and city-building efforts.[28]

Greenwood's other founding institutions included Rev. C. L. Netherland's barbershop on Boston Street; Thomas R. Gentry's real estate office on North Detroit Street; and, most notably, O. W. Gurley's grocery store on the corner of Archer and Greenwood Streets. Gurley soon added a one-story rooming house to the building and, before the race riot of 1921, enlarged the facility to four floors and diversified its set of services. The building became widely known within the African American community as the "Gurley Building."[29] By 1910, Afro-Tulsans counted a trade union (Hod Carriers Local No. 199); a newspaper, the *Weekly Planet*; a school for Black children; and the famous Williams' Dreamland Theater among the major institutions serving the city's Black community.

The proprietors of the Dreamland Theater, John and Loula Williams, originally from Mississippi and Tennessee, had migrated to Tulsa near the turn of the century. John became a skilled auto mechanic, while Loula employed her entrepreneurial skills in the development of a "confectionary," selling ice cream, candy, and soft drinks. In 1914, the Williamses built a new two-story brick building, not far from a three-story building that they owned on the northwest corner of Greenwood and Archer Avenues. A twenty-one-room boarding house occupied the second floor. The Dreamland Theater opened on the first floor under Loula's direction. Tulsa's first Black theater, it regularly featured silent movies with piano music and other forms of live entertainment.[30] As Greenwood's network of institutions expanded, the first two blocks north of Archer was dubbed "Deep Greenwood," representing the heart of Tulsa's Black community.[31] As shown in a photo taken in 1918, facing north from Archer Street,

> There were one, two and three story brick buildings located on both sides of the street for two blocks. The buildings served as offices for the doctors, law-yers and real estate as well as hotels, undertakers, drugstores, grocery stores,

dry goods store, cafes, newspaper, recreation parlors, theater, and beauty parlors—hair dressers, they were called in those days—while along Archer Street, east and west of Greenwood, other businesses were established. Brick churches were built in various sections of the community.[32]

The district's leisure world would not only "come alive" on traditional Friday and Saturday nights, but also on "Thursday nights and Sunday afternoons and evenings." These were the traditional "days off" for Black household workers living in white neighborhoods. When Mabel B. Little arrived in Tulsa from the all-Black town of Boley, Oklahoma in 1913, she later remembered "Deep Greenwood," a wide array of eateries, and "a panorama of lively dance halls, barber shops and theatres glittering in the night light." A visiting spokesman for the National Negro Business League described Tulsa's vibrant Black community, especially its night life, as "a regular Monte Carlo."[33]

By the eve of the infamous race riot of 1921, the Greenwood community enthusiastically reported, among a long list of institutions, "two Black schools, Dunbar and Booker T. Washington, one Black hospital, and two Black newspapers, the Tulsa *Star* and the Oklahoma *Sun* . . . thirteen churches and . . . two Black theaters and a Black library."[34] In 1918, one Tulsa resident, Mary Elizabeth Parrish, arrived in the city from Rochester, New York. She later recalled how she came to Tulsa not as many others had come, "lured by the dream of making money and bettering myself in the financial world, but because of the wonderful cooperation I observed among our people, and especially the harmony of spirit and action that existed between the business men and women."[35]

Miami's Colored Town also developed an impressive range of entrepreneurial, religious, fraternal, and mutual benefit organizations. Entrepreneur Henry Flagler helped to fuel the city's church-building movement when he donated small plots of uncleared land for the building of Black churches. As in the building of their own homes, however, it was the energetic investment of their own energy, labor, and resources that gave rise to Miami's African American religious infrastructure. Even more so than building their own homes, constructing imposing and even modest church buildings entailed years and sometimes decades of work before completion. Remarking on Miami's dynamic Black church-building movement, some residents described Colored Town as "a city of churches." Baptist churches dominated Miami's religious landscape, but significant numbers of Methodist, Episcopalian,

Pentecostal, Seventh Day Adventists, and a few other denominations rounded out the religious infrastructure of Black Miami.[36]

The Black church not only played an important role in the spiritual life of Miami's Black community but also helped to fuel the rise of Black businesses in the city. As early as 1904, Colored Town minister Rev. S. W. Brown, a migrant from South Carolina, launched one of the earliest Black businesses in the city, the Colored Town Bargain Store, a grocer. Brown owned the grocery building as well as several other properties in Colored Town. Miami's predominantly Black business district gradually took shape "along a half mile strip on Avenue G." During the 1920s, Avenue G was renamed Second Avenue. It gained increasing renown as Miami's "Little Broadway," a site of thriving jazz and blues night clubs, the Lyric Theater, and a number of movie houses and dance halls. It even had its own trolley car line.[37]

Second Avenue not only contained grocery and general merchandise stores, but also an ice cream parlor, a pharmacy, and a funeral parlor as well as "clubhouses, rooming houses, and an office of *The Industrial Reporter*, a Black newspaper." By World War I, prewar Black businesses and professional establishments were joined by a "soft drink plant, dentist and doctor offices, real estate firms, insurance companies, and a plethora of food, leisure time, and entertainment establishments."[38] In addition to grocer and minister S. W. Brown, leading Colored Town property and business owners included Henry Reeves, the Bahamian owner of the influential newspaper the *Miami Times*; funeral director and founder of the community's first cemetery Kelsey Pharr; and attorney Richard Toomey, South Florida's first Black lawyer, who later became vice president of the Negro National Bar Association.[39]

Houston's city-building process had deep roots in the antebellum years. In 1847, the enslaved man Elias Dibble, aided by white Methodists, founded the African Mission of the Houston Methodist Church. In 1865, Black Houstonians formed the Trinity African Methodist Episcopal Church, the city's first independent Black church congregation. Following the Civil War, Trinity purchased land at the corner of Travis and Bell Streets; it remained the nerve center of Black Methodism in the city through the early twentieth century. At about the same time, John Henry "Jack" Yates, a minister, former slave and migrant from Virginia, became the first "resident pastor" of Houston's Antioch Baptist Church, founded in 1866. Under the pastorship of Rev. Frederick Lee Lights (1894–1921), Antioch later built a brick edifice on Robin Street in the Fourth Ward. The congregation climbed in membership from 319 in 1894 to nearly 1,700 in 1915.[40]

The Church of God in Christ (COGIC) Pentecostal churches also gradually gained a footing in Houston before World War I. Unlike mainline Black Baptist, Methodist, and other denominations, the Pentecostal movement—characterized by "speaking in tongues" and extensive shouting—opened its doors to the pastorship of Black women. Located on Center Street in the Third Ward, Houston's first COGIC congregation emerged in 1909 and stimulated the growth of other churches, particularly during and after World War I. In the meantime, in 1887, Houston's Black Catholics formed St. Nicholas, their first church in the Third Ward. St. Nicholas remained the center of Black Catholicism until the 1920s, when refugees from the Great Flood of 1927 built Our Mother of Mercy in the Fifth Ward. By World War I, Houston reported no fewer than fifty-nine Baptist, eight Methodist Episcopal, five AME, two CME, one Catholic, and one Holiness congregations.[41]

Alongside the church and a variety of entrepreneurial activities, a broad range of fraternal orders and mutual benefit societies reinforced the city-building process. In addition to local branches of national organizations like the Prince Hall Masons, Grand Lodge of the Knights of Pythias, and the Grand United Order of Odd Fellows, Blacks in the urban Southwest and Southeast also formed their own local and regional mutual benefit societies, including most notably Houston's influential Ancient Order of Pilgrims. Formed in 1882, the Pilgrims eventually became a national fraternal order as the Great Migration got underway. In 1915, the order reported thirty-one chapters in the Houston area and across the nation. The Pilgrims not only provided mutual benefit, sick, burial, and health insurance for members, but also invested in real estate. By the 1920s, the order's four-story building housed a plethora of Black businesses and professional practices, including pharmacists, groceries, and law, dental, and medical offices. The company's value reached $200,000 before the Depression took its toll.[42]

Numerous women's auxiliaries, single-sex, and dual-sex orders broadened the network of mutual aid and benefit organizations. These orders took such names as the United Brothers of Friendship; the Knights and Daughters of Tabor; Sons and Daughters of Mercy; Sisters of the Mysterious Ten; the Household of Ruth; Grand Court of Calanthe; and Daughters of Czar.[43] While men spearheaded the bulk of Black business enterprises connected to fraternal orders and mutual benefit societies, women also advanced the entrepreneurial activities of these orders. In 1895, Black women formed Houston's Hermione #4, the female auxiliary of the Grand Lodge of the Knights of

Pythias. This organization not only established insurance policies and benefits for its women members; it also invested in real estate, stocks, and bonds. The Hermione #4 eventually reported an income of $600,000 and assets of $250,000—making it the wealthiest Black female fraternal society in America at that time. It was also a cross-class organization that "brought together migrant women from differing socioeconomic backgrounds, professions and education levels." As historian Bernadette Pruitt makes clear, Black women were "tireless community builders."[44]

By the early twentieth century, an extensive network of African American institutions had emerged not only as bulwarks against the Jim Crow order, but also as evidence of the ongoing vitality of the city-building process. But these extraordinary achievements emerged against tremendous odds. As elsewhere across urban America, southeastern and southwestern Blacks built their city in the face of white hostility from without and internal discord from within their own communities. Recurring acts of racial violence and internal social cleavages severely curtailed the African American push for their own independent self-sufficient city.

INTER- AND INTRA-RACIAL CONFLICT
AND POLITICS

In 1915, as African American homes encroached on Highland Park, a white neighborhood on the western boundary of Miami's Colored Town, armed white men "with masks and torches" visited some forty Black families along the contested border between Sixth and Fourth Streets and Avenue I and J, and delivered signs boldly declaring, "No N . . . . . can live in this house. Move out by Monday night or we will blow you up. Signed 200 white men."[45] Two years later in 1917, white mobs crossed over into Colored Town and bombed the Odd Fellows Hall. In 1920, Colored Town experienced another series of night invasions of their community, including dynamite explosions and bombings. When destructive storms hit Miami's expensive lakefront properties in 1926, authorities used the National Guard to "conscript" African Americans from Colored Town to restore and rebuild the homes and properties of white communities. At gunpoint, national guardsmen ordered Shaddie Ward and his three sons off the roof of their own house, where they were hard at work repairing storm damage. When Ward and his sons questioned the request, guardsmen aggressively insisted that they "get off their roof and climb in the back of the truck with a dozen other colored people already impressed into service."[46]

Police brutality against Black people sparked the Houston Race Riot of 1917. During the war years, the U.S. War Department constructed Camp Logan for the training of National Guard units preparing for active duty. Located three miles west of downtown Houston, Camp Logan and Ellington Field, an aviation training facility built at the same time, generated one million dollars in revenue for the city each month. The city's political and economic elites applauded the government's decision to locate these lucrative facilities in Houston. When the U.S. Army ordered members of the all-Black segregated Third Battalion of the 24th Infantry to Houston to guard the construction site, white Houstonians expressed widespread opposition to the decision. But the War Department prevailed, and the Army dispatched Black soldiers to Camp Logan.

While the Afro-Houstonians welcomed the Black troops, the 24th met a hostile reception from white residents. When a Black soldier sought to protect a Black Fourth Ward woman from police brutality, he was brutally assaulted by a white police officer and taken to jail, where he was again attacked. When another Black soldier and military policeman, Corporal Charles Baltimore, arrived on the scene to inquire about the fate of his fellow soldier, he was also beaten with a gun butt and arrested. Although officers later released Baltimore, rumors nonetheless spread among the Black soldiers that Baltimore had died in police custody. Some 100 armed Black men marched on the Houston police station, killing 16 white and Hispanic residents in the process, before authorities brought the revolt under control. In the wake of three separate court-martial tribunals, military authorities indicted 118 enlisted men; found 110 guilty; sentenced 29 to death (reduced to 19 when President Wilson intervened and commuted the sentence of 10 men); and sentenced 63 to life in federal prisons. No white civilians or law officers faced prosecution for their part in fomenting the violence.[47]

In May 1921, Tulsa mobs launched the deadliest attack on an African American urban community in the nation's history. The conflict emerged when a white female elevator operator accused a nineteen-year-old Black man, Dick Rowland, of physically assaulting her and "tearing her clothes." When authorities arrested the man and took him to the county jail, a white mob soon gathered near the facility. Fearing a lynching, several armed Blacks arrived on the scene and offered their services to the county sheriff. When members of the mob sought to disarm the Blacks, violence broke out. For a while, some 50 to 75 Blacks held their ground against an estimated 1,500 to 2,000 whites, who soon forced Blacks to retreat into their community, the Greenwood section of the city.[48]

Authorities deputized members of the mob, who assaulted, killed, jailed, and detained Blacks en masse. Under martial law, Adjutant General Charles F. Barrett of the state National Guard disbanded the special deputies but continued the internment of some 4,000 Blacks at the city's jail, convention center, and fairgrounds. At the same time, the National Guard released all but a few whites to return to their homes. Whites burned and looted the Black Greenwood District, destroying an estimated $500,000 in African American property, including the Gurley Hotel ($150,000), the Dreamland Theater and Williams Building ($100,000), and the Mount Zion Baptist Church ($85,000). Estimates of the number of dead and wounded ranged from 27 to over 250, but contemporary accounts in the *Tulsa Tribune* and the *New York Times* reported that 68 Blacks and 9 whites lost their lives.[49]

Tulsa's Democratic mayor T. D. Evans took the lead in casting blame for the violence on African Americans. The mayor claimed in vitriolic and racist language that the city's armed Black citizens threatened the safety of the white community and justified the mob's actions. In a June 14, 1921, speech before the Tulsa City Commission, Evans declared, "Let the blame for this negro uprising lie right where it belongs—on those armed negroes and their followers who started this trouble and who instigated it." Furthermore, the mayor said, "I say it was good generalship to let the destruction come to that section where the trouble was hatched up, put in motion and where it had its inception."[50]

In the face of destructive efforts to terminate the Black city-building movement, Tulsa's Black city builders fought back. They pledged to rebuild their "city on a hill." Some young people were especially determined to stay put and reclaim all that was lost. When one of these young men received a letter from his friend and $40 for a train ticket to Chicago, he swiftly replied, "True it is, we are facing a terrible situation. . . . They have destroyed our homes; they have wrecked our schools; they have reduced our churches to ashes and they have murdered our people . . . but they have not touched our spirit. . . . I came here and built my fortune with that SPIRIT, I shall reconstruct it here with that SPIRIT, and I expect to live on and die here with it."[51]

While not all victims of the Tulsa Riot were able to bounce back and rebuild, by the end of 1922, African Americans had rebuilt many of the burned-out buildings, extending north from Archer Street. Many of the new structures were also constructed of brick from the local Acme brickyard. Most of the new buildings weathered the storm of the Great Depression. However exposed and vulnerable to racial assaults it may have been, the Black metropolis provided a foundation for ongoing organized struggles against the white supremacist order. Grounded in their urban spaces, Houstonians, Tulsans, and Miamians forged not one but a variety of political as well as economic and spiritual strategies for securing their city and broadening their access to civil and human rights.

African Americans in the urban Southeast and Southwest claimed a substantial legacy of empowerment and participation in the formal electoral process during the early postbellum years. But the rise of Jim Crow and disfranchisement movements eclipsed these efforts and nearly drove Blacks from the body politic during this nadir in Black political history. Hence, increasing numbers of Black leaders in this period entered complicated negotiations with white elites over ways to improve the lives of Black people and "uplift the race" within the rigid and unequal confines of the white supremacist system. Although fraught with ongoing resistance from public authorities, white workers, and white homeowners, their efforts produced a gradually expanding number of all-Black publicly supported schools, social services, hospitals, public parks, and playgrounds. These institutions supplemented and enhanced, rather than diminished, the Black city-building movement. They reflected the impact of Black power and the rise of the Black metropolis on the political system during a time of widespread violence and rampant disfranchisement of Black people.

In their negotiations behind the color line, Black leaders displayed a fierce determination and even militance in advancing the interests of Black people. In 1900, to take one outstanding example, Miami's young Black professionals formed the Colored Board of Trade. They forged strong relations between Black property owners and white landlords. The board not only sought an agreement with white realtors that divided the real estate market *equitably* along the color line. It also insisted on barring white capital from "invading" the city's Black spaces and selling real estate directly to Black buyers. In the pages of the Miami *Herald*, the Colored Board of Trade declared, "We insist . . . upon a segregation that really does segregate, absolute and inviolate. . . . If we are to be shut in, simple justice demands that white people be shut out." When the Miami City Council declared its inability to "keep white capital out of Colored Town," the Colored Board of Trade angrily retorted that, "we would be unfair to ourselves and unworthy of our place in the body politic, if we did not frankly and emphatically protest."[52]

As African Americans sought to control the economy of the Black community and pushed for equal access to publicly supported institutions to supplement the building of the Black city, they did not relinquish their engagement in the formal electoral process. Encouraged by the rise of the Black Metropolis, African Americans continued to vote, participate in the affairs of the Republican Party, discuss political issues, and debate public policies that influenced their lives. A substantial legacy of postbellum electoral activism also informed the persistence of Black political engagement following the fall of the Republican Party in southern politics, the rise of the segregationist system, and the disfranchisement of Black voters.

In the wake of emancipation, Black Houstonians formed numerous political clubs and vigorously supported the Republican Party in municipal, state, and national politics. Houston's Black Republicans gained substantial influence in the Harris County Republican Club, a biracial organization formed in 1869. Blacks served as the club's vice president, secretary, and two of five members of the executive committee. Moreover, the initial meetings of the organization took place in Antioch Baptist Church, where African Americans outnumbered whites by margins as high as ten to one. Black Houstonians also enthusiastically mobilized their numbers and outdistanced white registered voters in the election of 1870, helping to remove Democrats from power in Houston and Harris County. Houston Blacks catapulted radical Republican Thomas R. Scanlon into the mayor's office. For the first time in the Bayou City's history, African Americans gained access to local political offices, with their ranks including councilmen, police officers, and the City Street Commissioner.

Even as they gained a footing in the Republican Party and received material benefits, African American activists forcefully called attention to the gap between their contributions to the party's success and returns on their loyal support. They also mobilized their numbers to wage a fight within the party to level the playing field. In the late 1860s and early 1870s, activists Matt Gaines and Richard Nelson roundly protested the party's failure to support an African American candidate from the predominantly African American congressional district. According to Gaines, "Negroes deserved at least one congressional seat." Equally important, following the removal of the radical government in 1873, African Americans did not disappear from the political arena. As historian James SoRelle notes, "radical rule in the Bayou City was over," but some Blacks continued their political activities through the nineteenth and early twentieth century within the Republican party and, to some degree, third-party movements.[53]

When the Democratic Party returned to power in Houston in 1873, Black Houstonians continued their engagement in electoral politics. In 1876 and again in 1884, Richard Allen, a building contractor, was appointed to the Republican Party's "rules committee." At the same time, some Black Houstonians supported third-party movements like the Greenback Party, formed in 1878, to help oust the Democratic Party from public office. By 1912, in addition to Richard Allen, other Black Houstonians—including John N. Adkins and M. H. Broyles—had served as delegates to the Republican Party's national convention. A decade later, the Texas legislature revised the state's primary election law and "expressly prohibited Black participation in Democratic primary elections." Following passage of the 1923 law, Afro-Texans, including Houstonians, launched a series of legal challenges to the white primary. But these challenges largely failed until April 1944, when the U.S. Supreme Court, in *Smith v. Allwright,* struck down the Texas primary law, declaring it a violation of the Fifteenth Amendment to the U.S. Constitution. In the summer of 1944, Houston Blacks voted for the first time in the Texas Democratic Party primary.[54]

In the meantime, the Houston Race Riot of 1917 and the explosive growth of the city's Black metropolis had served as catalysts for the emergence of the militant New Negro Movement in Houston during and following World War I. War and the revolt of Black soldiers opened a floodgate of African American militance and self-assertion. Formed in 1919, the Black newspaper the *Houston Informer* emerged in response to the fate of the Black soldiers following the Houston revolt. The new paper promised to protest "acts of discrimination" against Black people. The *Informer*, Richardson declared, condemned crime, Black and white, "but when police officers resort to undue methods and highhanded methods to prevent a thorough and impartial investigation of alleged crimes from all angles, they simply increase rather than diminish crimes, and also create additional contempt and disrespect for law and order, thereby becoming *particeps* criminals."[55]

In Oklahoma, from the outset of the early emancipation years, African Americans not only exercised the franchise, but gained election to the territorial legislature in 1870. In the same year, the territorial government enacted its first Jim Crow laws, segregating Blacks and whites in the institutional life of the state. But African Americans nonetheless retained the franchise until

1910, when the state disfranchised Black voters through the infamous "Grandfather Clause." When the U.S. Supreme Court struck down this mechanism for depriving Black people of the vote in 1915, Oklahoma sidestepped the law by establishing a very limited window of opportunity (only eleven days) for new voters to register. If they failed to register in this time frame, potential voters were then permanently and by law disfranchised.[56]

Nonetheless, as elsewhere, in the wake of ongoing efforts to remove Blacks from the body politic, Black Tulsans not only continued to vote; they also joined the cresting New Negro Movement during and after World War I and opened a new chapter in the political history of Blacks in the city. Ahead of the destructive race riot of 1921, Tulsa's Black community established a thriving chapter of the African Blood Brotherhood (ABB). Comprised of units spread across the U.S. and the Caribbean, the ABB urged African Americans to organize trade unions, establish cooperative businesses, and "create paramilitary units to safe guard the community" against lynch law. At the same time, the city's African American press, particularly the Tulsa *Star*, urged Black people to arm themselves and prevent mob violence "BEFORE and during," not after, a lynching and mob violence had erupted.[57]

At the beginning of Miami's history, African Americans voted in the city's incorporation election of 1896. They cast 44 percent of the 368 votes on the creation of Miami as an independent municipality. According to local historian Paul George, incorporation represented "the beginning and the end of meaningful Black involvement" in the formal political life of the city until the modern Black Freedom Movement following World War II. Black Miamians faced ongoing efforts to curtail their participation in municipal politics. In 1897 and again in 1901, the state legislature enabled the Democratic Party to exclude Blacks from full and equal participation in the political process. The new legislation allowed the Democratic Party to exclude Blacks from membership; bar them from the party's primary elections; and enforce a discriminatory poll tax that severely limited the Black vote in general elections. Thus, in 1920, African Americans reported only one registered voter for every 14 white voters.[58]

The dwindling roster of Black voters nonetheless underscored the ongoing though declining African American engagement in the city's electoral process. Driven by the rise of Miami's Black metropolis, voting nonetheless remained consequential for Colored Town's politics. Some members of the white supremacist Democratic Party sought to harness Black votes to their own political interests. Miami's third mayor, Democrat John Sewell (1903–

1907), called Black voters his "Black artillery," even against his Democratic rivals. Sewell gleefully described how he ensured that "about one hundred of my negroes registered and qualified to vote, and held them in reserve for emergencies."[59]

While Miami's disfranchisement movement did not entirely remove Blacks from engagement in formal political activities, Blacks held on to the franchise by an exceedingly thin thread, voting in only small numbers through the early 1930s. This thin thread nonetheless provided the basis for a militant challenge to Miami's white supremacy politics during the late 1930s. Emboldened by the grassroots solidarity of their Black metropolis, Miami's Black community registered some 1,700 new voters in 1939 and openly defied the usual Ku Klux Klan intimidation, threats, and violence designed to remove Blacks from the ballot and the ballot box.[60]

Despite extraordinary solidarity in their political responses to the Jim Crow order, building the Black metropolis entailed significant internal ideological, political, and social conflict. By the onset of World War I, African American institutions increasingly fragmented along class lines. The largest and most financially sound churches (Houston's Trinity Methodist Episcopal Church and Antioch Baptist Church, for example) attracted members of the city's expanding Black middle class as well as the better off sections of the Black working class, while the smaller churches served predominantly poor and working-class Blacks in "storefront, shot-gun house congregations" that often held worship services in "dreadfully dreary and desolate structures." Equally important, as elsewhere in late nineteenth- and early twentieth-century America, women were the principal ground troops in the African American city-building process. Yet, with a few exceptions like Houston's Lucy F. Farrow, a minister in the Holiness Church of God in Christ, African American women were routinely excluded from the top leadership positions in Black churches, fraternal orders, business enterprises, and political organizations.[61]

In addition to patterns of fragmentation that often resembled forms of dissent and friction in other late nineteenth- and early twentieth-century Black institutions, the urban Southeast and Southwest recorded some of the most painful episodes of intraracial strife. The cleavage between U.S. and Caribbean-born Blacks was quite wide, especially during the early years of the twentieth century. At its formation in 1900, the Colored Board of Trade excluded Black Bahamians and other Caribbean Blacks from membership. U.S. born Blacks regularly sought to marginalize Caribbean Blacks in the institutional and political life of Miami's Black community. For their part, Blacks from areas colonized by the British Empire sought to distance themselves from Black Americans. In 1919, Black Caribbeans joined their white counterparts in the formation of a Miami chapter of the Overseas Club, an organization that served British expatriates worldwide. Some Caribbean Blacks used the Overseas Club to claim a British identity as "Black British subjects" and sought to distance themselves from the constraints of the Jim Crow order that indiscriminately ensnared all people of African descent.[62]

In July 1920, Herbert Brooks, an Afro-Bahamian, faced charges of sexually assaulting a white woman. Brooks escaped the posse and bloodhounds into Colored Town, but a member of the Colored Board of Trade contacted the mayor's office and arranged to turn Brooks over to authorities with the promise that he would receive a lawful trial; lynch law would not prevail. Brooks, however, never made it to trial. He died, according to authorities, when he jumped to his death from a moving train. Afro-Bahamians and other Blacks from the West Indies responded violently to the death of Herbert Brooks. They roundly criticized and blamed U.S. Blacks for Brooks's murder. Some 400 Bahamians poured into the streets, threatening to destroy African American shops and places of business. Street fighting also broke out in some places between West Indian and U.S. Blacks. At the same time, Caribbean Blacks staged a boycott against African American businesses. One FBI agent reported that there was a virtual "state of war between English and American Negroes."

Despite substantial friction between diverse ethnicities within Miami's Black community, African Americans gradually built bridges to each other across these social divides. The Colored Board of Trade gradually opened membership to Caribbean Blacks by 1920. At the same time, intermarriage between the two groups proceeded apace. Moreover, an estimated 30 percent of all Black homes with boarders served a mix of Caribbean- and U.S.-born Black residents. More important, however, at the same time that Caribbean- and American-born Blacks clashed and complicated their own city-building efforts, they forged extraordinary bonds around the Junkano festival and parade and the Miami chapter of Marcus Garvey's Universal Negro Improvement Association (UNIA). They decried the ongoing conflicts between the Colored Board of Trade and the British and Caribbean Overseas Club. In the words of George Carter, branch president, the Garvey movement demonstrated how people from "the Bahamas and Native Americans could support a common cause, and realize that we were children of common parent stock, who were transplanted at different points in America." Before its demise after only a few years of intensive worldwide organizing, the Garvey movement demonstrated how the rise of the Black metropolis helped to lay the foundation for a variety of national and transnational Black liberation movements during the urban industrial age.[63]

. . .

Between the Civil War and the onset of World War I, African Americans built new communities in the ethnically and racially diverse cities of the urban Southeast and Southwest. The Black population had roots in antebellum Tulsa, Houston, and Miami, but the Black city-building movement escalated in the wake of emancipation and the subsequent explosion of urban capitalist development, immigration, and the rise of a new and more hostile system of racial apartheid. Even more so than elsewhere across the postbellum and Jim Crow South, Blacks in the urban Southeast and Southwest gradually gained access to land, space, and homes and built their metropolis against the backdrop of racial restrictions on access to land and homeownership; disfranchisement of Black voters; and mob violence, most notably the Tulsa Race Riot of 1921—often cited today as an emblematic case for reparations for industrial-era descendants of African people enslaved in America.

Against the odds, African American churches, fraternal orders, mutual benefit societies, and business enterprises not only proliferated. They also provided the institutional infrastructure for the ongoing fight against the injustices of Jim Crow. As disfranchisement movements reduced the presence of Blacks at the ballot box, African Americans retained a toehold in the electoral arena, even as they intensified their community-building activities as the principal bulwark against the white supremacist order. At the same time, internal divisions and conflicts along class, gender, ethnic, ideological, and political lines challenged the cohesiveness of the Black city-building project. But Blacks in the urban Southeast and Southwest repeatedly found ways to surmount such differences and advance the Black city-building process. During World War I and its early aftermath, Afro-Tulsans, Miamians, and Houstonians prepared to take their Black metropolis (along with their counterparts in the urban North, West, and South) into the era of the New Negro.

PART TWO

Northeast, Midwest, and West

FIVE

————

Building Their Own "City on the Hill"

THE QUEST FOR FREEDOM, LAND, homeownership, and institutional space animated the African American city-building process in the urban Northeast no less than the urban South. Land and homes not only offered subsistence to families and communities, but also provided opportunities to enter the market economy; create a measure of wealth; build institutions; and forge viable political movements for freedom and independence. By the mid-eighteenth century, growing numbers of African people, enslaved and free, gained access to the city as renters, modest property holders, and owners of their own burial grounds. Renters, property owners, and communal burial grounds fueled the emergence of the Black city in early New York (New Amsterdam), Philadelphia, and Boston. In the wake of the Revolutionary War and the rise of the United States as independent republic, the gradual manumission movement resulted in the emancipation of most Blacks in the Northeast two decades ahead of the Civil War.

From the vantage point of the contemporary reparations movement, this chapter underscores how the case for reparations for northern urban Blacks includes nearly two centuries of enslavement followed by a generation of political disfranchisement, economic inequality, and mob violence. This system of racialized capitalist development prevailed before the emancipation and enfranchisement of enslaved people nationwide. Except in the case of the African burial grounds, Black people responded to these conditions through informal but influential social networks rather than formal institutions before the onset of the American Revolution. Thereafter, however, they established their first churches, fraternal orders, mutual benefit associations, and business enterprises—all in the face of fierce white resistance.[1] Recalling John Winthrop's pledge to build a new "City on the Hill," African people

MAP 6. Until relatively recently, studies of American cities downplayed the Black experience before the onset of the twentieth-century Great Migration. This map delineates the major centers of Black urban life in the late colonial, revolutionary, and early Northeast. These antebellum cities—most notably New York, Philadelphia, and Boston—helped to set the stage for the Black city-building movement across the urban North in the years after the Civil War.

recognized the racial limits of that vision as carried out by the northeastern white elite descended from Winthrop and his fellow colonists, and quietly set about envisioning and constructing their own alternative "City on the Hill."[2]

ESTABLISHING A FOOTHOLD AND SHAPING THE BUILT ENVIRONMENT

As early as 1644, enslaved Africans waged a vigorous campaign for land and freedom against the Dutch West India Company in New Amsterdam. The company soon granted the men and their wives, and later their children, "half-freedom," including access to their own land. Located near an area called "Fresh Water Pond," title to the land not only helped to seed African

American city-building activities in what became New York City. It also foreshadowed their growing impact on the built environment of the urban Northeast.[3] In 1656, the free Black Bostonian B. Ken, or "Bus Bus," as he was called, not only owned "a house and lot" but also "four acres and a half of land planted in wheat." In 1701, another enslaved Bostonian named Adam fought and won a two-year court battle for his freedom and an opportunity to purchase land and take charge of his own life. At the same time, Black Philadelphians gradually occupied property in the city's emerging commercial district, where they eventually made their mark on the Quaker city's landscape.[4]

Alongside modest levels of early property ownership, it was the acquisition of burial grounds that strongly reinforced the city-building process and helped to spur the growth of Black communities across the early Northeast. Early burial grounds established informal African-inspired social and cultural relationships that would later power the construction of African American churches, fraternal orders, and businesses. In Boston, Philadelphia, and New York, burial plots and funeral services were calculated to build strong social networks among diverse people of African descent. In Boston, for example, the city's "Negro funeral processions" wended their way "all over town," deliberately avoiding "the most direct route to the grave" and maximizing contact among Blacks living in different parts of the city. "On Sundays, holidays, and fairdays," contemporary observers regularly remarked that African people "could be seen dividing into 'numerous little squads,' dancing after the manner of their several nations in Africa, and speaking and singing in their native dialects." These processions expressed a strong desire among enslaved African people to not only "preserve" the remains of their loved ones, but also to create an opportunity for the living to congregate and build community "in an area that was theirs alone."[5]

As African Americans shaped the cityscape through their burial grounds and homeownership, they also rented property in an expanding range of neighborhoods in the colonial and early American city. In New York, the general emancipation of half-free people and their children liberated families to move further out from "Fresh Water Pond" into rental and, to some extent, owner-occupied properties in the growing neighborhoods of the Fifth and Sixth Wards. In Philadelphia, the vast majority of Black people occupied homes within twenty blocks of the city's densest area of settlement, adjacent to leading white merchants, insurance salesmen, bankers, and proprietors of fashionable retail shops. Black Philadelphians, including pioneering Black ministers Richard Allen and Absalom Jones, later purchased land and homes in this commercial district that "stretched from Spruce to Vine streets along the Delaware River, extending west as far as Tenth Street." Black Philadelphians also moved into an older settlement north of the commercial core. Located between Arch and Vine Streets west of Fourth Street, this area housed about 30 of the city's 169 Black households by 1790.[6] Meanwhile, significant numbers of enslaved Black Bostonians occupied rental property in the poorest sections of the city's North End and later the West End near the docks, riverfronts, and alleys.[7]

Before the American Revolution and the rise of the New Republic, African people had developed a variety of informal economic, family, community, and cultural networks. These social relations not only connected them to each other, but also to their white elite and working-class counterparts. Broad community-wide leisure time and cultural interactions with Euro-Americans included, most notably, the Irish St. Patrick's Day, the Dutch Pinkster, and recurring funerals and Sabbath and market activities.[8] One contemporary observer noted how "all" of the "various languages of Africa, mixed with broken" English filled the air, "accompanied with music of the fiddle, tambourine, the banjo, [and] drum."[9] These diverse celebrations and festivals revealed the increasing confluence of African and western religious, social, and political ideas and practices in the colonial city.[10]

The advent of the American Revolution and the emergence of the new republic touched off the gradual manumission of enslaved people across the urban Northeast.[11] As the free Black population increased, both free and enslaved people of color intensified their campaigns for homes and rental properties in new areas of the city.[12] African Americans soon occupied two new and more densely settled areas on Philadelphia's north and south sides. By 1820, nearly 75 percent of Black Philadelphians lived in the north side neighborhood, described by historian Emma Lapsansky as the "Cedar Street Corridor." The number of independent Black households in the old urban core steadily declined to only about 64 families in 1810, although large numbers of live-in free Black household workers remained in the area among nearly 3,750 white households.[13] Meanwhile, New York City Blacks continued to move outward from the eastern Manhattan Dock Ward community into their own households in the Fifth and Sixth Wards toward the western part of Manhattan Island.

By the beginning of the War of 1812, African Americans lived in an area "between the Hudson River and Bowery Road in the Sixth Ward clustered around" Fresh Water Pond. As Black New Yorkers continued to move west on Manhattan Island, however, Fresh Water Pond increasingly evolved into New York City's "Five Points" neighborhood, named for the intersection of five streets in the area. Located in the Sixth Ward, Five Points boasted the largest concentration of Black people in early New York City. Given the area's proximity to the center of the city and to Broadway, however, white elites and middle-class reformers regarded Five Points as a dangerous area of interracial crime and sex that required close monitoring and policing.[14] In the mid-1820s, when the bootblack Andrew Williams purchased land from John Whitehead at the site of Seneca Village, other working-class Blacks soon followed suit and ultimately purchased about half of the fifty-lot real estate development. By the 1850s, Seneca Village had increased to nearly 300 Black residents and enjoyed a reputation as a stable Black landowning community.[15]

At about the same time that African Americans expanded their foothold in New York City, Black Bostonians occupied the north side of Beacon Hill, its "lower slopes" pejoratively described as "N . . . . . . Hill." Black and white Beacon Hill converged on Belknap Street (later Joy Street), "a narrow cobblestone way that climbed from Cambridge Street to the summit near the Statehouse." Nearly two-thirds of the city's Black population lived in this area by 1860. In the meantime, significant numbers of Blacks continued to live in the old North End neighborhood "near the wharves," while another important Black community emerged to the north of the Beacon Hill concentration. In addition to Cambridge Street, at the bottom of the hill, Blacks also settled on the streets "immediately to the north, in Ward Five, by then occupied by the Massachusetts General Hospital."[16]

Under the impact of the American Revolution, gradual emancipation, and the expansion of Black residential areas, African Americans increasingly formalized their institutional infrastructure. Black community-based institutions dramatically expanded and transformed the urban landscape. As Black churches, mutual benefit societies, schools, and business establishments dotted the landscape, they signaled the ongoing and deepening impact of the Black city-building process on the built environment. In the urban Northeast, as elsewhere, the church stood out as being among the most energetic and innovative Black city-builders. Pioneering Black churchmen Richard Allen and Absalom Jones, both born in slavery, emerged as major leaders in the independent Black church movement across the region and the nation.

Born in 1760, Richard Allen converted to Methodism as a young man in 1777. After traveling, working, and preaching across Pennsylvania, New Jersey, and Delaware, he returned to Philadelphia in 1786. When the white St. George's Church removed Blacks from their seats to make room for white worshippers, Allen and Jones spearheaded the founding of Philadelphia's Bethel African Methodist Episcopal Church (AME). By 1794, Black Philadelphians had built and dedicated their own independent AME church. Popularly known as Mother Bethel and headed by Richard Allen, the church occupied the east side of Sixth Street between Pine and Lombard. Meanwhile, under the leadership of Absalom Jones, Philadelphians established the St. Thomas Episcopal Church, which occupied its own building west of Fifth Avenue, between Spruce and Walnut.[17]

In 1795, New Yorkers established the independent African Methodist Episcopal Zion Church (AMEZ) under the pastorship of Peter Williams, Sr. During the early nineteenth century, the congregation purchased property for a new church home on the corner of Leonard and Church Streets in the Fifth Ward. In 1813, however, the Asbury Methodist Episcopal Church, led by William Miller and Thomas Sipkins, broke from the AME Zion Church. The new congregation soon bought a meeting place on Elizabeth Street, but that structure was destroyed by fire in 1827. The congregation then met in a series of rental properties before eventually building a permanent home.[18] Meanwhile, Black Episcopalians broke from the white Trinity Episcopalian Church in 1809. A decade later, the congregation had formed St. Phillip's Episcopal Church and built its first building on Collect Street. Peter Williams, Jr., son of Peter Williams, Sr., became its first pastor.

In 1807, New Yorkers also formed the historic Abyssinian Baptist Church, led by Rev. Thomas Paul of Boston, the founder of the First African Baptist Church.[19] In 1821, New York City's First Colored Presbyterian Church emerged under the leadership of Samuel Cornish, a student of Presbyterian theology and training in Philadelphia. In 1824, Cornish led the construction of a $13,000 brick building, partly through funds from white benefactors, but the church remained indebted for a huge portion of the building's cost and lost the building within two or three years. The congregation purchased another edifice in 1831. In sum, between 1796 and 1826, New York City Blacks had established four Methodist Episcopal, three Protestant Episcopal, two Baptist, and one Presbyterian churches.

Despite the often precarious financial foundation of independent Black churches, when they occupied their own buildings and opened their doors for service, they not only became magnets for new people moving into the city. They also became highly visible symbols of African American influence on the urban landscape. In addition to churches, a plethora of independent mutual benefit societies and fraternal orders reinforced the Black city-building process and its impact on the built environment. In 1820, for example, in New York City, the African Society for Mutual Relief purchased its first real estate on Orange Street. At the time of purchase, the lot contained a boarding house, from which the order collected rent. Behind this rental property, the society built its own meeting hall, which it used for its own activities as well as rental to other organizations seeking space for their work. The African Society also purchased and rented other properties outside its original Orange Street holdings.[20]

African Americans repeatedly used their access to land, homes, and rental properties to establish their own businesses and advance the city-building process through entrepreneurship.[21] Partly as a result of growing restrictions on their access to skilled jobs and the best household and domestic occupation following massive German and Irish immigration into the city during the early nineteenth century, increasing numbers of African Americans turned toward entrepreneurship as the best strategy for securing an economic footing in the urban political economy. Scores of Black washerwomen, cooks, coachmen, waiters, barbers, and hairdressers arranged their own contracts, lived independently, and employed other Black workers. In his study of nineteenth-century Philadelphia, W. E. B. Du Bois noted that "the whole catering business ... transformed the Negro cook and waiter into a public caterer and restauranteur, and raised a crowd of underpaid" workers to "a set of self-reliant, original business men, who amassed fortunes for themselves and won general respect for their people."[22]

Philadelphian Robert Bogle established his catering firm on Eighth Street near Sansom and "set the fashion of the day" for elite white families before the advent of "the millionaire and the French cook." Bogle's successor, Peter Augustine, an immigrant from the West Indies, paved the way for the emergence of a significant coterie of well-known Black caterers in Philadelphia. These included most notably the Jones, Dorsey, Minton, and Prosser families. In New York, Thomas Downing's Oyster Bar on Broad Street and Cato's Tavern in a nearby suburb became well-known for serving a predominantly white elite clientele, while others like the "African Grove," operated by

William Brown, a retired Black ship steward, served an all-Black clientele. Brown opened his "pleasure garden" in 1820 in the backyard of a home that he had rented on Thomas Street.[23]

Boston and Philadelphia claimed the most successful of the early nineteenth-century Black entrepreneurs. Boston's Paul Cuffee and Philadelphia's James Forten built upon their experiences as laborers in the seafaring industry to establish successful fishing and maritime businesses. Following the war, Cuffee purchased a fleet of ships and sailed to the Caribbean, Sweden, France, and Russia. In 1807, he also launched an ambitious effort to trade with the continent of Africa. By the time of his death in 1817, Cuffee owned or partially owned several vessels as well as a $3,500 farm and house. Cuffee's success owed a great deal to the support of his youngest sister, Freelove Slocum, who helped to finance many of the overseas voyages, sold the company's imported goods, and advised the family on investment opportunities.[24] Forten developed a successful sail-making firm, formerly owned by his employer Robert Bridges. Unlike so many other white employers of the day, Bridges acknowledged Forten's "skill, energy, diligence and good conduct" and rewarded him with promotion to foreman. By the time of Bridges's death in 1798, Forten had served as foreman of the workforce for twelve years. He eventually became full owner of the business; employed a workforce of some forty men, Blacks and whites; and amassed a fortune of $100,000 from his manufacture of sails for leading shipbuilders of the Northeast.[25]

In addition to religious, fraternal, and business organizations, the African American urban infrastructure included schools and a variety of social service institutions founded and supported by white reformers and philanthropists as well as African Americans themselves. In 1793, reformers in the Pennsylvania Abolition Society purchased a vacant lot on Cherry Street in the northern part of Philadelphia; moved a frame house to the site; and hired a Black teacher to instruct African American students there. At the turn of the nineteenth century, the PAS shifted its support away from the Cherry Street School to a new school located at Sixth and Walnut Streets. In Boston, in 1815, a Black teacher persuaded a white philanthropist to fund the building of a school for African American students. According to historians Horton and Horton, the merchant Abiel Smith willed "securities worth in excess of $4,000" to the city of Boston for Black education. With the acquisition of these funds, an earlier independent African American school, located in the basement of the city's African Meeting House, was renamed in Smith's honor.[26]

In 1842, when a fire destroyed the building of the New York Association for the Benefit of the Colored Orphans Asylum (purchased in 1837), the City of New York dropped its long-standing opposition to funding the facility and donated twenty lots of land "between Forty-third and Forty-fourth Streets and Fifth Avenue" to the organization. By 1843, the women founders of the organization had built a substantial building on Fifth Avenue which housed the orphanage until mobs destroyed the facility during the Race and Draft Riots of 1863.[27] In 1839, supported by the white American Seaman's Friendly Society, William Powell, the Black abolitionist and former sailor, established the Colored Sailors Home at the corner of John and Gold Streets in lower Manhattan. Powell, the free son of a New York slave father and a free mother, was born in New York City and founded the home to help improve the conditions of Black workers, including the establishment of a lodging house, employment, food, and other services.[28]

Establishing independent Black institutions was not easy. In addition to harnessing their own hard-earned resources and meager incomes, African Americans faced a series of fires, arson, mob violence, and discriminatory public policies that undermined their quest for independent religious, educational, fraternal, and social service organizations. Indeed, from the outset of European settlement of the Northeast, African Americans carved out their own living space and institutional infrastructure against extraordinary odds, including limits on their access to the most livable real estate and restrictions on the rights of citizenship as they made the transition from slavery to freedom. In short, African Americans constructed the Black city under siege.

CITY-BUILDING UNDER SIEGE

Fresh Water Pond, their initial area of settlement in New York, was named for a body of water ironically polluted by waste materials from a nearby tannery establishment. Although the city filled in the pond before the War of 1812, the area retained its reputation as a site of offensive odors and disease. In Boston, in 1742, only about 7 percent of Boston's total Black population was free, but those men and women lived in the city's almshouse at a rate "more than thirty-six times that of the white population." Moreover, as Blacks gained their freedom elsewhere and migrated to Boston, the city's selectmen warned off prospective Black newcomers—presumably to prevent them from becoming a social welfare burden on municipal institutions and the public treasury. African Americans were only 1 percent of the Massachusetts population, but they made up 3 percent of all persons warned away by the selectmen.[29]

Furthermore, in the wake of the British takeover of New Amsterdam, the slave codes of 1702 and 1712 closed down the Dutch system of "half-freedom" and undercut earlier strides toward the development of a free and independent Black community. The 1712 statute also prohibited Blacks from owning their own real estate. Enslaved Blacks in British New York found it increasingly difficult to secure their freedom from human bondage. The prosperous free Black Luycas Pieters, descendant of Fresh Water Pond landowners, gradually lost his land and even his freedom by 1738. "He lived as an indentured servant and his wife was forced to turn to the almshouse for assistance."[30] As early as 1726, the Pennsylvania legislature passed an "Act For the Better Regulating of Negroes in This Province." The statute declared that "tis found by experience that free negroes are an idle, slothful people and often prove burdensome to the neighborhood and afford ill examples to other negroes [slaves]" in the province. Thus, the law mandated that all manumitting slaveowners post a 30-pound bond to guarantee the maintenance of any freed person who might become indigent and "incapable of self-support." Moreover, the law empowered magistrates to bond out both "free adults" and "any free Black children" (until twenty-four years of age for males, and twenty-one for females) to white employers on an annual basis to ensure control over their labor and persons.[31]

White resistance to Black urban residence reinforced the incidence of unhealthy housing and living conditions for Black families and communities. Beginning with Philadelphia in 1798, most major cities instituted public waterworks to improve health and living conditions, but such works invariably bypassed the poorest neighborhoods with disproportionately large numbers of free people of color. In 1833, the Boston city directory listed one-third of Black residents as living in areas described as "alleys, courts, places, and rear buildings." Similarly, in the late 1840s, contemporary observer George G. Foster described how Black Philadelphians occupied the "lofts, garrets and cellars" as well as the "blind alleys and narrow courts" of the city's housing market. In New York's Five Points area, a physician reported the condition of a three-story building—"inhabited wholly by Negroes." Surrounded on three sides by "a number of pig styes and stables," the report stated, "the quantity of filth, liquid and otherwise" made the grounds "almost impassable."[32]

Passage of disfranchisement state legislation and the federal Fugitive Slave Act of 1850 placed new restrictions on the African American quest to build a free city. In July 1837, the Pennsylvania Supreme Court declared that free Blacks were not "freemen" as defined by the state's constitution of 1776 and 1790; therefore, the court concluded that free Blacks had no right to the franchise. During the state's new constitutional convention later in 1837–38, lawmakers revised the revolutionary era constitution and restricted the franchise to "white" men only by a vote of 77 to 45. When one sympathetic delegate to the disfranchisement convention introduced but failed to secure a provision permitting propertied Black men like James Forten to vote, he sadly concluded, "No amount of property, no talents, no personal worth, no service rendered the country, nothing will be admitted as a reason for relaxing the exclusion."[33] New York Blacks had exercised the franchise on the same basis as whites under the revolutionary constitution of 1777, but state legislators convened a new constitutional convention in 1821 and voted to increase the property tax requirement for Black voters to $250. While the state also imposed a term of militia service as well as a tax on white voters, the state removed these restrictions on white men in 1826; thereafter, only African Americans confronted the burden of a property requirement in order to qualify to vote.[34] Only in Massachusetts and three other New England states did Blacks retain unrestricted access to the franchise during the turbulent late antebellum years. African Americans bitterly protested removal from "a right peaceably enjoyed" for nearly fifty years following the American Revolution.[35]

The Fugitive Slave Law of 1850 strengthened the hand of slave catchers and weakened the social and political position of the Black community. The incidence of kidnapping and re-enslavement of free people of color escalated. In Boston, African Americans lamented the departure from the promise of freedom for all Blacks that had been symbolized in the death of Crispus Attucks during the struggle for the nation's independence. In the wake of the Fugitive Slave Law, Black Bostonians witnessed soldiers and policemen marching Black fugitives over the very ground of the 1770 massacre site as they were headed to Boston Harbor for transport to a life of slavery in the southern states. In multiple cities, firms proposing to take advantage of the new federal regulations proliferated. F. H. Pettis, a Virginian with a law practice in New York, boldly advertised his services as "IMPORTANT TO THE SOUTH." According to Pettis, New York City contained an estimated "5,000 Runaway Slaves." Furthermore, the ad stated that the new federal law "renders it easy for the recovery of such property." Allegedly focused on capturing fugitives, kidnapping rings emerged across the urban landscape, ensnaring growing numbers of free Black residents. Empire City abolitionists dubbed this informal network of man and woman stealers the "New York Kidnapping Club."[36]

The spread of human smuggling and people-stealing networks reveals how cities, slavery, and freedom became ever more tightly intertwined and the Black city-building process more precarious during the late antebellum years. As new waves of European immigrants arrived in the city, efforts to dislodge free people of color from the land intensified. The New York City Manumission Society, to take one example of a previously strong ally, spearheaded the formation of state and local chapters of the ACS and adopted its agenda before finally disbanding as a manumission-focused group altogether in 1849. In 1835, when the ACS encountered increasing difficulties funding its repatriation projects, the Pennsylvania and New York City chapters broke from the parent body and jointly sponsored their own African resettlement schemes. Shortly after William Lloyd Garrison launched the *Liberator* in 1831, ACS headquarters assigned Reverend Joshua N. Danforth to the post of agent for the New York and New England regions. Danforth soon opened an office in Boston, where the popular minister Lyman Beecher quickly gathered "a host of New England clergymen in proclaiming the merits of African colonization and asking God to prosper the cause."[37]

Between 1829 and 1849, African Americans faced nearly a dozen incidents of mob violence designed to unravel their expanding communities in New York, Philadelphia, and Boston. Compared to the countryside, where Blacks owned less personal and institutional property, African American homes, churches, schools, and social service organizations provided easy targets for early nineteenth century assaults on the Black urban community by poor and working-class white mobs, reinforced by some "gentlemen of property and standing." In the Philadelphia riots of 1834, mobs demolished three Black churches, while also attacking and looting the homes of 30 free Blacks and their families. In the same year, New York mobs destroyed the home of abolitionist Arthur Tappan; attacked the churches of Peter Williams, Henry Ludlow, and Samuel Cox (twice); and destroyed several homes of Black residents in the Five Points area.[38]

New Yorkers also demolished the hall of the African Society for Mutual Relief and a Black-owned barbershop. In antebellum Boston, mob violence broke out near North Square on Sunday August 27, 1843, when white sailors attacked a group of four Black men. When the Blacks defended themselves, a mob of several hundred whites descended on the area, as contemporary sources reported, "breathing out threatenings against the colored people, and every colored person that appeared in the street was beset and beaten, some nearly to death." In this case, authorities (fire and police forces) dispersed and arrested some of the largely Irish mob, but there were no sailors (presumably Anglo) or Blacks arrested in the aftermath of the violence.[39]

Assaults on the late antebellum Black community included the condemnation and demolition of Seneca Village, one of the nation's oldest independent Black communities. In 1853, the city of New York destroyed Seneca Village to make way for Central Park. Residents of the development received insufficient compensation for their homes and land to resettle as independent land and homeowners in other parts of the city's expensive real estate market. They scattered across the urban landscape, as the city razed their "churches, schools, and homes." The Seneca Village experience underscores how the Black city-building process involved recurring moments of destruction and rebuilding in the face of racially charged public policies, policing, and the law, as well as disastrous fires, real estate practices, and mob violence.

As they lost their grip on property ownership in Seneca Village, African American occupancy of rental properties increased. Exclusion from prime real estate in white communities as buyers and renters also accelerated. By 1860, over 85 percent of all New York City Blacks resided below Fourteenth Street (nearly half in a fifty-block area that included parts of the Third, Fifth, and Eighth Wards). About 75 percent of the city's streets counted "no Black residents at all." At the same time, African Americans dropped from just over 10 percent of New York's total population in 1800 to only 1.5 percent in 1860. The percentage of Blacks in Philadelphia peaked at 12 percent in 1830, dropping thereafter to less than 4 percent during the 1850s. Boston's Black percentage of the total also declined from its comparatively small 4 percent of the total in 1800 to less than 2 percent by 1860.[40]

In July 1863, what began as an attack on government buildings in protest against the military conscription law swiftly escalated into over five days of attacks on New York City's free Black community. Well over 100 African Americans died during the violence. Mobs also destroyed one of the most conspicuous symbols of African American institutional life in mid-nineteenth century New York City—the Colored Orphan Asylum, located on Fifth Avenue between Forty-Third and Forty-Fourth Streets. Crowds took possession of bedding, clothing, food, and other items of value and then set the building on fire. The orphanage burned to the ground before firefighters could squelch the blaze.[41] At the same time, landlords were evicting Black tenants from rental properties, "fearing the destruction" of their buildings. Moreover, when the proprietors of the Colored Orphan Asylum sought to rebuild in the same location in the aftermath of the violence, property owners forced them to relocate elsewhere—to Fifty-First Street for four years and then to 143rd Street between Amsterdam and Broadway, the future home of New York City's renowned African American community in Harlem.[42]

African Americans did not take legal and extralegal constraints on their quest for homeownership, land, and institutional infrastructure sitting down. Some free Blacks fled to Canada and others left for Africa in the wake of increasing racial conflict, but most free people of color stayed. They used their tenuous hold on urban space to organize a long and drawn-out fight for freedom, citizenship, and human rights on American soil. Although highly constrained in their institutional, social, and political struggles, both enslaved and free people of color forged movements to not only build but also to liberate the Black city and its residents from systems of inequality. During the colonial era, alongside early freedom petitions to European authorities, they staged desperate revolts and plots against human bondage and disfranchisement of free people of color.

LIBERATING THE BLACK CITY

Revolts and Plots to Revolt

Rebellion and plots to rebel broke out most notably in New York City in 1712 and again in 1741, and in Boston in 1738 and again in 1745. In these violent encounters, urban Blacks, enslaved and free, joined forces with small numbers of poor and working whites. The interracial character of these struggles suggested an alternative vision for the city than that of Euro-American political elites. As the ferment leading to the American Revolution intensified, enslaved urban Blacks lodged rising numbers of freedom petitions. They equated emancipation with property ownership, citizenship, and the potential for family, city, and even nation-building.[43] In 1773, for example, Boston Blacks delivered a petition to Governor Hutchinson and the General Court, stating, "We have no Property! We have no Wives! No children! We have no City! No Country!"[44]

From the outset of the new republic, African Americans not only built their religious, fraternal, educational, and business institutions to meet their specialized social, cultural, and spiritual needs. They also transformed these structures into centers of resistance to slavery and second-class citizenship for free people of color. They mobilized and utilized their institutions to shield the Black urban community (especially Black women and their children) from everyday forms of intimidation and mob violence.[45] Such abuse aimed to weaken African American claims on a place in the city, while also pressing them to accept offers of repatriation on African soil. But Blacks in the urban Northeast, as elsewhere across urban America, delivered a resounding "NO!" to the designs of the American Colonization Society.

Resisting the Colonization Movement

Following its formation in 1816, the vast majority of African Americans opposed the programs of the ACS. Taking the lead in opposing African resettlement schemes, the Free African Society (FAS) of Philadelphia counseled patience and faith in the future of the African race on American soil. Turning to biblical scriptures for justification and inspiration, the FAS declared, "the race is not to the swift, nor the battle to the strong; but that one who has on the shield of faith" and "shall chase a thousand, and two put ten thousand to flight. Here is encouragement of the African race."

Between 1817 and 1819, Black Philadelphians condemned colonization in a series of mass meetings at "Mother Bethel" AME church. In January 1817, some 3,000 Blacks packed the main floor and balcony surrounding the church on Sixth Street. When James Forten, chair of the gathering, called for a vote on the question of repatriation to Africa, in unison the throng delivered a resounding "No!" In resolutions adopted at the meeting, African Americans pledged to not only fight for full citizenship rights for free Blacks, but also to escalate their opposition to slavery across the land. The Philadelphia anticolonization meeting concluded with an appeal to the principles of the revolution and the ideas of the new nation. "Any measure or system of measures, having a tendency to banish" African Americans from the nation "would not only be cruel, but in direct violation of those principles, which have been the boast of this republic."[46]

In New York, on January 8, 1839, Blacks organized the "Great Anti-Colonization Meeting." The gathering described the ACS colonization scheme "as antirepublican, un-Christian, and 'contrary to reason' and asserted that the United States was the only logical home for free Blacks." One of the speakers, Philip Bell, an editor and member of the African

Society, urged the gathering to show the ACS that "we are freemen and we mean to be free." African Americans repeatedly reaffirmed their determination to defeat the ACS, declaring over and over again, "Here we were born, and here we will die." When he arrived in Boston from North Carolina during the mid-1820s, abolitionist David Walker found housing on Beacon Hill and joined the city's African Methodist Church, the Prince Hall Masonic Lodge, and the Massachusetts General Colored Association. He also became one of the most ardent anticolonizationists of his day. He spoke for many of his brothers and sisters when he blamed "Our Wretchedness" as a people in part on "the Colonizing Plan." New York City's Black newspaper, *Freedom's Journal*, not only published Walker's attacks on repatriation, but regularly opened its columns to anticolonizationists.[47]

Fighting for the Vote

The liberation politics of the early American city not only included mobilization against the colonization movement, but also a spirited effort to secure the franchise for free Black men. Partly because of their determined effort to exercise full citizenship in the new nation and defend Black urban communities against socioeconomic, cultural, and political assaults, free men of color retained the vote until 1821 in New York and 1836 in Philadelphia, but only Black Bostonians continued to vote through the onset of the Civil War.[48] African American access to the franchise during the early years after the American Revolution was by no means uncontested terrain, however. In 1811, New York's Democratic-Republican Party sought to stymie Black voters by enacting a voter fraud law to prevent "slaves from voting," but the law ensnared and harassed free Black voters by requiring new formal freedom certification by public officials and payment of a fee.[49] Nonetheless, free men of color voted in municipal and state elections and sometimes ran for public office in the early days of the republic. In 1800, a Boston newspaper reported an upsurge of support for the Federalist Party in a recent election. In a close analysis of the vote, the paper identified "a bloc" of "forty men of color" as a significant contributing factor.

Republicans and Federalists openly vied for African American support. In 1813, New York City's Republican Party accused the Federalists of bribing a Black leader to secure the votes of the free Black community. Indeed, Black New Yorkers did assure Federalist victory in the election of 1813. According to the recollections of one observer, the votes of "three hundred Negroes in the city of New York" not only "decided the election in favor of the Federalist party," but also "decided the character of the legislature of this state."[50]

Philadelphians retained access to the franchise through a property qualification that wealthy Blacks could meet. But white officials discouraged Blacks from voting or putting forward their own candidates for office by failing to assess Black property holders and thereby removing them from the roll of qualified voters. Nonetheless, some Black elites such as James Forten influenced the political process indirectly, not only through their elite white allies, but also through influence over their own white employees. On one occasion, Forten explained that he mobilized his white employees behind the campaign of one successful Philadelphia congressman. He described how he had taken "15 white men" to vote for his candidate. "In my sail loft," Forten said, "I have 30 persons at work . . . and among them are 22 journeymen—15 of whom are white. . . . All the white men went to the polls and voted for you." Still, Black Philadelphians were less direct participants in electoral politics than their counterparts in Boston and New York.[51]

Despite disfranchisement and partial disfranchisement of free Blacks in the urban Northeast, voting and nonvoting Blacks monitored party politics as part of their ongoing effort to secure a place in the urban political economy. In New York, where Black property holders retained the vote, African Americans regularly supported the elite Whig party over the proslavery but popular Democratic Party. African Americans complained that proslavery forces carried too much weight in both major parties. In 1839, following the formation of the antislavery Liberty Party in New York, African Americans, including editors of the Colored American, supported the party's presidential candidate James G. Birney over the Democratic and Whig party candidates. Following Birney's defeat in the election of 1840, Liberty Party members initiated a campaign to enfranchise more Black voters through various efforts to extend property ownership among free Blacks. One white abolitionist, Gerritt Smith, enabled some 3,000 Blacks to gain title to land in New York State and qualify to vote. In one subdivision near Lake Placid, African Americans named their settlement after an ancient West African city, calling it Timbuctoo.[52]

During the late antebellum years, urban Blacks launched new organizations to protect and strengthen the Black city in the face of increasing racial violence, the Fugitive Slave Law, and ongoing efforts to rid the city and country of people of color. While the church and fraternal orders continued to provide institutional support for the Black Freedom struggle, new organizations opened the

door for the development of stronger and more focused movements for liberation. Until about the late 1820s and early 1830s, the most influential Black
leaders were "based in and acted almost entirely through the organized
church," but thereafter Black leaders gained greater "organizational backing"
from new "anti-slavery groups as well as the church" and fraternal
organizations.[53]

The Movement to Abolish Slavery

Formed in 1826, the General Coloured Association of Massachusetts pushed
for equal rights for free Blacks and for the immediate abolition of slavery in
the South. Two years later, the organization provided a forum for David
Walker, a migrant from Wilmington, North Carolina, and proprietor of a
clothing store in Boston. Walker delivered a powerful antislavery address at
the organization's annual convention in 1829. Describing Black people in the
U.S. as "the most degraded, wretched, and abject set of beings that ever lived
since the world began," Walker strongly exhorted enslaved Black people to
throw off the yoke of slavery, by physical violence if necessary. Walker's
"Appeal," published as a pamphlet, became one of the most widely read and
influential antebellum political statements on the African American quest
for freedom and full citizenship rights.[54]

Walker and other radical Black abolitionists gradually attracted a new
generation of militant white allies in their effort to counter mounting opposition to their presence in the late antebellum city. Black abolitionists had
their most profound impact on the brothers Arthur and Lewis Tappan of
New York; William Lloyd Garrison of Boston and his newspaper the
Liberator (1831); the creation of the New England Anti-Slavery Society (1832),
founded at Boston's African Meeting House; and the American Anti-Slavery
Society, established in Philadelphia in 1833. Following the lead of Garrison
and radical Black abolitionists, the latter developed a vigorous program of
education, petitions, legislation, and boycotts to obtain immediate abolition
and equal rights for Black people.[55]

The creation of new interracial fugitive aid societies and vigilance com-
mittees broadened support for fugitives and free Blacks harassed by slave
catchers who sought to sell them into the slave South. These societies built,
sustained, and expanded "cities of refuge" for rising numbers of Black people
fleeing southern bondage. William Lloyd Garrison and other white abolitionists dominated large formal antislavery organizations like the American

Anti-Slavery Society, but fugitives and free Blacks stood at the center of the grassroots movement known as the underground railroad. In the 1840s, under the leadership of free Black abolitionist David Ruggles, New York Vigilance Committee members boarded a recently arrived ship from Brazil and helped three Portuguese-speaking slaves to escape. In 1842, the New England African Americans formed the Vigilance Freedom Association and enabled fugitive George Latimer and his family to move from Norfolk, Virginia, to Boston. When authorities arrested Latimer on charges of larceny filed by his owner, the committee raised sufficient funds to purchase Latimer's freedom; it also sent a massive petition, bearing the signatures of nearly 65,000 people, to the Massachusetts legislature, urging lawmakers to protect African Americans from fugitive slave catchers.[56]

Women, Gender, and Class Dynamics

Women played a vital role in all phases of the Black Freedom Movement and struggles to survive as an urban people. Activist Black women included the teacher Sarah Mapps Douglass of Philadelphia; the editor Mary Ann Shadd Cary, also of Philadelphia and later Canada; Harriet Tubman, the Maryland fugitive who moved to Philadelphia; the itinerant New York minister Sojourner Truth; and Maria W. Stewart, a resident of Boston and later New York, to name only a few. In February 1833 Sarah Douglass, along with several other Black women, attended a meeting to "consider the propriety" of setting up a female antislavery organization in Philadelphia. Ten months later seven Black and eleven white women launched the Female Anti-Slavery Society. Meanwhile, two years after the appearance of David Walker's *Appeal*, Bostonian Maria Stewart published her own pamphlet, *Religion and the Pure Principles of Morality, the Sure Foundation on Which We Must Build*. Neither gender nor color, Stewart said, should bar Black women from speaking out on behalf of the race. In one speech, she urged Black men to relinquish their "fear of offending the whites" and "let their voices be heard" and their hands "raised in behalf of their color."

Two of the most recognized voices among this company of women were those of Harriet Tubman and Sojourner Truth. Tubman, a fugitive from Maryland's Eastern Shore, became one of the most effective agents on the underground railroad after she escaped from slavery and made her way to Philadelphia where she obtained work as a domestic, saved her earnings, and made some twenty trips into slave territory to liberate relatives and friends.[57]

Tubman's elder counterpart Sojourner Truth advanced the cause of freedom through a long and effective career as an itinerant preacher and fighter for social justice. Born a slave in New York, Isabella Baumfree gained her freedom under the state's gradual Emancipation Act of 1817 and changed her name to Sojourner Truth in June 1843. "The Lord gave me Sojourner," she said, "because I was to travel up an' down the land showin' the people their sins an' bein' a sign unto them. . . . The Lord gave me Truth, because I was to declare the truth to the people." Truth's personal identity and politics were thoroughly grounded in the religious, social, and political ferment of New York City.[58]

Constraints on the city-building process emerged from within as well as outside the African American community. Internal ideological, color, and class differences would influence the community-building process through the onset of the Civil War. In the African American church, Black men repeatedly invoked the biblical injunction of the apostle Paul—that women should remain silent in the church and follow the guidance of men. Women like Maria Stewart often countered, "Did St. Paul know of our wrongs and deprivations? . . . I presume he would make no objection to our pleading in public for our rights." During the early 1840s, when the AME's annual Philadelphia Conference denied Julia Foote and other Black women permission to preach the gospel, Foote launched her career as an independent preacher and traveled widely across the northern states of New England and the mid-Atlantic. Similarly, after Maria Stewart strongly articulated ideas first enunciated by David Walker, Boston's Black community pressured her to leave the public arena. When she left the city for New York in the wake of such pressure, she staunchly defended the right of Black and white women to shape the political agenda of the larger community. It is not sex or color, she said, but "the principle formed in the soul" that made men and women.[59]

Gender dynamics—intertwined with growing philosophical, color, and economic differentiation within the Black urban community—posed some of the most daunting challenges to the solidarity of the Black city-building movement. By the late antebellum years, growing numbers of influential Black ministers like Richard Allen moved to curtail some of the major ideas and cultural practices of poor and working-class urban Blacks, such as the "shouting tradition" in African American churches, the consumption of alcohol, and widespread gambling as a leisure time pursuit. But the hostile and violent racial environment that Black urbanites faced as a people repeatedly muted such internal tensions and social conflict. This dimension of

Black city experience saw fresh expression in New York City as the Civil War got underway.[60]

Transnational Dimensions

The quest for a free and independent Black city was not limited to life in North America. Early on in the slave trade, Africans yearned for an opportunity to escape and return to the land of their birth, including cities that dotted the West Coast of Africa. Until the onset of the American Revolution, however, cities offered enslaved people few opportunities to seek freedom outside colonial North America. But the outbreak of the Revolutionary War radically changed the social and political context of the Black Freedom struggle and city-building movement. The persistence of slavery among the rebels, racial discrimination in the continental forces, and the increasing presence of the British army encouraged enslaved and free Blacks to advance their own liberation through participation in the imperial forces.[61]

Substantial numbers of enslaved and free people of color joined the British army and fought for their freedom under the Union Jack. An estimated 3,000 Black men and women left for Nova Scotia when the British evacuated New York City in 1783. Nearly 70 of these Black evacuees reported fleeing from slaveowners in the Philadelphia area. In Canada, African Americans not only sought freedom through the acquisition of farms, but also through the quest for urban property and opportunities to build their own city on Canadian soil. When racial animosity, including the Shelburn Riot of 1782, undercut their search for freedom in Canada, nearly 1,200 Black men, women, and children departed the province for the British-sponsored West African nation of Sierra Leone, where they became part of the founding generation of the city of Freetown.[62]

Still, most Black urbanites in the revolutionary era would stay put, cast their lot with the American rebels, and stake their claims to emancipation, full citizenship, and access to a free urban life on U.S. soil. With the deteriorating conditions of the late antebellum years, however, people of African descent again pondered the possibilities of building the Black city outside the U.S. As radical abolitionism gave way to moral reform approaches to the African American freedom struggle, urban Blacks reevaluated emigration on their own terms. Some African Americans had supported independent programs of resettlement in Africa from the outset of the revolutionary era. The free African Company of Boston expressed strong disapproval of whites "going [to] settle a place for us. . . . We think it would be better if we could charter a vessel and send some [of] our own Blacks." Just before the War of 1812, leading African Americans supported a plan for the resettlement of Black people in Sierra Leone. Under the leadership of Paul Cuffee, this program of repatriation gained the initial support of Richard Allen, James Forten, and Absalom Jones of Philadelphia and Thomas Paul, Prince Saunders, and Robert Roberts of Boston.

During the 1820s, even as they resisted white-dominated colonization efforts, free people of color forged independent resettlement projects— focused most notably on Haiti and Canada. Supporters of Cuffee's program of resettlement, including Forten, Allen, and Peter Williams, endorsed the development of a vigorous Haitian immigration proposal. Under the leadership of Prince Saunders, between 6,000 and 7,000 free Blacks departed for Haiti in 1824. After this project failed, nearly a third of the settlers returned to the United States. Another group of free Blacks met in Philadelphia in 1830 and proposed the exploration of Canada as a site for the relocation of Blacks from the United States. By the beginning of the Civil War, around 40,000 African Americans had resettled in Wilberforce, Windsor, Chatham, and a few other Canadian locations.[63]

· · ·

By the onset of the Civil War, a substantial but fragile Black city had developed in the urban Northeast. It emerged out of the ongoing interplay between Black people's resolve to gain a permanent place on American soil and the equally persistent efforts of Euro-Americans to roll back and defeat this effort. Massive European immigration, repatriation movements, and mob violence repeatedly undercut the promise of emancipation, citizenship, and human rights for African Americans in the region. Nonetheless, despite ongoing and relentless social, economic, and political pressures to quit the land, Black New Yorkers, Philadelphians, and Bostonians stayed put and fought for their own free and independent Black city. Their efforts laid the groundwork for the rise of the industrial city following the Civil War.

During the late nineteenth and early twentieth centuries, the urban Northeast became a major target of southern Black migration and the transformation of the city-building process. By World War I and the 1920s, New York City's Harlem had not only emerged as the largest Black metropolis in the world, African and Caribbean cities included. It was also the principal site of the twentieth-century cultural Black renaissance; militant "New Negro" politics; and the seedbed of national and transnational Black liberation movements, including movements for redress for past patterns of class and racial inequality. As this chapter demonstrates, however, the case for reparations in the urban Northeast must begin with the initial enslavement and emancipation of Black people in the years before the Civil War and the rise of the industrial age. Dynamic social movements and city-building activities were not limited to the urban Northeast. They were also integral parts of African American life and political struggles in Midwestern and West Coast cities, as we will see in chapters 6 and 7.

SIX

Establishing the Industrial Metropolis

THE NINETEENTH-CENTURY URBAN NORTHEAST set the stage for the rise of the industrial city following the Civil War and the emancipation of some four million enslaved people. But it was the Midwest that emerged as the most dynamic new center of African American migration, work, and city-building efforts. Although the Midwest Black metropolis had deep roots in the early nineteenth century, it dramatically expanded during the twentieth century Great Migration. Much like their northeastern counterparts, Midwestern Blacks built their own city against the violent backdrop of the white supremacist social order. They also harnessed the Black city to wage spirited campaigns against the new segregationist system. During the late nineteenth and early twentieth centuries, Black midwesterners increasingly redefined themselves as "New Negroes."[1]

Black midwesterners articulated a new and more militant resolve to secure their full citizenship rights even as they sought to strengthen the Black city. In 1920, they formed the Protective Circle of Chicago to fight white terrorism in the housing market. "In every legitimate and legal way," the organization's constitution stated, Blacks would combat "lawlessness that has recently been evidence in intimidation, bombing, threatening and coercion of Colored and white citizens of Chicago."[2] When white Milwaukeeans blocked African Americans from occupying homes that they had duly and legally purchased with their hard-earned money, the attorney and political activist George Hamilton declared, "I would have resorted to physical violence before I would have let them stop me from building my home. There are times when it would be better to be dead than to submit to such insults."[3]

The changing political consciousness of New Negroes was by no means entirely a product of the Great Migration and the rapid industrialization of

MAP 7. Whereas other regional maps in this book include a focus on Black life in three selected cities, this one identifies six cities for close analysis during the era of the Great Migration from World War I through the March on Washington Movement during World War II. A focus on Milwaukee, Chicago, Detroit, Cleveland, Pittsburgh, and Cincinnati enables us to capture the enormous impact of the Great Migration on the eastern and western parts of the Great Lakes as well as the urban Ohio Valley.

the Black population. Twentieth-century Midwestern Black politics built upon a substantial legacy of earlier nineteenth century social struggles. Nineteenth-century Black politics both inspired and reinforced the emergence of the modern Black Freedom Movement as a national and transnational phenomenon by the mid-twentieth century. These larger social struggles were also deeply anchored in the dynamics of the grassroots Black city-building process. Whereas the enslavement of Blacks constituted a key component of the case for reparations in the urban South and Northeast, the rationale for redress is based almost exclusively on the exploitation of Black labor in the manufacturing sector of the Midwest industrial metropolis. Still, we must not only consider the issue of labor exploitation. We must also acknowledge the dynamic role that underpaid Black workers and their communities played in creatively building their own metropolis, even as their work fueled the building of predominantly white metropolitan areas in Chicago, Detroit, Pittsburgh, and elsewhere across the region.

EXPANDING THEIR FOOTHOLD AGAINST
THE BARRIERS

Although the Midwest's Black metropolis had its origins in the late colonial and early nineteenth century, the onset of the Great Migration transformed the Black city-building process in Chicago, Detroit, and Milwaukee as well Cleveland, Cincinnati, and Pittsburgh. Between World War I and 1930, Chicago's Black population increased fivefold; it rose from 44,000 to 234,000 before the onset of the Great Depression. Cleveland, Milwaukee, Cincinnati, and Pittsburgh also witnessed rising numbers of southern Blacks moving into these Midwestern cities. But Detroit registered the most astounding population growth among the many Midwestern cities receiving Black newcomers. Black Detroit's population rose by 600 percent during the war years and another 200 percent during the 1920s. In real numbers, Detroit's African American population jumped from 6,000 to over 120,000 in less than two decades.[4]

As the Great Migration accelerated during the war and postwar years, homeowners and realtors determined to hold the line on African American access to homes in all-white areas. When legitimate means for excluding Blacks from the real estate market failed, white homeowners and realtors turned to violence. In addition to everyday acts of intimidation and harassment of Black residents, decisions to employ violence to keep white neighborhoods white were deeply anchored in a plethora of white supremacist homeowners' associations. These associations were particularly widespread in Chicago—including the Hyde Park and Kenwood Property Owners' Association; the Grand Boulevard Property Owners' Association; the Park Manor and Wakeford Improvement Association, among others—but Milwaukee and Detroit also established their share of racially exclusionary homeowner organizations to keep Black people out of their neighborhoods. Amid increasing use of violence, Black residents sometimes received warnings of impending violence. "We are going to BLOW these FLATS TO

HELL and if you don't want to go with them you had better move at once."
As part of its strategy for removing Black residents, the organization also
launched a boycott of white businesses that served Black residents in the
community.[5]

On July 27, 1919, a major riot erupted in Chicago when a fight broke out
between Blacks and whites along the shore of Lake Michigan. During the
confrontation, a Black youth, Eugene Williams, drowned after being stoned
by white youth. Violence soon spread into the larger community, when local
police refused to arrest any whites for the drowning and instead tried to
arrest Blacks. For the next seven days, violence rocked the city. When the
violence ceased, 23 Blacks and 15 whites had lost their lives. Another 500
persons, mostly Blacks, received serious injuries. The riot also left 1,000 persons homeless, underscoring the precarious nature of the Black city-building
process. As suggested by the Black and white causalities in the violence, however, African Americans were not the sole victims of racial violence.[6]

On June 20, 1943, over 100,000 people crowded Detroit's Belle Isle
Amusement Park. Beginning at the park's casino, ferry dock, playgrounds,
and bus stops, violence soon spilled over into the Black Paradise Valley area.
By early morning African Americans had smashed windows and looted
numerous white-owned stores on Hastings Avenue. Only the arrival of federal troops put down the violence, which resulted in 34 deaths, 675 injuries,
nearly 1,900 arrests, and an estimated $2 million in property damage. In the
Detroit riots, most of those killed, injured, or arrested were Blacks, while the
damaged property belonged almost exclusively to whites.[7] In June 1944,
when two Black families occupied their home in the Mt. Adams area of
Cincinnati, a mob of over 50 men and boys stoned the home, destroying all
the doors and windows. Described as the "first Negro residents" on the street,
the family had to vacate their home and flee for their lives. Sympathetic white
allies of African Americans were also victims of white mob violence. When
a white female neighbor publicly criticized whites for their actions, several
hundred whites marched to her home and hung an effigy of the woman.[8]

Partly because of low incomes as well as discriminatory real estate practices, the initial wave of newcomers typically moved into neighborhoods
within or adjacent to the cities' designated low-rent "red light" or "vice" districts.[9] Replete with an underground economy of gambling, brothels, dance
halls, and bootlegging establishments, these areas included the "bad lands"
on Milwaukee's West Side; Detroit's East Side, particularly the area around
Beaubien Street; and Chicago's South Side, between Wentworth and

Wabash, an area that catered to a predominantly white but mixed-race clientele. With passage of the Volstad Prohibition Law of 1919, the emergence of illegal bootlegging establishments, "speakeasies," or "blind pigs" proliferated. Following prohibition, "the illegal sale of liquor" became Detroit's second largest industry "after the production of automobiles." The city's "blind pigs" skyrocketed; there may have been fifteen to twenty thousand by the late 1920s. Chicago's chief of police declared that so long as gamblers, bootleggers, and especially prostitutes "confined their activities to the districts between Wentworth and Wabash, they would not be apprehended." In Chicago's so-called "Black Belt," city officials "mapped out on each side of the city wherein to intern vice." Authorities pushed the boundaries of illegal activities further south of the CBD, "placing it right in the heart of the Black Belt." In 1917, the *Detroit News* described the East Side as a declining area of "gambling clubs and countless numbers of disorderly houses."[10]

The advent of the New Deal Homeowner's Loan Corporation in 1933 enabled some African Americans to save their homes from foreclosure during the Depression, but federal housing policies did more to deepen the racially divided housing market than to mitigate its destructive effects. Housing authorities, influenced by powerful southern Democrats, insisted on racial segregation in federally funded units. In 1941, the Federal Public Housing Authority (FPHA) had approved Detroit's Sojourner Truth Housing Project. Named for the Black abolitionist leader and designated for Black occupancy, the project was located in a predominantly white working-class neighborhood. When local residents protested, federal authorities rescinded their decision and handed the project over to whites. Only the vigorous protests of the Black community secured the project for African Americans. On the other hand, the federal government established an all-white project at the Ford Motor Company's new Willow Run facility. Although Blacks fought to integrate these units, the FPHA opposed the movement and maintained the separation of Blacks and whites in public housing projects. Housing conflict became a major catalyst of the Detroit Race Riot of 1943.[11]

African Americans carved out a tenuous place in the Midwest metropolis within the larger context of this racially divided, hostile, and discriminatory housing market. The African American population not only increased but occupied homes in an expanding range of disproportionately Black neighborhoods. In 1910, the vast majority of Chicago's Black community lived in the Second and Third Wards on the city's South Side, making up about 50 percent of all Blacks in the city. Other African Americans lived in substantial numbers in the Sixth, Seventh, Fourteenth, Thirtieth, and Thirty-First Wards. During the interwar years, however, Cottage Grove and Fifty-Fifth Street marked its southern boundary as Blacks pushed into the previously all-white communities of Kenwood and Hyde Park to the east; Woodlawn, Park Manor, and Chatham further south; Englewood to the southwest; and Lawndale on the city's West Side. With relatively few people and little infrastructure before the 1880s, the West Side communities of North Lawndale, West Garfield Park, and Austin "filled with buildings and people between 1880 and 1920."[12] At about the same time, the East Side community remained the chief center of Black residence in Detroit, "bounded by Randolph Street on the west to Hastings Street on the east, and by Gratiot on the north to the river on the south."[13] As the migration picked up steam, new southern Black city-builders gradually moved into commodious homes in the northern portion of the East Side. Dubbed "Paradise Valley," this area offered a destination of "hope for the tens of thousands of black migrants who journeyed there to begin a new life" beyond St. Antoine Street, the so-called "Black Bottom" that was the poorest portion of the community, but still within the East Side neighborhood.[14]

In Pittsburgh, the Hill District made the transition from a predominantly white multiethnic neighborhood to a predominantly Black community. The Hill District's African American population dramatically increased by 14,000 residents in the Third and Fifth Wards, while the white, predominantly immigrant population, dropped by over 7,600 residents.[15] Whereas Cleveland's late nineteenth-century Black population took shelter in widely dispersed areas within three of the city's wards, the Great Migration witnessed the increasing concentration of the city's Black community in an area near the Central Business District, bounded by Euclid Avenue on the north, East 105th Street on the east, and Woodland Avenue on the south. Most of Cleveland's new southern Black city-builders took homes in the neighborhood west of East Fifty-Fifth Street, sandwiched between Euclid Avenue and the Cuyahoga River.[16] For its part, Cincinnati's West End absorbed the bulk of new southern Black migrants and city-builders. The total Black basin population increased from less than 13,000 in 1910 to over 32,700 in 1930, while the white basin population dropped from 137,500 in 1910 to an estimated 98,800 in 1920 and then to 59,000 in 1930.[17]

The Black city-building process was a dynamic cross-class phenomenon within the rapidly expanding Midwestern cities. Renowned poet Gwendolyn Brooks later illuminated the grassroots, cross-class dynamics of Chicago's

Black community-building efforts. Her father, a porter for a corporate firm, and her mother, a former schoolteacher, moved to Chicago's South Side on the eve of World War I. According to Brooks, her family "never accepted the racial status quo as so limiting" that it would squash their aspirations for a better life, including housing, for themselves and their children. After arriving in Chicago, the Brooks family rented a modest home in the small African American settlement in Hyde Park. During the early 1920s, however, the Brookses purchased their own home at 4332 S. Champlain Avenue, located in the Grand Boulevard community, an emerging site of Chicago's aspiring Black homeowners and community builders.[18]

BREACHING THE RESIDENTIAL COLOR LINE

The Brookses, and a wave of other "upwardly mobile" African American city-builders, pushed the boundaries of the African American community "outward and beyond" arbitrary limits set by white homeowners, realtors, and banking institutions. In the city's Douglas Community, an area that stretched from Twenty-Second Street to Thirty-Fifth Street and Federal Street to Lake Michigan, African Americans established homes among "clusters of whites" along the lakefront close to Thirty-Fifth Street. In 1922, Chicago's Alderman Louis B. Anderson and newspaper publisher Robert S. Abbott built some of the most expensive and elaborate homes in the city. Anderson's majestic "colonial revival style" home was at 3800 S. Calumet Avenue, while Abbott's $50,000 "baronial" Queen Anne style home was at 4742 Grand Boulevard. Abbott's biographer described his fourteen-room home as an "ivy-covered, three-story, red brick mansion trimmed in white stone."[19]

By the onset of World War I, rising numbers of poor and working-class Blacks took advantage of the region's expanding underground housing market to purchase lots and build their own modest homes on the outskirts of the metropolis. This informal housing market included land and real estate speculators, building materials companies, finance institutions, building and construction companies, and "an army of carpenters all willing to help low-income workers build their own homes." Land speculators and developers purchased large plots of land without water, sewer services, or roads in unincorporated areas; subdivided these properties into small lots; and sold them cheaply to poor and working-class African American residents.[20] In Cincinnati, Lincoln Heights emerged as an all-Black suburb of homeowners between roughly 1923 and 1944, when it gained status as an independent municipality. The Black population of the area rose from 57 residents in 1923 to over 6,600 by the end of World War II. African Americans creatively built their own homes "piecemeal—one or two rooms at a time." The factory worker Odell Boggs "purchased a lot, bought used lumber, and worked on his home in the evenings and on weekends with the help of friends." Boggs and his family moved into the house upon completing two rooms. In the following year, he hired a carpenter to help him complete the construction of his home.[21]

Cleveland Blacks also penetrated previously all-white neighborhoods and gradually gained access to better housing outside the city's major African American settlement on Central Avenue. According to the African American housing specialist Robert C. Weaver, some Forest City Blacks "could and did acquire desirable and used property in new areas," often "through a friendly white, since most white owners would not sell directly to Negroes." Moreover, African Americans usually financed such purchases with cash payments or with loans from individuals rather than racially exclusionary lending institutions. The city's more affluent Black residents moved out of the central area into rental and owner-occupied property east of East Seventy-Ninth Street and "east along Kinsman Avenue into Mt. Pleasant." Located among upwardly mobile immigrant workers and their families on the outer edge of the Black community, according to the Cleveland writer Charles Chestnut, African Americans purchased, rented, and occupied better housing "without objection and many of them own their own homes."[22]

Pittsburgh's Black community gained its most notable opportunities for purchasing new homes in the city's Upper Hill District. In 1923, the laborer James Coleman and his wife Lucy bought a lot at 845 Perry Street for $325; they took out a mortgage on the land. They retired the land mortgage in 1925 and took out "two new mortgages for $2,000 each to build a two-story brick veneer house." James and Lucy had completely paid off their debts by 1944. In 1925, for his part, the Georgia-born laborer Walker Pratt, purchased a lot at 819 Whitesides Road for $1050. A year later, he borrowed $7,500 to construct "a two-and-one-half story brick duplex."[23]

As the Great Depression got underway, disproportionately more Blacks than whites lost their homes to foreclosures. After increasing substantially between 1910 and 1930, African American homeownership rates declined in Cleveland, Chicago, and Detroit. In Chicago, one woman lamented the painful loss of her property as the Depression spread across the city and region. As she put it, "I've always been accustomed to having something, and I've had a mighty fall. You see I had such a fine home. I had to sell nearly all my fine furniture for almost nothing. I had my home under HOLC. That was my last chance to save it—and I lost it." In 1934, Pittsburgh homeowner Walker Pratt refinanced his debt with the assistance of the New Deal Home Owners' Loan Corporation. But as with the woman in Chicago, such support proved insufficient. Three years later, the Corporation foreclosed on Pratt's home.[24]

After a steep uphill climb to save their homes during the Depression years, African Americans revived their homeownership efforts during and after World War II. In Cincinnati, the wartime housing shortage and the increasing migration of white residents from the city's basin community resulted in "an easing of racial restrictions on real estate mortgages and a new willingness among realtors to sell to and rent houses and apartments to blacks in previously all-white neighborhoods." War and early postwar Black Cincinnatians spread even more widely across the city's hilltop and valley neighborhoods.[25]

A similar phenomenon emerged in Chicago, Pittsburgh, Detroit, and Cleveland. Between 1940 and 1960, over 400,000 whites abandoned central city Chicago for suburban locations, while African Americans increased by more than 270,000 during the same period. In each of the four-year periods between 1950 and 1954 and 1955 and 1959, more than seven thousand units transitioned from white to Black. As historian Arnold Hirsch notes, older restrictive covenants against Black housing occupancy in white neighborhoods became little more than "a fairly coarse sieve, unable to stop the flow of black population when put to the test." Similarly, in 1946, the popular Black weekly the *Chicago Defender* informed its readers of what it called "the rapidly tumbling restrictive covenants," which it further described as "falling apart at the seams."[26] Following the U.S. Supreme Court's ruling outlawing restrictive covenants in 1948, African Americans also gradually moved into owner-occupied and rental properties in previously all-white neighborhoods in the Motor City. In 1940, Blacks in Detroit claimed ownership of just over 5,000 homes out of a total of over 167,000 owner-occupied buildings in the city. By 1950, they owned over 21,600 homes out of a total of 276,300 for the city. By the mid-1950s, as historian Richard Walter Thomas notes, "private housing had taken over the lead and had become the major approach for solving housing problems for blacks."[27]

Although precarious, in constant flux, and fragile, African American access to urban land, housing, and neighborhoods provided the territorial context for the expansion of the Black city and its extensive institutional infrastructure. African Americans would use their increasing access to urban space as renters and as homeowners to forge their own independent community-based institutions. While a variety of new institutions would emerge under the impact of the Great Migration, as elsewhere, the independent Black church would play a major role in the development of the Black infrastructure in the urban Midwest. This rich institutional infrastructure would in turn establish the foundation for organizing new and more effective political movements against the Jim Crow system.

CREATING THE BLACK METROPOLIS/
TRANSFORMING THE CITYSCAPE

Across the urban Midwest, the industrial-era Black church built upon deep nineteenth-century roots and expanded its role as the cornerstone of the African American community and city-building process. Established churches flourished at the same time that a new generation of Black religious institutions emerged and helped to deepen the impact of Black religious life on the urban landscape. Despite the tremendous expansion of established Black churches and their profound impact on the built environment, however, they failed to fully meet the rising demand for church homes and social services among the city's increasing numbers of southern Black wage earners. Class and cultural biases among the larger AME and, to some extent, Baptist churches fueled the rise of a new generation of Black churches among dissatisfied newcomers to the city.[28]

Churches and Mutual Benefit and Social Service Organizations

Newcomers expressed their resolve to develop an independent religious life by building a plethora of new churches in their new homes. Milwaukee's newcomers spoke for many migrants across the urban Midwest and elsewhere when one resident boldly declared, "We shall prove to be citizens in helping to make Milwaukee one of the greatest religious cities of Wisconsin."[29]

Over the entire period, Black Milwaukeeans established no fewer than thirteen new congregations, predominantly Baptist, Holiness, and Spiritualist denominations. Between 1917 and 1922, they founded Galilee (later Greater Galilee); Mt. Zion; and St. Paul (later Tabernacle) Baptist churches. They followed in 1924 and 1925 with the establishment of Mt. Olive Baptist and the Church of God in Christ. Somewhat later in the decade, they also launched St. Matthew Colored Methodist Episcopal Church, a Seventh Day Adventist congregation, and several small storefront Holiness and Spiritualist bodies. When Galilee opened for service in 1920, it immediately embarked upon a vigorous campaign to build a $40,000 edifice to meet what church leaders described "the crying needs" of its "growing congregation," which had reached over 460 members by the mid-1920s.[30]

In Chicago, between 1916 and 1919 alone, migrants established five new Baptist congregations: Pilgrim, Monumental, Providence, Progressive, and Liberty. Beginning as prayer meetings in the homes of newcomers, by the late 1920s most of these churches had acquired "their own buildings and boasted memberships of over five hundred"; they profoundly influenced the urban landscape. At about the same time, in 1916, Elder Lucy Smith, a Georgia-born migrant, organized All Nations Pentecostal Church as a prayer meeting in her Chicago home. For ten years, the church moved from storefront to storefront until Smith initiated the building of a new edifice.[31] In 1926, a Detroit observer described the impact of the new churches on the cityscape: "As one walks through the several Negro neighborhoods, he finds numerous storefronts, basements, front rooms . . . platforms in vacant lots, and other small . . . places being used as church buildings."[32]

Supplementing and deepening the impact of Black churches was a growing range of mutual aid and benefit societies, fraternal orders, social clubs, and especially a plethora of new exceedingly diverse business and social service enterprises. These new industrial-era institutions had a profound impact on the Black city-building process. While most of these organizations were multiclass and mixed-sex institutions, some were distinctly business and professional clubs. Pittsburgh's popular Loendi Club, named after a lake in Africa, was a prime example of the elite's influence on the Black city-building process.[33]

By the mid-1920s, in Milwaukee, Detroit, and Chicago, the spread of new social welfare programs (including local branches of the National Urban League, among others) had helped to reshape the urban landscape. In Milwaukee, for example, in 1917, Rev. Jesse S. Woods, the minister of St. Mark's AME church, resigned his ministerial post and spearheaded the establishment of the city's Booker T. Washington Social and Industrial Center, "a three-story, forty-eight room boarding, lodging, and recreational facility." The organization provided a broad range of social services for new-

FIGURE 5. Pittsburgh's early twentieth-century elite Loendi Club, modeled after the city's leading industrialists' Duquesne Club. Courtesy of Teenie Harris Archive/Carnegie Museum of Art, Pittsburgh.

comers and their families until it was supplanted by the launch of the Milwaukee branch of the National Urban League during the mid-1920s.[34]

In Cleveland, African Americans established the Negro Welfare Association (NWA), an affiliate of the National Urban League. Formed in December 1917, the NWA soon delivered a broad range of economic and social services to the city's booming Black population. Launched with a $10,000 grant from the Mayor's Advisory War Board, the organization purchased a large house on Central Avenue and offered boarding and lodging space for Black veterans.[35] Formed on the eve of World War I, the Phillis Wheatley Association (PWA) offered the most extensive services to young Black women making the trek to the Forest City.

Founded under the leadership of pioneering Black social worker Jane Edna Hunter, the organization launched a fundraising drive as the wartime migration accelerated. It raised $25,000 and refurbished an old Central Avenue home that housed some 400 young women and offered job training facilities. During the mid-1920s, following a successful half-million-dollar fundraising campaign, the PWA built a nine-story facility on Cedar Avenue. The new building, completed in 1928, "contained separate schools for instruction in music, cooking, and cosmetology." It also housed "six times" as many young female residents as before.[36] Formed in 1918, the Urban League of Pittsburgh (ULP) not only opened its own office on Wylie Avenue in the Hill District; during its early years it also housed the Pittsburgh office of the Pennsylvania Department of Labor.[37]

Entrepreneurship

Closely intertwined with the development of religious, fraternal, and social service organizations, African Americans intensified the building of business enterprises. The twentieth century not only witnessed rising numbers of businesses serving a Black clientele, but also the increasing diversification of types of businesses established by African Americans. Black entrepreneurs supplemented earlier emphasis on barbering and catering services to white clients with a growing range of real estate, insurance, newspapers, barber and beauty shops, hotels, rooming houses, restaurants, and retail establishments serving the Black population. Before World War I, Milwaukee's small Black community did not yet have a funeral home, a building and loan association, a regular Black weekly newspaper, or a community pharmacy. In the wake of the Great Migration, the city witnessed the establishment of the Daniel W. and Nellie B. Raynor Funeral Home (later Raynor and Reed) at 414 Cherry Street; the cooperatively owned Community Drug Store at the corner of Seventh and Cherry Streets; a regular weekly, the *Wisconsin Enterprise Blade*; and most notably the Columbia Building and Loan Association. Under the proprietorship of Wilbur Halyard and his wife Ardie, the Columbia Building and Loan Association aimed to achieve two straightforward goals: 1) promote the "saving habit by providing each member with a place to invest their funds"; and 2) make loans to members who hoped "to build or purchase a home or pay off an existing mortgage on monthly payments." As late as 1932, the organization's board not only remained intact, but the association's assets had grown to $73,000 and about thirty mortgage loans amounting to $62,000 had been granted. The company also reported $6,900 worth of property.[38]

During World War I and the 1920s, the number of Black retail establishments in Cleveland increased nearly tenfold. Most of these businesses were small single-proprietor firms. In 1929, a survey of Black businesses in Forest City reported some 215 stores serving the city's Black population. But Cleveland's most successful enterprise, the Cleveland Realty, Housing, and Investment Company, formed under the proprietorship of Welcome Blue, Nahum Brascher, and other local Blacks, aimed to expand African American property ownership in the city's Central Avenue District. As early as 1917–18, the company reported ownership of "almost every apartment building on East Fortieth Street between Central and Scovill" and continued to expand along with the Great Migration into the city itself. Opened in 1921, the Empire Savings and Loan Company emerged as Cleveland's most successful migration-era Black business. Under the proprietorship of Georgia-born migrant Herbert Chauncey, it opened with substantial support for a roster of other Black entrepreneurs. It soon reported a growing volume of business; opened a branch office; and established a real estate company and "one of the first insurance companies in the Forest City." Like their white counterparts, however, Black realtors also rented to Black tenants at rates far above the earlier rents for their previous white residents. The Black weekly the *Cleveland Gazette* complained that Black realtors had increased rents "from three to even seven and ten dollars a month above what the 'rooms' were renting for up to the time they secured control of them."[39]

African American undertaking and cemetery firms also expanded during the period. By the late 1920s, Cleveland reported ten Black-owned funeral homes, the most successful of which was J. Walter Will's "House of Wills," located initially on Central Avenue; it later moved to larger quarters on East Fifty-Fifth Street. Will emerged as one of the wealthiest funeral directors in the state of Ohio. The Cleveland entrepreneur Alonzo Wright secured the first franchise to open a Standard Oil Company gas station in a predominantly Black community and soon introduced several innovations in customer service that would become hallmarks of the modern filling station—"free tire and radiator checks and windshield cleaning."[40]

During and after World War I, Cincinnati's Black community also built a thriving network of new businesses that catered to the expanding African American market and reinforced the city-building process. In his pioneering study of the city's Black community, *Cincinnati's Colored Citizens*, published in 1926, journalist and entrepreneur Wendell P. Dabney documented the lives of the city's most successful Black entrepreneurs, even as he roundly criticized this group for not taking full advantage of their opportunities to serve the increasing Black population. Dabney reported, "We have hundreds of business houses. A multiplicity of certain kinds of, a scarcity of others. Naturally, those necessitating small capital and of a type largely in demand are the most numerous . . . barber shops, beauty parlors, restaurants, lodging houses, and undertaking establishments." Most notably, Dabney underscored the emergence of a "Colored"-owned chain of drug stores; two lucrative cemetery enterprises, the Colored American Cemetery and the Union Baptist Cemetery; and several real estate firms, including the Industrial Loan and Savings Company and the Creative Realty Company, under the proprietorship of the Kentucky-born migrant Horace Sudduth.[41]

The entrepreneurial impact of Blacks on the city-building process was not limited to the activities of Black men. Black business and professional women also left their mark on the cityscape. Annie Turbo Malone's cosmetic business and school also thrived first in St. Louis and then in Chicago after she moved there in 1930. Built in 1918, Poro College included her business offices, manufacturing plant, training rooms, and space for community leisure-time activities. Like the more widely known Madam C. J. Walker, Malone also employed large numbers of agents in the United States and overseas. In Cincinnati, the Kentucky-born Madam J. H. Reider operated a successful hairdressing establishment. After learning the business as an agent of Walker's famous hair products company, Reider created her own scalp treatment system, known as "Reider's Wonderful Hair Restorer." Her agents worked in "various cities" and helped to establish her products on the market within and beyond Cincinnati.[42]

Detroit's Black community also developed an impressive range of new enterprises as the migration accelerated. The city's Black entrepreneurs launched a plethora of insurance, real estate, and hospitality companies, most notably the Great Lakes Insurance Company, incorporated in 1927; the Great Lakes Agency Company, which purchased the elegant Great Lakes Manor; and later the Great Lakes Country Club. By the start of World War II, the Great Lakes Insurance Company reported a 112-member Black workforce; $11 million of insurance in effect on $33,300 policyholders; and over $1.3 million in premiums. Detroit's 1920s Black enterprises also included the modern Biltmore Hotel; the Charles C. Diggs, Jr. Funeral business and later his affiliated Wayne County Better Homes, Inc.; the Dixon Brothers Superior Bottling Company; the three-hundred-room Gotham Hotel; and most notably, physician Robert Greenridge's chain of pharmacies. In 1911, Greenridge "established one of the first black chains of drug stores" in the city of Detroit. By 1924, he had not only encouraged the spread of Black-

owned Black-owned stores, but also mentored and encouraged young entrepreneurs to enter the business.[43]

In 1935, Greenridge spearheaded the movement of Detroit's Black businesses from the most dilapidated portion of the East Side community into a
new area "around East Warren Avenue, Canfield, and Hancock between
Beaubien and Russell." Greenridge opened a modern office building, the
"Walgreen," in the neighborhood. Located on the corner of East Warren and
Beaubien Streets, the Walgreen building was not only a modern structure,
but also a major employer of aspiring young Black professional and businesspeople. The Black weekly the *Detroit Tribune* praised Greenridge for his
accomplishments in shaping the growth of Detroit's expanding Black city:
"By investing in this modern office building and making it available to members of the race, Dr. Greenridge has rendered a real service to the community
which is worthy of our unstinted gratitude and support. Despite the business
depression . . . the colored men and women of this community are . . . coura-
geously pushing toward greater achievement. We congratulate them, one and
all. We also commend the masses of our people here who are so loyally giving
financial support to Negro business."[44]

In Chicago, Jesse Binga, Robert Abbott, and Anthony Overton emerged
at the center of the most lucrative new Black business enterprises during the
1920s. They built a series of businesses that helped to transform Chicago's
built environment, including the Overton Hygienic Building, a four-story
multipurpose building, near the center of the expanding Black metropolis at
3639 S. State Street. Overton also constructed another multistory building
that housed his journalistic enterprise, the *Chicago Bee*, at 3647–3655 S. State
Street. Built between 1929 and 1931, the *Bee* building featured elevator service, Art Deco design, and a "front elevation, composed of colored terra cotta"
that reflected the *Bee*'s and Overton's aesthetic notions about "modernity."
Born in Detroit, Jesse Binga became a Pullman porter and moved to Chicago
as a young man during the 1890s. He soon invested his earnings in real estate,
becoming a pioneer Black homeowner in all-white neighborhoods. During
the interwar years, he also became known for providing much needed rental
properties for poor and working-class Black residents. In 1924, Binga transformed his private banking establishment, located at Thirty-Sixth Place and
State Street, into a new "colonnaded" Binga State Bank building at 3455 S.
State Street. In 1929, just as the Depression got underway, Binga opened his
"Binga Arcade," a large building on the northwest corner of his banking
establishment. In its end of the year report for 1928, the Binga State Bank

reported nearly $1.5 million in deposits, including $800,000 in real estate loans that helped to expand Black home ownership before the crash of 1929. Before decade's end, Binga owned "1,200 leaseholds on flats and residences" and "more frontage on State Street south of 12th Street than any other person."[45]

African American architects and engineers also left their mark on the Midwest cityscape. Walter T. Bailey migrated to Chicago in 1924, after heading Tuskegee's architecture department and establishing his own firm in Memphis, Tennessee. Born in downstate Kewanee, Illinois, Bailey received a degree in science and architecture from the University of Illinois at Urbana-Champaign. He rented an office in the Overton Building and soon landed a job designing the new eight-story National Knights of Pythias Temple at 3745 S. State Street. Completed in 1928 and built at a cost of $859,000, the Pythian skyscraper covered a quarter of a city block. Charles S. Duke, an African American architectural and structural engineer, also influenced the city-building process through his own firm. Duke, who was originally from Alabama, received his early schooling at the prestigious St. Phillips Exeter Academy in New Hampshire and later graduated from Howard University in Washington, DC. He arrived in Chicago during the early years of the Great Migration, set up his own architectural business in 1922, and soon helped to shape the cityscape through his appointments to the Chicago Zoning Commission; as an engineer in the bridge department of the city of Chicago; and as a member of the Chicago Housing Commission. At the Chicago World's Fair in 1933–34, he also designed a replica of the original homestead of Chicago's first non-indigenous permanent resident—Haitian trader Jean Baptiste Pointe DuSable—for the predominantly female National De Saible Memorial Society.[46]

The African American press played a major role in the city-building process across the urban Midwest and elsewhere. The Black weeklies the *Pittsburgh Courier* and *Chicago Defender* emerged as the two most successful Black newspapers in the country. Only now, however, are we beginning to appreciate their profound impact on the Black city-building process and the built environment. In 1929, Robert L. Vann, editor and major stockholder in the *Pittsburgh Courier*, opened a new office and printing press at 2628 Centre Avenue in Pittsburgh's Hill District. The facility was completed at a cost of $104,000. According to Andrew Buni, Vann's biographer, it was "a splendid place, full of modern if second-hand equipment. . . . At a time when most black newspapers were coming out of small side-street shops with limited and inadequate equipment, Vann was doubly proud of his twenty-four-page Hoe Simplex Straightline Press that could turn out an astonishing fifteen thousand newspapers an hour."[47]

In May 1921, editor and founder of the *Chicago Defender* Robert Abbott moved his paper to 3435 Indiana Avenue. Abbott's paper occupied a facility valued at an estimated one million dollars. Located two blocks east of the State Street business corridor, the paper's building was remodeled "with a modern décor" consistent with Abbott's dream and outfitted with a combination of old and new presses valued at $150,000. In his innovative recent study, *A House for the Struggle*, historian E. James West places the *Defender* and the city's Johnson publishing firm at the center of "a dynamic rereading of the history of Chicago's press" and its "relationship to the built environment." When Abbott announced the opening of the new office and printing press, thousands of Chicagoans flocked to the South Side facility to hear Abbott reveal "the mysteries of a modern printing press" in the heart of the Black Belt.[48]

The Midwestern Black press and its impact on the urban landscape extended far beyond these two giants in the field of journalism and business advocacy. Despite its relatively small size compared to Chicago and Pittsburgh, for example, Cleveland's Black community developed a vibrant African American press. Forest City publications included, most notably, the *Cleveland Gazette*, founded in 1883 by the West Virginia–born migrant Harry C. Smith. The *Gazette* persisted as Cleveland's principal Black newspaper through World War II. In Cincinnati, Wendell P. Dabney, a migrant from Richmond, Virginia, founded the Dabney Publishing Company in 1907 and launched *The Union*, focused on the life and doings of Black Cincinnatians. Dabney launched the paper with backing from the city's Republican Party. His account of *The Union*'s history credits an energetic and able roster of young Black women staff for the paper's success.[49]

In Midwestern cities, then, a broad range of beauty salons, barbershops, and funeral homes; restaurants, retail outlets, and billiard halls; as well as a plethora of social service, labor, civic, civil rights, and political organizations occupied their own buildings, primarily as renters, but also as property owners, and reinforced the African American impact on the urban landscape. The cluster of social, civic, and political organizations included most notably local branches of the National Association for the Advancement of Colored People, the National Urban League, the National Association of Colored Women (NACW) with its self-help credo "lifting as we climb," the Brotherhood of Sleeping Car Porters and Maids, and, for a brief but extraordinary moment, the Universal Negro Improvement Association (UNIA) or Garvey move-ment.[50] During its short heyday during the early post–World War I years, the UNIA established its own popular Liberty Halls, businesses, and civic organizations across the urban Midwest. By 1923, the Chicago UNIA had opened branches on both the South Side and the West Side, claimed over 9,000 members, and occupied its own Liberty Hall headquarters at Forty-Ninth and State Streets on the South Side. It also operated a coterie of "relatively profitable businesses," especially restaurants to serve its growing membership. Drawing upon the earnings of Black auto workers, the Detroit UNIA purchased its own building and opened a restaurant, as its numbers rose to an estimated 4,000 members during the early 1920s. For its part, Milwaukee's small Black community opened its own Liberty Hall at Third and Walnut Streets north of the CBD.[51]

Not all Black enterprises in the Midwest metropolis were legal businesses. Some were underground establishments that transformed residences in and near the "red light" districts into thriving businesses that shaped the institu-tional infrastructure of the Black city. On the eve of World War I, the most lucrative business among Milwaukee's African American population was John L. Slaughter's Turf Hotel. Originally from Lynchburg, Virginia, Slaughter migrated to Milwaukee in 1890. After working for a while as a porter, he embarked on a gambling career and eventually opened his own establishment in 1894. By 1902, he had joined with a white partner and opened the New Turf European Hotel and Restaurant, a $50,000 gambling house. His decline as a businessman came after about 1908, when city officials launched a concerted campaign to "clean up the 'bad lands.'"

Slaughter left Milwaukee for Chicago just before the beginning of World War I but returned to the city during 1920s and resumed business. By the end of the interwar years, however, another entrepreneur of the informal econ-omy, Clinton (Joe) Harris, had emerged as "king" of Milwaukee's illegal but very lucrative "policy" game. Harris reported legal earnings of only $300 to $400 per month, but he owned the 711 Club at 711 W. Walnut Street. He also gained recognition as one of Milwaukee's wealthiest Blacks, who used his facilities to adjudicate potentially dangerous disputes among African Americans and made generous contributions to the community life of the Black metropolis. The popular Milwaukee minister and social worker Rev. Cecil A. Fisher asserted that nearly every Black church in Milwaukee had "enjoyed the benefaction" of Harris's hand.[52]

Even more so than in Milwaukee, African Americans in Detroit and Chicago supplemented their legitimate enterprises with lucrative underground establishments. In addition to cabarets and nightclubs, the policy game, also called "numbers," was a form of then-illegal gambling (now legalized as the "state lottery") that financed a plethora of grocery stores, restaurants, banks, insurance companies and even some churches, and provided jobs for workers as well as some Black professional people. Some of Detroit's storefront churches became well-known sites of illegal policy stations. Members later cited the policy game as an incentive for joining and maintaining their membership. "Before I joined this church," one member related, "I used to play as big as fifty cents almost every day ... and never hit. I went to this church, got a private reading. She told me to fast. I did three days; and one day I played fifty cents and won."[53] In Chicago, John "Mushmouth" Johnson's Emporium Saloon on State Street; Robert T. Motts's Pekin Theater, also on State Street; and Elijah Johnson's Dreamland Ballroom (later Dreamland Café) all developed in part out of earnings from the numbers game and other forms of gambling. Policy income also supported the growth of Jesse Binga's bank, the Chicago American Giants professional baseball team, and the formation of the National Negro Baseball League in 1920.

As in Detroit, Chicago's ministers of poor and working-class churches like Elder Lucy Smith chose not to "hold it against the people if they play policy numbers." "Conditions here," Lucy said, "are not good." As historian Davarian Baldwin notes, significant numbers of Black women "created indirect economies benefiting from policy, by giving consultations and selling dream books and other lucky products as spiritualist mediums."[54] Black women's participation in Chicago's underground economy extended well beyond the policy game and employment as sex workers and managers of brothels. They also operated lucrative "buffet flats" or "good time flats" that flourished in the wake of prohibition. "Called 'landladies' by urbanites-in-the-know, the operators of these flats did not directly compete with saloon-based after-hours clubs. Instead, they were part of the late-night party circuit and established their special niche by providing an assortment of racy amusements [including music, food, alcohol, and sex shows] to men and women ... [in] private dwellings, usually apartments."[55]

Great Migration–era Black midwesterners not only increasingly celebrated the rise of their own Black metropolis. They also used the dramatic expansion of Black urban infrastructure to launch new and more militant assaults against the segregationist system. As suggested at the outset of this chapter, by redefining themselves as "New Negroes," they waged a militant fight against class and racial inequality in the region's Black history. The fight for a broader, more inclusive, and more equitable city was not easy. It entailed significant ideological, class, and gender debates, conflicts, and disputes over the best path toward liberation, freedom, and independence. But Black midwesterners firmly united behind campaigns to demolish the Jim Crow social order.

MOBILIZING A NEW FREEDOM MOVEMENT

The twentieth-century politics of the Black metropolis gained increasing expression in the language and deeds of the "New Negro."[56] "New Negroes" advanced firm demands for full citizenship rights and equal access to all facets of the geography and political economy of the city even as they sought to strengthen the political and social infrastructure of the Black urban community. In June 1919, as soldiers began demobilizing after the First World War, J. Anthony Josey, activist editor of the *Wisconsin Enterprise Blade*, enthusiastically reprinted W. E. B. Du Bois's ringing editorial, "We Return Fighting," published in the NAACP's *Crisis* magazine: "This is the country to which we soldiers of Democracy return. . . . We return—We return from Fighting. We Return Fighting. Make way for Democracy, We saved it in France, and by the Great Jehovah, we will save it in the United States of America or know the reason why."[57] Josey, the Milwaukee branch of the NAACP, the Milwaukee Urban League, and other local leaders intensified demands for equal access to the city's full range of social services, health, and leisure-time facilities, but they vehemently opposed movements to serve Black people on a segregated and unequal basis.[58]

A group of Chicago college-educated Black intellectuals, authors, and activists coalesced around the *Chicago Whip*. Founded in 1919 by businessman William C. Linton and Yale Law School graduates Joseph D. Bibb and Arthur C. MacNeal, the *Whip* staunchly resisted "all forms of segregation" and advocated a "broadside attack on injustice and oppression" wherever it existed. The paper also adopted a form of economic radicalism and strongly urged poor and working-class Blacks to join the organized labor movement and fight for the liberation of Black and white workers. Linton, Bibb, and MacNeal embraced Marcus Garvey's movement to build "race pride" among

Black people, but they also firmly rejected his notion of "race first" over class unity across the color line. Despite its radical pronouncements on class and race, the *Whip* received solid financial backing from middle-class Black business and professional luminaries, including Anthony Overton, Jesse Binga, and Lacey Kirk Williams.[59]

Detroit's "New Negro" radicalism also gained voice in the work of the NAACP, the Garvey movement, and the merger of civil rights and labor activism. The Detroit NAACP emerged at the forefront of the city's civil rights and social justice movement following the Ossian Sweet case of 1925. When a mob attacked the home of dentist Henry Ossian Sweet in a previously all-white neighborhood of Detroit, the Sweets returned fire, killing one white man and wounding another. Authorities quickly moved in and arrested ten occupants of the Sweet household, including his pregnant wife Gladys, and placed them on trial for murder. The Detroit branch swiftly secured local and national support to free the Sweets from criminal prosecution for defending themselves and their home from mob violence. The branch's work on behalf of the Sweets resulted in their acquittal.[60]

Following the Sweet case, the Detroit NAACP amplified its attacks on racial injustice, including police brutality. In 1933, 1938, and 1939, it roundly protested the police killing of Black people in the city. In early 1939, at a mass meeting at a local church, the president of the North Detroit Youth Council of the NAACP told the crowd that "Negroes are being shot down like rats and unless we put up a bigger fight such conditions will continue to exist." Branch president Dr. James J. McClendon assured the audience that the case "will not be over until the policeman is punished for the slaying of [the Black worker] Jesse James." Reverend Horace White, pastor of the Plymouth Congregational Church and head of the NAACP's Legal Redress Committee, urged the crowd to "get mad about it, and then you'll get something done." Later, in the same year, an estimated 1,500 people crowded into Bethel AME Church to protest police brutality during a "Brutality Week" program planned by a coalition of activist organizations. At one mass meeting, the famous civil rights lawyer Charles Hamilton Houston urged the gathering to not only go after the policemen involved, but to "go after the [entire] City Hall gang." Rev. White had also admonished his audience to vote "for the one who promises to abolish police brutality."[61]

The African American struggle against racial barriers was not limited to protests against state violence and demands for equal access to social services. It also included "Don't Buy Where You Can't Work" boycotts of white merchants in order to expand employment opportunities for Black residents. Better jobs and higher wages were seen as critical to the success of the African American community-building movement. During the Depression years, inspired by the example of Harlem's Black community, for example, Fannie B. Peck and some 50 Black women met in the basement of the Bethel AME Church and formed Detroit's Housewives League. League women firmly believed that the League represented a shift in Black women's vision for their children, their families, and their communities. In addition to promoting education for Black youth, they would use their buying power and the boycott to open jobs that they could enter upon graduation. At the organization's founding, Peck declared that "it had been in the minds of our women that they, their husbands and children were victims of a vicious economic system." Activists associated with the *Chicago Whip* spearheaded a similar campaign under the slogan "Spend Your Money Where You Can Work." The paper implored Black people to boycott and picket businesses that refused to employ African Americans. Through an aggressive program of picketing and selective buying, the *Whip* helped to create an estimated two thousand jobs during the late 1920s and early 1930s.[62]

Some Black midwesterners advanced their political agenda through affiliation with the U.S. Communist Party (CP). By the late 1920s, a small coterie of Black workers, including Joseph Billups, Walter Hardin, and Paul Kirk, had joined the Communist Party–controlled Auto Workers Union (AWU). While the party made few inroads into the Black metropolis during the 1920s, it gained the attention of rising numbers of Black residents during the Depression, when CP members boldly assisted Black families in avoiding evictions from their homes. As Drake and Cayton reported in their massive study of Chicago, "When eviction notices arrived, it was not unusual for a mother to shout to the children, 'Run quick and find the Reds!'"[63]

African American engagement with the Communist Party peaked within the context of the organizing campaigns of the new Congress of Industrial Organizations (CIO) unions and the formation of the National Negro Congress (NNC). The NNC symbolized growing cross-class support for the labor movement. Formed in 1936, the NNC aimed to unite all existing African American organizations against the ravages of the Depression and racial inequality. Representatives from six hundred organizations selected A. Philip Randolph, president of the Brotherhood of Sleeping Car Porters and Maids, to spearhead this effort. While the organization aimed to achieve a variety of goals in the struggle for citizenship and launched its own antilynching campaign, it emphasized economic democracy and the unionization of Black workers as principal goals.[64] From its inception, under the leadership of Rev. Charles Hill of the Hartford Street Baptist Church, the Detroit chapter of the NNC recruited an energetic cadre of young activists, including Christopher Columbus Alston, Coleman Young, John Conyers, Sr., and Shelton Tappes, who became involved in the UAW's effort to organize Black workers in the auto industry. Until recently most scholarship on the NNC emphasized the heavy hand of the Communist Party in its programs and activities, but recent scholarship underscores the grassroots dimensions of the movement and the ways that rank-and-file Black members and activists played the principal role in shaping the politics of the organization. Historian Erik S. Gellman, for example, places "a black-led network at the center of a narrative usually dominated by white unionists, New Dealers, Communists, and other antifascist leaders."[65]

Few African Americans actually joined the CP, in the urban Midwest or elsewhere. The vast majority of Black labor activists joined the Congress of Industrial Organizations, but the CP did recruit three prominent Black communists in the Pittsburgh region. During the early Depression years, Ernest McKinney, the grandson of an active member of the United Mine Workers, joined a splinter group of the CP and participated in demonstrations on behalf of unemployed workers in Pittsburgh. Originally from Chattanooga, Tennessee, Ben Careathers, another Black CP recruit, had migrated to Pittsburgh before World War I; in succession he worked as a janitor and helper on the railroads, opened an upholstery shop, and joined the socialists and then the CP by the early 1930s. He also participated in the CP's unemployed councils. The Black Pullman porter William Scarville also joined the party in Pittsburgh and became well-known in the circle of white communists in western Pennsylvania.[66]

As the Black population increased and the Black metropolis expanded and consolidated, African Americans also mobilized to take power in local, state, and national politics. While they built political alliances primarily with whites in the Republican Party before the Great Depression and the Democratic Party thereafter, they also set out on their own and built independent political movements to strengthen their hand in municipal politics. In some cases, they supported the Communist and Socialist Parties. In Milwaukee, despite their small numbers, they regularly supported the Republican ticket at the state and national levels, while adopting flexible and quite independent voting records at the local level. During the entire interwar years, their votes enabled Milwaukee's Socialist Party to retain the mayor's office against recurring challenges from the Republican and Democratic parties. Moreover, while most northern Blacks shifted their support to Franklin Delano Roosevelt (FDR) and the Democratic Party in the presidential election of 1936, Milwaukee's small Black community made the transition to the Democratic Party in the election of 1932.[67]

In 1919, African Americans elected Robert H. Logan to Pittsburgh's city council. While he served only one term, his victory accented the efforts of Pittsburgh Blacks to transform segregation into a base of political empowerment and counter the Republican Party's neglect of its Black constituency. According to Robert Vann of the *Pittsburgh Courier*, Logan's election represented "a solid bloc" effort of Black voters. After suffering defeat in his own bid to become judge of the Court of Common Pleas of Allegheny County in 1921, Vann expressed even greater urgency for Black voters to mobilize in their own interests: "It is better to elect a Negro generally speaking than ANY white man. . . . [Far] better to have a Negro speaking in [the race's] behalf than any white man." By 1927, Pittsburgh Blacks had formed the Third Ward Voters' League under the leadership of Walter C. Rainey, and soon claimed a membership of 5,000 Black voters. Black people outnumbered whites in the Third Ward and expressed a determination to create more jobs and public offices for Blacks through aggressive participation in electoral politics.[68]

During the first two decades of the twentieth century, Cleveland's small but growing Black population mobilized behind the political leadership of Thomas W. Fleming and built a strong Black Republican machine. Fleming, born in Mercer, Pennsylvania in 1874, received early training as a barber. He quit school early and moved to Cleveland in 1892. At the young age of twenty-one, he had become the owner of his own shop. He later returned to school and earned a law degree. Armed with his new professional credentials, he soon formed the Twelfth Ward Republican Club as a vehicle to organize and "solidify the Afro-American voters" in the city. In 1906, Fleming spearheaded the formation of a new organization, the Attucks Republican Club.[69]

A citywide organization, the Attucks Club emerged as the centerpiece of Cleveland's Black Republican machine. In 1909, with the support of the city's white Republican boss Maurice Maschke, along with solid backing from Black voters, Fleming became Cleveland's first Black councilman. Although he was not reelected after his first term, he remained politically engaged in Republican Party politics and regained the office within a newly redrawn Eleventh Ward in 1915. He retained the post until the onset of the Great Depression in 1929. Fleming gained nearly unwavering support from the city's predominantly poor and working-class Black community, partly because he controlled patronage appointments allotted to African Americans through the Republican organization. In 1916, following his election to a council seat for the second time, Fleming not only dispensed traditional municipal sanitation and custodial crew jobs to Black supporters, but also "appointed seventy Negroes to replace whites as election officers in the Eleventh Ward." He also secured a number of clerkships and supervisory posts for African Americans in several municipal departments.[70]

Cincinnati's African American community also mobilized to curb Republican control of their votes at the local level. But the city's municipal politics changed with the adoption of the reform city charter of 1924, which abolished ward-based politics and instituted a city manager and a nine-member city council. The city adopted a complicated proportional representation approach to voting, which proponents argued would end "corrupt Republican" or "one party" domination of municipal government. Theoretically, any group, including African Americans, could obtain election to the city council by garnering one-tenth of total votes plus one vote. Under the new charter, African Americans mobilized behind the candidacy of Frank A. B. Hall, a retired detective. It was not until the early years of the Depression, however, that Blacks succeeded in electing Hall to city council.[71]

In Chicago, more so than elsewhere, the increasing concentration of Blacks on the South Side enabled them to challenge the regular Republican leadership for control of predominantly Black wards. A new generation of young Black Republican political leaders—including Edward H. Wright, Oscar De Priest, Robert R. Jackson, and Beauregard Moseley—forged an independent organization within the party and focused their attention on controlling wards with majority or near-majority Black populations. Black women, organized in the Alpha Suffrage Club, played a pivotal role in the politics of the South Side. Their efforts resulted in the election of Oscar De Priest as Chicago's first Black alderman in 1915, then a second in 1918. In 1924, Chicagoans elected their first Black state senator, and four years later sent De Priest to the U.S. Congress. The latter office not only symbolized the growth of Black power at the local level, but also signaled the resurgence of African Americans in national politics following the disfranchisement of southern Blacks and the ascendancy of Jim Crow. By 1930, African Americans controlled the Republican Party on Chicago's South Side, where they made up majorities of the Second, Third, and Fourth Wards.[72]

Chicago's political experience inspired Black politics in other Midwestern cities and beyond. In Milwaukee, as early as 1918, when the city's Black population had reached just over 2,000 residents, African Americans launched a movement to elect a Black alderman from the Sixth Ward, their area of highest concentration. As the weekly Black newspaper the *Wisconsin Enterprise Blade* declared, the rise of the Black community in the Sixth Ward would enable Milwaukee Blacks to replicate "what your people have done in the 2nd Ward of Chicago, where they have already one alderman and will soon have another." African Americans elected the Democrat LeRoy Simmons, a realtor, to the Wisconsin State Assembly in 1944, but the election of Milwaukee's first Black alderman would have to wait until the postwar years. The election of Blacks to the Detroit city council would also have to wait until the 1950s. Nonetheless, the interwar years set the stage for increasing African American challenges to white hegemony in those electoral districts where Blacks comprised majorities or near majorities. As historian Richard Walter Thomas makes clear, it was the "migrants, the generation of blacks born and reared between the world wars" that "sowed the first seeds of future black political control in Detroit."[73]

As early as 1923, Detroit's Black community organized the United Civic League and adopted the motto "Every Negro Vote in Every Election" to support Frank Murphy's campaign for a Recorders Court judgeship. An archopponent of Henry Ford and his Republican politics, prolabor attorney, Communist, and Democratic Party activist, Murphy not only won the judgeship but used African American support to build his own so-called "new deal" coalition well ahead of FDR's election as president in 1932. African Americans helped to elect Murphy to the mayor's office in 1930 and 1931. But this was just the tip of the iceberg. African Americans fueled Murphy's rise to governor of Michigan, U.S. attorney general, and U.S. Supreme Court Justice. In the meantime, in 1930, Charles Roxborough, one of the city's leading Black Republicans, gained election to the state senate. While white votes proved decisive in the election of Republican Henry Bass to the State Assembly in 1910, Roxborough became the first Black in Detroit and Michigan history to be elected by a predominantly Black constituency.

Under the leadership of Snow F. Grigsby, the South Carolina–born pharmacist and activist, a young generation of activists formed the Detroit Civic Rights Committee (CRC) and soon became a pivotal force in the political mobilization of Black Detroit. The CRC supplanted the earlier Booker T. Washington Trade Association (BTWTA), founded in 1930 by Reverend William Peck, the popular minister of Detroit's Bethel AME Church, the city's second oldest and second largest Black church. The BTWTA advocated a program of economic Black nationalism and focused mainly on strengthening Black businesses through "Buy Black" campaigns. As noted above, Peck's wife Fannie led Detroit's Housewives League and reinforced the activities of the movement to organize the buying power of Black women and their families. Unlike the BTWTA, as historian Beth Bates notes, the CRC "revitalized community organizing" by pressing established citywide institutions to open jobs for Black residents. In 1935, the organization supported the candidacy of Maurice Sugar—a prolabor white attorney and communist sympathizer—in its publication the *Civic Rights Bulletin*.

In addition to Grigsby, Peck, and the CRC, Sugar also gained the endorsement of L. C. Blount, president of the Detroit chapter of the NAACP, and Reverend Robert L. Bradby, considered by many historians to have been a staunchly loyal supporter of Henry Ford. In a mass mailing to his "Friends, as Citizens of Detroit and Wayne County," Bradby declared that African Americans "would manifest the basest ingratitude were we not unanimous and enthusiastic in favoring" the election of Maurice Sugar. Although Sugar lost his election bid in each case, his campaign underscored the increasing shift of the city's Black politics from a pro-Ford and corporate stance to one of closer alignment with the expanding interracial labor movement, as reflected in growing African American membership in the United Automobile Workers union (UAW). Somewhat similar to Milwaukee, there was a noticeable shift of Detroit's Black voters toward the Democratic Party in the presidential election of 1932. Detroit's Black population increased its vote for the Democratic Party from about 20 percent in the previous election to nearly 38 percent in 1932. The vast majority of Blacks would not vote for the Democratic Party until the elections of 1936 and 1940.[74]

As suggested above, African American politics produced tangible material benefits for Black residents, although far from sufficient to meet their needs and far, as well, from acknowledging the weight of their growing influence in municipal elections. Black Milwaukeeans used their support of the city's socialist regime to expand their access to patronage appointments. In addition to the usual sanitation department jobs, Black Milwaukeeans gradually expanded their employment in professional positions as social workers, nurses, and probation officers. They placed tremendous pressure on city agencies to secure these jobs. In 1941, under intense pressure from Black activists, Milwaukee built a large outdoor swimming pool, equipped with locker rooms, for African Americans at Tenth and Reservoir Streets. The city used funds provided by FDR's WPA program to construct the $250,000 facility. In Detroit, African Americans enabled John Smith, a staunch labor unionist and supporter of Frank Murphy, to win the mayor's office in 1924. Smith promised to address the demands of the city's Black community, including addressing police brutality by hiring Black policemen.

Following his election as mayor of Detroit with essential African American support, Smith responded to the demands of Black voters by expanding the number of African American employees in the Post Office; the Sanitary Division of the Public Works Department; and, to some extent, the Police Department. Despite the city's historic resistance to employing Black policemen, Detroit slowly added 32 Black officers to a force of over 3,000 white policemen.[75] At the same time, hundreds of Black Chicagoans took positions as teachers, clerks, policemen, and postal workers as well as the customary jobs as custodial employees and general laborers. Blacks made up about 7 percent of the city's total population as the Great Depression got underway but accounted for some 25 percent of all postal workers. At city hall, an African American held the position of Assistant Corporation Council and trial lawyer for property damage litigation totaling millions of dollars. Twenty other Blacks worked as legal investigators for the department. Moreover, in addition to municipal jobs, some African Americans gained police "protection for activities within the underground economy."[76]

Similar to the city-building process elsewhere, the Midwest Black metropolis emerged against the grain of significant divisions and conflicts within the Black urban community. Class and gender cleavages challenged the community-building project. These divisions gained substantial expression within mainstream Black churches, fraternal, social service, and entrepreneurial activities, where women often served under the leadership of Black men with severe limits on their ability to become ministers of major congregations or the principal officers in local branches of social service organizations like the National Urban League. Gender, class, and status distinction also surfaced in major Black nationalist and transnational movements like the Community Party, the Garvey movement, and a little later the Nation of Islam. Female Garveyites, for example, defied formal limits on their roles in the UNIA. Under the leadership of predominantly working-class members of the organization, the Garvey movement not only persisted well into and beyond the interwar years. It also fueled the rise of modern Black feminism against oppressive forms of patriarchy within Black urban politics and social movements during the industrial age.[77]

Likewise, working-class Black women embraced the Nation of Islam (but not necessarily its full range of gendered constraints) as part of their fight against gender as well as class and racial inequality within the larger urban community. As historian Ula Taylor notes in her pioneering study of NOI women, the vast majority of these women "were hardworking and unlettered black women determined to assist their men in the development of a black Islamic society." In her own words, for example, Sister Ruby Williams, a rank-and-file member of the NOI, revealed how she joined the Nation not only because of racist abuse at the hands of white men, but also because many Black men were "instrumental in making her plight worse."[78] Such gender tensions and friction were not limited to Black nationalist or mainstream Black religious and fraternal organizations. These divisions also gained expression in organizations that were ideologically committed to global struggles against class oppression. In his groundbreaking study of Black women in the U.S. Communist Party, historian Erik McDuffie shows how radical Black women pioneered the concept of "triple oppression" to both document and combat the strictures of class, race, and gender dynamics in progressive social and political organizations as well as the larger society of which they were an integral part. Much like Keisha Blain, he also underscores how these women helped to seed the rise of the Black feminist movement of the 1960s and 1970s.[79]

Despite significant conflicts along class, gender, ideological, and cultural lines, the Midwestern Black metropolis repeatedly bridged such differences in the interest of racial solidarity in the fight to dismantle the segregationist order. Although the Nation of Islam stood firmly against what Minister Malcolm X would later describe as "integration into a burning house," Midwestern Black urbanites enthusiastically joined the nationwide March on Washington Movement (MOWM). They closed ranks with African Americans from across the country to demand equal access to defense industry jobs and desegregation of the U.S. military services as World War II got underway. Helping to fuel the MOWM was the *Pittsburgh Courier*'s "Double-V" campaign to defeat fascism abroad and Jim Crow at home.[80] Under the leadership of A. Philip Randolph, the MOWM emerged in 1941 following a meeting of civil rights groups in Chicago.[81] By early June, the

MOWM had established march headquarters in cities across the country, from New York to San Francisco.[82]

The MOWM helped to mobilize the masses of Black working people as well as the middle and upper classes. According to Randolph, "The March on Washington Movement is essentially a movement of the people. It is all Negro and pro-Negro, but not for that reason anti-white or anti-Semitic, or anti-Catholic, or anti-foreign, or anti-labor. Its major weapon is the nonviolent demonstration of Negro mass power."[83] Moreover, Randolph further stated: "It was apparent . . . that some unusual, bold and gigantic effort must be made to awaken the American people and the President of the Nation to the realization that the Negroes were the victims of sharp and unbearable oppression, and that the fires of resentment were flaming higher and higher." Though the MOWM welcomed liberal white support, Randolph insisted that African Americans lead the movement. Randolph was wary of the labor movement, the major political parties, and the growing communist influence in Black organizations like the National Negro Congress.[84]

Although Roosevelt resisted the movement as long as he could, the MOWM finally succeeded. Roosevelt met with Black leaders A. Philip Randolph and Walter White of the NAACP on June 18, 1941. A week later FDR issued Executive Order 8802, banning racial discrimination in government employment, defense industries, and training programs. The order also established the Fair Employment Practices Committee (FEPC) to implement its provisions. Executive Order 8802 empowered the FEPC to receive, investigate, and address complaints of racial discrimination in the defense program.[85]

Executive Order 8802 represented an important turning point in Midwestern and African American political history and the city-building process. By strengthening the hand of Black workers and increasing their wage-earning power, it enhanced the institution and community-building activities of Black people. It also linked Blacks in the urban Midwest and elsewhere even more closely to the Democratic Party and helped to transform the federal government into a significant, albeit problematic, ally. It also helped to strengthen the bond between Black workers and organized labor, primarily through the unions of the Congress of Industrial Organizations. The CIO's leadership supported the FEPC claims of Black workers and helped them to break the job ceiling. At its annual convention in 1941, for example, the CIO denounced racially discriminatory hiring policies as a "direct attack against our nation's policy to build democracy in our fight against Hitlerism." A year later, the organization established its own Committee to Abolish Racial Discrimination and urged its affiliates to support national policy against discrimination: "When a decision to employ minority group workers is made, the union must be prepared to stand behind it." New, highly organized, interwar assaults on the Jim Crow order sowed the seeds for the rise of the modern Black Freedom Movement in the years following World War II, eventually resulting in the demolition of the Jim Crow system nationwide.[86]

REMEMBERING PREINDUSTRIAL ROOTS

As fresh and innovative as the "New Negro" roots of the twentieth century Black Freedom Movement may have been, earlier nineteenth-century social struggles both inspired and informed the modern Black liberation movement. A few prominent examples underscore this point. In 1837, for example, when Pennsylvania disfranchised Black citizens, African Americans in Pittsburgh and Western Pennsylvania filed one of the most militant protests of that day—"Memorial of the Free Citizens of Colony of Pittsburgh and Its Vicinity Relative to the Right of Suffrage" (July 1837). Seventy-nine area Blacks signed the petition exhorting the state to restore the franchise to Black people. The petition cited the contributions that Blacks had made to the state and argued forcibly that African Americans were as worthy and entitled as whites to exercise the vote. In January 1841, John Peck became president of a new effort to gain the franchise. A week later the group met at Bethel AME Church and proposed a statewide convention to continue the fight for suffrage. In August 1841, this convention indeed met at the same church, with John B. Vashon, Lewis Woodson, A. D. Lewis, and Martin Delany taking leadership roles.[87]

Similar struggles emerged in nineteenth-century Chicago, Detroit, Milwaukee, and elsewhere across the urban Midwest. On October 26, 1843, a statewide convention of Black people met at Detroit's Second Baptist Church and approved "An Address to the Citizens of the State of Michigan." The resolution "condemned the Negroes' loss of rights, endorsed the principles of the Declaration of Independence and called for equal civil and political rights" for Black people. In Chicago, following passage of the Fugitive Slave Law of 1850, 300 Black residents, over 50 percent of the permanent Black citizenry, met at Quinn Chapel AME church to plan a response to the new law. They organized a Liberty Association, established a vigilante group,

FIGURE 6. Pittsburgh's Old Bethel African Methodist Episcopal Church was the first AME congregation to organize services west of the Allegheny Mountains. This structure served the church until it was finally demolished under the destructive impact of urban renewal during the 1950s. Courtesy of Teenie Harris Archive/Carnegie Museum of Art, Pittsburgh.

and established seven six-person patrols, charging each with keeping "an eye out" for the slave catchers. The group also issued a stinging resolution, declaring their determination to resist the fugitive slave legislation, to the death if necessary. "We do not wish to offer violence to any person unless driven to the extreme, in which case we are determined to defend ourselves at all hazards, even should it be the shedding of human blood, and in doing thus, we will appeal to the Supreme Judge of the Social World to support us in the justice of our cause."[88] In October 1850, Black Milwaukeeans also met to plot a response to the 1850 Fugitive Slave Law. Under the leadership of the grocer Lewis Johnson, chair of the gathering, and Joseph Barquet, secretary, African Americans declared their intention to resist the measure, and, if necessary, to give their lives in the cause of liberty.[89]

· · ·

By the end of World War II, inspired partly by their early nineteenth-century struggles against slavery and discrimination against free people of color,

African Americans had not only built their own city against the powerful constraints of the new Jim Crow order. They had also achieved this feat against the limitations of their own internal differences and social conflicts along class, cultural, and ideological lines. Black people from different class, status, cultural, and political backgrounds perceived deep and persistent forms of racial inequality as evidence that people of African descent shared a common fate and that their class interests were closely intertwined with the imperatives of racial solidarity.

While the contemporary case for reparations in industrial America revolves around inequality of work, wages, housing, health, and social conditions for urban Blacks, this chapter shows how a full and more complete rationale for reparations in our times must also include the energetic efforts of Black urbanites in crafting their own city against the destructive backdrop of racial capitalism in the twentieth century. Although the Black city-building process unfolded mainly along the Black-white socioeconomic and political divide in the urban Midwest, African Americans also forged a West Coast metropolis through a complicated series of interactions with diverse people of Latinx, Asian, and Euro-American descent. Somewhat similar to the Southeast and Southwest, these dynamic class, ethnic, and race relations produced a unique Black city-building experience as compared to the Midwest, Northeast, and the South.

SEVEN

Constructing the Black City under "That Open Sky"

PEOPLE OF AFRICAN DESCENT ARRIVED in the urban West alongside the Spanish and later the English colonization of indigenous land and people in the region. But their numbers increased only slowly until the advent of World War II and the rise of the modern Black Freedom Movement during the 1950s and 1960s. Unlike the urban Northeast and Midwest, West Coast city-building entailed complicated social relations between African Americans, Native Americans, Asian Americans, Latinx people, and people of European descent. Such diverse ethnic and race relations deepened the transnational dimensions of Black urbanization; challenged African American efforts to build unified communities; and complicated movements to dismantle the segregationist system.[1] Nonetheless, as late as 2023, a statewide California study of systemic inequality revealed a stark pattern of economic, social, and institutional discrimination against Black Californians, including its principal urban areas, from the advent of statehood in 1850 to the present. As the report concludes, "Federal, California, and local government, acting in tandem and in parallel with private actors, created and intensified ... environmental harms, unequal educational and health outcomes, [a racial wealth gap], and over-policing of African American neighborhoods in California and across the nation."[2]

Nonetheless, early on higher rates of African American homeownership than those in the urban Northeast and Midwest buoyed the Black city-building process in the urban West. In 1913, after he visited Los Angeles, the scholar W. E. B. Du Bois reported in the *Crisis* that Black Angelenos were "the most beautifully housed group of Colored people in the United States."[3] Du Bois's assessment would largely hold for Seattle and the San Francisco Bay Area as well as Los Angeles across the span of the interwar years. Hence,

MAP 8. While the Black urban population had deep roots in the early American West, this map underscores the African American experience on the urban "Pacific rim." More so than elsewhere in urban America, West Coast cities—namely Los Angeles, the San Francisco Bay Area, and Seattle—would become sites of diverse social relations between Black people and a variety of European, Asian, Latinx, and indigenous American people. These complicated class, ethnic, and race relations would shape the rise of a unique Black western city-building experience.

more so than elsewhere, Blacks in the urban West would use their somewhat greater access to homeownership as well as rental spaces to build institutions to address their own social service, cultural, and political needs. Their city-building efforts also buttressed the nationwide African American movement to eclipse the segregationist order.

LAND AND HOMES: PROMISE AND LIMITS

Before the mid-twentieth century, the urban West offered few opportunities for African Americans to move to the city in large numbers, find viable employment, and take up permanent residence. Even so, early on in the commercial and industrial development of the region, small but significant numbers of Black newcomers gained access to land and homeownership. These pioneer urbanites gave some support to enthusiastic endorsements of the urban West as potential sites for the Black city-building movement.

Following the discovery of gold at Sutter's Fort in 1848, the first Black landowners and homeowners were single men without families, but this pattern soon changed as growing numbers of young men with wives and families migrated into the region.[4] At the outbreak of the Civil War, Afro-San Franciscans reported real estate and personal property worth $300,000. The African American newspaper the *Pacific Appeal* enthusiastically reported Black property ownership as tangible "evidence of thrift among our people" and "a source of much encouragement."[5]

Black property ownership was not limited to the most well-to-do elites among the city's small Black population, but included general laborers and household workers as well. In 1870, Russell Davis, a wagoner who could not read or write, claimed ownership of real estate valued at $25,000; an illiterate janitor, Ezekiel Cooper, reported ownership of $10,000 worth of small lots; and Mary Ellen "Mammy" Pleasant owned $30,000 worth of real estate, accrued with investment income from her popular boardinghouse. But the most successful of these early postbellum Black property owners was the porter Richard Barber, who claimed ownership of some $70,000 worth of property, most of it in real estate.[6]

As early as the 1850s, one newcomer described San Francisco as the "New York of the Pacific," partly because of its prosperous, albeit small, numbers of Black property holders. This very positive perception of life in the Bay Area endured through the early twentieth century. African American homeownership in the East Bay suburbs accelerated after the destructive San Francisco fire and earthquake at the turn of the century. The city's gradually expanding Black middle class and better-off members of the Black working class purchased homes and moved into previously all-white neighborhoods in Oakland, Richmond, and Sunset.[7]

Increasing numbers of poor and working-class Blacks also moved to East Bay suburbs where rents were lower and more affordable than in the Bay City. East Bay towns offered "larger homes, more space for yards and children, and suffered from less noise and congestion" than their San Francisco counterparts. In the opening years of the twentieth century, J. S. Francis, editor of the African American newspaper the *Western Outlook*, declared that no "strong color line" prevented Blacks from occupying homes in predominantly white communities. Into the 1940s, according to sociologist Charles S. Johnson, "No rigidly segregated Negro community existed in the city." East Bay migrants, both renters and homeowners, became "urban dwellers in a rural land." They also became suburbanites at a time when the United States had just become a majority urban nation.[8]

Seattle's early Black community also waged an aggressive drive for home-ownership. As the Black population increased from only 19 people in 1880 to nearly 300 by 1890, significant numbers of families rather than single men or "transients" moved into the city. Elizabeth Grose, the granddaughter of one of the early Black pioneers, later recalled that the 1880s and 1890s brought "a steady stream of Black families" into the city.[9] By 1900, as renters and to some extent land and homeowners, Black Seattleites expanded their access to the city's housing market. The Grose family occupied their own hotel "near the waterfront as did Robert Dixon, the hotel barber, and William Davis, the hotel cook." Some twenty years earlier William Grose, the principal property owner in the district, had purchased a twelve-acre farm in the heavily wooded and undeveloped area just outside the city limits.[10]

With the advent of cable car service to the area, more of Seattle's Black middle-class families purchased lots from Grose and built their own homes "around the farmhouse of Seattle's oldest Black family." At the same time, middle-class and some working-class families moved into their own homes in the East Madison Street area on the northeastern edge of the city. By the early 1900s, East Madison housed the largest concentration of Seattle's Black homeowners. Meanwhile, the Yesler-Jackson neighborhood on the other side of East Madison was home to the city's predominantly poor and working-class Black community. The two communities slowly expanded toward each other and eventually converged into the single contiguous African American community called the "Central District" by the mid-twentieth century.[11]

African Americans also purchased their own homes at the beginning of their residence in the city of "Our Lady the Queen of the Angels," Los Angeles. Most of the city's first settlers were "Colored" people of mixed African, Indian, and Spanish lineage. Early Black Angelenos were deter-mined to buy land, build their own homes, and raise their families in the urban West. Among these, the family of Robert Owens arrived in the city from Texas in 1853. A former slave who had purchased his own freedom and that of his wife and three children, Owens soon purchased land in the city, and by 1860 he reported real estate holdings "valued at five thousand dollars." At about the same time, the popular Black midwife and nurse Biddy Mason accumulated a substantial savings and purchased real estate "on the edge of town, land that would become the heart of downtown" Los Angeles.[12]

FIGURE 7. Public housing became a distinct feature on the landscape of Black America during and after World War II. It was also a product of the politics of the expanding Black city. This is an aerial view of Seattle's Yesler Terrace neighborhood in 1941. Courtesy of Museum of History and Industry, Seattle.

One pioneer white resident declared that Biddy Mason "left to her family and heirs a handsome fortune." According to editor Charlotta Bass, early Black settlers "bought land and built beautiful homes in all sections of the city free from restrictions." Another resident also later recalled that early Black residents "lived everywhere, as there were no special districts then." In 1904, in African American newspaper the *Liberator*, a Black realtor wrote that "the Negroes of the city have prudently refused to segregate themselves into any locality, but have scattered and purchased homes in sections occupied by wealthy cultured white people, thus not only securing the best fire, water and police protection, but also the more important benefits that accrue from refined and cultured surroundings."[13]

Even in their area of highest concentration along Central Avenue, south of downtown, African Americans occupied "a sort of middling area that represented some of the best property on the Eastside. The Central Avenue District was on high, flat ground, neither swampy nor prone to floods." While some homes in the district were "shacks and housed the very poor," the majority of houses "were nice, however, and some were excellent."[14] By 1930, in Seattle, Los Angeles, and San Francisco, respectively, about 39, 34, and 14 percent of African Americans owned their own homes, compared to about 6 percent in Milwaukee and New York, 11 percent in Chicago, and a high of 17 percent in Detroit.[15] As one Black Seattle resident recalled, although exaggerated: "Practically everyone owned their homes.... They wasn't making no money but they owned homes and they were taking ten to fifteen years paying $15 per month."[16]

In the wake of World War II, during the escalating modern Black Freedom Movement, African Americans gradually moved into new predominantly white neighborhoods within and beyond the established city limits. In Los Angeles, rising numbers of middle- and working-class Blacks moved from the Eastside into the West Adams district, a northern offshoot of the West Jefferson neighborhood. As the older Central Avenue neighborhood lost population, its institutional infrastructure declined, but African Americans quickly undertook a new wave of institution-building activities in the new areas.[17] At the same time that some Blacks aimed toward new white neighborhoods, others headed for nearly exclusively Black private housing developments.

In early postwar Richmond, African Americans moved into a new development located in the northwest section of the city. According to historian Shirley Ann Moore, it was "the first subdivision in the city where Blacks could purchase homes." Under the leadership of Rev. Guthrie John Williams, an accomplished carpenter by trade, African Americans had persuaded the white land developer Fred Parr to fund a land development project for potential Black homeowners. Dubbed Parchester Village, this development included 409 houses and advertised itself as a multiracial "home community for all Americans," but it was a predominantly Black development. After it opened in 1950, African Americans praised Parchester Village as an "oasis" in a sea of restrictive covenants banning Black people from all-white neighborhoods.[18]

But the color line in the western real estate market had much deeper and more painful historical roots than contemporary popular opinion would lead us to believe. Despite higher levels of Black homeownership on the West Coast than elsewhere, most African Americans lived in rental rather than owner-occupied properties—and even these were rough. As early as 1889, when the ex-slave George Washington Dennis calculated his considerable real estate worth, white journalist Richard C. O. Benjamin reported that San Francisco was just "as prejudiced as the south." "Right here in San Francisco," Benjamin said, "it is impossible for respectable negro families to rent homes except in certain communities." Nearly two decades later, the Oakland *Sunshine* made the same point: "To live in either of the [Bay] cities, it is almost necessary for you to own your own home; rents are high and real estate agents do not care to rent to Negroes."[19] During the 1920s, another Black San Franciscan declared that racial discrimination "made it all but impossible" for African Americans to secure any living space except "run-down" dwellings often hardly fit for human habitation.[20]

During World War II, Afro-San Franciscans became the principal target of racially exclusionary practices as Japanese Americans left the city under internment orders. Grassroots white neighborhood groups, merchant associations, and so-called "improvement clubs" moved aggressively to restrict African American living space within the boundaries of the Fillmore district and Hunter's Point, both in San Francisco. Bay Area developers, realtors, and property owners increasingly barred Blacks from their neighborhoods. In 1943, according to a front-page story in the *Christian Science Monitor*, San Franciscans practiced segregation "almost rigidly with the use [of] occupancy clauses in deeds and leases restricting colored races to certain rather well defined areas of the city." One scholar estimated that 80 to 90 percent of the city's residential areas were "closed to non-Caucasian entry."[21]

Despite their wide dispersal across Seattle's landscape, the vast majority of Black residents concentrated within a relatively few neighborhoods. By 1900 African Americans occupied homes in each of the city's fourteen wards, but the majority lived in the First and Ninth Wards. In 1905, Seattle's white home-owners moved to prevent Black attorney J. Edward Hawkins from occupying his home on Capitol Hill, considered "the most prestigious neighborhood in the city." Five years later, a Seattle realtor filed a lawsuit against the influential and popular family of Horace Cayton. The suit claimed that the Cayton family's movement into a home on Capitol Hill had depressed real estate values and deprived them of their property rights protected by law. Accordingly, the suit asked authorities to evict the Caytons from their home. While the Caytons won their case, later in the same year another Black family was not so lucky: the developer the Hunter Tract Company brought suit against a family moving into a home that they had purchased in a development in the Mount Baker neighborhood, and the court sided with the company.[22]

Efforts to confine Seattle's Black population to the Yesler and Jackson Streets communities accelerated during and after World War I.[23] In 1938, in a revealing recollection of her experience in Seattle, Elva Moore Nicholas underscored the practice of racial discrimination among white realtors and homeowners. According to Nicholas, "An old lady ... showed me a place where the paper was peeling off the walls. . . . It was old and dirty. . . . I said, 'This is not fit for a dog to live in.' She [the landlady] says . . . 'its good enough for n . . . . . .' "[24] In the same year, a restrictive covenant on property on Twenty-Third Avenue mandated that the "purchaser must be of the white or Caucasian race and . . . the property is not to be sold, encumbered, conveyed, leased or rented to any person who is not of the white or Caucasian race. . . . This is also binding on the heirs, administration, successors and assigns of the purchaser." Consequently, during the 1920s and 1930s, African Americans endured rising difficulties finding suitable rental and homeownership opportunities, not only because of the economic devastation of the Great Depression and regular downturns in the business cycle, but also because of racial discrimination in the housing market. Again, in the words of Elva Nicholas, quoted above, "We walked our heels off looking for 'For Rent' or 'For Sale' signs. You couldn't buy out of the central district."[25]

African Americans also occupied the least desirable rental and home ownership properties in early twentieth century Los Angeles. L.A. residents later described their West Jefferson neighborhood as "swampy," "fever-ridden," and an "undesirable land area." In the Boyle Heights and West Temple neighborhoods, they also remembered occupying their own homes as well as rental properties "knee-deep" in mud and later surrounded by oil wells. These early Black residential areas "had a rough reputation." One resident later recalled, "When I came to this place, it was perhaps the filthiest, the most barren, the most disagreeable spot on God's earth; but it suited our pocketbook, so we stayed, built our homes, and reared our children." Housing in the City of Angels was largely unrestricted by race before World War II, "but only in the less desirable" neighborhoods in the city.[26]

When African American Angelenos moved into better homes in previously all-white neighborhoods, they usually encountered hostile and even violent resistance from their new neighbors. Some of L.A. County's white residents took extreme measures to prevent African Americans from owning their own homes in previously all-white communities. In 1902, a mob visited a Black family on Hooper Avenue and Thirty-Third Street, but this family resisted pressure to move out and other Black families soon moved into the area. Three years later, the home of a Black family burned down when they purchased in an all-white area. In 1908, when a Black family arrived in another all-white L.A. neighborhood, "vandals wrecked" the place. In the East Hollywood area, a dozen "prominent" members of the community paid

FIGURE 8. Los Angeles, 1952. Over more than two centuries, African Americans constructed their own Black city against the backdrop of recurring and persistent forms of class and racial hostility. This photo shows William Bailey (*left*), a schoolteacher and veteran of World War II, sorting through the wreckage of his home at 2130 Dunsmuir Street following a bomb explosion calculated to drive him and his wife out of the previously all-white neighborhood. Courtesy of Bettmann.

one Black family an unfriendly visit, with the ringleader declaring, "I come from Texas . . . where the N . . . . . s have no rights. You've got to get out."[27]

In 1925, the African American entrepreneur and physician Dr. Wilbur C. Gordon and nine Black realtors launched an all-Black housing development on a 213-acre plot of land. Located in the southwestern part of the county, the project gained financial backing from the white-owned Liberty Building and Loan Company. Black and white financiers formed "a seven-million-dollar syndicate" to develop what became known as "Gordon Manor." While a few of the proposed homes were geared toward middle-class Black families (at an average cost of about $3,500), most of the homes would sell for "$22,000 to $32,000," making them luxury homes for the emerging new Black elites.

The development was located north of the town of Torrence, which housed a large oil refinery, and an elite white neighborhood further south known as Palos Verdes. Despite its substantial distance from Gordon Manor, a group of white residents of Palos Verdes, including the famous landscape architect Frederick Law Olmsted, successfully lobbied the L.A. County Board of Supervisors to condemn Gordon Manor's land and transform it into a public park for white people. One member of the elite Palos Verdes group, the influential attorney Henry O'Melveny, conceded that the plan to block Gordon Manor "involved plain, downright fraud." Unlike so many homeowner developments for all-Black occupancy, this one included from the outset investments in "streets, curbs, sidewalks, ornamental street lighting, water lines, and fire hydrants."[28]

During and following World War II, neighborhood conditions in the urban West increasingly converged with those in the urban Midwest and Northeast. The postwar urban West witnessed the increasing stratification of urban communities along the Black-white divide, with Japanese, Chinese, and to some extent Latinx Americans gaining greater access to previously all-white areas. In Los Angeles, Watts moved from nearly equal proportions of African Americans, Mexicans, and Euro Americans at the outset of World War II to 95 percent Black two decades later. At the same time, the Central Avenue District "pushed south" as Watts "expanded northward." By the late 1960s, the two communities had "effectively joined" geographically, representing "a seven-mile stretch of African American neighborhoods locked between Main Street and Alameda."[29]

Racial discrimination reinforced segregation and the confinement of Black people to a limited segment of the urban housing market. Under the influence of the Second Great Migration, Blacks in the urban West "finally faced the problem that had plagued eastern cities since World War I. . . . The 'Negro problem' emerged full-blown, and the area's singularity and belief in its non-racial ways disappeared." As World War II got underway, just under 50 percent of African Americans lived in San Francisco's Fillmore district. By the early 1960s, the vast majority of Bay Area Blacks resided in the Western Addition, a narrow strip of land "along Fillmore Street from McAllister to Sutter, bordered by Divisadero Street and Webster Street."[30]

As early as 1950, Seaton Manning, director of the local branch of the National Urban League, had complained to national headquarters that he and his family were "unable to find a house or apartment in San Francisco. . . . Anything that is any good is restricted" by race. Fifteen years later, the liberal Bay Area columnist Herb Caen lamented, "The Negro, now representing one-tenth of the city's population, is largely restricted to a single section of substandard old housing—centering on, and radiating from, Fillmore Street." Meanwhile, with the addition of some 11,000 newcomers to the city's Black population, the proportion of African Americans living in Seattle's

Central District (specifically, 10 of the city's 118 census tracts) jumped from 69 percent during the war and its early aftermath to 80 percent in 1960.[31]

At the same time the racial divide intensified, African American communities also experienced a process of neighborhood dissolution and displacement under the impact of federal public housing and urban renewal programs. Such programs resulted in the demolition of older segments of the housing and institutional infrastructure of the Black metropolis. While the construction of federally financed public housing projects gradually relieved the acute housing problems confronting some newcomers to the city, it targeted predominantly Black neighborhoods for demolition to make way for the new developments and reinforced the racially divided housing market. Moreover, while several public housing projects initially admitted both Black and white residents, such steps toward integration in public housing soon gave way to explicitly segregationist policies designed to separate Black and white tenants across the urban West.

Urban renewal projects also heightened the spread of racially segregated neighborhoods. In the urban West, urban renewal decimated the Chavez Ravine community in Los Angeles and the historic West Oakland neighborhood in the Bay Area. As early as August 1949, Black Bay Area resident Lola Bell Sims wrote to President Harry Truman expressing fear of displacement. "Just now here in Oakland," she said, "the colored people are much confused and very unhappy ... thinking that they are going to lose their all and all by the U.S. government taking their property by force whether or not they want to give it up." In 1959, the Oakland Redevelopment Agency confirmed her fears, when it "defined all of the predominantly Black West Oakland neighborhood as blighted."[32] City council approved the plan for renewal and listed the African American community among the first sites scheduled for the bulldozer.[33] Despite protests from Black residents and civil rights organizations like the NAACP, the city of Oakland soon demolished the West Oakland area to make way for commercial and industrial development. But the city had failed to erect a single new housing unit on the property as late as 1969.[34]

Despite these limitations, and after beginning gradually before World War II, the massive Black migration to the West Coast cities picked up steam during the 1950s and 1960s. Profound demographic changes in the mix of African American, Latinx, Asian American, and Euro-American groups fueled the transformation of ethnic, class, and race relations in the region. By the end of World War II, the number of southern Blacks moving to the major cities of the urban West nearly matched the number moving to the leading cities of the urban Midwest.[35] Los Angeles's Black population mushroomed from 64,000 during World War II to 335,000 in 1960 to over 500,000 in 1970, an increase from just 4.2 percent of the total in 1940 to nearly 18 percent by the late 1960s. At about the same time, the Los Angeles suburb of Compton emerged as a predominantly Black community under the impact of the Second Great Migration. Starting from only a handful of residents during the 1940s, Compton's Black population increased by nearly 30,000 during the 1950s and rose to nearly 56,000 in 1970. It had increased from 39 percent of the total in 1960 to 71 percent in 1970.[36]

Meanwhile, San Francisco's Black community escalated from under 5,000 in 1940 to 74,400 in 1960 and to nearly 100,000 by 1970, an increase from less than 1 percent of the total in 1940 to over 13 percent by the late 1960s. Suburban Oakland's Black community experienced even more explosive growth than that in San Francisco; it rose from nearly 8,500 in 1940 to over 83,600 in 1960 and to nearly 125,000 in 1970, an increase from just under 3 percent of the total in 1940 to 23 percent in 1960 and to 34 percent in 1970.[37] For its part, Seattle's Black population jumped from under 4,000 in 1940 to nearly 27,000 in 1960 to 38,000 in 1970, an increase from just 1 percent of the total in 1940 to 7 percent by the late 1960s. In the nearby industrial suburb of Bremerton, the Black population rose from fewer than 100 residents in 1940 to over 4,600 five years later, a figure that exceeded Seattle's total Black population at the outset of World War II.[38]

As African Americans gained a foothold, however precarious, in the housing and labor markets of the western city, they soon undertook the construction of their own institutional infrastructure. The independent Black church movement, fraternal orders, social clubs, and entrepreneurial activities flourished. However, whereas the rise of autonomous Black religious, mutual benefit, and entrepreneurial organizations had deep roots in early nineteenth century northeastern and Midwestern cities, the independent Black institution-building movement slowly reached the urban West during the late nineteenth century.

ORGANIZING INSTITUTIONS/TRANSFORMING THE LANDSCAPE

Churches

During the early 1870s, Black Angelenos launched their independent church-building movement with the simultaneous founding of the First African

Methodist Episcopal Church and the Second Baptist Church. So named to establish its identity and independence from the all-white First Baptist Church, Second Baptist soon built its own two-story brick edifice at 740 Maple Avenue "near the corner of Maple and 8th Street, south of downtown, a little east of Main Street." As the first Great Migration got underway during and after World War I, Second Baptist gave rise to several new Baptist churches, including New Hope Baptist, Mount Zion Baptist, St. Paul Institutional Baptist, and Tabernacle Baptist Church. Under the leadership of Rev. H. D. Prowd, between 1915 and 1920, the church played an influential role in L.A., California, and the nation through its prominent activities within the National Baptist Convention, formed in Atlanta in 1895.

However, unlike in most cities, L.A.'s Black Methodists outnumbered their Baptist counterparts. In 1872, Black Methodists came together to form L.A.'s First African Methodist Episcopal Church. Organized in the home of entrepreneur Biddy Mason, the First AME Church became a key pillar in the institutional development of Black Los Angeles. By the turn of the twentieth century, influential Black Methodist bodies included the AME, the AME Zion, and the Colored Methodist Episcopal churches. Before the onset of World War I, the First AME Church built the city's most imposing African American church at Eighth and Towne Streets, just two blocks east of the *New Age* newspaper's headquarters.[39]

Most Afro-Angelenos referred to the new church edifice as the "Eighth and Town" church. Not only its architectural brilliance, but also its deep civic engagement with a broad cross section of the African American community brought widespread attention and lots of members to the church. In 1903, First AME launched its famous Los Angeles Sunday Forum. Known simply as "the Forum," this organization reached out beyond the church to the larger Black community in Los Angeles. Open to "everyone in the community regardless of religion, income, gender, politics, or social status," the Forum provided a major opportunity for diverse members of the community to voice their opinions on a wide range of issues affecting the city's Black community: "The Forum was a kind of regularly scheduled town-hall meeting for the city's Black community, an open space for debate, indignation, and organization and an important venue for Black activism." Indicative of the Forum's effort to bridge diverse constituents within the African American community, it regularly met every Sunday afternoon at the African American Odd Fellows Hall, a two story wooden structure located on Eighth Street between Maple Avenue and San Pedro Street.[40]

FIGURE 9. Within the context of ongoing barriers to their quest for equal access to urban space, across all regions and across all time periods, the Black church played a vital role in the African American city-building process, including its impact on the larger built environment and politics of the city. In this photo, the choir poses outside the First African Methodist Episcopal Church, Los Angeles. Built in 1902 at Eighth and Towne (and often referred to as the Eighth and Towne Church), First AME soon became the site of the famous Los Angeles Sunday Forum, an instrument of political mobilization across all sectors of the early twentieth-century Black community. Courtesy of Smithsonian National Museum of African American History and Culture, Gift of First AME Church of Los Angeles.

Baptist and Methodist congregations dominated the Black church-building movement in San Francisco and Seattle as well. Founded in 1886 and 1890, respectively, the First African Methodist Episcopal Church and the Mount Zion Baptist Church claimed the lion's share of Black churchgoers in Seattle well into the era of the Great Migration. Under the leadership of Rev. Seaborn Collins, a skilled carpenter and machinist, the church soon built its own edifice (replete with "Italian windows and pews") on what is now Fourteenth Street. During the 1920s, the church also purchased two additional plots of land adjacent to the building. In 1933, in the depths of the Depression years, Seattle Blacks also founded the Ebenezer AME Zion Church. Ebenezer soon took its place among the four largest and most influential congregations in the city.[41]

In San Francisco, three churches, all founded during the early 1850s, comprised the institutional core of the Bay City's early African American city-building process. In addition to the Third Baptist Church, the city's first Black church, these churches included the First African Methodist Zion Church and the Bethel African Methodist Episcopal Church. Elite commentators and the local Black press downplayed the spread of small Methodist and Baptist churches into the Bay Area communities of Richmond and Oakland, but the church-building movement in these outlying suburban communities also enhanced the Black city-building process. As southern Black migration escalated during and after World War II, these churches—the North Richmond Missionary Baptist Church (NRMBC), along with the North Richmond Colored Methodist Episcopal Church and the Church of God in Christ (COGIC)—would gain increasing power and influence in the life of the African American community in the San Francisco Bay Area.[42]

While Baptist and Methodist bodies dominated the religious life of Blacks in the urban West, as elsewhere, these congregations did not exhaust the range of spiritual experiences and church-building activities among the region's African American people. In Seattle, for example, although the Emerald City reported only ten Black churches by the 1940s, the city's Black religious life included the Church of God in Christ; the Full Gospel Pentecostal Mission; St. Phillips Chapel Episcopal Church; the Grace Presbyterian Church; and Father Divine's Temple of Peace. This diversity characterized Black churches in L.A. and the San Francisco Bay Area as well. L.A. played an important role in expanding the Pentecostal and Holiness movement nationwide. The city's Black community, particularly the Texas migrant Rev. William J. Seymour, took a leading role in founding the popular Azusa Street Mission, an integrated religious organization that welcomed all ethnic and racial groups to worship under one roof.

During the first decade of the new century, the influence of the Azusa Street Mission and its popular three-year revival had spread across the country. It stimulated the emergence of several new Holiness and Pentecostal denominations. Rather than joining any of the new organizations, Seymour formed the Apostolic Faith Gospel Mission at the Azusa Street location. While the new mission welcomed all ethnic and racial groups, it also helped birth the all-Black Pentecostal Church of Christ (Holiness) U.S.A. Although the new body opened headquarters in Arkansas, it maintained its publishing enterprise in Los Angeles.[43]

As elsewhere, African American churches across the urban West were the seedbeds of fraternal orders, mutual benefit societies, women's clubs, and a plethora of entrepreneurial activities. In Los Angeles, Seattle, and the San Francisco Bay Area, the Masons, Elks, Odd Fellows, and other fraternal orders and mutual benefit societies erected their own lodge halls and made a deep impression on the urban landscape and the rise of the western Black metropolis. In Los Angeles, as noted above, the First AME's popular Los Angeles Forum regularly met every Sunday afternoon at the African American Odd Fellows Hall. By the mid-1920s, the lodge halls of Seattle's African American Elks and Masons became prominent landmarks in the Central District. At the same time, Black women's clubs, affiliated with the National Association of Colored Women, also shaped the built environment by occupying and maintaining their own facilities like Seattle's Sojourner Truth Home for single women.[44]

Business Establishments

Integral to the efflorescence of the Black city in the West was the dramatic expansion of African American entrepreneurial activities. From the outset of their sojourn in the urban West, African Americans built a variety of businesses. The ex-slave George Washington Dennis arrived in San Francisco before statehood and purchased his freedom from his owner, who was also his father. As a free man, he opened the Custom House Livery Stable at Sansom and Washington Streets and later established the successful Cosmopolitan Coal and Wood Yard at 340 Broadway. He sold fuel both wholesale and retail and by 1889 reported an estimated $50,000 in property. In 1902, a husband-and-wife team (the Phillipses) operated a successful bath, barber, and beauty shop at 218 Post Street in San Francisco. Contemporary reports described the firm as "very elaborately fitted up." It featured "all the modern conveniences—electric lighting, electric hair dryers, and private booths, five for hairdressing and two for manicuring." The company also enthusiastically reported $3,000 in stock. During World War I and its aftermath, the funeral business of John Howard Butler and Luther M. Hudson emerged as another major "source of both pride and employment" for Black residents.[45]

In the meantime, following the exodus of Black people from San Francisco to the East Bay, Oakland became a new energetic center of Bay Area African American entrepreneurship. The East Bay city was described as a "beehive of industry" among Black people, while San Francisco's Black business community tended to stagnate. Emblematic of East Bay Black entrepreneurship was the elaborate restaurant of William L. Vance and Simon A. Dedrick, two Texas-born migrants to the city. Following the earthquake and fire of 1906, the two men invested $4,000 into remodeling, including increasing the seating capacity of the dining room that seated 60 people and a dozen private rooms to accommodate another 54 patrons. Electric chandeliers, fans, and high ceilings enhanced the ambience and comfort of the restaurant that "served one thousand meals daily." However, it was another Black business, the Silver Dollar Trading Company, under the proprietorship of the North Carolinian Brittain Oxendine, that claimed the mantle as the largest employer of African American workers in the Bay City, although it apparently reported only 10 men on its payroll at the turn of the twentieth century.[46]

In 1909, Samuel C. Rogers, a migrant from Ohio, moved to Richmond and opened the Bay Area's most successful Black building and construction firm. Four years earlier, E. H. Oliphant had opened the Richmond Café on Washington Avenue and soon advertised the business as serving "the best meal in the city." By the beginning of the Great Depression, Oakland reported over 100 Black owned enterprises: "Fifteen eating establishments, two undertakers, two insurance companies, sixteen real estate agents, five printers, sixteen barbershops, and thirteen beauty parlors." At about the same time, as elsewhere, Seattle's small Black population developed its own nascent Black business district within the city's larger CBD. In addition to a plethora of barber and beauty shops, grocers, and real estate, and funeral businesses serving an African American clientele, a range of new and more diverse entrepreneurial firms developed during the interwar years: the Anzier/Gala Theater; the sixty-two-room Golden West Hotel, enthusiastically promoted as the best "colored" hotel west of Chicago; and the transnational Liberian-West African Transportation and Trading Company, launched in 1927, to name a few. But it was the *Northwest Enterprise*, the Black weekly newspaper, discussed below, that emerged as the city's most successful African American business.[47]

Los Angeles developed the most illustrious Black business community in the urban West. A standout among turn-of-the-century businesses was A. J. Jones's two-story hotel and restaurant, valued at $23,000. Ahead of the hotel's construction, the *California Eagle* enthusiastically reported that one of the most important marks of progress for Black Angelenos was "the brick building now being constructed at the junction of San Pedro and First Streets."

But it was the businessman Sidney P. Dones who claimed the mantle for helping to establish Central Avenue as a BBD during the first leg of the Great Migration. Dones, originally from Marshall, Texas, moved to L.A. in 1905. After a brief return to Texas, he emerged as perhaps Los Angeles's most prominent African American entrepreneur, realtor, and businessman. In 1916, Dones erected the Booker T. Washington Building at Tenth Street and Central Avenue; it was a three-story structure with a variety of shops on the street level and a plethora of offices and apartments above. The newspaper man Joe Bass described the Dones building as the largest and most imposing edifice on Central Avenue. Bass also lauded Dones's accomplishments as a service "procured" specifically for "Colored Business Men." At about the same time, Ida Wills established the Southern Hotel between Twelfth and Pico Streets and F. A. Williams and his business partner bought the Angelus Theater, dubbed the "only Show House owned by Colored Men in the Entire West." Joe Bass announced the arrival of Central Avenue from Eighth to Twentieth Streets as "one of the most remarkable Negro business sections in the country."[48]

During the 1920s, African American businesses in L.A. not only continued to expand, but also diversified and became more elaborate. In 1927, the dentist John Alexander Sommerville built a new 150-room hotel and office building at Forty-First and Central Avenue, well beyond the Twelfth and Central Avenue core of the Black business district at the time. The *California Eagle* described the new Sommerville Hotel as "the beauty spot of Los Angeles, the monument to Negro enterprise." From the sidewalk, observers marveled at the five-story structure, but "unseen were the basement level for storerooms and a rooftop garden." Established in 1925, the Golden State Guaranteed Insurance Company emerged as the most outstanding new enterprise in Afro-Los Angeles during the interwar years. The company developed under the dynamic leadership of Texas-born William Nickerson, Jr., and his able assistants Norman O. Houston, the Oakland, California–born migrant (a business student at the University of California–Berkeley before leaving college for military service) and George Beavers, Jr., originally from Atlanta, Georgia. Golden State initially occupied "just one room in . . . a little . . . two-story frame building over on [1435] Central Avenue and Newton Street." Three years later, the company built its own "magnificent" new headquarters at 4111 Central Avenue, employing both Black architects and Black building contractors to design and construct the facility. The business weathered the Depression storm and in 1948, the African American architect Paul Williams designed a new Golden State Mutual Life Insurance Company building "far to the west" of the Central District. A "tall, strong, elegant structure," the Golden State office attracted rising numbers of other Black homeowners and institutions into the neighborhood. Williams also later designed a new home for the city's First AME Church, located not far from the Golden State building.[49]

Informal Economy

The African American business community was by no means limited to legitimate enterprises. As elsewhere in urban America, an underground cadre of Black entrepreneurs emerged in L.A., Seattle, and the San Francisco Bay Area. In addition to serving as home to early Black legitimate enterprises, discussed above, the L.A. "block" also reflected the impact of illegal underground entrepreneurship on the Black city-building process. The equivalent of the so-called "red light districts" in cities across the country, the "block" became a major target of white and Black reformers. Middle-class Blacks and their white allies regularly complained about illegal gambling, prostitution, and alcohol consumption in the area. The *Los Angeles Times* published a scathing condemnation of the district in 1904, describing the area as the "negro tenderloin." African American–owned private clubs bore the brunt of the *Times*'s scathing attacks. According to the *Times*, at Ben's Place, an African American–owned business, "Hell begins cooking at dark and boils on until dawn." During the 1930s, Lucius Lomax, a migrant and gambler from Chicago, established the lucrative but illegal policy or numbers game in L.A. He became well-known and well-liked because he used the wealth he gained to support legitimate Black businesses and newspapers, including the *California Eagle* and the *Sentinel*. When it appeared that the Sommerville Hotel would go under as the Depression took its toll on Black businesses, Lomax purchased the hotel and renamed it the Dunbar Hotel in honor of the African American poet Paul Lawrence Dunbar.[50]

Before World War II, except for the sex trade, in San Francisco, it was the Chinese population that became the principal target of white reformers. According to historian Albert Broussard, the Bay Area's white press repeatedly portrayed Chinese community "as a cesspool of vice, prostitution, gambling, and drugs, particularly opium." Under the impact of World War II and the Second Great Migration, the pattern flipped. As Broussard notes, Black residents "expressed growing dismay that the Fillmore district had become a cesspool of crime and vice." The Black weekly newspaper, the *Sun Reporter*, launched a spirited campaign to reform the Fillmore district. At the same time, the Black press and middle-class elites grudgingly admitted and even embraced the employment benefits of the underground economy of "gambling, crapshooting, bookmaking, and lotteries."[51]

The *Sun Reporter* gave substantial space to African American critics of Chinese residents who profited from gambling and other illicit activities in the Fillmore district. One reader wrote, "We don't want the Chinaman taking over the Fillmore district. . . . How long do you think a Negro could run a dice game in Chinatown?" An editorial bluntly declared, "Get the Record Straight. . . . We are not berating the Chinese—we have great respect for them, but we are unalterably opposed to any group becoming a parasite on the lifeline of the [African American] community." Furthermore, it was widely believed within the Bay Area that Carlton Goodlet, editor of the *Sun Reporter*, had won controlling interest in the paper in a poker game with a white San Franciscan who originally owned the paper.[52]

The East Bay also reported an expanding informal economy. White and Black elites decried how the Second Great Migration disrupted the "once quiet neighborhoods in the area." Wartime bars and night clubs, according to historian Shirley Ann Moore, "raked in monthly profits totaling eight thousand dollars" as Richmond's cash-flush war workers flocked to "liquor, gambling, and other illicit" enterprises. One city judge focused special attention on young women who used these establishments to proposition clients and turned nearby rooming houses into sites of paid sex work. But Richmond's informal economy of gambling, alcohol, and sex was not new. As early as 1911, the Women's Improvement Club had campaigned to close all the city's "saloons, brothels, and gambling houses" as the San Francisco fire and earthquake stimulated the increasing movement of the city's Black and white residents to the East Bay.[53]

Seattle's "red light" district had emerged by the 1890s in an area dubbed the "tide flats," located on lower Jackson Street. As historian Quintard Taylor notes, some of Seattle's most lucrative Black enterprises sprang up in the tide flats. "These brothels, gambling houses, and saloons employed numerous musicians, bouncers, maids, cooks, and janitors, and provided more jobs than the barbershops, restaurants, and other 'respectable' establishments." Saloon owners Denver Ed Smith, Richard Roman, and N. F. Butts operated some of the city's most successful African American enterprises. Such underground businesses also included the entrepreneurial activities of Black women. Mary

Thompson operated the popular Minnehaha Saloon. Outfitted with an upstairs suite of rooms for the use of prostitutes, Thompson's business generated substantial profits and placed her among the city's wealthiest Black residents.[54]

The Black Press

A vibrant Black press emerged early on as both a business undertaking as well as a promoter of Black enterprises catering to the needs of African Americans, their families, and their communities. While many of these new businesses were short-lived, underfinanced, and irregular in production and delivery of products and services to their Black clientele, they nonetheless helped to forge connections between diverse constituents within the Black community; promoted the virtues of owning and operating businesses to serve the African American public, however modest; and reinforced the Black city-building process.[55] A variety of "race papers," as they were called, emerged in the urban West long before and during World War II. In 1894, Horace R. Cayton founded the popular *Seattle Republican*, a paper that combined his scathing attacks on the Jim Crow system with firm support for the party of Lincoln.

By the turn of the century, Cayton and his wife Susie, the paper's associate editor, had emerged as the most widely known African American Seattleites on a regional and national scale. Seattle's first African American newspaper, the exceedingly short-lived *Seattle Standard*, had been founded in 1890 by Brittain Oxendine, a migrant from North Carolina and former member of the state legislature, who had moved to Seattle in 1889. But it was the *Northwest Enterprise* that became Seattle's most successful African American weekly as both a business and source of information and support for African American communities across the urban Northwest. Founded in 1920 under the leadership of entrepreneur and journalist William H. Wilson, the *Northwest Enterprise* swiftly expanded its circulation to the entire Pacific Northwest. Before the stock market crash of 1929, the paper reported 25,000 subscribers in far flung African American communities in Montana, Oregon, and Idaho, as well as Washington state.[56]

Beginning with the publication of the *Mirror of the Times* (1857), Afro-San Franciscans had launched many weekly newspapers by the turn of the twentieth century. These included most notably the *Pacific Appeal* (1862–1879) and the *Elevator* (1865–1898), under the editorship of Phillip A. Bell.

Editor Bell moved to the Bay Area following a distinguished professional career on the East Coast. As a young man, he not only worked as an agent for William Lloyd Garrison's the *Liberator*, but founded the New York *Weekly Advocate* and later the *Colored American*, described by contemporaries as the "chief" newspaper of the "colored people." During the late nineteenth and early twentieth century, Bay Area Blacks founded a new round of weekly news organs serving the African American community. In addition to two newspapers in San Francisco, the *Western Appeal* (ca. 1918–1927) and the *Spokesman* (1931–1935), Black journalists launched several newspapers in the East Bay, including the Oakland *Western Outlook* (1894–1924); the *Sunshine* (1900–1923); the *Times* (1923–1930); the *Western American* (1926–1929); the *Independent* (1929–1931); and the *California Voice*. Published under editor E. A. Daly and his wife beginning in 1919, the *California Voice* persisted over the next half century. Rounding out the list of early-to-mid-twentieth century African American newspapers in the East Bay area, Richmond's first Black newspaper, the *Richmond Guide*, was founded by the shipyard worker Margaret Starks, from Arkansas, in 1944.[57]

As it did with business and community-building activities in general, Los Angeles developed the most impressive roster of Black weekly newspapers. As early as 1889, the former slave John J. Niemore migrated to L.A. from Texas and set up the city's first African American–owned newspaper, the *Owl*. By 1910, after the collapse of the *Owl* and several other newspapers, including the *Advocate* and the *Southern California Guide*, Niemore launched the *California Eagle*. Located in what one observer described as a "shack" on Central Avenue, the *Eagle* passed into the hands of Charlotta Bass following Niemore's death in 1912. Other Black newspapers serving L.A.'s Black community included the *Weekly Observer*, the *Liberator*, and the *New Age*.[58]

Founded under the editorship of Oscar Hudson, the *New Age* was sold to journalist and entrepreneur Frederick Roberts in 1912. As Flamming concludes, the *Eagle* and the *New Age* helped to anchor the African American community on Central Avenue. The *Eagle*'s printing office at 814 Central Avenue "became an unofficial community center, a place where Race men and women dropped in to discuss the issues of the day. It was frequented by political lieutenants, Club women, striving business people, and visitors to the community. It was a place to see and be seen. The same was true of Robert's *New Age* office on San Pedro Street, only a few blocks away."[59]

During the interwar years contemporary observers acknowledged that the urban West had embarked upon its own city-building activities, even if less extensively than elsewhere. It also invited comparisons with counterparts in other cities across the urban Northeast and Midwest. As early as the 1920s, the New York journalist and activist Chandler Owens visited the region and later declared that he had discovered a "veritable little Harlem" among Black Angelenos.[60]

African Americans in the urban West built their business infrastructure against the backdrop of stiff competition with Euro- and Asian American competitors. The Emerald City's Japanese community's Nehonmachi enterprises both overshadowed and constrained the development of Seattle's African American business community. Moreover, white businessmen never relinquished the segregated African American market to Black entrepreneurs. Competition with white firms represented an ongoing challenge for Black businesspeople—magnified during and after the 1920s, when chain grocery stores like Safeway spread into African American neighborhoods across urban America. In L.A., for example, in 1925, Safeway did not operate any stores near Central Avenue. Five years later, six Safeway stores catered to L.A.'s Black community. Commercial chains represented a double-edged sword, however. They offered African American consumers a broader range of product and service options than Black businesses could. At the same time, they undercut the customer base of struggling neighborhood-based grocery stores.[61]

Notwithstanding certain fluidity along the color line in West Coast cities, African Americans waged ongoing struggles against Jim Crow West. Their challenges to the racially divided metropolis had significant beginnings before the Civil War but escalated during the Great Migration and the emergence of the industrial age. As elsewhere across twentieth-century urban America, the social and political struggles of the urban West facilitated the rise of the modern Black Freedom Movement nationwide. Partly inspired by their own nineteenth-century battles for social justice and full citizenship rights, Seattle, San Francisco, and Los Angeles became important sites in the escalating fight to dismantle the white supremacist order.

CHALLENGING WHITE SUPREMACY/THE CITY AS POLITICAL RESOURCE

In rapid succession during the inter-war years, African Americans formed a plethora of new organizations to combat racial injustice across the urban West. As elsewhere during the era of the Great Migration, these organizations included local branches of the NAACP, the National Urban League, Garvey's Universal Negro Improvement Association during the 1920s, the Communist Party-inspired National Negro Congress, the Congress of Racial Equality (CORE), the March on Washington Movement, and Double-V campaigns for victory at home and abroad during World War II.[62]

Inspired by the wartime March on Washington Movement as well as persistent socioeconomic disparities in the early postwar urban political economy, African Americans and their white allies forged a vigorous nonviolent direct-action movement for racial equality. Beginning during the late 1940s and early 1950s, nonviolent direct-action protests picked up steam during the late 1950s and early 1960s. In the spring and summer of 1964, California chapters of CORE coordinated a statewide campaign against the discriminatory policies of Bank of America. The organization picketed branch offices in San Francisco, Los Angeles, and San Diego, where CORE members were arrested for defying a court injunction. Its chairman, Harold Brown, served a sixty-day jail sentence. At about the same time, in Los Angeles, a coalition of seventy-six social justice organizations conducted "sit-ins," "study-ins," and "sing-ins" at the Board of Education, demanding an end to racially segregated schools.[63]

In collaboration with the local branch of the NAACP and other groups in the postwar years, the Seattle CORE also staged nonviolent direct-action protests for jobs, education, housing, and equal protection of the law. In addition to protests against grocery stores like A&P, Seattle activists mounted some of their most militant struggles against discrimination in the city's housing market. The fight against the Jim Crow housing system unfolded with support from a broad range of interracial civil rights and social justice organizations: the Seattle Urban League; the Fair Housing Listing Service; the Christian Friends for Racial Equality; and the NAACP, among others. This coalition targeted the giant Picture Floor Plans (PFP) Real Estate Agency for a series of intensive demonstrations over nearly three months from March to May 1964. Owned by the president of the Seattle Real Estate Board, PFP was the city's largest real estate firm at the time. But the movement soon collapsed under the weight of increasing police harassment of protesters and a court-ordered injunction against the sit-ins at the company's offices.[64]

Despite setbacks and partial victories from campaign to campaign and from city to city, the urban West reinforced the nationwide fight that toppled the segregationist order. By the mid-1960s, passage of a series of landmark federal Civil Rights Acts (1964, 1965, and 1968) outlawed racial discrimination in employment, housing, and public accommodations. At about the same time, however, the confluence of a variety of national forces—the outbreak of violent urban revolts in cities across the nation, the rise of influential Black nationalist organizations like the Nation of Islam and its young charismatic minister Malcolm X, and the assassination of both Malcolm and Martin Luther King—led to the rise of the Black Power phase of the modern Black Freedom Movement. The new politics also transformed the African American city-building process in the urban West and nationwide. While organizations like CORE, the Student Nonviolent Coordinating Committee (SNCC), and a proliferation of militant college and university-based campus organizations would play important roles in the rise of the Black Power Movement as a local, regional, national, and increasingly transnational phenomenon, the new politics of the Black city gained its most powerful expression in the Black Panther Party (BPP).

In 1966, Huey P. Newton and Bobby Seale, students at Oakland's Merritt College, founded the Black Panther Party (BPP) for Self Defense. The BPP incorporated the Nation of Islam's "Wants and Beliefs" into the party's "Ten-Point Program" for the attainment of armed self-defense, political control of the Black community, economic independence, and institutional and cultural autonomy. In addition to launching armed community patrols to monitor Black-police interactions and prevent police brutality, the BPP established liberation schools, free health clinics, and free breakfast programs.[65]

Although it was inspired by the Nation of Islam and a variety of national and transnational developments in African American and U.S. history, the Black Panther Party and its affiliated chapters in Los Angeles, San Francisco, and Seattle were fundamentally rooted in the local culture, economy, and politics of the Black city. As discussed above, western cities had experienced explosive Black population growth during the second wave of the Great Migration. Increasing numbers of West Coast Blacks gained jobs in the manufacturing sector of the urban economy. But they also occupied the cellar of the workforce and enjoyed limited opportunities for upward mobility. At the same time, like Blacks in other major metropolitan areas, western Blacks confronted increasing residential segregation, inequality in the schools, displacement by urban renewal, and police brutality.[66]

Though it began as a local organization, inspired by broader currents of political thought and action, by decade's end the BPP had become a national and international force, and its militant call for Black Power could be heard around the globe in such diverse countries as the United Kingdom, Israel, Australia, and India.[67] In New Zealand, the Polynesian Panther Party adopted the U.S. Black Panther's Ten Point Program and clearly articulated its ideas: "We cannot have Black and white unity until we have Black unity."[68]

. . .

By the mid-twentieth century, African Americans had built new communities across the ethnically and racially diverse cities of the urban West—somewhat similar to but quite distinct from the urban Southeast and Southwest, where the power of the state formally propped up the segregationist order. Although the Black western metropolis had its origins in the late antebellum and Civil War years, the Black city-building movement escalated in the wake of emancipation and the subsequent explosion of urban capitalist development, immigration, and the rise of a new and more hostile system of racial apartheid. The Black western metropolis gradually emerged within this larger context of restrictions on access to land, homeownership, and civil rights. As elsewhere, however, African Americans used their urban spaces and institutions to seed the emergence of the modern Black Freedom Movement. During World War II and its aftermath, all along the urban West Coast, the escalating Black Freedom struggle undercut the segregationist system and opened the door to the increasing movement of African Americans into previously all-white communities.

The gradual desegregation of white neighborhoods and the emergence of racially mixed communities hinted at the possibility of creating broader and more inclusive multiracial neighborhoods. But the notion of a Black metropolis soon gained fresh new expression. "Freedom Now" and the integrationist phase of the Black liberation movement increasingly gave way to "Black Power" and the quest for Black control of Black communities. West Coast cities became important sites of late twentieth-century demands for redress for past practices of social inequality. But the case for reparations in the urban West, no less than elsewhere across urban America, must acknowledge the creative ways that African Americans built their own Black metropolis and helped to transform the built environment "under that open sky."[69]

Conclusion

REFLECTIONS ON THE POSTINDUSTRIAL AGE

FROM THE OUTSET OF THE EUROPEAN settlement of North America through the advent of the modern Black Freedom Movement, people of African descent built their own Black cities across urban America. Replete with its own extensive institutional infrastructure, the Black city influenced the built environment of the larger predominantly white city. As seen throughout this study, creation of the Black metropolis represented a major accomplishment for people of African descent, formerly enslaved and later segregated in the modern urban social system. They accomplished this important feat against the persistent but changing backdrop of white supremacist ideology and social practices. Through a variety of creative strategies, African Americans gained access to space as both renters and homeowners and also constructed urban communities against the grain of their own internal ideological, class, and social differences and conflicts. Most important, however, Black urbanites used their institutional infrastructure as a launching pad, forged powerful civil and human rights movements, and helped to demolish the institution of slavery during the nineteenth century and Jim Crow during the industrial age.

During the late twentieth and early twenty-first century, a new postindustrial Black metropolis slowly took shape. After nearly a century of intensive migration and city-building efforts, majority- or near-majority-Black cities became the norm. Between 1970 and the early twenty-first century, Detroit, Cleveland, New Orleans, Baltimore, Birmingham, and Atlanta became majority-Black cites. At the same time, the numbers of Blacks living in the central cities started to decline. Between 2000 and 2010, the central cities of the fifteen largest metropolitan areas lost 300,000 African Americans. As demographer William H. Frey notes, this was "the first absolute population decline" among African Americans in these cities "as a group." New York City's African American population peaked at 2.1 million people in 1990 but dropped to 2.0 million in 2010. Cleveland's Black population declined from 288,000 in 1970 to 212,000 four decades later. Over the same period, Black Angelenos dropped from over 500,000 to 365,000. And Washington, DC's Black population dropped precipitously from over 70 percent of the total to only 45 percent.[1] Growing numbers of northern and western Blacks migrated to the South—not the old rural South but the expanding urban South. During the 1970s alone, the South added over a million manufacturing jobs at the same time that increasing northeastern and midwestern industries closed their doors—some of them relocating to the South and Southwest. The new southern migrants, some returnees from the era of the Great Migration, worked in offices, shops, and factories of the urban South, and "navigated the streets and alleys of the inner city."[2]

The demolition of federal public housing projects as well as deindustrialization reinforced the loss of inner-city Black residents by the turn of the twentieth century. In 1992, the U.S. Department of Housing and Urban Development launched a $5 billion low-income housing program, "Homeownership and Opportunity for People Everywhere," popularly known as HOPE VI. Widely regarded as one of "the most ambitious urban redevelopment" projects in the nation's history, HOPE VI leveraged federal dollars to dismantle and replace what authorities described as "severely distressed public housing projects," occupied mainly by poor and working-class African Americans and other people of color. The new federal effort at public housing reform promised to relocate existing tenants to "redesigned mixed-income housing" and provide vouchers for some residents to rent apartments in the private housing market. Between the program's inception and its demise in 2010, HOPE VI housing development projects demolished some 98,600 units in over 160 cities across the country.

The impact of HOPE VI on the African American city-building process varied from city to city. In Pittsburgh, for example, authorities designated two Hill District projects—Allequippa Terrace and Bedford Dwellings—for demolition and redevelopment. The bulldozer quickly razed Allequippa Terrace, but grassroots activists organized an effective protest movement against the destruction of Bedford Dwellings, ensuring that authorities modified demolition plans and eased the transition of residents from their old homes into new structures within and beyond the construction site. In Chicago, by 2007, sociologist Mary Pattillo notes that HOPE VI projects had already demolished most of the public housing in the city's North Kenwood–Oakland community "to make way for row houses and apartment buildings." This process was tightly interwoven with the larger gentrification of the area, but unfolded here, as Pattillo argues, "with a decidedly black flavor." Still, despite evidence of variation on the process, the massive destruction of public housing projects played an important role in reshaping the city-building process during the emerging postindustrial age.[3]

As suggested by Pattillo's observations, in addition to new public housing programs, gentrification also unanchored some Black urban residents from their earlier homes in the city. Well-to-do American-born whites and Blacks moved into the city from elsewhere. They claimed space in the same areas undergoing renovation by African American residents who stayed. White, and, to some extent, Black gentrifiers with capital purchased the old central city buildings; drove real estate prices beyond the means of most poor people; and made it impossible for them to stay in their rapidly changing communities. Mostly young urban professionals claimed living space in large renovated Victorian homes, previously occupied by poor and working-class Blacks, in the central cities. The arrival of young white and to some extent Black "moneyed" and "creative classes" nudged poor and working-class Black residents out into inner-ring previously all-white suburbs on the peripheries of New York, Boston, San Francisco, Philadelphia, Savannah, Charleston, and Baltimore among other cities.

Key inner-ring suburban communities became Blacker and increasingly poorer, while the old inner city became whiter and increasingly richer, but other aspects of postindustrial Black suburbanization also complicate the unfolding shape of the city-building process and its impact on the built environment, urban politics, and social struggles. The percentage of Blacks living in suburban areas nationwide increased from less than 10 percent during the 1960s and early 1970s to 23 percent in 1980. By the turn of the new millennium, that figure had increased to over one-third. In 2010, for the first time in the nation's history, the majority of African Americans lived in suburbs. "In size, speed, and significance," suburban historian Andrew Wiese declared, "the suburbs was the next Great Migration."[4]

Black suburbanites earned over 50 percent more than African American residents of the central cities. Indeed, in Atlanta, Chicago, and Washington, DC, Black suburbanites reported higher levels of income and education attainment than their white counterparts. According to the pioneering journalist of Black suburbanization, Joel Garreau, late twentieth-century

America witnessed the rise of a huge "churchgoing, home-owning, childrearing, backyard barbecuing, traffic-jam-cursing black middle class." On Stone Mountain, Georgia, near Atlanta, birthplace of the twentieth-century Ku Klux Klan, "pine forest and pasture land" gave way to a subdivision of suburban homes built for African American families "seeking homes above $200,000." Prince George's County, Maryland emerged as the nation's first majority-Black suburban county, where African Americans occupied "deluxe building tracts and sprawling subdivisions." By the end of the century, the *Washington Post* reported that the District of Columbia's African American "intelligentsia and business leaders, and, indeed, the rock-ribbed middle class of teachers, federal workers and salespeople, [were] grounded firmly in the suburbs of the city."[5]

But African American life on the most livable parts of the periphery was by no means secure, even for prominent Black property owners. The economic recession of 2008 wiped out the homeownership and modest wealth building gains of large numbers of Black people. An estimated 11 percent of Blacks and 7 percent of whites lost their homes to foreclosures between roughly 2008 and 2012. They were the chief victims of what historian Keeanga-Yamahtta Taylor describes as "predatory inclusion" in the nation's real estate and housing market. As historian Jacqueline Jones so aptly put it, "Predatory lenders sought to make money via a perverse reversal of earlier 'redlining' efforts. Now, instead of denying mortgages to black credit-seekers whether or not they were qualified, banks aggressively marketed toxic financial products to blacks regardless of their financial condition.... Some banks considered the ideal mark to be an older, single black woman."[6]

Between 2005 and 2009, with the vast majority of their wealth invested in homeownership, the median wealth of Black households declined by 53 percent (about $12,000 to $6,000) compared to 16 percent for white households (about $135,000 to $113,000). White households reported retirement funds, pension accounts, and stocks, among other sources of wealth besides homeownership. Their wealth also cushioned them against unexpected crises, particularly involving health care, while increasing numbers of Black families lived on the perilous edge of the nation's class and racially divided medical system.[7]

The rise of outlying urban neighborhoods and suburban communities entailed substantial conflict as well as cooperation among African Americans from different class and cultural backgrounds. The initial waves of Black suburbanites included substantial numbers of middle-class and better-off working-class African Americans, but subsequent movement to outlying areas included increasing numbers of poorer Blacks, including many single women with children. As the class composition of the African American suburban population shifted in favor of the poorest Black residents, internal social conflicts increased. However, rather than mounting hostile organized movements to block the in-migration of poor and working-class residents into their new suburban neighborhoods, most middle-class residents intensified their campaigns to "educate" and curtail the behavior of poor residents. In some cases, however, efforts to hold the line against the movement of poor and working-class Blacks into an area touched off major conflict, as in Prince George's County, where African American suburbanites gained national media attention when they hired policemen to bar inner-city Black youth from the local recreational facilities. Still, as historian Andrew Wiese concludes, "Notwithstanding gates and security guards at a few local subdivisions, black Prince Georgians rarely approached exclusivity with the ferocity or self-righteousness of their white peers."[8]

As the twenty-first century unfolded and the distinctive features of the new city came into sharper focus, African Americans harnessed their resources and forged new social justice campaigns. In the wake of Barack Obama's second term in office and that of his successor, ultra-conservative Donald J. Trump, as president of the United States, a variety of events opened a new chapter in African American political history, race, and the city-building process. These developments included, most notably, the persistence of the carceral state and the rise in African American deaths in police custody, and the deadly impact of the COVID-19 pandemic on the lives of Black people and other communities of color. Postindustrial-era Black communities intensified their demands for compensation for past and present injustices and violations of their civil and human rights. Their efforts gained potent expression in the emergence of the Black Lives Matter movement, a new and more dynamic organized reparations movement, and escalating local as well as national demands for redress across all sectors of the country's institutional life.

Similar to earlier liberation politics, twenty-first century Black social struggles turned to historic community-based Black institutions for inspiration and support. Following the national conventions of the Republican and Democratic parties in the summer of 2020, for example, a coalition of over one hundred groups joined the Black Lives Matter Electoral Justice Project. Ahead of the general election, the BLM electoral justice project attracted close to 500,000 participants for a virtual 2020 Black National Convention. On this and other occasions, COVID-era activists repeatedly underscored the significance of community-based organizing and institutions for the long-term success of movements designed to eradicate systemic inequality and social injustice. According to Spencer Overton, president of the Joint Center for Political and Economic Studies, any battle plan for progress "must incorporate building and fortifying Black institutions. . . . Strong Black institutions allow us to weather the storms, exercise agency and leadership, debate, participate and fully take advantage of opportunities."[9]

The postindustrial Black city continues to unfold before our eyes on a day-to-day basis. In addition to documenting African American urban life over three centuries, *Building the Black City* hopefully also enables us to see much more clearly how the Black city, built by and for Black people, is an extraordinary achievement. It not only supports current calls for reparative justice programs for people suffering from past and present forms of class and racial inequality. It also reinforces and strengthens the case for reparations based on the inequities of unpaid slave labor and later underpaid wage labor of free African Americans over several centuries of time; in all regions of the country; and across all segments of the workforce, social, and political system. In short, by accenting the creative energy, ideas, and city-building work of Black Americans, this study adds another equally compelling pillar to the rapidly evolving rationale for reparations for descendants of African people enslaved in America; in northern and western as well as southern cities; and, most important, in industrial, preindustrial, and recent postindustrial America.

NOTES

INTRODUCTION

1. St. Clair Drake and Horace R. Cayton, *Black Metropolis: A Study of Negro Life in a Northern City* (1945; repr., Chicago: University of Chicago Press, 1993), 12.

2. Leslie M. Harris, Clarence Lang, Rhonda Y. Williams, and Joe William Trotter, Jr., eds., *Black Urban History at the Crossroads: Race and Place in the American City* (Pittsburgh: University of Pittsburgh Press, 2024).

3. Leslie M. Harris to C. Lang, R. Y. Williams, and J. W. Trotter, email correspondence, July 27, 2023. We are also indebted to Leslie for suggesting a scholarly forum on the notion of the "Black City," as a means of clarifying the issue and establishing a framework for future research on the subject.

4. See, for example, Selden Richardson, *Built by Blacks: African American Architecture and Neighborhoods in Richmond* (Charleston, SC: History Press, 2007, 2008, and 2011); Camilla Hawthorne and Jovan Scott Lewis, eds., *The Black Geographic: Praxis, Resistance, Futurity* (Durham: Duke University Press, 2023); Brian D. Goldstein, *The Roots of Urban Renaissance: Gentrification and the Struggle over Harlem* (Cambridge, MA: Harvard University Press, 2017); Tara A. Dudley, *Building Antebellum New Orleans: Free People of Color and Their Influence* (Austin: University of Texas Press, 2021); E. James West, *A House for the Struggle: The Black Press and the Built Environment in Chicago* (Urbana: University of Illinois Press, 2022); Walter Hood and Grace Mitchell Tada, eds., *Black Landscapes Matter* (Charlottesville: University of Virginia Press, 2020); Sean Anderson and Mabel O. Wilson, *Reconstructions: Architecture and Blackness in America* (New York: The Museum of Modern Art, 2021); Irene Cheng, Charles L. Davis, II, and Mabel O. Wilson, eds., *Race and Modern Architecture: A Critical History from the Enlightenment to the Present* (Pittsburgh: University of Pittsburgh Press, 2020). Also see Paul Wellington, *Black Built: History and Architecture in the Black Community*, ed. Karen Boston (n.p.: Paul Wellington, 2019).

5. Marcus Anthony Hunter, *Black Citymakers: How the Philadelphia Negro Changed Urban America* (New York: Oxford University Press, 2013); Marcus A. Hunter and Zandria F. Robinson, "The Sociology of Urban Black America," *Annual*

Review of Sociology 42 (2016): 385–405; Marcus A. Hunter and Zandria F. Robinson, *Chocolate Cities: The Black Map of American Life* (Berkeley: University of California Press, 2018); and Angel David Nieves and Leslie M. Alexander, eds., *"We Shall Independent Be": African American Place-Making and the Struggle to Claim Space in the United States* (Boulder: University of Colorado Press, 2008).

6. Hunter and Robinson, *Chocolate Cities*, x.

7. Nieves and Alexander, *"We Shall Independent Be,"* 5–6.

8. Goldstein, *The Roots of Urban Renaissance*, 11.

9. Leslie M. Harris, *In the Shadow of Slavery: African Americans in New York City, 1626–1863* (Chicago: University of Chicago Press, 2003); Leslie Alexander, *African or American? Black Identity and Political Activism in New York City, 1784–1861* (Urbana: University of Illinois Press, 2008); Catherine McNeur, *Taming Manhattan: Environmental Battles in the Antebellum City* (Cambridge, MA: Harvard University Press, 2014), 203–9.

10. William A. Darity, Jr., and A. Kirsten Mullen, *From Here to Equality: Reparations for Black Americans in the Twenty-First Century* (Chapel Hill: University of North Carolina Press, 2020), 9–27. Also see "Interpreting the African American Working-Class Experience: Essay on Sources," in Joe William Trotter, Jr., *Workers on Arrival: Black Labor in the Making of America* (Oakland: University of California Press, 2019), 185–210.

11. Gwendolyn L. Wright, Lucas Hubbard, and William A. Darity, Jr., *The Pandemic: How Covid Increased Inequality in America* (Durham: Duke University Press, 2022); Darity and Mullen, *From Here to Equality*; Barbara Ransby, *Making All Black Lives Matter: Reimaging Freedom in the 21st Century* (Oakland: University of California Press, 2018).

12. Henry Louis Taylor, ed., *Race and the City: Work, Community, and Protest in Cincinnati, 1820–1970* (Urbana: University of Illinois Press, 1993), xiv.

13. Albert S. Broussard, *Black San Francisco: The Struggle for Racial Equality in the West, 1900–1954* (Lawrence: University Press of Kansas, 1993), 30; Douglas Flamming, *Bound for Freedom: Black Los Angeles in Jim Crow America* (Berkeley: University of California Press, 2005), 98; Quintard Taylor, *The Forging of a Black Community: Seattle's Central District from 1870 through the Civil Rights Era* (Seattle: University of Washington Press, 1994), 178–79.

14. Matthew Desmond, *Evicted: Poverty and Profit in the American City* (New York: Crown Publishers, 2016); Peter Moskowitz, *How to Kill a City: Gentrification, Inequality, and the Fight for the Neighborhood* (New York: Nation Books, 2017); Richard Rothstein, *The Color of Law: A Forgotten History of How Our Government Segregated America* (New York: Liveright Publishing, 2017); Keeanga-Yamahtta Taylor, *Race for Profit: How Banks and the Real Estate Industry Undermined Black Homeownership* (Chapel Hill: University of North Carolina Press, 2019); Waverly Duck, *No Way Out: Precarious Living in the Shadow of Poverty and Drug-Dealing* (Chicago: University of Chicago Press, 2015).

15. Michelle Alexander, *The New Jim Crow: Mass Incarceration in the Age of Colorblindness* (New York: The New Press, 2010); Elizabeth Hinton, *From the War*

on Poverty to the War on Crime: The Making of Mass Incarceration in America (Cambridge, MA: Harvard University Press, 2016); and Simon Balto, *Occupied Territory: Policing Black Chicago from Red Summer to Black Power* (Chapel Hill: University of North Carolina Press, 2019).

16. Ransby, *Making All Black Lives Matter*. Also, for keen insight into the deep urban-industrial roots of recent changes in metropolitan-wide Black politics and liberation struggles, see Clarence Lang, *Grassroots at the Gateway: Class Politics and Black Freedom Struggle in St. Louis, 1936–75* (Ann Arbor: University of Michigan Press, 2009); Keona K. Ervin, *Gateway to Equality: Black Women and the Struggle for Economic Justice in St. Louis* (Lexington: University Press of Kentucky, 2017); Rhonda Y. Williams, *Concrete Demands: The Search for Black Power in the 20th Century* (New York: Routledge, 2015); and Clarence Lang, *Black America in the Shadow of the Sixties: Notes on the Civil Rights Movement, Neoliberalism, and Politics* (Ann Arbor: University of Michigan Press, 2015).

CHAPTER ONE

1. Kimberly S. Hanger, *Bounded Lives, Bounded Places: Free Black Society in Colonial New Orleans, 1769–1803* (Durham: Duke University Press, 1997), 166, 168; Bernard E. Powers, Jr., *Black Charlestonians: A Social History, 1822–1885* (Fayetteville: University of Arkansas Press, 1994), 52–54; Wilma King, *The Essence of Liberty: Free Black Women during the Slave Era* (Columbia: University of Missouri Press, 2006), 28–29; H. E. Sterkx, *The Free Negro in Ante-Bellum Louisiana* (Rutherford: Fairleigh Dickinson University Press, 1972), 271; Amrita Chakraborty Myers, *Forging Freedom: Black Women and the Pursuit of Liberty in Antebellum Charleston* (Chapel Hill: University of North Carolina Press, 2011), 11.

2. Emma Hart, *Building Charleston: Town and Society in the Eighteenth-Century British Atlantic World* (Charlottesville: University of Virginia Press, 2010); Robert Olwell, *Masters, Slaves, and Subjects: South Carolina Low Country, 1740–1790* (Ithaca: Cornell University Press, 1998); Ras M. Brown, *African-Atlantic Cultures and the South Carolina Lowcountry* (New York: Cambridge University Press, 2012); Philip D. Morgan, *Slave Counterpoint: Black Culture in the Eighteenth-Century Chesapeake and Low Country* (Chapel Hill: University of North Carolina Press, 1998); Ari Kelman, *A River and Its City: The Nature of Landscape in New Orleans* (2003; repr., Berkeley: University of California Press, 2006); Thomas C. Buchanan, *Slaves, Free Blacks, and the Western Steamboat World* (Chapel Hill: University of North Carolina Press, 2004); D. H. Usner, Jr., *Indians, Settlers, and Slaves in a Frontier Exchange Economy: The Lower Mississippi Valley before 1783* (Chapel Hill: University of North Carolina Press, 1992); Gwendolyn Midlo Hall, *Africans in Colonial Louisiana: The Development of Afro-Creole Culture in the Eighteenth Century* (Baton Rouge: Louisiana State University Press, 1992); Nan A. Rothschild and Diana deZerega Wall, *The Archaeology of American Cities*

(Gainesville: University Press of Florida, 2014); Rebecca Scott, *Degrees of Freedom: Louisiana and Cuba after Slavery* (Cambridge, MA: Harvard University Press, 2005); Shirley E. Thompson, *Exiles at Home: The Struggle to Become American in Creole New Orleans* (Cambridge, MA: Harvard University Press, 2009); Jay Gitlin, Barbara Berglund, and Adam Arenson, eds., *Frontier Cities: Encounters at the Crossroads of Empire* (Philadelphia: University of Pennsylvania Press, 2013); Arnold R. Hirsch and Joseph Logsdon, eds., *Creole New Orleans: Race and Americanization* (Baton Rouge: Louisiana State University Press, 1992), 74, 78–87; Donald Everett, "Free Persons of Color in Colonial Louisiana," *Louisiana History* 7, no. 1 (1966): 21–50; Daniel E. Walker, *No More, No More: Slavery and Cultural Resistance in Havana and New Orleans* (Minneapolis: University of Minnesota Press, 2004); John W. Blassingame, *Black New Orleans, 1860–1880* (Chicago: University of Chicago Press, 1973); Leslie M. Harris and Daina R. Berry, eds., *Slavery and Freedom in Savannah* (Athens: University of Georgia Press, 2014); Whittington B. Johnson, *Black Savannah, 1788–1864* (Fayetteville: University of Arkansas Press, 1996); Jacqueline Jones, *Saving Savannah: The City and the Civil War* (New York: Knopf, 2008); Dylan C. Pinningroth, *The Claims of Kinfolk: African American Property and Community in the Nineteenth-Century South* (Chapel Hill: University of North Carolina Press, 2003); Loren L. Schweninger, *Black Property Owners in the South, 1790–1915* (Urbana: University of Illinois Press, 1990).

3. Hart, *Building Charleston*, 89; Olwell, *Masters, Slaves, and Subjects*, 69; R. Brown, *African-Atlantic Cultures and the South Carolina Lowcountry*, 43, 62, 75, 77; Philip D. Morgan, "Black Life in Eighteenth Century Charleston" (Institute Colloquium, Kellock Library, February 1984); Morgan, *Slave Counterpoint*, 20, 34 (quote), 62, 76–77, 444–46, 449.

4. Kelman, *A River and Its City*, 12–15, 19–28; Buchanan, *Slaves, Free Blacks, and the Western Steamboat World*, 28–31; Daniel H. Usner, Jr., "From African Captivity to American Slavery: The Introduction of Black Laborers to Colonial Louisiana," *Louisiana History* 20 (1979): 38–47; Usner, *Indians, Settlers, and Slaves in a Exchange Economy*, 31–34, 54–56; Midlo Hall, *Africans in Colonial Louisiana*, 126–27, 179.

5. Rothschild and Wall, *The Archaeology of American Cities*, 44–46; Scott, *Degrees of Freedom*, 34–35, 78; Thompson, *Exiles at Home*, 4–5; Daniel Usner, "Colonial Projects and Frontier Practices," in Gitlin, Berglund, and Arenson, eds., *Frontier Cities*, 27–45; Hirsch and Logsdon, *Creole New Orleans*, 74, 78–87; Everett, "Free Persons of Color in Colonial Louisiana," 21–50; Walker, *No More, No More*, 2–3; Robert C. Reinders, "The Free Negro in the New Orleans Economy, 1850–1860," *Louisiana History* 6, no. 3 (1965); Roger A. Fischer, "Racial Segregation in Ante-Bellum New Orleans," *American Historical Review* 74, no. 3 (1969); Sterkx, *The Free Negro in Ante-Bellum Louisiana*.

6. Harris and Berry, eds., *Slavery and Freedom in Savannah*, 1, 9, 15; Johnson, *Black Savannah*, 85–105, 183–89; Jones, *Saving Savannah*, 15–20.

7. Pinningroth, *The Claims of Kinfolk*, 46, 144–45.

8. Dudley, *Building Antebellum New Orleans*, 16.

9. Schweninger, *Black Property Owners in the South*, 20–21, 113, 115–16.

10. Dudley, *Building Antebellum New Orleans*, 19.

11. Thompson, *Exiles at Home*, 112.

12. Dudley, *Building Antebellum New Orleans*, 20, 69, 115–16; Thompson, *Exiles at Home*, 111–13 (quotes, 112 and 113), 129–30; Blassingame, *Black New Orleans*, 11; W. Johnson, *Black Savannah*, 5, 38, 44, 59–68, 68–76.

13. W. Johnson, *Black Savannah*, 21, 85, 115–16.

14. Feay S. Coleman, "Salley and Her Children: Maria, Emma, and John Charles Gibbons," in Harris and Berry, *Slavery and Freedom in Savannah*, 89–90; Powers, *Black Charlestonians*, 28, 38; Morgan, "Black Life in Eighteenth Century Charleston," 26–29; Myers, *Forging Freedom*, 60; Ira Berlin, *Slaves without Masters: The Free Negro in the Antebellum South* (1974; repr., New York: The New Press, 1992), 109.

15. Powers, *Black Charlestonians*, 246–47, 251.

16. Myers, *Forging Freedom*, 24; Powers, *Black Charlestonians*, 246–47, 251.

17. Leonard P. Curry, *The Free Black in Urban America, 1800–1850: The Shadow of the Dream* (Chicago: University of Chicago Press, 1981), 70; Richard C. Wade, *Slavery in the Cities: The South, 1820–1860* (New York: Oxford University Press, 1964), 69–70, 75–79; Powers, *Black Charlestonians*, 246–47.

18. Bernard L. Herman, *Town House: Architecture and Material Life in the Early American City* (Chapel Hill: University of North Carolina Press, 2005), 119–20, 154. In Herman's view, southern urban architectural controls both limited and facilitated movements for liberation among enslaved people.

19. Berlin, *Slaves without Masters*, 257; Blassingame, *Black New Orleans*, 16–17.

20. Myers, *Forging Freedom*, 25.

21. Usner, "From African Captivity to American Slavery," 38, 40–41, 46, 47; Hall, *Africans in Colonial Louisiana*, 126–27, 179; Usner, "Colonial Projects and Frontier Practices," 27–45; Sterkx, *The Free Negro in Ante-Bellum Louisiana*, 16–35; Berlin, *Slaves without Masters*, 3–4; Hirsch and Logsdon, *Creole New Orleans*, 74, 78–87; Everett, "Free Persons of Color in Colonial Louisiana," 2–3, 1–30, quote, 1; Carl Bridenbaugh, *Cities in the Wilderness: The First Century of Urban Life in America, 1625–1742* (New York: The Ronald Press Company, 1938), 379–80; Ira Berlin, *Many Thousands Gone: The First Two Centuries of Slavery in North America* (Cambridge, MA: Harvard University Press, 1998), 26, 78–79, 81–88, 212–75; Curry, *The Free Black in Urban America, 1800–1850*, 57, 59.

22. Paul Harvey, *Through the Storm, through the Night: A History of African American Christianity* (Lanham, MD: Rowman and Littlefield, 2011), 31–32, 203; Sylvia R. Frey, *Water from the Rock: Black Resistance in a Revolutionary Age* (Princeton: Princeton University Press, 1991), 21, 24, 75, 204.

23. Powers, *Black Charlestonians*, 20–21, 61; Myers, *Forging Freedom*, 71; Douglas R. Egerton, *He Shall Go Out Free: The Lives of Denmark Vesey* (1999; rev. ed., New York: Rowman and Littlefield, 2004), 109–25; Edward A. Pearson, *Designs against Charleston: The Trial Record of the Denmark Vesey Slave Conspiracy of 1822*

(Chapel Hill: University of North Carolina Press, 1999), 49–53; Margaret Washington Creel, *"A Peculiar People": Slave Religion and Community-Culture among the Gullahs* (New York: New York University Press, 1988), 131, 153–54, 162–63; W. Johnson, *Black Savannah, 1788–1864*, 7–10. Whereas most Black churches resulted from an irreconcilable "schism" between Blacks and whites "within a biracial church," historian Whittington Johnson shows how Savannah's Black church "was begun by African Americans, mainly slaves," but also free Blacks who accepted slave leadership and desired the freedom of their own "church home."

24. W. Johnson, *Black Savannah*, 12.

25. W. Johnson, *Black Savannah*, 3; Blassingame, *Black New Orleans*, 13–14; Curry, *The Free Black in Urban America, 1800–1850*, 181, 184–85.

26. W. Johnson, *Black Savannah*, 121; Blassingame, *Black New Orleans*, 11; Powers, *Black Charlestonians*, 51. Because of the restricted nature of the Brown Fellowship's efforts to reach poor free people of color, dark-skinned free people of color took steps to organize for their own social welfare with the creation of the Society of Dark Men or the Humane Brotherhood (Powers, *Black Charlestonians*, 52.)

27. W. Johnson, *Black Savannah*, 25; Harris and Berry, *Slavery and Freedom in Savannah*, 26; Powers, *Black Charlestonians*, 51.

28. Curry, *The Free Black in Urban America, 1800–1850*, 160–61; Powers, *Black Charlestonians*, 54; Harris and Berry, *Slavery and Freedom in Savannah*, 126, 134–35; Blassingame, *Black New Orleans*, 11. In 1770, the Georgia legislature passed its first colonial era law prohibiting the teaching of enslaved people to read and write (Harris and Berry, *Slavery and Freedom in Savannah*, 134–35). In 1817, the Savannah city council prohibited the teaching of free Blacks and slaves, and in 1829, the Georgia legislature followed suit with passage of its own law against the teaching of free and enslaved Blacks to read and write (126).

29. Schweninger, *Black Property Owners in the South*, 21–22; Rothschild and Wall, *The Archaeology of American Cities*, 84–85.

30. Myers, *Forging Freedom*, 95–96; Hanger, *Bounded Lives, Bounded Places*, 63–65; Alisha Cromwell, "Enslaved Women in the Marketplace," in Harris and Berry, *Slavery and Freedom in Savannah*, 54–55; Pinningroth, *The Claims of Kinfolk*, 61–65; W. Johnson, *Black Savannah*, 69; Tania Sammons, "Andrew Cox Marshall," in Harris and Berry, *Slavery and Freedom in Savannah*, 102–3; John Ingham and Lynne B. Feldman, *African-American Business Leaders: A Biographical Dictionary* (Westport: Greenwood Publishing Company, 1994), 410–11; Juliet E.K. Walker, *The History of Black Business in America: Capitalism, Race, Entrepreneurship*, vol. 1, *To 1865*, 2nd ed. (Chapel Hill: University of North Carolina Press, 2009), 113; W. Johnson, *Black Savannah*, 11–12, 46–47, 82.

31. W. Johnson, *Black Savannah*, 67, 135; Cromwell, "Enslaved Women in the Marketplace," 54–55; Powers, *Black Charlestonians*, 23–24; Myers, *Forging Freedom*, 96–97.

32. Powers, *Black Charlestonians*, 23–24; Myers, *Forging Freedom*, 96–97.

33. Schweninger, *Black Property Owners in the South*, 20, 48.

34. Powers, *Black Charlestonians*, 43; Walker, *The History of Black Business in America*, 48–49, 113, 136–37, 150; Sammons, "Andrew Cox Marshall," 102–3; Ingham and Feldman, *African-American Business Leaders*, 410–11; W. Johnson, *Black Savannah*, 11–12, 46–47, 82.

35. King, *The Essence of Liberty*, 12, 70–71, 73; Walker, *The History of Black Business in America*, 178; W. Johnson, *Black Savannah*, 72–73.

36. Schweninger, *Black Property Owners in the South*, 50–51.

37. Dudley, *Building Antebellum New Orleans*, 4–5.

38. Powers, *Black Charlestonians*, 246–47; Wade, *Slavery in the Cities*, 69–70, 75–79; Robert S. Starobin, *Industrial Slavery in the Old South* (New York: Oxford University Press, 1970), 10–18, 28–33, 63–65; Shane White and Graham White, *Stylin': African American Expressive Culture from Its Beginnings to the Zoot Suit* (Ithaca: Cornell University Press, 1998).

39. Harris and Berry, *Slavery and Freedom in Savannah*, 123, 127.

40. Berlin, *Slaves without Masters*, 123.

41. Berlin, *Slaves without Masters*, 124–25; Bell and Schafer, cited in Myers, *Forging Freedom*, 62n86; Scott, *Degrees of Freedom*, 16; Curry, *The Free Black in Urban America*, 250.

42. Wade, *Slavery in the Cities*, 326–27; Harris and Berry, *Slavery and Freedom in Savannah*, 15, 48, 130; Johnson, *Black Savannah*, 183–84; Powers, *Black Charlestonians*, 267.

43. Myers, *Forging Freedom*, 40.

44. Harris and Berry, *Slavery and Freedom in Savannah*, 28–29, 125–26; Berlin, *Slaves without Masters*, 109, 114–16

45. Harris and Berry, *Slavery and Freedom in Savannah*, 126–27; W. Johnson, *Black Savannah*, 82; Powers, *Black Charlestonians*, 28; Berlin, *Slaves without Masters*, 117.

46. Trotter, *Workers on Arrival*, 42.

47. Sterkx, *The Free Negro in Ante-Bellum Louisiana*, 289–94 (quote, 294); P.J. Staudenraus, *The African Colonization Movement, 1816–1865* (New York: Columbia University Press, 1961), 146–49.

48. Annette Gordon-Reed, *The Hemingses of Monticello: An American Family* (New York: W. W. Norton and Company, 2008), 653–54.

49. W. Johnson, *Black Savannah*, 150–53.

50. Powers, *Black Charlestonians*, 64–65.

51. Morgan, "Black Life in Eighteenth Century Charleston," 36; W. Johnson, *Black Savannah*, 120; Powers, *Black Charlestonians*, 12–13.

52. D.L. Chandler, "Profiles of Courage: The Rich History of African American Firefighters," *NewsOne: Social Justice*, online, January 28, 2014; Wade, *Slavery in the Cities*, 45–46; Jacqueline Jones, *American Work: Four Centuries of Black and White Labor* (New York: W. W. Norton, 1998), 212; W. Johnson, *Black Savannah*, 120.

53. Morgan, "Black Life in Eighteenth Century Charleston," 3–4, 36, 39; Powers, *Black Charlestonians*, 37.

54. Carl P. Borick, *A Gallant Defense: The Siege of Charleston, 1780* (Columbia: University of South Carolina Press, 2003), 18, quote, 40–43, 122–23, 136; Jacqueline Jones, *A Dreadful Deceit: The Myth of Race from the Colonial Era to Obama's America* (New York: Basic Books, 2013), 89; Frey, *Water from the Rock*, 172–73; Jones, *American Work*, 104.

55. Frey, *Water From The Rock*, 37–38, 84, 86–87, 96–98, 106.

56. W. Johnson, *Black Savannah*, 8.

57. Trotter, *Workers on Arrival*, 42.

58. Joe William Trotter, Jr., *The African American Experience* (Boston: Houghton Mifflin Company, 2001), 253.

59. Trotter, *Workers on Arrival*, 49.

60. Trotter, *Workers on Arrival*, 49.

61. Scott, *Degrees of Freedom*, 29.

62. Scott, *Degrees of Freedom*, 34–35; Schweninger, *Black Property Owners in the South*, 20–21, 23, 101–2, 213. Similar to their white counterparts, these Black slaveowners also "bought, sold, mortgaged, willed, traded, and transferred" their enslaved kinsmen, while also requiring long hours of labor in workshops and fields. They also dispensed harsh discipline to counter resistance and challenges to their authority to command slave labor (105–6).

63. Blassingame, *Black New Orleans*, 11; Schweninger, *Black Property Owners in the South*, 23; W. Johnson, *Black Savannah*, 80–82; Myers, *Forging Freedom*, 24.

64. Walker, *No More, No More*, 139–43; Hanger, *Bounded Lives, Bounded Places*, 1–2, 11–23, 145–47, 163.

65. W. Johnson, *Black Savannah*, 156–58; Powers, *Black Charlestonians*, 66.

66. Powers, *Black Charlestonians*, 60, 66–67; Johnson, *Black Savannah*, 149.

67. Egerton, *He Shall Go Out Free*, 154–202; John Lofton, *Denmark Vesey's Revolt: The Slave Plot that Lit a Fuse to Fort Sumter* (1964; Kent: Kent State University Press, 1983), 131–55, 182–240; Pearson, *Designs against Charleston*, 1–9, 64–65, 77–79; Powers, *Black Charlestonians*, 29–33; Curry, *The Free Black in Urban America, 1800–1850*, 96–98.

68. J. William Harris, *The Hanging of Thomas Jeremiah: A Free Black Man's Encounter with Liberty* (New Haven: Yale University Press, 2009), 92–97; Schweninger, *Black Property Owners in the South*, 31–32.

69. Willard B. Gatewood, *Aristocrats of Color: The Black Elite, 1880–1920* (Fayetteville: University of Arkansas Press, 2000), 40; Constance M. Green, *The Secret City: A History of Race Relations in the Nation's Capital* (Princeton: Princeton University Press, 1967), 16–17, 23–24, 38–44; Berlin, *Slaves without Masters*, 58, 130 (quote); Powers, *Black Charlestonians*, 51–52; C. Eric Lincoln and Lawrence H. Mamiya, *The Black Church in the African American Experience* (Durham: Duke University Press, 1990), 52–53.

70. Hanger, *Bounded Lives, Bounded Places*, 166, 168; Powers, *Black Charlestonians*, 52–54; King, *The Essence of Liberty*, 28–29; Sterkx, *The Free Negro in Ante-Bellum Louisiana*, 271; Myers, *Forging Freedom*, 11.

CHAPTER TWO

1. Mariana L. R. Dantas, *Black Townsmen: Urban Slavery and Freedom in the Eighteenth-Century Americas* (New York: Palgrave Macmillan, 2008); Gregg D. Kimball, *American City, Southern Place: A Cultural History of Antebellum Richmond* (Athens: University of Georgia Press, 2000); Kate Masur, *An Example for All the Land: Emancipation and the Struggle over Equality in Washington, D.C.* (Chapel Hill: University of North Carolina Press, 2010); Stanley Harrold, *Subversives: Antislavery Community in Washington, D.C., 1828–1865* (Baton Rouge: Louisiana State University Press, 2003); Midori Takagi, *"Rearing Wolves to Our Own Destruction": Slavery in Richmond, Virginia* (Charlottesville: University Press of Virginia, 1999); Joshua D. Rothman, *Notorious in the Neighborhood: Sex and Families across the Color Line in Virginia, 1787–1861* (Chapel Hill: University of North Carolina Press, 2003); Seth Rockman, *Scraping By: Wage Labor, Slavery, and Survival in Early Baltimore* (Baltimore: Johns Hopkins University Press, 2009); Christopher Phillips, *Freedom's Port: The African American Community of Baltimore, 1790–1860* (Urbana: University of Illinois Press, 1997); Jeffrey Kerr Ritchie, *Freedpeople in the Tobacco South: Virginia, 1860–1900* (Chapel Hill: University of North Carolina Press, 1999); T. Stephen Whitman, *The Price of Freedom: Slavery and Manumission in Baltimore and Early National Maryland* (Lexington: University Press of Kentucky, 1997); Chris Myers Asch and George Derek Musgrove, *Chocolate City: A History of Race and Democracy in the Nation's Capital* (Chapel Hill: University of North Carolina Press, 2017); Barbara Jeanne Fields, *Slavery and Freedom: Maryland during the Nineteenth Century* (New Haven: Yale University Press, 1985); Rothschild and Wall, *The Archaeology of American Cities*; Herman, *Town House*; Gary M. Fink and Merle E. Reed, *Race, Class, and Community in Southern Labor History* (Tuscaloosa: University of Alabama Press, 1994); Green, *The Secret City*; Wade, *Slavery in the Cities*; Curry, *The Free Black in Urban America, 1800–1850*; Claudia Goldin, *Urban Slavery in the American South: 1820–1860* (Chicago: University of Chicago Press, 1976).

2. Christopher Phillips, *Freedom's Port: The African American Community of Baltimore, 1790–1860* (Urbana: University of Illinois Press, 1997), 37, 38–63, 73–74; Curry, *The Free Black in Urban America*, 1–7, 244–51; Wade, *Slavery in the Cities*, 325–30; Whitman, *The Price of Freedom*, 63–69; Dantas, *Black Townsmen*, 108–9.

3. Asch and Musgrove, *Chocolate City*, 17; Harrold, *Subversives*, 7, 30; Letitia Brown, *Free Negroes in the District of Columbia, 1790–1846* (New York: Oxford University Press, 1972); Robert H. Gudmestad, *A Troublesome Commerce: The Transformation of the Interstate Slave Trade* (Baton Rouge: Louisiana State University Press, 2003), 8–34, 209–10; Michael Tadman, *Speculators and Slaves: Masters, Traders, and Slaves in the Old South* (Madison: University of Wisconsin Press, 1989), 5–10; Harrold, *Subversives*, 6, 30–31; Masur, *An Example for All the Land*, 13–18; Lawrence Larsen, *The Urban South: A History* (Lexington: University Press of Kentucky, 1990), 37; Wade, *Slavery in the Cities*, 107–208; Frederic Bancroft, *Slave-Trading in the Old South* (Baltimore: J. H. Furst Company, 1931), 382–40; Walter Johnson, *River of Dark Dreams: Slavery and Empire in the Cotton Kingdom*

(Cambridge: Harvard University Press, 2013), 1–17; Claudia D. Goldin, *Urban Slavery in the American South, 1820–1860: A Quantitative History* (Chicago: University of Chicago Press, 1976), 11–27.

4. Gregg D. Kimball, *American City, Southern Place: A Cultural History of Antebellum Richmond* (Athens: University of Georgia Press, 2000), 3–36, 124–58; Midori Takagi, *"Rearing Wolves to Our Own Destruction": Slavery in Richmond, Virginia, 1782–1865* (Charlottesville: University Press of Virginia, 1999), 9–36; Jeffrey R. Kerr-Ritchie, *Freedpeople in the Tobacco South: Virginia, 1860–1900* (Chapel Hill: University of North Carolina Press, 1999), 13–30; Suzanne Schnittman, "Black Workers in Antebellum Richmond," in Fink and Reed, eds., *Race, Class, and Community in Southern Labor History*, 72–86.

5. Schweninger, *Black Property Owners in the South, 1790–1915*, 13.

6. Brown, *Free Negroes in the District of Columbia*, 18–19; Schweninger, *Black Property Owners in the South*, 13, 16–17, 76–77, 111, 202; Phillips, *Freedom's Port*, 87–98, 153–54; Walker, *The History of Black Business in America*, 178–79; Whitman, *The Price of Freedom*, 136; Kimball, *American City, Southern Place*, 139.

7. Phillips, *Freedom's Port*, 153; Dantas, *Black Townsmen*, 158–59.

8. Schweninger, *Black Property Owners in the South*, 66, 111; Walker, *The History of Black Business in America*, 137, 151–52, 178–79; Curry, *The Free Black in Urban America*, 269; Phillips, *Freedom's Port*, 99, 153–54.

9. Takagi, *"Rearing Wolves to Our Own Destruction,"* 100; Curry, *The Free Black in Urban America*, 271. By contrast, in the same year, in New Orleans, free people of color reported the ownership of 2,351 slaves, while nearly 75 percent of Charleston's free Black households owned slaves (Phillips, *Freedom's Port*, 94).

10. Phillips, *Freedom's Port*, 102–5.

11. Curry, *The Free Black in Urban America*, 70; Wade, *Slavery in Cities: The South*, 69–70, 75–79; Brown, *Free Negroes in the District of Columbia*, 8–9; James Borchert, *Alley Life in Washington: Family, Community, Religion, and Folklife in the City, 1850–1970* (Urbana: University of Illinois Press, 1980), 3–6.

12. Takagi, *"Rearing Wolves to Our Own Destruction,"* 39–41, 96–98; Wade, *Slavery in the Cities*, 135–36; Kimball, *American City, Southern Place*, 74–75, 171–74; Curry, *The Free Black in Urban America*, 138–39, 273; Ronald L. Lewis, *Coal, Iron, and Slaves: Industrial Slavery in Maryland and Virginia, 1715–1865* (Westport, CT: Greenwood Press, 1979), 154–5; Starobin, *Industrial Slavery in the Old South*, 62–68; Todd L. Savitt, *Medicine and Slavery: The Diseases and Health of Blacks in Antebellum Virginia* (Urbana: University of Illinois Press, 1978), 80–82.

13. Phillips, *Freedom's Port*, 83–84, 232; Curry, *The Free Black in Urban America*, 216–22; Dantas, *Black Townsmen*, 1–2; Wade, *Slavery in the Cities*, 106–10.

14. Brown, *Free Negroes in the District of Columbia*, 140; Walker, *The History of Black Business in America*, 161–62; Asch and Musgrove, *Chocolate City*, 69 (in 1837, the DC city council passed a more restrictive code designed to control the growing free Black population); Curry, *The Free Black in Urban America*, 97–98, 109–11; Dorothy Provine, "The Economic Position of the Free Blacks in the District of Columbia, 1800–1860," *Journal of Negro History* 58, no. 1 (1973): 61–72; Sandra

Fitzpatrick and Maria R. Goodwin, *The Guide to Black Washington: Places and Events of Historical and Cultural Significance in the Nation's Capital* (New York: Hippocrene Books, 1990), 20, 39, 41, 199.

15. Asch and Musgrove, *Chocolate City*, 56–58; Phillips, *Freedom's Port*, 211; Claude A. Clegg III, *The Price of Liberty: African Americans and the Making of Liberia* (Chapel Hill: University of North Carolina Press, 2004), 30–31; Staudenraus, *The African Colonization Movement*, 234–39, 196–97.

16. Takagi, *"Rearing Wolves to Our Own Destruction,"* 116–17; Wade, *Slavery in the Cities*, 327; Kimball, *American City, Southern Place*, 31; Curry, *The Free Black in Urban America*, 246.

17. Phillips, *Freedom's Port*, 131–43; Green, *The Secret City*, 24–25; Curry, *The Free Black in Urban America*, 178; Lincoln and Mamiya, *The Black Church in the African American Experience*, 22–27, 58; Berlin, *Slaves without Masters*, 288–89; Harvey, *Through the Storm, through the Night*, 38–39; Clarence E. Walker, *A Rock in a Weary Land: The African Methodist Episcopal Church during the Civil War and Reconstruction* (Baton Rouge: Louisiana State University Press, 1982), 8–9; Harry Reed, *Platform for Change: The Foundations of the Northern Free Black Community, 1775–1865* (East Lansing: Michigan State University Press, 1994), 32–33; Frey, *Water from the Rock*, 294–97; Wade, *Slavery in the Cities*, 168–69, 240.

18. Asch and Musgrove, *Chocolate City*, 60; Harrold, *Subversives*, 41.

19. Takagi, *"Rearing Wolves to Our Own Destruction,"* 53–69, 103–12, 120; Kimball, *American City, Southern Place*, 44–45, 70–71, 124–25, 126–27.

20. Phillips, *Freedom's Port*, 118, 121.

21. Phillips, *Freedom's Port*, 124–25, 129, 133–35, 137–38; C. Walker, *A Rock in a Weary Land*, 4–11; Julie Winch, *Philadelphia's Black Elite: Activism, Accommodation, and the Struggle for Autonomy, 1787–1848* (Philadelphia: Temple University Press, 1988), 4–15; Curry, *The Free Black in Urban America*, 75–78, 181, quote, 177.

22. Joe W. Trotter, "African American Fraternal Associations in American History: An Introduction," and Theda Skocpol and Jennifer L. Oser, "Organization Despite Adversity: The Origins and Development of African American Fraternal Associations," in special issue, *Social Science History* 28, no. 3 (Fall 2004): 355–66, 373–87; Phillips, *Freedom's Port*, 170–71; Asch and Musgrove, *Chocolate City*, 60–61.

23. Curry, *The Free Black in Urban America*, 25–36, 200–1, 208–11; Berlin, *Slaves without Masters*, 234–41; Curry, *The Free Black Urban America*, 25–36; Philip S. Foner, *Organized Labor and the Black Worker, 1619–1973* (New York: Praeger Publishers, 1974), 10–11; Philip S. Foner and Ronald L. Lewis, eds., *The Black Worker to 1869, Vol. 1* (Philadelphia: Temple University Press, 1978), 236–41, 245–46; Phillips, *Freedom's Port*, 78, 170–72, 202; Takagi, *"Rearing Wolves to Our Own Destruction,"* 106; Charles H. Wesley, *Negro Labor in the United States, 1850–1925: A Study in American Economic History* (1927; repr., New York: Russell and Russell, 1967), 55–62; Walker, *The History of Black Business in America*, 116, 132.

24. Green, *The Secret City*, 17, 23–24, 50–51.

25. Phillips, *Freedom's Port*, 164–67; Harrold, *Subversives*, 26–27. Some white Baltimoreans embraced Black education, as suggested by one newspaper advertisement

for a "Colored Man, to act as Porter," adding "None need apply unless they can read, write, and understand figures" (Phillips, 165).

26. Phillips, *Freedom's Port*, 78.

27. Brown, *Free Negroes in the District of Columbia*, 131–32; Phillips, *Freedom's Port*, 102.

28. Berlin, *Slaves without Masters*, 22–36, 108–16; Curry, *Free Black in Urban America*, 1–7, 244–51; Wade, *Slavery in the Cities*, 325–30; Brown, *Free Negroes in the District of Columbia*, 98, 246; Dantas, *Black Townsmen*, 108–09; Green, *The Secret City*, 16; Darlene Clark Hine and Kathleen Thompson, *A Shining Thread of Hope: The History of Black Women in America* (New York: Broadway Books, 1998), 95–96; Kathleen Thompson, "Elizabeth Keckley (1818–1907)," in Darlene Clark Hine, Elsa Barkley Brown, and Roslyn Terborg-Penn, eds., *Black Women in America: An Historical Encyclopedia* (Brooklyn: Carlson Publishing Inc., 1993), 672–73; Jennifer Fleischner, "Keckley, Elizabeth Hobbs," in Henry Louis Gates Jr. and Evelyn Brooks Higginbotham, eds., *African American National Biography*, vol. 5 (New York: Oxford University Press, 2008), 45–46; Asch and Musgrove, *Chocolate City*, 109–10.

29. John Ingham, "Wormley, James," in Gates and Higginbotham, eds., *African American National Biography*, vol. 8, 441–44; Walker, *The History of Black Business in America*, 152, 162.

30. Walker, *The History of Black Business in America*, 137, 152–51. This informal economy had deep roots in the rural Upper South. In 1770, a Maryland planter complained that it was nearly impossible for him to raise hogs or sheep because enslaved Blacks constantly killed them "to sell to some white people who are little better than themselves" (Schweninger, *Black Property Owners in the South*, 14). Upper South urban Blacks even launched a few short-lived transnational enterprises, including most notably, in Baltimore, Daniel Coker's Liberian trading business on the West Coast of Africa. and Hezekiah Grice's Chesapeake and Liberia Trading Company. The Maryland-based Haytian Company focused on opening up commercial relations with the republic of Haiti (Walker, 154–56).

31. Kimball, *American City, Southern Place*, xx, 8, 126, 129, 186, 257; Tikagi, *"Rearing Wolves to Our Own Destruction,"* 61–65, 68–69; Gerald W. Mullin, *Flight and Rebellion: Slave Resistance in Eighteenth-Century Virginia* (1972; repr., New York: Oxford University Press, 1975), 140–63, quote, 148–49.

32. Phillips, *Freedom's Port*, 221, 229.

33. C. Peter Ripley, et al., *Witness for Freedom: African American Voices on Race, Slavery, and Emancipation* (Chapel Hill: University of North Carolina Press, 1993), 2–3; Peter P. Hinks, *To Awaken My Afflicted Brethren: David Walker and the Problem of Antebellum Slave Resistance* (University Park: Pennsylvania State University Press, 1997), 184n30, 91; Asch and Musgrove, *Chocolate City*, 57–58; Harrold, *Subversives*, 28; Green, *Secret City*, 34; Phillips, *Freedom's Port*, 214, 220–26, quote 225.

34. Kimball, *American City, Southern Place*, 144–47; Phillips, *Freedom's Port*, 213–14, 220–26; Ripley, ed., *Witness for Freedom*, 3–4. In Virginia, any slave manumitted after 1806 had to leave the state within one year or face re-enslavement (Asch and Musgrove, *Chocolate City*, 58).

35. Phillips, *Freedom's Port*, 225.

36. Phillips, *Freedom's Port*, 220–26; Ripley, ed., *Witness for Freedom*, 3–4.

37. Phillips, *Freedom's Port*, 214–15, 218, 223–24, 226.

38. Harrold, *Subversives*, 1, 17–19; Phillips, *Freedom's Port*, 229.

39. Phillips, *Freedom's Port*, 231.

40. Harrold, *Subversives*, 2–4, 22–23, 141; Phillips, *Freedom's Port*, 131, 218–19; L. Brown, *Free Negroes in the District of Columbia*, 1–5, 141.

41. Phillips, *Freedom's Port*, 30–31; Green, *The Secret City*, 13–23, 28, 37; Constance M. Green, *American Cities in the Growth of the Nation* (New York: J. De Graff, 1957), 216–41; Gilbert Osofsky, ed., *Puttin' On Ole Massa: The Slave Narrative of Henry Bibb, William Wells Brown, and Solomon Northup* (New York: Harper and Row Publishers, 1969), quote, 241; Masur, *An Example for All the Land*, 13–17.

42. Asch and Musgrove, *Chocolate City*, 86–88; Harrold, *Subversives*, 74–75, 79.

43. Harrold, *Subversives*, 118–19.

44. Harrold, *Subversives*, 118–19.

45. Harrold, *Subversives*, 64, 97–99, 118–19, 132, 136–37, 144, 166; Asch and Musgrove, *Chocolate City*, 90–92. The Compromise of 1850 banned the slave trade from Washington, DC (Asch and Musgrove, 93–94).

46. Takagi, *"Rearing Wolves to Our Own Destruction,"* 21.

47. L. Brown, *Free Negroes in the District of Columbia*, 140; Phillips, *Freedom's Port*, 169, 227–28.

48. Phillips, *Freedom's Port*, 208, 233.

49. Phillips, *Freedom's Port*, 137–38; Asch and Musgrove, *Chocolate City*, 61.

50. Phillips, *Freedom's Port*, 63, 98–99, 140.

51. Phillips, *Freedom's Port*, 147.

52. Phillips, *Freedom's Port*, 156–58, 160–61.

CHAPTER THREE

1. Henry M. McKiven, Jr., *Iron and Steel: Class, Race, and Community in Birmingham, Alabama, 1875–1920* (Chapel Hill: University of North Carolina Press, 1995); Brian Kelly, *Race, Class, and Power in the Alabama Coalfields, 1908–1921* (Urbana: University of Illinois Press, 2001); Jonathan M. Wiener, *Social Origins of the New South: Alabama, 1860–1885* (Baton Rouge: Louisiana State University Press, 1978); Edward L. Ayers, *The Promise of the New South: Life After Reconstruction* (New York: Oxford University Press, 1992); Lynne B. Feldman, *A Sense of Place: Birmingham's Black Middle Class Community, 1890–1930* (Tuscaloosa: University of Alabama Press, 1999); Tera W. Hunter, *To 'Joy My Freedom: Southern Black Women's Lives and Labors after the Civil War* (Cambridge, MA: Harvard University Press, 1997); Ronald H. Bayor, *Race and the Shaping of Twentieth-Century Atlanta* (Chapel Hill: University of North Carolina, 1996); Georgina Hickey, *Hope and Danger in the New South City: Working Class Women and Urban Development in Atlanta, 1890–1940* (Athens: University of Georgia Press, 2003); Gregory Mixon, *The Atlanta Riot: Race,*

Class, and Violence in a New South City (Gainesville: University Press of Florida, 2005); Jean Bradley Anderson, *Durham County: A History of Durham County, North Carolina* (Durham: Duke University Press, 1990); Leslie Brown, *Upbuilding Black Durham: Gender, Class, and Black Community Development in the Jim Crow South* (Chapel Hill: University of North Carolina Press, 2008); Ronald Lewis, *Black Coal Miners in America: Race, Class, and Community Conflict, 1780–1980* (Lexington: University of Kentucky Press, 1987); Daniel Letwin, *The Challenge of Interracial Unionism: Alabama Coal Miners, 1878–1921* (Chapel Hill: University of North Carolina Press, 1998); Howard N. Rabinowitz, *Race Relations in the Urban South, 1865–1890* (Urbana: University of Illinois Press, 1980); Allison Dorsey, *To Build Our Lives Together: Community Formation in Black Atlanta, 1875–1906* (Athens: University of Georgia Press, 2004); Alexa B. Henderson, *Atlanta Life Insurance Company: Guardian of Black Economic Dignity* (Tuscaloosa: University of Alabama Press, 1990).

2. McKiven, *Iron and Steel*, 9–10, 57–60, 102–3; Kelly, *Race, Class, and Power in the Alabama Coalfields*, 1–3; Wiener, *Social Origins of the New South*, 137–60, 163–73, 181–85; Ayers, *The Promise of the New South*, 59, 64, 110–11; Feldman, *A Sense of Place*, 8.

3. Hunter, *To 'Joy My Freedom*, 241; Bayor, *Race and the Shaping of Twentieth-Century Atlanta*, 7; Hickey, *Hope and Danger in the New South City*, 18–19; Mixon, *The Atlanta Riot*, 114–20.

4. Anderson, *Durham County*, 263, 480; Brown, *Upbuilding Black Durham*, 16, 41, 89; Charles E. Hall, *Negroes in the United States, 1920–1932* (U.S. Bureau of the Census, 1935; repr., New York: Arno Press and the New York Times, 1969), table 11, 62; Lawrence Larsen, *The Urban South: A History* (Lexington: University Press of Kentucky, 1990), 80.

5. Hunter, *To 'Joy My Freedom*, 7, 82–83, 127, 241; Brown, *Upbuilding Black Durham*, 11, 41–43; Wiener, *Social Origins of the New South*, 198; Hickey, *Hope and Danger in the New South City*, 9–18; Hunter, *To 'Joy My Freedom*, 7, 82, 127, 241; Ayers, *The Promise of the New South*, 322–27.

6. Kelly, *Race, Class, and Power in the Alabama Coalfields*, 32; Feldman, *A Sense of Place*, 7–9; McKiven, *Iron and Steel*, 2, 18–19, 42–47; Lewis, *Black Coal Miners in America*, 39–41, 167–93; Letwin, *The Challenge of Interracial Unionism*, 23.

7. Feldman, *A Sense of Place*, 25, 43, 45–47. Over the next two decades, Black homeownership (about 5 percent) continued to fall below the rate of white homeownership (about 11 percent).

8. Feldman, *A Sense of Place*, 9, 19, 24, 25 (map), 26–27, 29, 32, 34, 40, 71; Rabinowitz, *Race Relations in the Urban South*, 105–6; Roger L. Rice, "Residential Segregation by Law, 1910–1917," *Journal of Southern History*, 34, no. 2 (May 1968): 179–82, quote, 182; Hunter, *To 'Joy My Freedom*, 44–50, 45, 48, 64–65; Douglass Massey and Nancy Denton, *American Apartheid: Segregation and the Making of the Underclass* (Cambridge, MA: Harvard University Press, 1993), 20–22.

9. Hunter, *To 'Joy My Freedom*, 22–23, 44–50, 45, 48, 64–65, 100–3; Dorsey, *To Build Our Lives Together*, 166; Bayor, *Race and the Shaping of Twentieth-Century Atlanta*, 12, 39–43.

10. Anderson, *Durham County*, 155–57.

11. Anderson, *Durham County*, 132, 156–58. Markum later returned to the area and lived in his own home near the church and school that he had helped to found years earlier. African American property holders in Hayti gradually expanded after about 1877, when John Daniels purchased a lot and built his home on Fayetteville Street, where he lived for the remainder of his life (155–57).

12. Feldman, *A Sense of Place*, 43–45; Dorsey, *To Build Our Lives Together*, 45.

13. Brown, *Upbuilding Black Durham*, 141, 144–45, 149, map, 189; Feldman, *A Sense of Place*, 9, 19, 24, 26–27, 32, 34, 40, 43–45, 71; Rabinowitz, *Race Relations in the Urban South*, 105–6; Rice, "Residential Segregation by Law, 1910–1917," 179–82, quote, 182; Hunter, *To 'Joy My Freedom*, 44–50; Massey and Denton, *American Apartheid*, 20–22.

14. Feldman, *A Sense of Place*, 9, 19, 26–27, 42–45, 65–68; Rabinowitz, *Race Relations in the Urban South*, 105–6; Rice, "Residential Segregation by Law, 1910–1917," 179–82, quote, 182; Hunter, *To 'Joy My Freedom*, 44–50; Massey and Denton, *American Apartheid*, 20–22.

15. Feldman, *A Sense of Place*, 64–66.

16. Feldman, *A Sense of Place*, 130.

17. Hunter, *To 'Joy My Freedom*, 68; Zandra L. Jordan, "A Guide to Atlanta's Black History, Heritage and Culture," Spelman College, 3–4; Dorsey, *To Build Our Lives Together*, 57–58, 66.

18. Feldman, *A Sense of Place*, 141–42.

19. Dorsey, *To Build Our Lives Together*, 60–61, 65–66.

20. Brown, *Upbuilding Black Durham*, 33–34, 36; "White Rock Baptist Church," website, February 16, 2020.

21. Joe W. Trotter, "African-American Fraternal Associations and the History of Civil Society in the United States: An Introduction," *Social Science History* 28, no. 3 (Fall 2004); Hunter, *To 'Joy My Freedom*, 70; Feldman, *A Sense of Place*, 155, 170–71.

22. Brown, *Upbuilding Black Durham*, 33, 36; "White Rock Baptist Church," website, February 16, 2020.

23. Dorsey, *To Build Our Lives Together*, 76–77; Brown, *Upbuilding Black Durham*, 173; Anderson, *Durham County*, 169, 260–61.

24. Brown, *Upbuilding Black Durham*, 3, 31, 39–41.

25. Ingham and Feldman, *African-American Business Leaders*, 550–54, quote, 552; Walter B. Weare, *Black Business in the New South: A Social History of the North Carolina Mutual Life Insurance Company* (Urbana: University of Illinois Press, 1973), 29–102, quote, 30.

26. Anderson, *Durham County*, 160, 519n4.

27. Brown, *Upbuilding Black Durham*, 141, 144–45, 149, map, 189; E. Franklin Frazier, "Durham: Capital of the Black Middle Class," in Alain Locke, ed., *The New Negro: Voices of the Harlem Renaissance* (1925; repr., 1992), 333–40, quote, 340.

28. Feldman, *A Sense of Place*, 28, 61–63, 64–66.

29. Feldman, *A Sense of Place*, 9, 19, 26–27, 61–63; Rabinowitz, *Race Relations in the Urban South*, 105–6; Rice, "Residential Segregation by Law, 1910–1917," 179–82,

quote, 182; Hunter, *To 'Joy My Freedom*, 44–50; Massey and Denton, *American Apartheid*, 20–22. Much like Birmingham's early CBD, Smithfield's African American population initially lived "alongside recent immigrants from Italy, England, and Germany, who also shared space with native-born whites," in an area bounded on the north, south, east, and west, respectively, by Martha Street, Sallie Avenue, Joseph Street, and William Street.

30. Hickey, *Hope and Danger in the New South City*, 62–63; Feldman, *A Sense of Place*, 68–69, 86–87; Clifford M. Kuhn, Harlon E. Joye, and E. B. West, *Living Atlanta: An Oral History of the City, 1914–1948* (Athens: Atlanta Historical Society and University of Georgia Press, 1990), 37–42, 301–2; Eileen Southern, *The Music of Black Americans: A History* (New York: W. W. Norton and Company, 1971), 358, 376, 382; Roland E. Wolseley, *The Black Press, U.S.A.*, 2nd ed. (Ames: Iowa State University Press, 1990), 75–78; Henderson, *Atlanta Life Insurance Company*, 63–99.

31. Dorsey, *To Build Our Lives Together*, 49–52. By 1900, Alonzo Herndon reported a net worth of $12,750, some $5,000 ahead of the next tier of Black property holders. Ten years later, Herndon's net worth had increased to $10,300. He owed 97 percent of his wealth to real estate investments within the city of Atlanta. Other wealthy Black men also invested an estimated 80 to 90 percent of their wealth in real estate.

32. Mark R. Schneider, *Boston Confronts Jim Crow, 1890–1920* (Boston: Northeastern University Press, 2019), 73–76; August Meier, *Negro Thought in America, 1880–1915* (Ann Arbor: University of Michigan Press, 1963), 124–27; Weare, *Black Business in the New South*, 144–45; Brown, *Upbuilding of Black Durham*, 116; Hickey, *Hope and Danger in the New South City*, 62–63; Feldman, *A Sense of Place*, 68–69, 86–87; Kuhn, Joye, and West, *Living Atlanta*, 37–42, 301–2. Also see Southern, *The Music of Black Americans*, 358, 376, 382; Wolseley, *The Black Press, U.S.A.*, 75–78; Henderson, *Atlanta Life Insurance Company*, 63–99.

33. Bayor, *Race and the Shaping of Twentieth-Century Atlanta*, 5, 7, 18; Dorsey, *To Build Our Lives Together*, 128–30, 138–39, 153. (No Blacks would serve on Atlanta's city council again until the 1950s.)

34. Feldman, *A Sense of Place*, 9–11.

35. Brown, *Upbuilding Black Durham*, 41, 47, 73.

36. Mixon, *The Atlanta Riot*, 85–100, 107–8; Dorsey, *To Build Our Lives Together*, 158–62; Ayers, *The Promise of the New South*, 436; Paul A. Gilje, *Rioting in America* (Bloomington: Indiana University Press, 1996), 109–10; Herbert Shapiro, *White Violence and Black Resistance: From Reconstruction to Montgomery* (Amherst: University of Massachusetts Press, 1988), 100–101.

37. Bayor, *Race and the Shaping of Twentieth-Century Atlanta*, 8, 11–12; Dorsey, *To Build Our Lives Together*, 144, 161.

38. Dorsey, *To Build Our Lives Together*, 123–24, quote, 123, 127–29, 130–32, 140–41.

39. Dorsey, *To Build Our Lives Together*, 129, 131–33, 141.

40. Feldman, *A Sense of Place*, 10.

41. Brown, *Uplifting Black Durham*, 41, 46–47, 49.

42. Brown, *Uplifting Black Durham*, 41.

43. Feldman, *A Sense of Place*, 106–7; Dorsey, *To Build Our Lives Together*, 122–23, 149–50.

44. Feldman, *A Sense of Place*, 78–79, 106–8.

45. Feldman, *A Sense of Place*, 12, 13, 78–79, 91, 106–8.

46. Dorsey, *To Build Our Lives Together*, 138, 151, 153, 163; Bayor, *Race and the Shaping of Twentieth-Century Atlanta*, 4, 7, 18; Feldman, *A Sense of Place*, 12, 79–80.

47. Feldman, *A Sense of Place*, 113–14, 120–21.

48. Brown, *Upbuilding Black Durham*, 58, 68.

49. Bayor, *Race and the Shaping of Twentieth-Century Atlanta*, 4–5; Dorsey, *To Build Our Lives Together*, 130–31, 140–41, citing Bacote, 140.

50. Hickey, *Hope and Danger in the New South City*, 62–63; Feldman, *A Sense of Place*, 68–69, 86–87, 106–7; Kuhn, Joye, and West, *Living Atlanta*, 37–42, 301–2; Southern, *The Music of Black Americans*, 358, 376, 382; Wolseley, *The Black Press, U.S.A.*, 75–78; Henderson, *Atlanta Life Insurance Company*, 63–99.

51. Dorsey, *To Build Our Lives Together*, 135–40, quote (139, 156, quote (166); Feldman, *A Sense of Place*, 42–43; Bayor, *Race and the Shaping of Twentieth-Century Atlanta*, 12.

CHAPTER FOUR

1. Bernadette Pruitt, *The Other Great Migration: The Movement of Rural African Americans to Houston, 1900–1941* (College Station: Texas A&M University Press, 2013), 25; D. G. McComb, *Houston: A History* (Austin: University of Texas Press, 1981); Kimberley Green Weathers, "Houston, Texas," in David Goldfield, ed., *American Urban History: An Encylopedia* (Thousand Oaks: Sage Publications, 2007), 362–63.

2. Pruitt, *The Other Great Migration*, 6–7; Weathers, "Houston, Texas," 362–63.

3. Scott Ellsworth, *Death in a Promised Land: The Tulsa Race Riot of 1921* (Baton Rouge: Louisiana State University Press, 1982), 10, 11; Alfred Brophy, *Reconstructing the Dreamland: The Tulsa Riot of 1921* (New York: Oxford University Press, 2002), 1–3; Dennis McClendon, "Tulsa, Oklahoma," in Goldfield, *American Urban History*, 809–11.

4. N. D. B. Connolly, *A World More Concrete: Real Estate and the Remaking of Jim Crow South Florida* (Chicago: University of Chicago Press, 2014), 5.

5. Connolly, *A World More Concrete*, 5, 19, 21, 45–47, 66; M. Dunn, *Black Miami in the Twentieth Century* (Gainesville: University of Florida Press, 1997), 46–47; Raymond Mohl, "Miami, Florida," in Goldfield, *American Urban History*, 467–70.

6. James SoRelle, "The Darker Side of 'Heaven': The Black Community in Houston, Texas, 1917–1945" (PhD diss., Kent State University, 1980), 3–4, 18; Pruitt, *The Other Great Migration*, 6–7.

7. Hannibal B. Johnson, *Black Wall Street: From Riot to Renaissance in Tulsa's Historic Greenwood District* (Fort Worth: Eakin Press, 1998), 5–6.

8. Ellsworth, *Death in the Promised Land*, 12–13; H. Johnson, *Black Wall Street*, 5–6.

9. H. Johnson, *Black Wall Street*, 12–13; Kendra T. Field, *Growing Up with the Country: Family, Race, and Nation after the Civil War* (New Haven: Yale University Press, 2018), 24–25.

10. Connolly, *A World More Concrete*, 19, 24–25; Paul S. George, "Colored Town: Miami's Black Community, 1896–1930," *Florida Historical Quarterly* 56, no. 4 (April 1978): 432–33; Hall, *Negroes in the United States*, 55.

11. SoRelle, "The Darker Side of 'Heaven,'" 107; Hall, *Negroes in the United States*, 55; Connolly, *A World More Concrete*, 24–45; Ellsworth, *Death in the Promised Land*. For a positive take on jobs in Miami see George, "Colored Town," 433.

12. Connolly, *A World More Concrete*, 2, 58.

13. Connolly, *A World More Concrete*, 26, 46–47; Henry Whitlow, "The History of the Greenwood Era in Tulsa," paper presented to the Tulsa Historical Society, March 29, 1974, 1–5, online access.

14. Pruitt, *The Other Great Migration*, 67; SoRelle, "The Darker Side of 'Heaven,'" 48–49; Peter M. Rutkoff and William B. Scott, *Fly Away: The Great African American Cultural Migrations* (Baltimore: Johns Hopkins University Press, 2010), 252.

15. Whitlow, "The History of the Greenwood Era in Tulsa," 1–5; Ellsworth, *Death in the Promised Land*, 14–16; H. Johnson, *Black Wall Street*, 10.

16. Whitlow, "The History of the Greenwood Era in Tulsa," 1–5; Ellsworth, *Death in the Promised Land*,16; H. Johnson, *Black Wall Street*, 53.

17. Connolly, *A World More Concrete*, 27–28.

18. Connolly, *A World More Concrete*, 26–27, 36.

19. H. Johnson, *Black Wall Street*, 80.

20. Pruitt, *The Other Great Migration*, 43–44, 61, 67–68, 73 (quote), 74–77, 161–62; SoRelle, "The Darker Side of 'Heaven,'" 48–49; Rutkoff and Scott, *Fly Away*, 252–53.

21. Pruitt, *The Other Great* Migration, 63–64 (map 3).

22. Pruitt, *The Other Great* Migration, quotes, 57, 65.

23. Pruitt, *The Other Great* Migration, 72–73.

24. Congressman D. Beyer, chair, "The Economic Legacy of the 1921 Tulsa Race Massacre: Today's Racial Wealth Gap" (J.E.C., U.S. Congress, 2019); C. E. Hall, *Negroes in the United States, 1920–1932* (New York: Arno Press and NYT, 1969), 276; Whitlow, "The History of the Greenwood Era in Tulsa," 1–5; Ellsworth, *Death in the Promised Land*, quote, 16; Connolly, *A World More Concrete*, 26, 76–78.

25. Connolly, *A World More Concrete*, quote, 41, 46–47.

26. Whitlow, "The History of the Greenwood Era in Tulsa," 1–5; Ellsworth, *Death in the Promised Land*; H. Johnson, *Black Wall Street*, 10.

27. H. Johnson, *Black Wall Street*, 89.

28. H. Johnson, *Black Wall Street*, 83–85.

29. Ellsworth, *Death in the Promised Land*, 13–14.

30. Ellsworth, *Death in the Promised Land*, 1–3.

31. Whitlow, "The History of the Greenwood Era in Tulsa," 1–5; Ellsworth, *Death in the Promised Land*, 12, 15.

32. Whitlow, "The History of the Greenwood Era in Tulsa," 2.

33. Ellsworth, *Death in the Promised Land*, 15–16.

34. H. Johnson, *Black Wall Street*, 13–14; Whitlow, "The History of the Greenwood Era in Tulsa," 2.

35. H. Johnson, *Black Wall Street*, 10.

36. Connolly, *A World More Concrete*, 26; George, "Colored Town," 437.

37. George, "Colored Town," 438, 440.

38. George, "Colored Town," 438, 440.

39. George, "Colored Town," 438.

40. Rutkoff and Scott, *Fly Away*, 253; Pruitt, *The Other Great Migration*, 100, 112; SoRelle, "The Darker Side of 'Heaven,'" 51–52.

41. SoRelle, "The Darker Side of 'Heaven,'" 48–50, 53; Pruitt, *The Other Great Migration*, 65, 72, 74–75, 77–80, 113, 115–16.

42. Pruitt, *The Other Great Migration*, 102–3, 243, fig. 45.

43. Pruitt, *The Other Great Migration*; George, "Colored Town," 439; Ellsworth, *Death in the Promised Land*, 13–14.

44. Pruitt, *The Other Great Migration*, 105–6, 116.

45. Connolly, *A World More Concrete*, 33.

46. Connolly, *A World More Concrete*, 40, 50–51.

47. Pruitt, *The Other Great Migration*, 141–47.

48. This section is based on Trotter, *The African American Experience*, 406.

49. Ellsworth, *Death in the Promised Land*, 45–69; Trotter, *The African American Experience*, 406.

50. H. Johnson, *Black Wall Street*, 69–70.

51. H. Johnson, *Black Wall Street*, vii, 30; Ellsworth, *Death in the Promised Land*, 108–9.

52. Connolly, *A World More Concrete*, 31, 33, 35; Pruitt, *The Other Great Migration*, 22.

53. SoRelle, "The Darker Side of 'Heaven,'" 39–41.

54. SoRelle, "The Darker Side of 'Heaven,'" 43–44, 173, 214–15; Darlene Clark Hine, *Black Victory: The Rise and Fall of the White Primary in Texas* (Columbia: University of Missouri Press, 2003).

55. Pruitt, *The Other Great Migration*, 150.

56. Ellsworth, *Death in the Promised Land*, 19.

57. Ellsworth, *Death in the Promised Land*, 24–25.

58. George, "Colored Town," 433–35; Connolly, *A World More Concrete*, 20.

59. George, "Colored Town," 433–35; Connolly, *A World More Concrete*, 20.

60. Raymond Mohl, "The Pattern of Race Relations in Miami Since the 1920s," in David R. Colburn and Jane L. Landers, eds., *The African American Heritage in Florida* (Gainesville: University of Florida Press, 1995), 346–47; George, "Colored Town," 433–35; Connolly, *A World More Concrete*, 170, 177–78.

61. Pruitt, *The Other Great Migration*, 111–13; Bettye Collier-Thomas, *Jesus, Jobs, and Justice: African American Women and Religion* (New York: Alfred A. Knopf, 2011), xv–xxxiv.

62. Connolly, *A World More Concrete*, 56–59.

63. Connolly, *A World More Concrete*, 54–55, 60–62.

CHAPTER FIVE

1. Harris, *In the Shadow of Slavery*; Alexander, *African or American?*; Carla L. Peterson, *Black Gotham: A Family History of African Americans in Nineteenth-Century New York City* (New Haven: Yale University Press, 2011); Edwin G. Burrows and Mike Wallace, *Gotham: A History of New York City to 1898* (New York: Oxford University Press, 1999); Craig Steven Wilder, *In the Company of Black Men: The African Influence on African American Culture in New York City* (New York: New York University Press, 2005); George Walker, *The Afro-American in New York City, 1827–1860* (New York: Garland Publishing, 1993); Gary B. Nash, *Forging Freedom: The Formation of Philadelphia's Black Community 1720–1840* (Cambridge, MA: Harvard University Press, 1988); Lorenzo J. Greene, *The Negro in Colonial New England, 1620–1776* (1942; repr., New York: Atheneum, 1968); Bridenbaugh, *Cities in the Wilderness*; William D. Piersen, *Black Yankees: The Development of an Afro-American Subculture in Eighteenth-Century New England* (Amherst: University of Massachusetts Press, 1988); Jorge Cañizares-Esguerra, Matt D. Childs, and James Sidbury, eds., *The Black Urban Atlantic in the Age of the Slave Trade* (Philadelphia: University of Pennsylvania Press, 2013); James O. and Lois E. Horton, *Black Bostonians: Family Life and Community Struggle in the Antebellum North* (New York: Holmes and Meier, 1979); Serena Zabin, *Dangerous Economies: Status and Commerce in Imperial New* York (Philadelphia: University of Pennsylvania Press, 2009); Joyce Goodfriend, *Before the Melting Pot: Society and Culture in Colonial New York City, 1664–1730* (Princeton: Princeton University Press, 1992); Douglas R. Egerton, *Death of Liberty: African Americans and Revolutionary America* (New York: Oxford University Press, 2009); W. E. B. Du Bois, *The Philadelphia Negro: A Social Study* (1899; repr., Philadelphia: University of Pennsylvania, 1996); Winch, *Philadelphia's Black Elite*; James Oliver Horton and Lois E. Horton, *In Hope of Liberty: Culture, Community, and Protest among Northern Free Blacks, 1700–1860* (New York: Oxford University Press, 1997); Shane White, *Somewhat More Independent: The End of Slavery in New York City, 1770–1810* (Athens: University of Georgia Press, 1991); Michael A. Gomez, *Exchanging Our Country Marks: The Transformation of African Identities in the Colonial and Antebellum South* (Chapel Hill: University of North Carolina Press, 1998); Michael Gomez, *Black Crescent: The Experience and Legacy of African Muslims in the Americas* (Cambridge: Cambridge University Press, 2005); James Sidbury, *Becoming African in America: Race and Nation in the Early Black Atlantic* (New York: Oxford University Press, 2007); Stephen Kantrowitz, *More Than Freedom: Fighting for Black*

Citizenship in a White Republic, 1829–1889 (New York: Penguin Press, 2012); Curry, *The Free Black in Urban America.*

2. For Winthrop's notion of the "City on the Hill," see Schneider, *Boston Confronts Jim Crow,* 3–4.

3. Harris, *In the Shadow of Slavery,* 23–24, 42, 74, 248, 260–61; Alexander, *African or American?,* 4–7; Peterson, *Black Gotham,* 50–55; Burrows and Wallace, *Gotham,* 32–33; Wilder, *In the Company of Black Men,* 33–35.

4. Nash, *Forging Freedom,* 8–15, quotes, 8, 13; Greene, *The Negro in Colonial New England,* 309, 312; Scott Hancock, "Claiming the Courtroom: Space, Race, and Law, 1808–1856," in Nieves and Alexander, *"We Shall Independent Be,"* 143; Bridenbaugh, *Cities in the Wilderness,* 201–2.

5. Nash, *Forging Freedom,* 8–15, quotes 8, 13; Greene, *The Negro in Colonial New England, 1620–1776,* 312; Piersen, *Black Yankees,* 77–78.

6. Harris, *In the Shadow of Slavery,* 24, 42, 74, 248, 260–61; Nash, *Forging Freedom,* 14, 164–65.

7. Piersen, *Black Yankees,* 25, 46–47; Horton and Horton, *Black Bostonians,* 4.

8. Shane White, "African Grove Theater," in Ira Berlin and Leslie M. Harris, eds., *Slavery in New York* (New York: The New Press, 2005), 174; Harris, *In the Shadow of Slavery,* 41–43, 78–79; Cañizares-Esguerra, Childs, and Sidbury, *The Black Urban Atlantic,* 1–2; Zabin, *Dangerous Economies,* 11–13, 58–62; Goodfriend, *Before the Melting Pot,* 121–22; Piersen, *Black Yankees,* 102–3; Egerton, *Death of Liberty,* 25; Du Bois, *The Philadelphia Negro,* 15.

9. Harris, *In the Shadow of Slavery,* 41–43; Berlin, *Many Thousands Gone,* 192–93; Piersen, *Black Yankees,* 117–40; Horton and Horton, *In Hope of Liberty,* 31–36; White, *Somewhat More Independent,* 96–100; Egerton, *Death of Liberty,* 22–25.

10. Gomez, *Exchanging Our Country Marks,* 66, 72–74; Gomez, *Black Crescent,* 132–47; Richard C. Rath, *How Early America Sounded* (Ithaca: Cornell University Press, 2003), 7; Sidbury, *Becoming African in America,* 22–27, quote, 27; Nash, *Forging Freedom,* 8–40; Creel, *"A Peculiar People,"* 86.

11. Curry, *The Free Black in Urban America,* 5–6, 249–50; Kantrowitz, *More Than Freedom,* 7, 101–8; Nash, *Forging Freedom,* 71; Harris, *In the Shadow of Slavery,* 102; Edgar J. McManus, *Black Bondage in the North* (Syracuse: Syracuse University Press, 1973), 161–67; Edgar J. McManus, *A History of Negro Slavery in New York* (Syracuse: Syracuse University Press, 1966), 174–79; Horton and Horton, *In Hope of Liberty,* 71–76; Leon Litwack, *North of Slavery: The Negro in the Free States, 1790–1860* (Chicago: University of Chicago Press, 1961), 7–15; Arthur Zilversmit, *The First Emancipation: The Abolition of Slavery in the North* (Chicago: University of Chicago Press, 1975), 113–16, 124–37, 176–84, 208–14; Gary Nash, "The Social Evolution of Preindustrial American Cities, 1700–1820," in Raymond A. Mohl, ed., *The Making of Urban America,* 2nd ed. (Wilmington: Scholarly Resources, 1997), 19–21. Between 1800 and 1830, the free Black population rose from 4,200 to 9,800 in Philadelphia; 3,500 to 14,000 in New York City; and from 1,200 to about 2,000 in Boston.

12. Curry, *The Free Black in Urban America,* 163.

13. Nash, *Forging Freedom*, 163–65, 168–69.

14. Harris, *In the Shadow of Slavery*, 42, 74, 252–52.

15. Harris, *In the Shadow of Slavery*, 74–75.

16. Nash, *Forging Freedom*, 161; Du Bois, *Philadelphia Negro*, 238–39; Harris, *In the Shadow of Slavery*, 76, 144–45, 265–66; Curry, *The Free Black in Urban America*, 100, 124–25, 132–34; Horton and Horton, *Black Bostonians*, 2–4, 25. The early Black urban community was not limited to rental and owner-occupied properties, however. It also included the residence of free people in private homes as household workers, orphanages, homes for the elderly, and early prisons. Some occupied boarding houses, hotels, hospitals, and even nearby military installations.

17. Nash, *Forging Freedom*, 163–65, 168–69.

18. Richard Allen of Philadelphia's Mother Bethel AME Church organized a church in New York City in 1820, but competition with New York's own independent Black church movement undermined its growth (see Harris, *In the Shadow of Slavery*, 85).

19. For this and the next paragraph, see Harris, *In the Shadow of Slavery*, 76, 82, 84–86, 87–88.

20. Harris, *In the Shadow of Slavery*, 87–88.

21. White, "African Grove Theater," 174; Harris, *In the Shadow of Slavery*, 41–43, 78–79; Cañizares-Esguerra, Childs, and Sidbury, eds., *The Black Urban Atlantic*, 1–2; Zabin, *Dangerous Economies*, 11–13, 58–62; Goodfriend, *Before the Melting Pot*, 121–22; Piersen, *Black Yankees*, 102–3; Egerton, *Death of Liberty*, 25; Du Bois, *The Philadelphia Negro*, 15.

22. Du Bois, *The Philadelphia Negro*, 33–34.

23. Nash, *Forging Freedom*, 148–54; Harris, *In the Shadow of Slavery*, 77–78.

24. James Campbell, *Middle Passages: African American Journeys to Africa, 1787–2005* (New York: Penguin Press, 2006), 30–39, 44; P. J. Staudenraus, *The African Colonization Movement, 1816–1865* (1961; repr., New York: Octagon Books, 1980), 21–29; Horton and Horton, *Black Bostonians*, 97–98; Freelove Slocum to Paul Cuffee, December 9, 1816, in Dorothy Sterling, ed., *We Are Your Sisters: Black Women in the Nineteenth Century* (New York: Norton and Company, 1984), 100–101; Sheldon Harris, *Paul Cuffee: Black America and the African Return* (New York: Simon and Schuster, 1972), 11–23.

25. John N. Ingham and Lynne B. Feldman, *African-American Business Leaders: A Biographical Dictionary* (Westport: Greenwood Press,1994), 236–39; Nash, *Forging Freedom*, 51–52, 148–49; Campbell, *Middle Passages*, 44.

26. Nash, *Forging Freedom*, 203–5; Horton and Horton, *Black Bostonians*, 76–77.

27. Harris, *In the Shadow of Slavery*, 145, 148.

28. Harris, *In the Shadow of Slavery*, 238; Curry, *The Free Black in Urban America*, 124, 132.

29. Harris, *In the Shadow of Slavery*, 42, 74, 252–52; Piersen, *Black Yankees*, 22, 25, 46–47; Horton and Horton, *Black Bostonians*, 4; Greene, *The Negro in Colonial New England*, 41, 208, 299, 311–12; Nash, "The Social Evolution of Preindustrial

Cities," 20; Richard Archer, *As If an Enemy's Country: The British Occupation of Boston and the Origins of Revolution* (New York: Oxford University Press, 2010), 119–20; Piersen, *Black Yankees*, 22.

30. Harris, *In the Shadow of Slavery*, 17, 23–28, 30–33, 37–39; Goodfriend, *Before the Melting Pot*, 117–26; Burrows and Wallace, *Gotham*, 149.

31. Nash, *Forging Freedom*, 8–12, quote, 8, 34–35; Kali N. Gross, *Colored Amazons: Crime, Violence, and Black Women in the City of Brotherly Love, 1880–1910* (Durham: Duke University Press, 2006), 13–22.

32. Curry, *Free Black in Urban America*, 49–57, quotes, 49–52; Horton and Horton, *Black Bostonians*, 16–19; Harris, *In the Shadow of the Slavery*, 251–55; Nash, *Forging Freedom*, 165–69; Martin V. Melosi, *The Sanitary City: Urban Infrastructure in America from Colonial Times to the Present* (2000; abridged ed., Pittsburgh: University of Pittsburgh Press, 2008), 22–25; Howard P. Chudacoff, Judith E. Smith, and Peter C. Baldwin, *The Evolution of American Society*, 7th ed. (Boston: Prentice Hall, 2010), 50; Walker, *The Afro-American in New York City*, 8–13.

33. Winch, *Philadelphia's Black Elite*, 140.

34. Harris, *In the Shadow of Slavery*, 119.

35. Du Bois, *The Philadelphia Negro*, 370–72; Winch, *Philadelphia's Black Elite*, 134–36; Harris, *In the Shadow of Slavery*, 116–19; George Levesque, *Black Boston: African American Life and Culture in Urban America, 1750–1860* (London: Routledge, 1994), 318.

36. Kantrowitz, *More Than Freedom*, 1–7, 176–98; Fergus M. Bordewich, *The Underground Railroad and the War for the Soul of America* (New York: HarpersCollins, 2005), 169–72; Wilbur Siebert, *The Underground Railroad from Slavery to Freedom* (1898; reprt. New York: Arno Press and the New York Times, 1968), 17–40, 308–9; Claude A. Clegg III, *The Price of Liberty: African Americans and the Making of Liberia* (Chapel Hill: University of North Carolina Press, 2004), 171–77; Ripley, *Witness for Freedom*, 179–84; Harris, *In the Shadow of Slavery*, 271–73.

37. Harris, *In the Shadow of Slavery*, 134–35; Clegg, *The Price of Liberty*, 145–46; Staudenraus, *The African Colonization Movement*, 234–38; Stephen M. Best, *The Fugitive's Properties: Law and the Poetics of Possession* (Chicago: University of Chicago Press, 2004), quote and discussion of Stowe's position, 1–2.

38. Curry, *The Free Black in Urban America*, 101; Harris, *In the Shadow of Slavery*, 197–99, 250–51.

39. Curry, *The Free Black in Urban America*, 100–1; Nash, *Forging Freedom*, 275–79; Du Bois, *The Philadelphia Negro*, 27–29; Leonard L. Richards, *"Gentlemen of Property and Standing": Anti-Abolition Mobs in Jacksonian America* (New York, 1970), 155; Harris, *In the Shadow of Slavery*, 197–98.

40. Curry, *Free Black in Urban America*, 244–51.

41. Harris, *In the Shadow of Slavery*, 280–81.

42. Harris, *In the Shadow of Slavery*, 285–86,

43. Harris, *In the Shadow of Slavery*, 43–46; Goodfriend, *Before the Melting Pot*, 127–32; Burrows and Wallace, *Gotham*, 176; Roi Ottley and William J. Weatherby, *The Negro in New York: An Informal Social History* (New York: New York Public

Library and Oceana Publications, Inc., 1967), 36–37; Nash, *Forging Freedom*, 38–39; Egerton, *Death of Liberty*, 46; Benjamin L. Carp, *Rebels Rising: Cities and the American Revolution* (New York: Oxford University Press, 2007), 21–22, 172–212; Sidney Kaplan and Emma Nogrady Kaplan, *The Black Presence in the Era of the American Revolution* (Amherst: University of Massachusetts Press, 1989), 6–15, 30–31; Marcus Rediker, "A Motley Crew of Rebels: Sailors, Slaves, and the Coming of the American Revolution," in Ronald Hoffman and Peter J. Albert, eds., *The Transforming Hand of Revolution: Reconsidering the American Revolution as a Social Movement* (Charlottesville: U.S. Capitol Historical Society and University of Virginia Press, 1995), 155–56, 192.

44. Horton and Horton, *In Hope of Liberty*, 55–56; Greene, *The Negro in Colonial New England*, 241.

45. Horton and Horton, *Black Bostonians*, 30–31; Horton and Horton, *In Hope of Liberty*, 141–42; Curry, *The Free Black in Urban America*, 184–85; Reed, *Platform for Change*, 25–26; Horton and Horton, *Black Bostonians*, 28–29; Harris, *In the Shadow of Slavery*, 89–90; White, *Somewhat More Independent*, 95–106.

46. Nash, *Forging Freedom*, 101–3, 237–38; Staudenraus, *The African Colonization Movement*, 32–35; Floyd J. Miller, *The Search for a Black Nationality: Black Emigration and Colonization, 1787–1863* (Urbana: University of Illinois Press, 1975), 47–53; Winch, *Philadelphia's Black Elite*, 35–36.

47. Ripley et al., *Witness for Freedom*, 2–3; Hinks, *To Awaken My Afflicted Brethren*, 184n30, 91; Alexander, *African or American?*, 206n15, 211n66; Horton and Horton, *Black Bostonians*, 88–89.

48. Harris, *In the Shadow of Slavery*, 97–99, 128–29.

49. Harris, *In the Shadow of Slavery*, 102.

50. Kantrowitz, *More Than Freedom*, 7, 101–8; Harris, *In the Shadow of Slavery*, 102.

51. Winch, *Philadelphia's Black Elite*, 140.

52. Walker, *The Afro-American in New York City*, 41–45, 133–47; Harris, *In the Shadow of Slavery*, 275–78; Horton and Horton, *In Hope of Liberty*, 243.

53. Horton and Horton, *Black Bostonians*, 48.

54. Hinks, *To Awaken My Afflicted Brethren*, 91–115; Curry, *Free Black in Urban America*, 226–27; Harris, *In the Shadow of Slavery*, 174–75; Ripley et al., eds., *Witness for Freedom*, 42–46.

55. Nash, *Forging Freedom*, 276–79; Staudenraus, *The African Colonization Movement*, 188–206; Harris, *In the Shadow of Slavery*, 135, 153–54, 171, 197–99, 219–21; Daniel Feller, "A Brother in Arms: Benjamin Tappan and the Antislavery Democracy," *Journal of American History* 88, no. 1 (2001): 48–74; Van Goose, "'As a Nation, the English Are Our Friends': The Emergence of African American Politics in the British Atlantic World," *American Historical Review* 113, no. 1 (2008): 48–71; Ripley, *Witness for Freedom*, 4–6; Paul A. Gilje, *Rioting in America* (Bloomington: Indiana University Press, 1996), 81–82; Harris, *In the Shadow of Slavery*, 197–99; Horton and Horton, *Black Bostonians*, 225–26; Richards, *"Gentlemen of Property and Standing,"* 155.

56. Bordewich, *The Underground Railroad and the War for the Soul of America*, 167–78, 367; Harris, *In the Shadow of Slavery*, 206–15; Shirley J. Yee, *Black Women Abolitionists: A Study in Activism, 1828–1860* (Knoxville: University of Tennessee Press, 1992), 98–100; Walker, *The Afro-American in New York*, 170–72; Thomas D. Morris, *Free Men All: The Personal Liberty Laws of the North, 1780–1861* (Baltimore: Johns Hopkins University Press, 1974), 42–58, 73–76, 109–11.

57. Yee, *Black Women Abolitionists*, 95–96, 115–16, 125, 141–42; Marilyn Richardson, *Maria W. Stewart: America's First Black Woman Political Writer* (Bloomington: Indiana University Press, 1987), xiii–xvii, 3–27; Hine and Thompson, *A Shining Thread of Hope*, 106–7; Sterling, ed., *We Are Your Sisters*, 66–69, 151, 153–59; Paula Giddings, *When and Where I Enter: The Impact of Black Women on Race and Sex in America* (New York: Bantam Books, 1985), 49–54; Yee, *Black Women Abolitionists*, 95–96, 115–16, 125; Catherine Clinton, "'Slavery Is War': Harriet Tubman and the Underground Railroad," in David Blight, *Passages to Freedom: The Underground Railroad in History and Memory* (Washington, DC: Smithsonian Books, 2006), 195–209.

58. Nell Irvin Painter, *Sojourner Truth: A Life, a Symbol* (New York: W. W. Norton and Company, 1996), quotes, 7–8, 167; Erlene Stetson and Linda David, *Glorying in Tribulation: The Lifework of Sojourner Truth* (East Lansing: Michigan State University Press, 1994), 57–80, 88–120.

59. King, *The Essence of Liberty*, 120; Jane Rhodes, *Mary Ann Shadd Cary: The Black Press and Protest in the Nineteenth Century* (Bloomington: Indiana University Press, 1998), 74–75; Yee, *Black Women Abolitionists*, 14, 116, 121–22, 126–27, 169n69; Hine and Thompson, *A Shining Thread of Hope*, 106–7; Sterling, *We Are Your Sisters*, 66–69, 151, 170–71; Bettye Collier-Thomas, *Daughters of Thunder: Black Women Preachers and Their Sermons, 1850–1979* (San Francisco: Jossey-Bass Publishers, 1998), 57–68, 46–53; Harris, *In the Shadow of Slavery*, 178–79; Deborah Gray White, "Simply Truths: Antebellum Slavery in Black and White," in Blight, *Passages to Freedom*, 59–60; Clinton, "'Slavery Is War'"; Painter, *Sojourner Truth*, 7–8, 167.

60. Harris, *In the Shadow of Slavery*, 280–85; Gilje, *Rioting in America*, 92–94; Iver Bernstein, *The New York City Draft Riots: Their Significance for American Society and Politics in the Age of the Civil War* (New York, 1990), 1–42; Judith Giesberg, *Army at Home: Women and the Civil War on the Northern Home Front* (Chapel Hill: University of North Carolina Press, 2009), 127–30.

61. Jones, *A Dreadful Deceit*, 48.

62. Egerton, *Death or Liberty*, 74–88, 214–16; Judith L. Van Buskirk, *Generous Enemies: Patriots and Loyalists in Revolutionary New York* (Philadelphia: University of Pennsylvania Press, 2002), 137–49, 164–75; Christopher Clark, *Social Change in America: From the Revolution Through the Civil War* (Chicago: Ivan R. Dee, 2006), 49; Burrows and Wallace, *Gotham*, 248–49; Harris, *In the Shadow of Slavery*, 53–56; Benjamin Quarles, *The Negro in the American Revolution* (1961; repr., Chapel Hill: University of North Carolina Press, 1996), 51–67; Nash, *Forging Freedom*, 52; John Daniels, *In Freedom's Birthplace* (1914; repr., New York: Arno Press and the New

York Times, 1969), 12–14; Robin Winks, *The Blacks in Canada*, 2nd ed. (Montreal: McGill-Queens University Press, 1999).

63. Nash, *Forging Freedom*, 102–3, 184–85, 242–45; Horton and Horton, *Black Bostonians*, 97–98; Winch, *Philadelphia's Black Elite*, 35; Staudenraus, *The African Colonization Movement*, 9–11; Floyd Miller, *The Search for a Black Nationality: Black Emigration and Colonization, 1787–1863* (Urbana: University of Illinois Press, 1975), 47–50; Ashli White, *Encountering Revolution: Haiti and the Making of the Early Republic* (Baltimore: Johns Hopkins University Press, 2010), 209–10.

CHAPTER SIX

1. Christopher Robert Reed, *The Rise of Chicago's Black Metropolis, 1920–1929* (Urbana: University of Illinois Press, 2011), 30–31; Allan H. Spear, *Black Chicago: The Making of a Negro Ghetto* (Chicago: University of Chicago Press, 1967); Arnold Hirsch, *Making the Second Ghetto: Race and Housing in Chicago, 1940–1960* (Chicago: University of Chicago Press, 1983); Davarian L. Baldwin, *Chicago's New Negroes: Modernity, the Great Migration, and Black Urban Life* (Chapel Hill: University of North Carolina Press, 2007); St. Clair Drake and Horace R. Cayton, *Black Metropolis: A Study of Negro Life in a Northern City* (New York: Harcourt, Brace and World, Inc., 1945); David M. Katzman, *Before the Ghetto: Black Detroit in the Nineteenth Century* (Urbana: University of Illinois Press, 1973); Amanda I. Seligman, *Block by Block: Neighborhoods and Public Policy on Chicago's West Side* (Chicago: University of Chicago Press, 2005); Kenneth L. Kusmer, *A Ghetto Takes Shape: Black Cleveland, 1870–1930* (Urbana: University of Illinois Press, 1976); Kimberley L. Phillips, *AlabamaNorth: African-American Migrants, Community, and Working-Class Activism in Cleveland, 1915–45* (Urbana: University of Illinois Press, 1999); Todd Michney, *Neighborhoods: Black Upward Mobility in Cleveland, 1900–1980* (Chapel Hill: University of North Carolina Press, 2016); Richard Walter Thomas, *Life for Us Is What We Make It: Building Black Community in Detroit, 1915–1945* (Bloomington: Indiana University Press, 1993); Victoria Wolcott, *Remaking Respectability: African American Women in Interwar Detroit* (Chapel Hill: University of North Carolina Press, 2001); Thomas J. Sugrue, *The Origins of the Urban Crisis: Race and Inequality in Postwar Detroit* (Princeton: Princeton University Press, 1996); Beth T. Bates, *The Making of Black Detroit in the Age of Henry Ford* (Chapel Hill: University of North Carolina Press, 2012); Dominic J. Capeci, Jr., and Martha Wilkerson, *Layered Violence: The Detroit Riot of 1943* (Jackson: University of Mississippi Press, 1991); William Tuttle, Jr., *Race Riot: Chicago in the Red Hot Summer of 1919* (New York: Atheneum, 1970); Keisha N. Blain, *Set the World on Fire: Black Nationalist Women and the Global Struggle for Freedom* (Philadelphia: University of Pennsylvania Press, 2018); Taylor, *Race and the City*; John Bodnar, Roger Simon, and Michael Weber, *Lives of Their Own: Blacks, Italians, and Poles in Pittsburgh, 1900–1960* (Urbana: University of Illinois Press, 1982); William Powell Jones, *The March on Washington: Jobs, Freedom, and the Forgotten History of Civil*

Rights (New York: W. W. Norton, 2014); Joe William Trotter, Jr., *River Jordan: African American Urban Life in the Ohio Valley* (Lexington: University Press of Kentucky, 1998); Joe William Trotter, Jr., *Black Milwaukee: The Making of an Industrial Proletariat, 1915–45* (1985; repr., Urbana: University of Illinois Press, 2007); Ula Y. Taylor, *The Promise of Patriarchy: Women and the Nation of Islam* (Chapel Hill: University of North Carolina Press, 2017), 1–6; Erik S. McDuffie, *Sojourning for Freedom: Black Women, American Communism, and the Making of Black Left Feminism* (Durham: Duke University Press, 2011), 1–24; Ashley D. Farmer, *Remaking Black Power: How Black Women Transformed an Era* (Chapel Hill: University of North Carolina Press, 2017); Deborah Gray White, *Too Heavy a Load: Black Women in Defense of Themselves, 1894–1994* (New York: W. W. Norton, 1999).

2. Reed, *The Rise of Chicago's Black Metropolis*, 30–31; Spear, *Black Chicago*, 221.

3. "Petition Parley Is Stormy One: Opposed Playground Plan in Areas in Which Negroes Have Bought Lots," October 10, 1944; "Plan for Play Area Assailed: Negro Group Resolution," September 1944; "Rally Attacks 'Racial Action': City Hall is Target," September 11, 1944, all in *Milwaukee Journal*.

4. Joe W. Trotter, "African Americans in Cities," in Goldfield, *Encyclopedia of American Urban History*, 9–15.

5. Jeffrey Hegelson, *Crucibles of Black Empowerment: Chicago's Neighborhood Politics from the New Deal to Harold Washington* (Chicago: University of Chicago Press, 2014), 31; Reed, *The Rise of Chicago's Black* Metropolis, 29–30; Spear, *Black Chicago*, 22, 25, 150, 210–12.

6. Baldwin, *Chicago's New Negroes*, 15–16; Tuttle, *Race Riot*; Spear, *Black Chicago*, 214–15.

7. Capeci and Wilkerson, *Layered Violence*, 3–31; Sugrue, *The Origins of the Urban Crisis*, 73–74; Thomas, *Life for Us Is What We Make It*, 146–47.

8. Trotter, *River Jordan*, 143.

9. Robin F. Bachin, *Building the South Side: Urban Space and Civic Culture in Chicago, 1890–1919* (Chicago: University of Chicago Press, 2004), quote, 256; Khalil Gibran Muhammad, *The Condemnation of Blackness: Race, Crime, and the Making of Modern Urban America* (Cambridge, MA: Harvard University Press, 2010), 226–27; Cynthia M. Blair, *I've Got to Make My Livin': Black Women's Sex Work in Turn-of-the-Century Chicago* (Chicago: University of Chicago Press, 2010), 53–57, 59, 146, 149–51; Kevin Mumford, *Interzones: Black/White Sex Districts in Chicago and New York in the Early Twentieth Century* (New York: Columbia University Press, 1997), 20–21, 23. Historian Kevin Mumford defines the "vice districts" as "interzones," where "tolerating prostitution" and other forms of vice "served to create a new complex of racial and gendered politics" (21). More specifically, Mumford concludes that interzones were simultaneously "marginal and central," located within African American neighborhoods of often transient residents, Black and white, homosexual and heterosexual, prostitutes and clients (20).

10. Wolcott, *Remaking Respectability*, 103; Trotter, *Black Milwaukee*, 24; Patrick D. Jones, *The Selma of the North: Civil Rights Insurgency in Milwaukee* (Cambridge, MA: Harvard University Press, 2009), 18–20; Katzman, *Before the Ghetto*, 73;

Thomas, *Life for Us Is What We Make It*, 89–93, 110, quote; Olivier Zunz, *The Changing Face of Inequality: Urbanization, Industrial Development, and Immigrants in Detroit, 1880–1920* (Chicago: University of Chicago Press, 1982), 64–65, 392–93; Bates, *The Making of Black Detroit*, 32–36; Spear, *Black Chicago*, 25.

11. Capeci and Wilkerson, *Layered Violence*, 3–31; Sugrue, *The Origins of the Urban Crisis*, 73–74; Thomas, *Life for Us Is What We Make It*, 146–47.

12. Hirsch, *Making the Second Ghetto*, 3–5, 17; Spear, *Black Chicago*, 5, 11–21, 223; Seligman, *Block by Block*, quote, 14–15, 16–17.

13. Katzman, *Before the Ghetto*, 13, 26, 59.

14. Katzman, *Before the Ghetto*, 74, 77–78; Bates, *The Making of Black Detroit*, 101–3, quote, 101.

15. Trotter, *River Jordan*, 106; Joe W. Trotter and Jared N. Day, *Race and Renaissance: African Americans in Pittsburgh since World War II* (Pittsburgh: University of Pittsburgh Press, 2010), 13.

16. Kusmer, *A Ghetto Takes Shape*, 61–65, 135; Phillips, *AlabamaNorth*, 146–48.

17. Trotter, *River Jordan*, 106.

18. Reed, *The Rise of Chicago's Black Metropolis*, 27, 63.

19. Reed, *The Rise of Chicago's Black Metropolis*, 28, 39.

20. Henry Louis Taylor, Jr., "City Building, Public Policy, the Rise of the Industrial City, and Black Ghetto Formation in Cincinnati, 1850–1940," in Taylor, *Race and the City*, 174–75; Henry Louis Taylor, "Creating the Metropolis in Black and White: Black Suburbanization and the Planning Movement in Cincinnati, 1900–1950," in H. L. Taylor and Walter Hill, eds., *Historical Roots of the Urban Crisis: African Americans in the Industrial City, 1900–1950* (New York: Garland Publishing Company, 2000), 55.

21. Taylor, "Creating the Metropolis in Black and White," 59–63, and "City Building, Public Policy," 175.

22. Phillips, *AlabamaNorth*, 135–36.

23. Bodnar, Simon, and Weber, *Lives of Their Own*, 179.

24. "Black Home Ownership Rates in Selected Cities," in Quintard Taylor, *In Search of the Racial Frontier: African Americans in the American West, 1528–1990* (New York: W. W. Norton, 1998), 233; Drake and Cayton, *Black Metropolis*, 663–64; Bodnar, Simon, and Weber, *Lives of Their Own*, 179.

25. Taylor, "Introduction," in Taylor, *Race and the City*, 14.

26. Hirsch, *Making the Second Ghetto*, 128–30.

27. Thomas, *Life for Us Is What We Make It*, 316–17.

28. Spear, *Black Chicago*, 91–93, 178; Trotter, *Black Milwaukee*, 129–30; Thomas, *Life for Us Is What We Make It*, 178.

29. Trotter, *Black Milwaukee*, quote, 129–30.

30. Trotter, *Black Milwaukee*, 130–31; Thomas, *Life for Us Is What We Make It*, 178–79.

31. Wallace D. Best, *Passionately Human, No Less Divine: Religion and Culture in Black Chicago, 1915–1952* (Princeton: Princeton University Press, 2005), 1–11,

71–93, 118–46; Milton C. Sernett, *Bound for the Promised Land: African American Religion and the Great Migration* (Durham: Duke University Press, 1997), 101–3; Spear, *Black Chicago*, 175–79; Reed, *The Rise of Chicago's Black Metropolis*, 186–200; Collier-Thomas, *Jesus, Jobs, and Justice*, 84, 117–18. On Urban League programs to reshape the culture of poor and working class black migrants, see Touré Reed, *Not Alms but Opportunity: The Urban League and the Politics of Racial Uplift, 1910–1950* (Chapel Hill: University of North Carolina Press, 2008), 35.

32. Thomas, *Life for Us Is What We Make It*, 178–79.

33. Theda Skocpol, Ariane Liazos, and Marshall Ganz, *What a Might Power We Can Be: African American Fraternal Groups and the Struggle for Racial Equality* (Princeton: Princeton University Press, 2006), 1–20; Joe William Trotter, Jr., "African American Fraternal Orders in American History: An Introduction," *Social Science History* 28, no. 3 (January 2004): 355–66; Spear, *Black Chicago*, 107–8; Trotter, *Black Milwaukee*, 31–32, 131–32; Katzman, *Before the Ghetto*, 147–49.

34. Trotter, *Black Milwaukee*, 64–65, 72; Joe William Trotter, Jr., *Pittsburgh and the Urban League Movement: A Century of Social Service and Activism* (Pittsburgh: University of Pittsburgh Press, 2020), 34; Andrew Buni, *Robert L. Vann of the Pittsburgh Courier: Politics and Black Journalism* (Pittsburgh: University of Pittsburgh Press, 1974), 32.

35. Kusmer, *A Ghetto Takes Shape*, 254–55.

36. Phillips, *AlabamaNorth*, 92–95, 157–58; Kusmer, *A Ghetto Takes Shape*, 257.

37. Trotter, *River Jordan*, 88; Trotter, *Pittsburgh and the Urban League Movement*, 34.

38. Trotter, *Black Milwaukee*, 83–93, quote, 91.

39. Kusmer, *A Ghetto Takes Shape*, 192–95.

40. Kusmer, *A Ghetto Takes Shape*, 193–95.

41. Wendell Dabney, *Cincinnati's Colored Citizens* (1926; reprt. New York: Negro Universities Press, 1970), 142–43, 193, 237.

42. Dabney, *Cincinnati's Colored Citizens*, 241, 284, 290, 291, 293, 303.

43. Thomas, *Life for Us Is What We Make It*, 203–4.

44. Thomas, *Life for Us Is What We Make It*, 185, 203–4. Some of Detroit's Black entrepreneurs operated businesses in the heart of the East Side, but lived elsewhere. See Capeci and Wilkerson, *Layered Violence*, 109–10.

45. Reed, The Rise of Chicago's Black Metropolis, 96.

46. Reed, *The Rise of Chicago's Black Metropolis*, 54, 77–78, 96, 98–99, 116; Baldwin, *Chicago's New Negroes*, 44–52.

47. Buni, *Robert L. Vann of the Pittsburgh Courier*, 171–73.

48. West, *A House for the Struggle*, 2–3.

49. Kusmer, *A Ghetto Takes Shape*, 130–32, 194; Dabney, *Cincinnati's Colored Citizens*, 188–90, 197–98, 404.

50. White, *Too Heavy a Load*; Hine and Thompson, *A Shining Thread of Hope*; Kevin Gaines, *Uplifting the Race: Black Leadership, Politics, and Culture in the Twentieth Century* (Chapel Hill: University of North Carolina Press, 1996); David Levering Lewis, *W. E. B. Du Bois: Biography of a Race, 1868–1919* (New York: Henry

Holt and Company, 1993); David Levering Lewis, *W. E. B. Du Bois: A Biography, 1868–1963* (New York: Henry Holt, 2000); Charles F. Kellogg, *NAACP: A History of the National Association for the Advancement of Colored People* (Baltimore: Johns Hopkins Press, 1967); Reed, *Not Alms but Opportunity*; Shawn Leigh Alexander, *An Army of Lions: The Civil Rights Struggle before the NAACP* (Philadelphia: University of Pennsylvania Press, 2013).

51. Reed, *Rise of Chicago's Black Metropolis*, 183; Thomas, *Life for Us Is What We Make It*, 197; Trotter, *Black Milwaukee*, 125.

52. William T. Green, "Negroes in Milwaukee," in Milwaukee County Historical Society, ed., *The Negro in Milwaukee: A Historical Survey* (Milwaukee: Milwaukee County Historical Society, 1968), 5–11; "Bios of Important People," the Learning Center, the Wisconsin Black Historical Society, online, August 2020; Trotter, *Black Milwaukee*, 19–20, 206.

53. Thomas, *Life for Us Is What We Make It*, 116–17.

54. Baldwin, *Chicago's New Negroes*, 44–52, 209–23, quotes, 50; Blair, *I've Got to Make My Livin'*, 159–75; Harold F. Gosnell, *Negro Politicians; The Rise of Negro Politics in Chicago* (Chicago, University of Chicago Press, 1967), 115–35.

55. Blair, *I've Got to Make My Livin'*, 175–76.

56. Davarian Baldwin and Minkah Makalani, eds., *Escape from New York: The New Negro Renaissance beyond Harlem*, with a foreword by Robin D. G. Kelley (Minneapolis: University of Minnesota Press, 2013); Gaines, *Uplifting the Race*; Locke, *The New Negro*,; and Baldwin, introduction to *Chicago's New Negroes*, 1–19.

57. Reprint of W. E. B. Du Bois's *Crisis* editorial, "We Return Fighting," *Wisconsin Enterprise Blade*, June 5, 1919.

58. Trotter, *Black Milwaukee*, 106–7, 108.

59. Spear, *Black Chicago*, 185–86, 193.

60. Spear, *Black Chicago*, 185–86, 193; Kevin Boyle, *Arc of Justice: A Saga of Race, Civil Rights, and Murder in the Jazz Age* (New York: H. Holt, 2004), 17–43; Thomas, *Life for Us Is What We Make It*, quote, 138–40, 230–31.

61. Thomas, *Life for Us Is What We Make It*, 230–32.

62. Arvarh E. Strickland, *History of the Chicago Urban League* (Columbia: University of Missouri Press, 1966), 95–96; Wolcott, *Remaking Respectability*, 176–79, quote, 176; Baldwin, *Chicago's New Negroes*, 237–39; Jeffrey Helgeson, *Crucibles of Black Empowerment: Chicago's Neighborhood Politics from the New Deal to Harold Washington* (Chicago: University of Chicago Press, 2014), 55–58.

63. Drake and Cayton, *Black Metropolis*, 87. Also see Thomas, *Life for Us Is What We Make It*, 96; Dianne M. Pinderhughes, *Race and Ethnicity in Chicago Politics: A Reexamination of Pluralist Theory* (Urbana: University of Illinois Press, 1987), 123–24.

64. Erik S. Gellman, *Death Blow to Jim Crow: The National Negro Congress and the Rise of Militant Civil Rights* (Chapel Hill: University of North Carolina Press, 2012), 1–17.

65. Gellman, *Death Blow to Jim Crow*, 6, 17, 19, 206–7; Thomas, *Life for Us Is What We Make It*, 232, quote, 251–52, 280, 298; Helgeson, *Crucibles of Black Empowerment*, 67–70.

66. Steve Nelson, James R. Barrett, and Rob Ruck, *Steve Nelson: American Radical* (Pittsburgh: University of Pittsburgh Press, 1992), 25; Philip Bonosky, "The Story of Ben Careathers," *Masses and Mainstream*, 6 (July 1953): 34–44, repr. in Philip S. Foner and Ronald L. Lewis, eds., *The Black Worker from the Founding of the CIO to the AFL-CIO Merger 1936–1955, Vol. II* (Philadelphia: Temple University Press, 1983), 46–48; Philip S. Foner, *Organized Labor and the Black Worker, 1619–1973* (New York: Proeger Publishers, 1974), 219–237.

67. Trotter, *Black Milwaukee*, 120–22.

68. Buni, *Robert L. Vann of the Pittsburgh Courier*, 127–128.

69. Kusmer, *A Ghetto Takes Shape*, 145–48. Cf. Phillips, *AlabamaNorth*, 20, 164–65, 200.

70. Kusmer, *A Ghetto Takes Shape*, 145–48.

71. Trotter, *River Jordan*, 116.

72. Helgeson, *Crucibles of Black Empowerment*, 35–37; Spear, *Black Chicago*, 118–28; Gosnell, *Negro Politicians*, 163–80; Reed, *The Rise of Chicago's Black Metropolis*, 147–62; Lisa G. Matterson, *For the Freedom of Her Race: Black Women and Electoral Politics in Illinois, 1877–1932* (Chapel Hill: University of North Carolina Press, 2009), 95–96.

73. Trotter, *Black Milwaukee*, 120–22, 211–12; Thomas, *Life for Us Is What We Make It*, 229.

74. Thomas, *Life for Us Is What We Make It*, 253–54; Bates, *The Making of Black Detroit*, 5, 124, 173–74 178–79, 196–98; August Meier and Elliott Rudwick, *Black Detroit and the Rise of the UAW* (1979; repr., Ann Arbor: University of Michigan Press, 2007), 40–44.

75. Trotter, *Black Milwaukee*, 121–22, 1; Thomas, *Life for Us Is What We Make It*, 67–68, 253–54, 258.

76. Gosnell, *Negro Politicians*, 29–36; Buni, *Robert L. Vann of the Pittsburgh Courier*, 174–202; Drake and Cayton, *Black Metropolis*, 351–76; Martin Kilson, "Politics Change in the Negro Ghetto, 1900–1940s," in Nathan Huggins et al., eds., *Key Issues in the Afro-American Experience: Vol. 2* (New York: Harcourt Brace Jovanovich, 1971), 189–91; Hanes Walton, *Black Politics: A Theoretical and Structural Analysis* (Philadelphia: Lippincott Company, 1972), 115–16; Nancy J. Weiss, *Farewell to the Party of Lincoln: Black Politics in the Age of FDR* (Princeton: Princeton University Press, 1983), 78–95, 186–208; Reed, *Rise of Chicago's Black Metropolis*, 148–49; Gosnell, *Negro Politicians*, 67–114, 136–52; Spear, *Black Chicago*, 186–92; Weiss, *Farewell to the Party of Lincoln*, 3–33.

77. Blain, *Set the World on Fire*, 1–10.

78. Taylor, *The Promise of Patriarchy*, 3–6.

79. McDuffie, *Sojourning for Freedom*, 3–23; Farmer, *Remaking Black Power*, 14, 21, 20–28, 42.

80. Jones, *The March on Washington*, 41–78; Jervis Anderson, *A. Philip Randolph: A Biographical Portrait* (1972; reprt. Berkeley: University of California Press, 1986), 241–73; Foner, *Organized Labor and the Black Worker*, 239–42; Harvard Sitkoff, *A New Deal for Blacks: The Emergence of Civil Rights as a National Issue: The Depression Decade* (New York: Oxford University Press, 1978), 314–15.

81. Jones, *The March on Washington*, ix–xxi; Buni, *Robert L. Vann of Pittsburgh Courier: Politics and Black Journalism* (Pittsburgh: University of Pittsburgh Press, 1974), 325–26; Richard M. Dalfiume, "The Forgotten Years of the Negro Revolution," in Bernard Sternsher, ed., *The Negro in Depression and War: Prelude to Revolutin, 1930–1945* (Chicago: Quadrangle Books, 1969), 298–316.

82. A. Philip Randolph, "March for a Fair Share: The March on Washington Movement, 1941," repr. in Thomas R. Frazier, ed., *Afro-American History: Primary Sources* (Chicago: Dorsey Press, 1988), 291–98.

83. A. Philip Randolph, "Why Should We March," *Survey Graphic*, 31 (November 1942), repr. in Foner and Lewis, eds., *The Black Worker*, 251–52.

84. Randolph, "March for a Fair Share," quote, 295.

85. Anderson, *A. Philip Randolph*, 256–58.

86. Foner, *Organized Labor and the Black Worker*, 256; William H. Harris, *The Harder We Run: Black Workers since the Civil War* (New York: Oxford University Press, 1982), 113–22; Foner and Lewis, eds., *The Black Worker*, 251–300.

87. Trotter, *River Jordan*, 44–45.

88. Katzman, *Before the Ghetto*, 38–39; Drake and Cayton, *Black Metropolis*, 32, 34–35.

89. Trotter, *Black Milwaukee*, xlii.

CHAPTER SEVEN

1. Douglas Flamming, *Bound for Freedom: Black Los Angeles in Jim Crow America* (Berkeley: University of California Press, 2005); Albert S. Broussard, *Black San Francisco: The Struggle for Racial Equality in the West, 1900–1954* (Lawrence: University Press of Kansas, 1993); Douglas H. Daniels, *Pioneer Urbanites: A Social and Cultural History of Black San Francisco* (Philadelphia: Temple University Press, 1980); Shirley Ann Wilson Moore, *To Place Our Deeds: The African American Community of Richmond, California, 1910–1963* (Berkeley: University of California Press, 2000); Quintard Taylor, *The Forging of a Black Community: Seattle's Central District from 1870 through the Civil Rights Era* (Seattle: University of Washington Press, 1994); Taylor, *In Search of the Racial Frontier*; Pruitt, *The Other Great Migration*; SoRelle, "The Darker Side of 'Heaven'"; Connolly, *A World More Concrete*; Rutkoff and Scott, *Fly Away*; Ellsworth, *Death in the Promised Land*; H. Johnson, *Black Wall Street*; Donna Murch, *Living for the City: Migration, Education, and the Rise of the Black Panther Party in Oakland, California* (Chapel Hill: University of North Carolina Press, 2010); Charles E. Jones, *The Black Panther Party [Reconsidered]* (Baltimore: Black Classic Press, 1998); Peniel E. Joseph, *Waiting 'til the Mid-*

night Hour: A Narrative History of Black Power in America (New York: Henry Holt, 2006); Joshua Bloom and Waldo Martin, *Black Against Empire: The History and Politics of the Black Panther Party* (Berkeley: University of California, 2013); Robyn Spencer, *The Revolution Has Come: Black Power, Gender, and the Black Panther Party in Oakland* (Durham: Duke University Press, 2016); Mindy T. Fullilove, *Root Shock: How Tearing Up City Neighborhoods Hurts America, and What We Can Do about It* (New York: Ballantine Books, One World, 2005); Joshua Sides, *L.A. City Limits* (Berkeley: University of California Press, 2003); Robert Self, *American Babylon: Race and the Struggle for Postwar Oakland* (Princeton: Princeton University Press, 2003); Scott Kurashige, *The Shifting Grounds of Race: Politics and Society in Modern America* (Princeton: Princeton University Press, 2010); Peniel E. Joseph, ed., *The Black Power Movement: Rethinking the Civil Rights–Black Power Era* (New York: Routledge, 2006); Nico Slate, ed., *Black Power beyond Borders: The Global Dimensions of Black Power* (New York: Palgrave Macmillan, 2012).

2. State of California, *Task Force to Develop Reparations Proposals for African Americans: Final Report* (2023), 78.

3. Flamming, *Bound for Freedom*, 51.

4. Broussard, *Black San Francisco*, 11.

5. Daniels, *Pioneer Urbanites*, 25.

6. Daniels, *Pioneer Urbanites*, 25–26; Broussard, *Black San Francisco*, 14.

7. Daniels, *Pioneer Urbanites*, 26, 30; Broussard, *Black San Francisco*, 14.

8. Daniels, *Pioneer Urbanites*, 24, 99.

9. Broussard, *Black San Francisco*, 29–30.

10. Broussard, *Black San Francisco*, 29–30.

11. Taylor, *The Forging of a Black Community*, 17, 19.

12. Flamming, *Bound for Freedom*, 20–21, 23, quotes, 66.

13. Flamming, *Bound for Freedom*; Taylor, *The Forging of a Black Community*, 34–35.

14. Flamming, *Bound for Freedom*, 20–21, 23, quotes, 66.

15. Flamming, *Bound for Freedom*, 68, 78–81.

16. By 1910, some 36 percent of Black Los Angelenos owned their own homes, the largest percentage in the state and more than double and even triple the rate in the northeast and midwest (Flamming, *Bound for Freedom*, 51).

17. Taylor, *Forging of a Black Community*, 86.

18. Flamming, *Bound for Freedom*, 377.

19. Moore, *To Place Our Deeds*, 113–14.

20. As elsewhere, Black urban westerners rented property and built their own homes against the backdrop of extraordinary forms of housing discrimination along the color line. By 1930, about 14 percent of Afro-San Franciscans owned their own homes compared to 35 percent for American-born whites and about 42 percent for immigrants. According to historian Albert Broussard, African Americans were "several notches down the ladder" from whites in housing quality, but the Chinese occupied "the bottom rung. . . . The Chinese perhaps suffered most in their pitifully overcrowded conditions" (*Black San Francisco*, 31).

21. Daniels, *Pioneer Urbanites*, 102–3.

22. Daniels, *Pioneer Urbanites*, 169, Broussard, *Black San Francisco*, 167, 172.

23. Taylor, *The Forging of a Black Community*, 32, 82.

24. Taylor, *The Forging of a Black Community*, 83–84, 87.

25. Taylor, *The Forging of a Black Community*, 32–34, 82, 84.

26. Taylor, *The Forging of a Black Community*, 84.

27. Flamming, *Bound for Freedom*, 66–67.

28. Flamming, *Bound for Freedom*, 221–25.

29. Flamming, *Bound for Freedom*, 239–41.

30. Broussard, *Black San Francisco*, 30–31, 222–39; Flamming, *Bound for Freedom*, 98, 101–2, 155–56; Daniels, *Pioneer Urbanites*, 104, 170; Taylor, *Forging a Black Community*, 67, 177–78, 230–31.

31. Daniels, *Pioneer Urbanites*, 170; Broussard, *Black San Francisco*, 30–31.

32. Broussard, *Black San Francisco*, 30–31, 222, 239; Flamming, *Bound for Freedom*, 98, 101–2, 155–56; Daniels, *Pioneer Urbanites*, 104, 170; Taylor, *Forging of a Black Community*, 67, 177–78, 230–31.

33. Broussard, *Black San Francisco*, 175.

34. Fullilove, *Root Shock*, 4–5; Sides, *L.A. City Limits*, 118–20; Self, *American Babylon*, quote, 137.

35. Self, *American Babylon*, 137–49.

36. Flamming, *Bound for Freedom*, 378; Isabelle Wilkerson, *The Warmth of Other Suns: The Epic Story of America's Great Migration* (New York: Random House, 2010), 8–15; Rutkoff and Scott, *The Great African American Migration*, 11–14; James N. Gregory, *The Southern Diaspora: How the Great Migrations of Black and White Southerners Transformed America* (Chapel Hill: University of North Carolina Press, 2005), 11–41; Ira Berlin, *The Making of African America: The Four Great Migrations* (New York: Viking Books, 2010), 152–200.

37. Sides, *L.A. City Limits*, 121, 127; Taylor, *In Search of the Racial Frontier*, 286–87; Kurashige, *The Shifting Grounds of Race*, 274–75.

38. Taylor, *In Search of the Racial Frontier*, 254, 286–87; Taylor, *The Forging of a Black Community*, 160, 192; Daniels, *Pioneer Urbanites*, 165; Broussard, *Black San Francisco*, 24.

39. Taylor, *In Search of the Racial Frontier*, 254, 286–87; Taylor, *Forging of a Black Community*, 160, 170, 192; Daniels, *Pioneer Urbanites*, 165; Broussard, *Black San Francisco*, 24.

40. Flamming, *Bound for Freedom*, 110–13. The first AME church represented a major architectural landmark in the city: "From the street, a broad sweep of steps climbed to three large doorways, which led into an expansive sanctuary four stories high, with a slanting A-frame ceiling and an elegant bank of stained-glass windows on the street side. Adjacent to the main foyer, a commanding bell tower reached even higher, capped by four dramatic spires. In back of all that were the offices, Sunday-school rooms, and other departments of the church, all topped by another towering steeple."

41. Flamming, *Bound for Freedom*, 26, 113.

42. Taylor, *Forging of a Black Community*, 137–39, 242; "First African Methodist Episcopal (AME) Church, Seattle, Washington," church website, January 2, 2021.

43. Reyhan Harmanci, "Celebrating Where San Francisco's Black Roots Run Deepest," *New York Times*, March 3, 2012; "Third Baptist Church of San Francisco," thirdbaptist.org/update/history, January 2, 2021; Net Ministries Network, "First African Methodist Episcopal Zion Church," online, January 2, 2021.

44. Broussard, *Black San Francisco*, 54–55, 63–64; Moore, *To Place Our Deeds*, 27, 113, 140; Daniels, *Pioneer Urbanites*, 112–13, 118–19; Gretchen Lemke-Santangelo, *Abiding Courage: African American Migrant Women and the East Bay Community* (Chapel Hill: University of North Carolina Press, 1996), 159–60; Flamming, *Bound for Freedom*, 115.

45. Flamming, *Bound for Freedom*, 26; Taylor, *Forging of a Black Community*, 139–40.

46. Daniels, *Pioneer Urbanites*, 30, 46, 48; Broussard, *Black San Francisco*, 56–57.

47. Daniels, *Pioneer Urbanites*, 47–48.

48. Moore, *To Place Our Deeds*, 22; Santangelo, *Abiding Courage*, 73–74; Taylor, *Forging of a Black Community*, 71–73.

49. Flamming, *Bound for Freedom*, 87, 118, 121–22, 284, 296–97, 377.

50. Flamming, *Bound for Freedom*, 25, 119, 306.

51. Broussard, *Black San Francisco*, 233.

52. Broussard, *Black San Francisco*, 28, 46, 182–83, 232–34.

53. Moore, *To Place Our Deeds*, 14–15, 74–75.

54. Taylor, *Forging of a Black Community*, 28, 30–31.

55. As early as 1888, the Los Angeles *Weekly Observer* roundly applauded the opening of Frank Blackburn's "coffee and chop house" at First and Los Angeles Streets and urged Black people to patronize this and other Black businesses in the city (Flamming, *Bound for Freedom*, 118).

56. Taylor, *Forging of a Black Community*, 19–21, 71–73.

57. Daniels, *Pioneer Urbanites*, 116, 217; Moore, *To Place Our Deeds*, 50.

58. Flamming, *Bound for Freedom*, 26–27, 104.

59. Flamming, *Bound for Freedom*, 108.

60. Flamming, *Bound for Freedom*, 117.

61. Flamming, *Bound for Freedom*, 253; Robert E. Weems, Jr., *Desegregating the Dollar* (New York: New York University Press, 1998), 18–19; Lizabeth Cohen, *A Consumers' Republic: The Politics of Mass Consumption in Postwar America* (New York: Alfred A. Knopf, 2003), 44–47; Taylor, *Forging of a Black Community*, 198–99.

62. See Broussard, *Blacks in San Francisco*, 92–112; Flamming, *Bound for Freedom*, 321–22; Taylor, *Forging of a Black Community*, 102–4; Connolly, *A World More Concrete*, 91–93; Pruitt, *The Other Great Migration*, 271–74

63. Trotter, *The African American Experience*, 548, 550.

64. Joan Singler, Jean C. Durning, Bettylou Valentine, and Martha (Maid) J. Adams, *Seattle in Black and White: The Congress of Racial Equality and the Fight for*

Equal Opportunity (Seattle: University of Washington Press, 2011), 8–9, 126–33; Taylor, *Forging of a Black Community*, 205–6.

65. Jones, *The Black Panther Party [Reconsidered]*, 37; Joseph, *Waiting 'til the Midnight Hour*, 66–67, 92–94; Bloom and Martin, *Black against Empire*, 197–98; Spencer, *The Revolution Has Come*, 52–55.

66. Spencer, *The Revolution Has Come*, quote, 1, 25–34; 52–55; Murch, *Living for the City*, 4–5, 15–68; Self, *American Babylon*, 217–55; Jones, *The Black Panther Party [Reconsidered]*, 37; Bloom and Martin, *Black against Empire*, 146–47 (Seattle), 149–48 (Los Angeles), 197.

67. Murch, *Living for the City*, 4; Self, *American Babylon*, 217; Jeffrey O. G. Ogbar, "Rainbow Radicalism: The Rise of the Radical Ethnic Nationalism," in Joseph, *The Black Power Movement*, 193–228; Slate, *Black Power beyond Borders*, 1–33.

68. Nico Slate, "The Dalit Panthers: Race, Caste, and Black Power in India," 127–28; Robbie Shillian, "The Polynesian Panthers and the Black Power Gang: Surviving Racism and Colonialism in Aotearoa New Zealand," 107–11; Oz Frankel, "The Black Panthers of Israel and the Politics of the Radical Analogy," 81–83, all in Slate, *Black Power beyond Borders*.

69. Taylor, *In Search of the Racial Frontier*, 315.

CONCLUSION

1. William H. Frey, *Diversity Explosion: How New Racial Demographics Are Remaking America* (Washington, DC: Brookings Institution, 2015), 17, 154–55; U.S. Census Bureau Reports, 1970–2010.

2. Berlin, *The Making of African America*, 201–2; Wilkerson, *The Warmth of Other Suns*, 486–87; Gregory, *The Southern Diaspora*, 322–23; James S. Hirsch and Suzanne Alexander, "Reverse Exodus: Middle Class Blacks Quit Northern Cities and Settle in the South," *Wall Street Journal*, May 22, 1990; Michelle Nickerson and Darren Dochuk, eds., *Sunbelt Rising: The Politics of Space, Place, and Region* (Philadelphia: University of Pennsylvania Press, 2011), 1–28; Carol Stack, *Call to Home: African Americans Reclaim the Rural South* (New York: Basic Books, 1996), xi–xii, 25–26, 118; Sabrina Pendergrass, *The Black Reverse Migration Unfolds: Black Americans Move to the Urban South* (New York: Oxford University Press, forthcoming).

3. Mary Pattillo, *Black on the Block: The Politics of Race and Class in the City* (Chicago: University of Chicago Press, 2007), 4–5; Fullilove, *Root Shock*, 188; Trotter and Day, *Race and Renaissance*, 154, 182–83.

4. Andrew Wiese, *Places of Their Own: African American Suburbanization in the Twentieth Century* (Chicago: University of Chicago Press, 2004), 254.

5. Wiese, *Places of Their Own*, 256–57.

6. Taylor, *Race for Profit*, 1–23; Jones, *A Dreadful Deceit*, 292.

7. Jones, *A Dreadful Deceit*, 292; Sabrina Deitrick, "Cultural Change in Pittsburgh: A Demographic Analysis at City and County Scales," working paper, PDF, vol. 53, no. 2 (Fall-Winter 2015), 80, accessed online, February 10, 201; Urban League

of Pittsburgh, *Annual Report: 1999* (Pittsburgh, PA), 8–9; Jim McKinnon, "Ex-foes Unite against Sanders Agreement," *Pittsburgh Post-Gazette*, May 4, 1999, accessed online, January 25, 2018; Urban League of Pittsburgh, *Annual Report: 2000* (Pittsburgh, PA), 8–9, 15–19; Hesalyn Hunts, Ralph Bangs, and Ken Thompson, "The Health Status of African Americans in Allegheny County: A Black Paper for the Urban League of Pittsburgh," January 2002; Trista N. Sims, "Health Problems among African American Women Age 35–64 in Allegheny County: A Black Paper for the Urban League of Pittsburgh," January 2002.

8. Wiese, *Places of Their Own*, 282–84; Todd Michney, *Surrogate Suburbs: Black Upward Mobility and Neighborhood Change in Cleveland, 1900–1980* (Chapel Hill: University of North Carolina Press, 2017), 207–12.

9. Donna M. Owens, "Activists Chart Course for Black America's Progress after a Year of Turmoil," *USA Today*, February 1, 2021.

SELECTED BIBLIOGRAPHY

Alexander, Leslie M. *African or American? Black Identity and Political Activism in New York City, 1784–1861.* Urbana: University of Illinois Press, 2008.

Alexander, Michelle. *The New Jim Crow: Mass Incarceration in the Age of Colorblindness.* New York: The New Press, 2010.

Anderson, Jean Bradley. *Durham County: A History of Durham County, North Carolina.* Durham: Duke University Press, 1990.

Anderson, Sean, and Mabel O. Wilson. *Reconstructions: Architecture and Blackness in America.* New York: The Museum of Modern Art, 2021.

Asch, Chris Myers, and George Derek Musgrove. *Chocolate City: A History of Race and Democracy in the Nation's Capital.* Chapel Hill: University of North Carolina Press, 2017.

Ayers, Edward L. *The Promise of the New South: Life after Reconstruction.* New York: Oxford University Press, 1992.

Bachin, Robin F. *Building the South Side: Urban Space and Civic Culture in Chicago, 1890–1919.* Chicago: University of Chicago Press, 2004.

Baldwin, Davarian L. *Chicago's New Negroes: Modernity, the Great Migration, and Black Urban Life.* Chapel Hill: University of North Carolina Press, 2007.

Balto, Simon. *Occupied Territory: Policing Black Chicago from Red Summer to Black Power.* Chapel Hill: University of North Carolina Press, 2019.

Bates, Beth T. *The Making of Black Detroit in the Age of Henry Ford.* Chapel Hill: University of North Carolina Press, 2012.

Bayor, Ronald H. *Race and the Shaping of Twentieth-Century Atlanta.* Chapel Hill: University of North Carolina, 1996.

Berlin, Ira. *The Making of African America: The Four Great Migrations.* New York: Viking Books, 2010.

———. *Many Thousands Gone: The First Two Centuries of Slavery in North America.* Cambridge, MA: Harvard University Press, 1998.

———. *Slaves without Masters: The Free Negro in the Antebellum South.* 1974; repr., New York: The New Press, 1992.

Blain, Keisha N. *Set the World on Fire: Black Nationalist Women and the Global Struggle for Freedom*. Philadelphia: University of Pennsylvania Press, 2018.

Blair, Cynthia M. *I've Got to Make My Livin': Black Women's Sex Work in Turn-of-the-Century Chicago*. Chicago: University of Chicago Press, 2010.

Blassingame, John W. *Black New Orleans, 1860–1880*. Chicago: University of Chicago Press, 1973.

Bloom, Joshua, and Waldo Martin. *Black against Empire: The History and Politics of the Black Panther Party*. Berkeley: University of California, 2013.

Bodnar, John, Roger Simon, and Michael Weber. *Lives of Their Own: Blacks, Italians, and Poles in Pittsburgh, 1900–1960*. Urbana: University of Illinois Press, 1982.

Bordewich, Fergus M. *The Underground Railroad and the War for the Soul of America*. New York: HarpersCollins, 2005.

Bridenbaugh, Carl. *Cities in the Wilderness: The First Century of Urban Life in America, 1625–1742*. New York: The Ronald Press Company, 1938.

Broussard, Albert S. *Black San Francisco: The Struggle for Racial Equality in the West, 1900–1954*. Lawrence: University Press of Kansas, 1993.

Brown, Leslie. *Upbuilding Black Durham: Gender, Class, and Black Community Development in the Jim Crow South*. Chapel Hill: University of North Carolina Press, 2008.

Brown, Letitia. *Free Negroes in the District of Columbia, 1790–1846*. New York: Oxford University Press, 1972.

Brown, Ras M. *African-Atlantic Cultures and the South Carolina Lowcountry*. New York: Cambridge University Press, 2012.

Buchanan, Thomas C. *Slaves, Free Blacks, and the Western Steamboat World*. Chapel Hill: University of North Carolina Press, 2004.

Buni, Andrew. *Robert L. Vann of the Pittsburgh Courier: Politics and Black Journalism*. Pittsburgh: University of Pittsburgh Press, 1974.

Burrows, Edwin G., and Mike Wallace. *Gotham: A History of New York City to 1898*. New York: Oxford University Press, 1999.

Campbell, James. *Middle Passages: African American Journeys to Africa, 1787–2005*. New York: Penguin Press, 2006.

Cañizares-Esguerra, Jorge, Matt D. Childs, and James Sidbury, eds. *The Black Urban Atlantic in the Age of the Slave Trade*. Philadelphia: University of Pennsylvania Press, 2013.

Capeci, Dominic J., Jr., and Martha Wilkerson. *Layered Violence: The Detroit Riot of 1943*. Jackson: University of Mississippi Press, 1991.

Carp, Benjamin L. *Rebels Rising: Cities and the American Revolution*. New York: Oxford University Press, 2007.

Cheng, Irene, Charles L. Davis II, and Mabel O. Wilson, eds. *Race and Modern Architecture: A Critical History from the Enlightenment to the Present*. Pittsburgh: University of Pittsburgh Press, 2020.

Clegg, Claude A., III. *The Price of Liberty: African Americans and the Making of Liberia*. Chapel Hill: University of North Carolina Press, 2004.

Collier-Thomas, Bettye. *Jesus, Jobs, and Justice: African American Women and Religion*. New York: Alfred A. Knopf, 2010.

Connolly, N. D. B. *A World More Concrete: Real Estate and the Making of Jim Crow South Florida*. Chicago: University of Chicago Press, 2014.

Creel, Margaret Washington. *"A Peculiar People": Slave Religion and Community-Culture among the Gullahs*. New York: New York University Press, 1988.

Curry, Leonard. *The Free Black in Urban America, 1800–1850: In the Shadow of the Dream*. New York: University of Chicago Press, 1981.

Dabney, Wendell. *Cincinnati's Colored Citizens*. 1926; repr., New York: Negro Universities Press, 1970.

Daniels, Douglas H. *Pioneer Urbanites: A Social and Cultural History of Black San Francisco*. Philadelphia: Temple University Press, 1980.

Dantas, Mariana L. R. *Black Townsmen: Urban Slavery and Freedom in the Eighteenth-Century Americas*. New York: Palgrave Macmillan, 2008.

Darity, William A., Jr., and A. Kirsten Mullen. *From Here to Equality: Reparations for Black Americans in the Twenty-First Century*. Chapel Hill: University of North Carolina Press, 2020.

Desmond, Matthew. *Evicted: Poverty and Profit in the American City*. New York: Crown Publishers, 2016.

Dorsey, Allison. *To Build Our Lives Together: Community Formation in Black Atlanta, 1875–1906*. Athens: University of Georgia Press, 2004.

Drake, St. Clair, and Horace R. Cayton. *Black Metropolis: A Study of Negro Life in a Northern City*. 1945; repr., Chicago: University of Chicago Press, 1993.

Du Bois, W. E. B. *The Philadelphia Negro: A Social Study*. 1899; repr., Philadelphia: University of Pennsylvania, 1996.

Duck, Waverly. *No Way Out: Precarious Living in the Shadow of Poverty and Drug-Dealing*. Chicago: University of Chicago Press, 2015.

Dudley, Tara A. *Building Antebellum New Orleans: Free People of Color and Their Influence*. Austin: University of Texas Press, 2021.

Egerton, Douglas R. *Death of Liberty: African Americans and Revolutionary America*. New York: Oxford University Press, 2009.

———. *He Shall Go Out Free: The Lives of Denmark Vesey*. 1999; rev. ed., New York: Rowman and Littlefield, 2004.

Ellsworth, Scott. *Death in the Promised Land: The Tulsa Race Riot of 1921*. Baton Rouge: Louisiana State University Press, 1982.

Ervin, Keona K. *Gateway to Equality: Black Women and the Struggle for Economic Justice in St. Louis*. Lexington: University Press of Kentucky, 2017.

Everett, Donald. "Free Persons of Color in Colonial Louisiana." *Louisiana History* 7, no. 1 (1966): 21–50.

Farmer, Ashley D. *Remaking Black Power: How Black Women Transformed an Era*. Chapel Hill: University of North Carolina Press, 2017.

Feldman, Lynne B. *A Sense of Place: Birmingham's Black Middle Class Community, 1890–1930*. Tuscaloosa: University of Alabama Press, 1999.

Fields, Barbara Jeanne. *Slavery and Freedom: Maryland during the Nineteenth Century.* New Haven: Yale University Press, 1985.

Fink, Gary M., and Merle E. Reed. *Race, Class, and Community in Southern Labor History.* Tuscaloosa: University of Alabama Press, 1994.

Flamming, Douglas. *Bound for Freedom: Black Los Angeles in Jim Crow America.* Berkeley: University of California Press, 2005.

Foner, Philip S. *Organized Labor and the Black Worker, 1619–1973.* New York: Proeger Publishers, 1974.

Foner, Philip S., and Ronald L. Lewis, eds. *The Black Worker from the Founding of the CIO to the AFL-CIO Merger 1936–1955, Vol. II.* Philadelphia: Temple University Press, 1983.

Frey, Sylvia R. *Water from the Rock: Black Resistance in a Revolutionary Age.* Princeton: Princeton University Press, 1991.

Frey, William H. *Diversity Explosion: How New Racial Demographics Are Remaking America.* Washington, DC: Brookings Institution, 2015.

Fullilove, Mindy Thompson. *Root Shock: How Tearing Up City Neighborhoods Hurts America, and What We Can Do about It.* New York: Ballantine, 2004.

Gaines, Kevin. *Uplifting the Race: Black Leadership, Politics, and Culture in the Twentieth Century.* Chapel Hill: University of North Carolina Press, 1996.

Gellman, Erik S. *Death Blow to Jim Crow: The National Negro Congress and the Rise of Militant Civil Rights.* Chapel Hill: University of North Carolina Press, 2012.

George, Paul S. "Colored Town: Miami's Black Community, 1896–1930." *Florida Historical Quarterly* 56, no. 4 (April 1978).

Gilje, Paul A. *Rioting in America.* Bloomington: Indiana University Press, 1996.

Gitlin, Jay, Barbara Berglund, and Adam Arenson, eds. *Frontier Cities: Encounters at the Crossroads of Empire.* Philadelphia: University of Pennsylvania Press, 2013.

Goldfield, David, ed. *Encyclopedia of American Urban History.* Thousand Oaks: Sage Publications, 2007.

Goldin, Claudia. *Urban Slavery in the American South: 1820–1860.* Chicago: University of Chicago Press, 1976.

Goldstein, Brian D. *The Roots of Urban Renaissance: Gentrification and the Struggle over Harlem.* Cambridge, MA: Harvard University Press, 2017.

Gomez, Michael. *Black Crescent: The Experience and Legacy of African Muslims in the Americas.* Cambridge: Cambridge University Press, 2005.

———. *Exchanging Our Country Marks: The Transformation of African Identities in the Colonial and Antebellum South.* Chapel Hill: University of North Carolina Press, 1998.

Goodfriend, Joyce. *Before the Melting Pot: Society and Culture in Colonial New York City, 1664–1730.* Princeton: Princeton University Press, 1992.

Gosnell, Harold F. *Negro Politicians: The Rise of Negro Politics in Chicago.* Chicago: University of Chicago Press, 1967.

Green, Constance M. *The Secret City: A History of Race Relations in the Nation's Capital.* Princeton: Princeton University Press, 1967.

Greene, Lorenzo J. *The Negro in Colonial New England, 1620–1776.* 1942; repr., New York: Atheneum, 1968.

Gregory, James N. *The Southern Diaspora: How the Great Migrations of Black and White Southerners Transformed America.* Chapel Hill: University of North Carolina Press, 2005.

Gudmestad, Robert H. *A Troublesome Commerce: The Transformation of the Interstate Slave Trade.* Baton Rouge: Louisiana State University Press, 2003.

Hall, Charles E. *Negroes in the United States, 1920–1932.* U.S. Bureau of the Census, 1935; repr., New York: Arno Press and the New York Times, 1969.

Hall, Gwendolyn Midlo. *Africans in Colonial Louisiana: The Development of Afro-Creole Culture in the Eighteenth Century.* Baton Rouge: Louisiana State University Press, 1992.

Hanger, Kimberly S. *Bounded Lives, Bounded Places: Free Black Society in Colonial New Orleans, 1769–1803.* Durham: Duke University Press, 1997.

Harris, Leslie M. *In the Shadow of Slavery: African Americans in New York City, 1626–1863.* Chicago: University of Chicago Press, 2003.

Harris, Leslie M., and Daina R. Berry, eds. *Slavery and Freedom in Savannah.* Athens: University of Georgia Press, 2014.

Harris, Leslie M., Clarence Lang, Rhonda Y. Williams, and Joe William Trotter, Jr., eds. *Black Urban History at the Crossroads: Race and Place in the American City.* Pittsburgh: University of Pittsburgh Press, 2024.

Harrold, Stanley. *Subversives: Antislavery Community in Washington, D.C., 1828–1865.* Baton Rouge: Louisiana State University Press, 2003.

Hart, Emma. *Building Charleston: Town and Society in the Eighteenth-Century British Atlantic World.* Charlottesville: University of Virginia Press, 2010.

Harvey, Paul. *Through the Storm, through the Night: A History of African American Christianity.* Lanham, MD: Rowman and Littlefield, 2011.

Hawthorne, Camilla, and Jovan Scott Lewis, eds. *The Black Geographic: Praxis, Resistance, Futurity.* Durham: Duke University Press, 2023.

Helgeson, Jeffrey. *Crucibles of Black Empowerment: Chicago's Neighborhood Politics from the New Deal to Harold Washington.* Chicago: University of Chicago Press, 2014.

Henderson, Alexa B. *Atlanta Life Insurance Company: Guardian of Black Economic Dignity.* Tuscaloosa: University of Alabama Press, 1990.

Herman, Bernard L. *Town House: Architecture and Material Life in the Early American City, 1780–1830.* Chapel Hill: University of North Carolina Press, 2005.

Hickey, Georgina. *Hope and Danger in the New South City: Working-Class Women and Urban Development in Atlanta, 1890–1940.* Athens: University of Georgia Press, 2003.

Hine, Darlene Clark, and Kathleen Thompson. *A Shining Thread of Hope: A History of Black Women in America.* New York: Broadway Books, 1998.

Hinks, Peter P. *To Awaken My Afflicted Brethren: David Walker and the Problem of Antebellum Slave Resistance.* University Park: Pennsylvania State University Press, 1997.

Hinton, Elizabeth. *From the War on Poverty to the War on Crime: The Making of Mass Incarceration in America*. Cambridge, MA: Harvard University Press, 2016.

Hirsch, Arnold. *Making the Second Ghetto: Race and Housing in Chicago, 1940–1960*. Chicago: University of Chicago Press, 1983.

Hirsch, Arnold R., and Joseph Logsdon, eds. *Creole New Orleans: Race and Americanization*. Baton Rouge: Louisiana State University Press, 1992.

Hood, Walter, and Grace Mitchell Tada, eds. *Black Landscapes Matter*. Charlottesville: University of Virginia Press, 2020.

Horton, James O., and Lois E. Horton. *Black Bostonians: Family Life and Community Struggle in the Antebellum North*. New York: Holmes and Meier, 1979.

———. *In Hope of Liberty: Culture, Community, and Protest among Northern Free Blacks, 1700–1860*. New York: Oxford University Press, 1997.

Hunter, Marcus Anthony. *Black Citymakers: How the Philadelphia Negro Changed Urban America*. New York: Oxford University Press, 2013.

Hunter, Marcus A., and Zandria F. Robinson. *Chocolate Cities: The Black Map of American Life*. Berkeley: University of California Press, 2018.

———. "The Sociology of Urban Black America." *Annual Review of Sociology* 42 (2016): 385–405.

Hunter, Tera W. *To 'Joy My Freedom: Southern Black Women's Lives and Labors after the Civil War*. Cambridge, MA: Harvard University Press, 1997.

Ingham, John, and Lynne B. Feldman. *African-American Business Leaders: A Biographical Dictionary*. Westport: Greenwood Publishing Company, 1994.

Johnson, Hannibal B. *Black Wall Street: From Riot to Renaissance in Tulsa's Historic Greenwood District*. Fort Worth: Eakin Press, 1998.

Johnson, Whittington B. *Black Savannah, 1788–1864*. Fayetteville: University of Arkansas Press, 1996.

Jones, Charles E. *The Black Panther Party [Reconsidered]*. Baltimore: Black Classic Press, 1998.

Jones, Jacqueline. *A Dreadful Deceit: The Myth of Race from the Colonial Era to Obama's America*. New York: Basic Books, 2013.

———. *Saving Savannah: The City and the Civil War*. New York: Knopf, 2008.

Jones, William Powell. *The March on Washington: Jobs, Freedom, and the Forgotten History of Civil Rights*. New York: W. W. Norton, 2014.

Joseph, Peniel E., ed. *The Black Power Movement: Rethinking the Civil Rights–Black Power Era*. New York: Routledge, 2006.

———. *Waiting 'til the Midnight Hour: A Narrative History of Black Power in America*. New York: Henry Holt, 2006.

Kantrowitz, Stephen. *More Than Freedom: Fighting for Black Citizenship in a White Republic, 1829–1889*. New York: The Penguin Press, 2012.

Kaplan, Sidney, and Emma Nogrady Kaplan. *The Black Presence in the Era of the American Revolution*. Amherst: University of Massachusetts Press, 1989.

Katzman, David M. *Before the Ghetto: Black Detroit in the Nineteenth Century*. Urbana: University of Illinois Press, 1973.

Kelly, Brian. *Race, Class, and Power in the Alabama Coalfields, 1908–1921.* Urbana: University of Illinois Press, 2001.

Kelman, Ari. *A River and Its City: The Nature of Landscape in New Orleans.* 2003; repr., Berkeley: University of California Press, 2006.

Kimball, Gregg D. *American City, Southern Place: A Cultural History of Antebellum Richmond.* Athens: University of Georgia Press, 2000.

King, Wilma. *The Essence of Liberty: Free Black Women during the Slave Era.* Columbia: University of Missouri Press, 2006.

Kuhn, Clifford M., Harlon E. Joye, and E. B. West. *Living Atlanta: An Oral History of the City, 1914–1948.* Athens: Atlanta Historical Society and University of Georgia Press, 1990.

Kurashige, Scott. *The Shifting Grounds of Race: Politics and Society in Modern America.* Princeton: Princeton University Press, 2010.

Kusmer, Kenneth L. *A Ghetto Takes Shape: Black Cleveland, 1870–1930.* Urbana: University of Illinois Press, 1976.

Lang, Clarence. *Black America in the Shadow of the Sixties: Notes on the Civil Rights Movement, Neoliberalism, and Politics.* Ann Arbor: University of Michigan Press, 2015.

———. *Grassroots at the Gateway: Class Politics and Black Freedom Struggle in St. Louis, 1936–75.* Ann Arbor: University of Michigan Press, 2009.

Lause, Mark A. *Free Labor: The Civil War and the Making of an American Working Class.* Urbana: University of Illinois Press, 2015.

Letwin, Daniel. *The Challenge of Interracial Unionism: Alabama Coal Miners, 1878–1921.* Chapel Hill: University of North Carolina Press, 1998.

Lewis, Ronald. *Black Coal Miners in America: Race, Class, and Community Conflict, 1780–1980.* Lexington: University of Kentucky Press, 1987.

Lincoln, C. Eric, and Lawrence H. Mamiya. *The Black Church in the African American Experience.* Durham: Duke University Press, 1990.

Massey, Douglass, and Nancy Denton. *American Apartheid: Segregation and the Making of the Underclass.* Cambridge, MA: Harvard University Press, 1993.

Masur, Kate. *An Example for All the Land: Emancipation and the Struggle over Equality in Washington, D.C.* Chapel Hill: University of North Carolina Press, 2010.

McDuffie, Erik S. *Sojourning for Freedom: Black Women, American Communism, and the Making of Black Left Feminism.* Durham: Duke University Press, 2011.

McKiven, Henry M., Jr. *Iron and Steel: Class, Race, and Community in Birmingham, Alabama, 1875–1920.* Chapel Hill: University of North Carolina Press, 1995.

Michney, Todd. *Neighborhoods: Black Upward Mobility in Cleveland, 1900–1980.* Chapel Hill: University of North Carolina Press, 2016.

Mixon, Gregory. *The Atlanta Riot: Race, Class, and Violence in a New South City.* Gainesville: University Press of Florida, 2005.

Morgan, Philip D. *Slave Counterpoint: Black Culture in the Eighteenth-Century Chesapeake and Low Country.* Chapel Hill: University of North Carolina Press, 1998.

Moskowitz, Peter. *How to Kill a City: Gentrification, Inequality, and the Fight for the Neighborhood*. New York: Nation Books, 2017.

Muhammad, Khalil Gibran. *The Condemnation of Blackness: Race, Crime, and the Making of Modern Urban America*. Cambridge, MA: Harvard University Press, 2010.

Mumford, Kevin. *Interzones: Black/White Sex Districts in Chicago and New York in the Early Twentieth Century*. New York: Columbia University Press, 1997.

Murch, Donna. *Living for the City: Migration, Education, and the Rise of the Black Panther Party in Oakland, California*. Chapel Hill: University of North Carolina Press, 2010.

Myers, Amrita Chakraborty. *Forging Freedom: Black Women and the Pursuit of Liberty in Antebellum Charleston*. Chapel Hill: University of North Carolina Press, 2011.

Nash, Gary B. *Forging Freedom: The Formation of Philadelphia's Black Community, 1720–1840*. Cambridge, MA: Harvard University Press, 1988.

Nickerson, Michelle, and Darren Dochuk, eds. *Sunbelt Rising: The Politics of Space, Place, and Region*. Philadelphia: University of Pennsylvania Press, 2011.

Nieves, Angel David, and Leslie M. Alexander, eds. *"We Shall Independent Be": African American Place-Making and the Struggle to Claim Space in the United States*. Boulder: University of Colorado Press, 2008.

Olwell, Robert. *Masters, Slaves, and Subjects: South Carolina Low Country, 1740–1790*. Ithaca: Cornell University Press, 1998.

Painter, Nell Irvin. *Sojourner Truth: A Life, a Symbol*. New York: W. W. Norton and Company, 1996.

Pattillo, Mary. *Black on the Block: The Politics of Race and Class in the City*. Chicago: University of Chicago Press, 2007.

Pearson, Edward A. *Designs against Charleston: The Trial Record of the Denmark Vesey Slave Conspiracy of 1822*. Chapel Hill: University of North Carolina Press, 1999.

Pendergrass, Sabrina. *The Black Reverse Migration Unfolds: Black Americans Move to the Urban South*. New York: Oxford University Press, forthcoming.

Peterson, Carla L. *Black Gotham: A Family History of African Americans in Nineteenth-Century New York City*. New Haven: Yale University Press, 2011.

Phillips, Christopher. *Freedom's Port: The African American Community of Baltimore, 1790–1860*. Urbana: University of Illinois Press, 1997.

Phillips, Kimberley L. *AlabamaNorth: African-American Migrants, Community, and Working-Class Activism in Cleveland, 1915–45*. Urbana: University of Illinois Press, 1999.

Piersen, William D. *Black Yankees: The Development of an Afro-American Subculture in Eighteenth-Century New England*. Amherst: University of Massachusetts Press, 1988.

Pinningroth, Dylan C. *The Claims of Kinfolk: African American Property and Community in the Nineteenth-Century South*. Chapel Hill: University of North Carolina Press, 2003.

Powers, Bernard E., Jr. *Black Charlestonians: A Social History, 1822–1885.* Fayette-ville: University of Arkansas Press, 1994.

Pruitt, Bernadette. *The Other Great Migration: The Movement of Rural African Americans to Houston, 1900–1941.* College Station: Texas A&M University Press, 2013.

Rabinowitz, Howard N. *Race Relations in the Urban South, 1865–1890.* Urbana: University of Illinois Press, 1980.

Ransby, Barbara. *Making All Black Lives Matter: Reimagining Freedom in the 21st Century.* Oakland: University of California Press, 2018.

Reed, Christopher Robert. *The Rise of Chicago's Black Metropolis, 1920–1929.* Urbana: University of Illinois Press, 2011.

Reich, Steven A. *A Working People: A History of African American Workers since Emancipation.* Lanham, MD: Rowman and Littlefield, 2013.

Rice, Roger L. "Residential Segregation by Law, 1910–1917." *Journal of Southern History,* 34, no. 2 (May 1968): 179–82.

Richardson, Selden. *Built by Blacks: African American Architecture and Neighbor-hoods in Richmond.* Charleston, SC: History Press, 2007, 2008, and 2011.

Ripley, C. Peter, et al. *Witness for Freedom: African American Voices on Race, Slav-ery, and Emancipation.* Chapel Hill: University of North Carolina Press, 1993.

Ritchie, Jeffrey Kerr. *Freedpeople in the Tobacco South: Virginia, 1860–1900.* Chapel Hill: University of North Carolina Press, 1999.

Rockman, Seth. *Scraping By: Wage Labor, Slavery, and Survival in Early Baltimore.* Baltimore: Johns Hopkins University Press, 2009.

Rothman, Joshua D. *Notorious in the Neighborhood: Sex and Families across the Color Line in Virginia, 1787–1861.* Chapel Hill: University of North Carolina Press, 2003.

Rothschild, Nan A., and Diana deZerega Wall. *The Archaeology of American Cities.* Gainesville: University Press of Florida, 2014.

Rothstein, Richard. *The Color of Law: A Forgotten History of How Our Government Segregated America.* New York: Liveright Publishing, 2017.

Rutkoff, Peter M., and William B. Scott. *Fly Away: The Great African American Cultural Migrations.* Baltimore: Johns Hopkins University Press, 2010.

Schneider, Mark R. *Boston Confronts Jim Crow, 1890–1920.* Boston: Northeastern University Press, 1997.

Schweninger, Loren L. *Black Property Owners in the South, 1790–1915.* Urbana: University of Illinois Press, 1990.

Scott, Rebecca. *Degrees of Freedom: Louisiana and Cuba after Slavery.* Cambridge, MA: Harvard University Press, 2005.

Self, Robert. *American Babylon: Race and the Struggle for Postwar Oakland.* Princ-eton: Princeton University Press, 2003.

Seligman, Amanda I. *Block by Block: Neighborhoods and Public Policy on Chicago's West Side.* Chicago: University of Chicago Press, 2005.

Sidbury, James. *Becoming African in America: Race and Nation in the Early Black Atlantic.* New York: Oxford University Press, 2007.

Sides, Joshua. *L.A. City Limits*. Berkeley: University of California Press, 2003.

Slate, Nico, ed. *Black Power beyond Borders: The Global Dimensions of Black Power*. New York: Palgrave Macmillan, 2012.

SoRelle, James. "The Darker Side of 'Heaven': The Black Community in Houston, Texas, 1917–1945." PhD diss., Kent State University, 1980.

Southern, Eileen. *The Music of Black Americans: A History*. New York: W.W. Norton and Company, 1971.

Spear, Allan H. *Black Chicago: The Making of a Negro Ghetto*. Chicago: University of Chicago Press, 1967.

Spencer, Robyn. *The Revolution Has Come: Black Power, Gender, and the Black Panther Party in Oakland*. Durham: Duke University Press, 2016.

Stack, Carol. *Call to Home: African Americans Reclaim the Rural South*. New York: Basic Books, 1996.

Starobin, Robert S. *Industrial Slavery in the Old South*. New York: Oxford University Press, 1970.

Staudenraus, P.J. *The African Colonization Movement, 1816–1865*. 1961; repr., New York: Octagon Books, 1980.

Sterkx, H.E. *The Free Negro in Ante-Bellum Louisiana*. Rutherford: Fairleigh Dickinson University Press, 1972.

Sterling, Dorothy, ed. *We Are Your Sisters: Black Women in the Nineteenth Century*. New York: Norton and Company, 1984.

Stetson, Erlene, and Linda David. *Glorying in Tribulation: The Lifework of Sojourner Truth*. East Lansing: Michigan State University Press, 1994.

Sugrue, Thomas J. *The Origins of the Urban Crisis: Race and Inequality in Postwar Detroit*. Princeton: Princeton University Press, 1996.

Tadman, Michael. *Speculators and Slaves: Masters, Traders, and Slaves in the Old South*. Madison: University of Wisconsin Press, 1989.

Takagi, Midori. *"Rearing Wolves to Our Own Destruction": Slavery in Richmond, Virginia*. Charlottesville: University Press of Virginia, 1999.

Taylor, Henry Louis, ed. *Race and the City: Work, Community, and Protest in Cincinnati, 1820–1970*. Urbana: University of Illinois Press, 1993.

Taylor, Keeanga-Yamahtta. *Race for Profit: How Banks and the Real Estate Industry Undermined Black Homeownership*. Chapel Hill: University of North Carolina Press, 2019.

Taylor, Quintard. *The Forging of a Black Community: Seattle's Central District from 1870 through the Civil Rights Era*. Seattle: University of Washington Press, 1994.

———. *In Search of the Racial Frontier: African Americans in the American West, 1528–1990*. New York: W.W. Norton, 1998.

Taylor, Ula Y. *The Promise of Patriarchy: Women and the Nation of Islam*. Chapel Hill: University of North Carolina Press, 2017.

Thomas, Richard Walter. *Life for Us Is What We Make It: Building Black Community in Detroit, 1915–1945*. Bloomington: Indiana University Press, 1993.

Thompson, Shirley E. *Exiles at Home: The Struggle to Become American in Creole New Orleans*. Cambridge, MA: Harvard University Press, 2009.

Towers, Frank. *The Urban South and the Coming of the Civil War*. Charlottesville: University of Virginia Press, 2004.

Trotter, Joe William, Jr. *The African American Experience*. Boston: Houghton Mifflin Company, 2001.

———. "African American Fraternal Associations in American History: An Introduction." *Social Science History* 28, no. 3 (Fall 2004): 355–66.

———. *Black Milwaukee: The Making of an Industrial Proletariat, 1915–45*. 1985; repr., Urbana: University of Illinois Press, 2007.

———. *Pittsburgh and the Urban League Movement: A Century of Social Service and Activism*. Lexington: University Press of Kentucky, 2020.

———. *River Jordan: African American Urban Life in the Ohio Valley*. Lexington: University Press of Kentucky, 1998.

———. *Workers on Arrival: Black Labor in the Making of America*. Oakland: University of California Press, 2019.

Trotter, Joe William, and Jared N. Day. *Race and Renaissance: African Americans in Pittsburgh since World War II*. Pittsburgh: University of Pittsburgh Press, 2010.

Tuttle, William, Jr. *Race Riot: Chicago in the Red Hot Summer of 1919*. New York: Atheneum, 1970.

Usner, D. H., Jr. "From African Captivity to American Slavery: The Introduction of Black Laborers to Colonial Louisiana." *Louisiana History* 20 (1979): 38–47.

———. *Indians, Settlers, and Slaves in a Frontier Exchange Economy: The Lower Mississippi Valley before 1783*. Chapel Hill: University of North Carolina Press, 1992.

Wade, Richard C. *Slavery in the Cities: The South, 1820–1860*. New York: Oxford University Press, 1964.

Walker, Clarence E. *A Rock in a Weary Land: The African Methodist Episcopal Church during the Civil War and Reconstruction*. Baton Rouge: Louisiana State University Press, 1982

Walker, Daniel E. *No More, No More: Slavery and Cultural Resistance in Havana and New Orleans*. Minneapolis: University of Minnesota Press, 2004.

Walker, George. *The Afro-American in New York City, 1827–1860*. New York: Garland Publishing, 1993.

Walker, Juliet E. K. *The History of Black Business in America: Capitalism, Race, and Entrepreneurship*. Vol. 1, *To 1865*. 2nd ed. Chapel Hill: University of North Carolina Press, 2009.

Weare, Walter B. *Black Business in the New South: A Social History of the North Carolina Mutual Life Insurance Company*. Urbana: University of Illinois Press, 1973.

Wellington, Paul. *Black Built: History and Architecture in the Black Community*. Edited by Karen Boston. n.p.: Paul Wellington, 2019.

West, E. James. *A House for the Struggle: The Black Press and the Built Environment in Chicago*. Urbana: University of Illinois Press, 2022.

White, Deborah Gray. *Too Heavy a Load: Black Women in Defense of Themselves, 1894–1994*. New York: W. W. Norton, 1999.

White, Shane. *Somewhat More Independent: The End of Slavery in New York City, 1770–1810*. Athens: University of Georgia Press, 1991.

Whitman, T. Stephen. *The Price of Freedom: Slavery and Manumission in Baltimore and Early National Maryland*. Lexington: University Press of Kentucky, 1997.

Wiener, Jonathan M. *Social Origins of the New South: Alabama, 1860–1885*. Baton Rouge: Louisiana State University Press, 1978.

Wiese, Andrew. *Places of Their Own: African American Suburbanization in the Twentieth Century*. Chicago: University of Chicago Press, 2004.

Wilder, Craig Steven. *In the Company of Black Men: The African Influence on African American Culture in New York City*. New York: New York University Press, 2005.

Wilkerson, Isabel. *The Warmth of Other Suns: The Epic Story of America's Great Migration*. New York: Random House, 2010.

Williams, Rhonda Y. *Concrete Demands: The Search for Black Power in the 20th Century*. New York: Routledge, 2015.

Wilson Moore, Shirley Ann. *To Place Our Deeds: The African American Community of Richmond, California, 1910–1963*. Berkeley: University of California Press, 2000.

Winch, Julie. *Philadelphia's Black Elite: Activism, Accommodation, and the Struggle for Autonomy, 1787–1848*. Philadelphia: Temple University Press, 1988.

Wolcott, Victoria. *Remaking Respectability: African American Women in Interwar Detroit*. Chapel Hill: University of North Carolina Press, 2001.

Wright, Gwendolyn L., Lucas Hubbard, and William A. Darity, Jr. *The Pandemic: How Covid Increased Inequality in America*. Durham: Duke University Press, 2022.

Yee, Shirley J. *Black Women Abolitionists: A Study in Activism, 1828–1860*. Knoxville: University of Tennessee Press, 1992.

Zabin, Serena. *Dangerous Economies: Status and Commerce in Imperial New York*. Philadelphia: University of Pennsylvania Press, 2009.

INDEX

Abbott, Robert S., 152, 161, 163
abolition movement: in New York, Boston,
    and Philadelphia during early nine-
    teenth century, 5; in Northeast, 140–41.
    See also emancipation
Abrahams, Emanuel, 14
Abyssinian Baptist Church (NYC), 128
Act of 1836 (Washington, DC), 46
Adam (enslaved person), 125
Adams, Oscar W., 90
Adkins, John N., 115
African Academy, 51
African American Episcopal Church
    (Charleston), 36
African American Methodist churches
    (New Orleans), 19
African Blood Brotherhood (ABB), 116
African Civilization Society, 50
African Friendship Society for Social
    Relief, 50
African Institute, 51
African Masonic Lodge, 50
African Methodist Church (Boston), 138
African Methodist Episcopal (AME)
    church, 19, 22, 32, 37, 48, 49, 55–56, 64;
    in Birmingham, 77; in West, 246n40
African Methodist Episcopal Zion Church
    (AMEZ), 48, 128
African Society for Mutual Relief, 129
African Wesleyan Church, 61
African Wesleyan Society (DC), 48
Afro-Christianity: Afro-Baptist Church,
    77, 80; Great Awakenings and, 18. *See*

also African Methodist Episcopal
    (AME) church; Baptist churches
AIDS, 8
Alabama: Black labor in, 72; constitutional
    convention, 85, 90; as Deep South,
    12*map*; Duke, Charles S., 162; migrants
    to Miami from, 100; suffrage, 88. *See
    also* Birmingham; Deep South
Alexander, Leslie, 2–3
Allen, Richard, 49, 115, 127–28, 234n18
Allequippa Terrace (Pittsburgh), 208
alley housing: in Deep South, 14, 16, 17; in
    New South, 80, 208; in Northeast, 126,
    132; in Upper South, 44, 45, 53
Alpha Suffrage Club, 171
Alston, Christopher Columbus, 169
American Colonization Society (ACS):
    Liberia relocation program, 28, 29–30,
    38, 47; New Orleans chapter, 29; in
    Northeast, 134, 137–38; resistance to, 38,
    54, 55–58, 137–38; Savannah and, 29–30;
    in urban Upper South, 46–47, 54
American Tobacco Company, 71
Ancient Order of Pilgrims, 109
Anderson, Jean, 82
Anderson, Louis B., 152
Andrews, Ethan Allen, 60
Andry plantation, 11
Anglicanism, 18
antebellum era: African American quest
    for urban space, city-building, and
    freedom in Deep South in, 4, 11,
    38; African American responses to

Charleston (SC) *(continued)*
    mixed-race people in, 66; the Neck, 4,
    16; Negro Act of 1749 (Charleston), 23;
    percentage of enslaved people in ante-
    bellum era in, 27; racially diverse neigh-
    borhoods, 15–17; radicalizing of Black
    community in, 32; Reid Street, 17;
    rental properties in, 15–16; during
    Revolutionary War, 31–32; slavery/slave
    trade in, 13; suburbanization of Black
    people, 209; as turn of nineteenth
    century majority/near-majority Black
    city, 4; Vesey revolt of 1822, 19, 29, 31, 32
Charles Town, 13
Chauncey, Herbert, 159
Cherokee Nation, 99
Chestnut, Charles, 153
Chevalier, Albert, 104
Chicago: Black architects and engineers,
    162; Black businesses in, 161–62; Black
    church movement in, 156; Black city-
    building process in, 1–2, 3*map*, 147*map*,
    148, 151–52; Black communities in, 154;
    Black population in, 148; Douglas
    Community, 152; entrepreneurship in,
    160, 161–62; gentrification in, 209;
    Great Migration and, 148; HOPE VI
    and, 208–9; Lincoln Heights, 152–53;
    MOWM, 175–76; North Side commu-
    nities of, 7; preindustrial struggles in,
    177–78; prohibition, 150; riot of 1919,
    149; South Side communities, 7, 149–
    50, 152, 163, 164, 171–72; underground
    establishments, 165; Universal Negro
    Improvement Association (UNIA),
    164; voting in, 171–72; West Side com-
    munities, 7, 151, 164. *See also* Midwest
Chocolate Cities (Hunter and Robinson), 2
Christ Church Parish (Charleston), 14
Christian Benevolent Society, 21
Christian Civic League, 91
churches: banning of Black churches, 19;
    biracial churches, 19, 48, 54, 218n23; in
    Deep South, 19, 33, 77; free people of
    color and, 19; Great Migration and,
    192–93; in Midwest, 156, 164, 173, 174;
    in New South, 77, 78, 78–79, 80–81; in
    Northeast, 127–28; Pentecostal

churches, 109, 156, 194; segregation in,
    19; in Southeast and Southwest, 105–6,
    107–9; in Upper South, 48; in West,
    191–95. *See also* Baptist churches; Black
    church movement; Catholic Church;
    specific churches
Church of God in Christ (COGIC), 109,
    194
Cincinnati: Black businesses in, 163; Black
    city-building in, 3*map*, 147*map*; Black
    city-building process in, 148; Black
    communities in, 7, 154; Black popula-
    tion in, 148; as dual-border city, 7;
    entrepreneurship in, 160, 163; Great
    Migration and, 148; riot of 1944, 149;
    voting in, 171
CIO (Congress of Industrial Organiza-
    tions), 168, 169, 176–77
citizenship rights: African American quest
    for, 94; civil rights, 3, 63; events used to
    press for, 5; exclusions from, 45–46
city-building process. *See* Black city-build-
    ing process
City on the Hill vision, 123–24
Civic Rights Committee (CRC), 172–73
Civil War: African American armed strug-
    gle and, 29, 32–33; African American
    responses to challenges in Northeast
    during, 7; African Americans in urban
    Upper South at onset of, 53–54; Black
    population during antebellum era in,
    47; Blacks in support of Confederate
    war effort, 32–36; community institu-
    tions in Upper South at onset of,
    48–49, 50, 53; education by end of, 51;
    enslaved people in South before, 11;
    housing at onset of, 53; rebuilding of
    industrial cities after, 6; southern Blacks
    in support of Union war effort, 33, 34;
    urban-industrial South after, 5, 68; in
    urban Upper South, 39, 44, 66–67
class inequality: African American
    responses to challenges of, 7, 174; Black
    Freedom movement and, 141–43; hous-
    ing and, 44; postbellum commitment
    to improving, 5–6
Cleveland: Attucks Club, 170; Black busi-
    nesses in, 158–60, 163; Black city-build-

ing process in, 3*map*, 147*map*, 148;
Black communities in, 7, 151, 153, 154;
Black population in, 148, 151, 207, 208;
entrepreneurship in, 158–60, 163; Great
Migration and, 148; as majority-Black
city, 207; Negro Welfare Association
(NWA), 157; voting in, 170; West End,
151. *See also* Midwest
Clinton, Henry, 31
Cochran, Sophia, 17
Coconut Grove, 102
Coffee, T. W., 90
Coker, Daniel, 49, 51, 55, 57, 58, 64, 65,
224n30
Coleman, Feay S., 15
Coleman, James and Lucy, 153
Coles, Edward, 60
colonial era: antebellum centers of urban
Black life during, 124*map*; city-building
process in, 7; development of Black life
in urban South during, 4; free Black
population during, 27; in Lower South,
11; principal urban centers in Deep
South in, 12*map*
colonization movement, 30, 38, 47, 59, 67,
134, 137–38. *See also* American Coloni-
zation Society (ACS); Liberia relocation
program; repatriation; resettlement
color blind inequality, 4
color consciousness, 65
Colored Baptist Church, 19
Colored Board of Trade, 113–14, 117, 118
Colored Citizens League, 90
Colored Cooperative League, 91
Colored Man's Suffrage Association, 88
Colored Methodist Society, 49
Colored Orphans Asylum, 131, 135–36
Colored Sailors Home, 131
Colored Town (Miami), 6, 101, 102, 104,
107–8, 110, 116
commercial businesses: rice and indigo
production, 12–13; in urban Deep
South, 22. *See also* Black businesses;
entrepreneurship
Communist Party (US), 168, 169, 174, 175
Congo Square (New Orleans), 4, 17
Congressional Compromise of 1850, 62,
225n45

Congress of Industrial Organizations
(CIO), 168, 169, 176–77
Conyers, John, Sr., 169
Cordeviolle, Etienne, 14
Cornish, Samuel, 128
Costin, William, 43, 63
COVID-19 pandemic, 8, 211, 212
Covington, Jennie and Benjamin J., 104
Cox, Samuel, 134
Creek Nation, 98, 99
Cuban emigres, 28
Cuffee, Paul, 130
culture: Black cultural networks in North-
east, 126; of Black New Orleans, 17;
conflicting cultures in suburbs, 210–11;
diversity of, 2; of early Lower South
cities, 12
Cumberland Street Methodist Church
(Charleston), 21
Cunningham, Henry, 36
Cunningham, Virginia, 43
Curry, Leonard, 18

Dabney, Wendell P., 159–60, 163
Dailey, Joseph, 43, 53
Danforth, Joshua N., 134
Daniels, John, 75, 227n11
Datcher, Francis, 43
Daughters of Friendship, 81
Daughters of Jerusalem, 50
David, Thomas, 23
Davus, Noah, 51
Decatur Street district (Atlanta), 5
Deep South: African American communities during late antebellum era in, 4, 38;
African American quest for urban
space, city-building, and freedom in
antebellum era in, 11, 38; African Americans from, 99; Black church movement
in, 19–21, 38; Black city-building process
and, 3*map*, 6, 38; Black organizations in,
21, 38; Black population in, 208; Black
slaveholders in, 34, 38; building infrastructure, 18–26, 38; cities as political
lever, 28–38; claiming space, 12–18;
comparisons to Upper South, 39; constraints on emancipation in, 26–27;
emigres from Caribbean in, 27–28;

First Congregational Church (Birmingham), 77, 79
First Ward (Charleston), 16
Fisher, Carl, 98
Fisher, Cecil A., 164
Fitzgerald, Cornelia, 81
Fitzgerald, Pauline and Sallie, 81
Fitzgerald, Richard, 80, 82, 88
Five Points neighborhood (NYC), 127, 132, 134
Flagler, Henry, 98, 101, 102, 107
Fleming, Thomas W., 170–71
food vendors, 22
Ford, Henry, 172, 173
Fort Dallas, 100
Forten, James, 130, 137
Fort McAllister, 36
Fort Pulaski, 33
Fourth Ward (Atlanta), 74
Fourth Ward (Houston), 6, 104, 108, 111
fraternal organizations: building of, 4; in Deep South, 21; in Midwest, 156, 163; in New South, 80; in Northeast, 130–31; in Southeast and Southwest, 109–10; in Upper South, 50, 53–54
Frazier, E. Franklin, 82–83
Free African Society (FAS), 137
free Blacks: AME church in Charleston, 19; in antebellum South, 11; declines in populations of, 27; free Black militia, 26; property ownership by, 14–15; repatriation of, 28, 47
freedom: in Cincinnati, 7; obstacles and fight for free city, 26–28; obtained in urban Upper South, 5; purchasing of, 5; quest for after Civil War in urban-industrial South, 5; struggles in Upper South for, 54–55, 66. See also Black Freedom struggles
Freeman Town (Houston), 6, 101
free Negro immigration restrictions, 26
free Negro militia, 26
free people of color: American Colonization Society and, 28–30, 47, 54, 58–59; in Baltimore, 39, 42–44; benevolent societies of, 21, 50; Black churches and, 19; in British Army during Revolutionary War, 143; Brown Fellowship and,

218n26; business establishments of, 52–53; from Caribbean in urban Deep South, 27–28; in Charleston, 13–14, 17, 27; citizenship rights and, 28, 45; community-based institutions of, 28–29; Confederate war effort and, 32–36; discrimination against, 178–79; disfranchisement of, 29, 45–46, 67, 136, 137; in District of Columbia, 43; education of, 21–22; housing in Northeast of, 234n16; Humane Brotherhood, 218n26; increase in number of, 27; independent resettlement projects of, 144; in Louisiana, 26, 27; marriages, 65; National Convention of the Free People of Color, 59; in New Orleans, 11, 14, 17–18, 25–26, 36–37; in New York City, 132, 133–34; in poorest urban neighborhoods, 132; protecting interests of, 11, 38; public school systems in middle ground and, 63–64; re-enslavement of, 47, 59, 133–34; registration of, 46; repatriation of, 28, 47; resistance network and, 61; restrictions against, 46, 54; revolts/plots to revolt and, 37, 38; in Richmond (VA), 39, 42, 47; in Savannah, 13, 15, 16, 21, 27; as slaveowners, 34–35, 43; Society of Free Dark Men, 37, 218n26; as threat in Deep South, 30; underground and informal businesses serving, 54; in urban Upper South, 5; in Washington, DC, 39, 44, 62–63
French colonization, 13
Frenchtown (Houston), 104
Fresh Water Pond (NYC), 7, 124, 125, 127, 131, 132
Frey, Sylvia, 32
Frey, William H., 207–8
Friendship Baptist Church (Atlanta), 81
Friendship Lodge of Free Masons, 50
Fugitive Slave Act of 1850, 47, 133, 177
Fulton Bag and Cotton company, 70

Gailard, L. S., 83
Gaines, Matt, 114
Garden, Alexander, 18
Garner, Jesse, 52
Garreau, Joel, 209–10

Garrison, William Lloyd, 58, 59, 134
Garvey, Marcus, 166–67
Garvey movement, 118–19, 164, 166–67, 174
Gayarré, Charles-Étienne, 29
Gellman, Erik S., 169
gender: Black Freedom movement and, 141–43; Black urban community challenges and, 174; Nation of Islam and, 175. *See also* women
Genius of Universal Emancipation (periodical), 58
gentrification, 209
Gentry, Thomas R., 106
George, David, 32
George, Paul, 116
Georgia: Black suburbanization in, 210; British occupation of, 32; Constitution Convention, 87; early prohibition of slavery/slave trade in, 13; Equal Rights and Educational Association, 87; Guardianship Law of 1808, 26; prohibition of teaching enslaved people, 218n28; during Revolutionary War, 32; slavery/slave trade in, 13; voting restrictions in, 85. *See also* Atlanta; Savannah
Georgia Real Estate Loan and Trust Company, 84
Gibbons, John Charles, 15
Gibbons, William, 15
Goldstein, Brian, 3
Good Samaritans, 50
Goodson, C. L., 83
Gough, John (Goff/Goffe), 14
gradual manumission legislation: in Northeast, 123, 126, 127; in Upper South, 5; urban Upper South rejection of, 5
Grady, Henry, 72
Graham, George, 87
grassroots activism: Bedford Dwellings project and, 208; of Black city-building process, 147; of Black community-building efforts, 151–52; of demands for redress, 8; of Miami's Black community, 117; of National Negro Congress (NNC), 169; against old planter class, 88; racial injustice and, 4; of underground railroad, 141
Great Awakening, 18

Great Depression: Black voters in Midwest during, 169–70, 171; Miami and, 98; in Midwest, 148, 153–54, 168; in West, 187, 193, 196
Great Lakes, 147*map. See also* Chicago; Cleveland; Detroit; Milwaukee
Great Migration: Black Business Districts and, 197; Black churches and, 192–93; Black community-building process before, 2; Black organizations against racial injustice in urban West during, 202–3; fraternal organizations and, 80, 109; to Houston, 99, 109; Houston and, 99; impact on Midwest cities, 147*map*, 148–52, 155; impact on Midwest entrepreneurship, 158–66; influence of Second Great Migration, 189, 191, 198–99, 204; Midwest Black metropolis expansion during, 146; New Negroes and, 146; in New South, 80; New South political movements and, 68, 94, 95; struggles against Jim Crow in West during, 202; suburbs as next, 209
Green, Constance M., 51
Green, Thomas, 43, 58
Greenback Party, 115
Greener, Jacob, 58
Greenridge, Robert, 160–61
Greenwood District (Tulsa), 6, 101, 102–3, 104, 105–7, 112
Grice, Hezekiah, 58, 59, 224n30
Grigsby, Snow F., 172–73
grog shops, 17, 23, 37, 53
Guardianship Law of 1808 (Georgia), 26
Guiana, 58
Gun, Henrietta, 43
Gurley, O. W., 106

Haiti, 28, 32, 55, 144, 162, 224n30
Haitian Revolution, 27–28, 54, 55
half-freedom system, 132
Hall, Frank A. B., 171
Hall, Prince, 50
Halyard, Wilbur and Ardie, 158
Hamilton, George, 146
Hardin, Walter, 168
Harlem, 3, 82–83, 136, 144, 168, 202
Harper, Robert Goodloe, 47

Harris, Clinton (Joe), 164
Harris, Leslie M., 2, 213n3
Harrold, Stanley, 58, 61, 62
Haynes, March, 33
Hayti (African American community), 5,
74–75, 80, 81, 88
Henderson, Dempsey, 75
Herndon, Alonzo F., 83, 84, 228n31
Hill, Charles, 169
hiring-out system, 54–55
Hirsch, Arnold, 154
HIV, 8
Holloway, Richard, 34
homeowners associations, 148
homeownership. *See* Black property
ownership
Hope, Mary, 43
HOPE VI (federal housing program),
208–9
Hose, Sam, 86
household servants, 24
Housewives League, 168, 173
housing: Black homeownership, 226n7,
227n11; in Midwest, 150; in New South,
72–76; in Northeast, 132; public housing programs, 8, 150, 208–9; racial
discrimination in, 8, 245nn16,20. *See
also* Black property ownership; rental
properties; *specific cities*
Houston: Black businesses in, 103–4, 108;
Black city-building process in, 3*map*, 6;
Black communities in, 101; Black land
and homeownership in, 103, 104; Black
migrants in, 6; Black population in, 103,
104; building institutions in, 108–10;
Fifth Ward, 6, 103, 104; Fourth Ward,
6, 104, 109, 111; Freemantown, 6;
Frenchtown, 104; Great Migration and,
99; industrial capitalism and, 97; oil
industry in, 97; politics in, 114; race
riot, 111; railroad industry in, 97, 103;
rental properties, 104; as Southwest city,
96, 97*map*; Third Ward, 103, 104, 109.
See also Southeast
Houston, Charles Hamilton, 167
Houston, Georgia, 103–4
Houston, Joshua, Jr., 103
Houston Race Riot of 1917, 111

Howard, David T., 83
Howard, Robert, 24, 35
Hudson, Burton and Hattie, 79
Huma incident, 29–30
Humane Brotherhood, 218n26
Hunter, Jane Edna, 157
Hunter, Marcus, 2
Hunter Tract Company, 186

Indian territory, 99–100
indigo production, 12–13, 31
industrial capitalism, 6, 68
industrial era, 7, 68
industrial metropolis. *See* Midwest
infrastructure. *See* building infrastructure
inner-ring suburbs, 209
institutional infrastructure: of African
American communities in Deep South,
4, 18; of African American communities in Upper South, 39; diversity of, 2;
postbellum rebuilding of, 69
institution building: Afro-Baptist Church
and, 77; Black metropolis strengthening
by, 7; in Deep South, 18–26; in West,
191–202. *See also* churches
International Cotton Exposition, 70
intrapreneurs, 24
Israel Bethel Colored Methodist Episcopal
Church, 48

Jackson, A. F., 83
Jackson, Alfred, 91
Jackson, Robert R., 171
Jackson, Seetha, 76
Jacobs, Curtis W., 64
Jacobs bills, 64
Jakes, Henry, 43
James, Clinton, 53
Jasper, John, 48
Jefferson, Thomas, 29, 52
Jenningstown, 74
Jeremiah, Thomas, 37
Jim Crow system: assaults on, 89, 96, 177;
Black metropolis and struggle to end, 8,
165–66, 179; destructive impact of, 1, 6,
171; fight against, 90–91, 94, 110, 175;
New Jim Crow, 8, 179; in New South,
72; in Oklahoma, 115–16; in postbellum

urban South, 68; rise of, 11, 113; social movements against, 4; in Southeast and Southwest, 119. *See also* white supremacist system

Johnson, Callie and Columbus, 74
Johnson, Elijah, 165
Johnson, John "Mushmouth," 165
Johnson, Lewis, 178
Johnson, Whittington, 30, 218n23
Johnsontown, 74
Jones, Absalom, 127, 128
Jones, Jacqueline, 210
Jones, Jehu, 23
Jones family, 129
Josey, J. Anthony, 166

Keckly, Elizabeth, 52–53
Ken, B. "Bus Bus," 125
King, Boston, 31
King, Charles, 43
King, Rhonda, 43
Kirk, Paul, 168
Knights of Pythias, 80, 81, 109, 162
K Street rule, 44
Ku Klux Klan, 117, 210

Lacroix, Francois, 14
Lang, Clarence, 2
Lapsansky, Emma, 126
Latinx communities, 6
Leary, Samuel L., 82
legislation: "Act For the Better Regulating of Negroes" (PA), 132; Act of 1836 (Washington, DC), 46; as attacks on rights of free people of color, 63; ban on Black institutions in Louisiana, 19; ban on slave manumissions in Virginia, 42; Congressional Compromise of 1850, 62; Fugitive Slave Act of 1850, 133; gradual manumission legislation in Upper South, 5; Guardianship Law of 1808 (Georgia), 26; Jacobs bills, 64; limiting manumission in Charleston, 26; Negro Act of 1749 (Charleston), 23; residential segregation and, 44–45; restrictive legislation, 16, 22; Texas election law, 115
Leslie, Charles C., 36
Lewis, A. D., 177

liberation: abolition movement, 140–41; fighting for the vote, 138–40; Herman on, 217n18; liberating the Black city in Northeast, 144–45; resisting colonization movement, 137–38; revolts/plots to revolt, 136–37; rise of Black metropolis and movements for, 7; road to, 5; transnational dimensions of, 143–44; variations in politics of, 5; women, gender, and class dynamics of, 141–43; working for in Upper South, 58. *See also* revolts/plots to revolt
Liberia relocation program, 28, 29–30, 38, 47, 55, 56, 57, 64, 65. *See also* American Colonization Society (ACS)
Liberty City (Miami), 6
Lights, Frederick Lee, 108
Lincoln, Mary Todd, 53
Lincoln Heights (Chicago), 152
Linton, William C., 166
literacy: prohibitions on, 218n28; in urban Deep South, 21; in urban Upper South, 52
Little, Mabel B., 102–3, 107
Little, Pressley, 102–3
Little Ark church (DC), 48
live-in servants, 16
Loendi Club, 156, 157*fig.*
Logan, Robert H., 170
Los Angeles: Black businesses in, 196–98, 247n55; Black city-building in, 3*map*; Black population in, 191, 208; Black property ownership in, 180, 183–84; Central Avenue area, 8, 184, 185, 189, 197, 201
Los Angeles Sunday Forum,
Louisiana: ban on Black institutions in, 19; free Black population increase in, 27; Great Migration and, 99; laws prohibiting manumissions, 27; laws removing rights and privileges of free POC, 26; laws requiring departure of emancipated Blacks, 27; legislation on repatriation, 29; Louisiana Native Guard, 33–34; Louisiana Purchase, 13; slavery/slave trade in, 13. *See also* New Orleans
Louisiana Territory, 13

Lower South: African American urbanization in, 4; Black city-building process in, 10; emancipation in, 5; free Blacks in antebellum era in, 11. *See also* Charleston (SC); Deep South; New Orleans; Savannah

Ludlow, Henry, 134

Lundy, Benjamin, 56, 58, 59

lynchings: antilynching campaigns, 91, 168–69; guarding against, 111, 116; in New South, 84, 86

Lyons, Sandy, 106

Macedonia Baptist Church, 105

Mackey, Sam and Lucy, 101

MacNeal, Arthur C., 166

Magic City. *See* Miami

majority/near-majority Black cities, 2, 4, 10. *See also* Deep South

Malone, Annie Turbo, 160

Mangum and Son Company (Durham), 82

manufacturing sector, 166–67, 12–13

manumission of slaves: gradual manumission legislation and, 42; Jacobs bills, 64; in Northeast, 123, 134; South Carolina laws limiting, 26; in Virginia, 224n34; Virginia ban on, 42. *See also* emancipation

March on Washington Movement (MOWM), 175

Markum, Molly, 81

Markum (Markham), Edian, 75, 81, 226n7, 227n11

Maryland: ACS in, 47; Black suburbanization in, 210, 211; enslaved people's farming in, 42; gradual manumission legislation and, 5; Jacobs bills, 64; slavery/slave trade in, 5; working for liberation in, 58. *See also* Baltimore; Upper South

Maryland Abolition Society, 51

Maryland State Colonization Society, 47

Maschke, Maurice, 170

Masonic Order, 50

mass incarceration, 8

McAllister (San Francisco), 8

McCabe, Edward, 99

McClendon, James J., 167

McDuffie, Aaron, 82

McDuffie, Erik, 175

McGill, George R., 57–58

McHenry, Jackson, 87, 92

McKenny, William, 56

McKinney, Ernest, 169

McKiven, Henry, 72

McPherson, Christopher, 53

Memminger, Christopher, 30

Merrick, John, 82, 88

Methodism: Afro-Baptist Church and, 77; in Charleston, 19, 21; in Durham (NC), 75, 80; in Houston, 108; in Midwest, 155–56; in New South, 77; revival services, 37; slavery and, 18; spread across South of, 18; in urban Upper South, 48, 49, 64–65. *See also* African Methodist Episcopal (AME) church

Metropolitan AME Zion church (Birmingham), 77

Metropolitan Homes company, 83

Mexican laborers, 99

Meyer, Amrita, 37

Miami: Black businesses in, 108; Black city-building process in, 3*map*, 6, 102; Black communities in, 101; Black land and homeownership in, 102, 104; Black migrants in, 6; Black population in, 100; Black residential building in, 102; Brownsville, 6; building institutions in, 107–8; Colored Board of Trade, 113–14, 117, 118; Colored Town, 6, 101, 102, 104, 107–8, 110, 116; interracial ethnicity in, 100; investment capitalists and, 98; Liberty City, 6; Overtown, 6; population growth, 98; as Southeast city, 96, 97*map*; voting issues, 116

Michigan, 172. *See also* Detroit

middle ground. *See* Upper South

Midwest: Black churches in, 174; Black city-building process in, 151–52, 179; Black population in, 207, 208; breaching residential color line in, 152–55; entrepreneurship in, 158–66, 174; establishing the industrial metropolis in, 146–48, 178–79; expanding foothold against barriers in, 148–52; fraternal organizations, 156, 163, 174; Great

Migration and, 147*map*, 208; institution building in, 155–58; March on
Washington Movement (MOWM)
and, 175–76; mobilizing New Freedom
Movement, 166–77; preindustrial
struggles in, 177–78; rise of Black
metropolis in, 7; smaller urban Black
settlements in, 7; social, civic, and
political organizations in, 163, 174;
underground establishments, 164. *See
also* Chicago; Cleveland; Detroit; Great
Migration; Milwaukee; Pittsburgh
military service, 26
Miller, William, 128
Milwaukee: Black businesses in, 158; Black
churches in, 155–56, 164; Black city-
building process in, 3*map*, 147*map*, 148;
Black population in, 148; entrepreneurship in, 158; Great Migration and, 148;
low-rent districts of, 149; NAACP in,
166; North Side, 7; preindustrial struggles in, 177, 178; social welfare programs
in, 156; underground establishments,
164; Universal Negro Improvement
Association (UNIA), 164; Urban
League, 166; voting in, 170, 172, 173–74;
WPA programs, 174. *See also* Midwest
Miner, Charles, 60
Miner, Myrtilla, 51
Minor's Moralist Society, 21, 22
Minton family, 129
Mirault, Lewis (Louis), 28
Mitchell, James, 14
mixed-race people: Confederate war effort
and, 35; emancipation of women and
children of, 5; influence on Deep South
city-building process, 11; manumission
of women and children, 27; marriages
of, 65; slaveholding by, 11; as slaveown-
ers, 34–35; slaveowners and, 15; in urban
Upper South, 39, 65, 65–66
Monumental City. *See* Baltimore
Moore, Aaron M., 88, 92
Moore, Shirley Ann, 185, 199
Morehead School, 82
Moseley, Beauregard, 171
Mother Bethel church (Philadelphia),
49–50, 77, 137, 234n18

Motor City. *See* Detroit
Mott, Robert T., 165
Mount Zion United Methodist Church
(DC), 48
Mt. Vernon Baptist Church (Durham), 80
Mt. Zion Baptist Church (Tulsa), 106
mulattos. *See* mixed-race people
multiracial context: biracial institutions, 19,
218n23; interracial ethnicity in Miami,
100; in urban West, 7. *See also* mixed-
race people
Mumford, Kevin, 239n9
Murphy, Frank, 172, 174
Mutual Life Insurance Company (NC), 82

NAACP (National Association for the
Advancement of Colored People), 90,
163, 166, 167, 173, 176
NACW (National Association of Colored
Women), 163, 195
National Association for the Advancement
of Colored People (NAACP), 90, 163,
166, 167, 173, 176
National Association of Colored Women
(NACW), 163, 195
National Negro Business League, 84
National Negro Congress (NNC), 168–69,
176
National Urban League, 156, 157, 163, 166,
174
Nation of Islam, 174, 175
near-majority Black cities. *See* majority-
Black cities
the Neck (Charleston), 4, 16
Negro Act of 1749 (Charleston), 23
Negro Convention Movement, 59
Negro Republican Convention, 88
Negro Suffrage Leagues, 88
Negro Welfare Association (NWA), 157
neighborhoods. *See* Black neighborhoods
Nella, A. P., 89
Nelson, Richard, 114
Netherland, C. L., 106
New Amsterdam, 123, 124–25, 132. *See also*
New York (city)
New Bethel Baptist Church (Durham), 80
New Deal, 95, 150, 154
New Jim Crow, 8, 179

New Negroes: Black Midwesterners as, 146, 166; new freedom movement mobilization by, 166–77; political consciousness of, 146–47

New Negro Movement: Black city-building process and, 119; Black Tulsans and, 116; emergence of, 115; Harlem and politics of, 145; innovation of, 177

New Orleans: ACS and, 29; Black church movement in, 19; Black city-building in, 3*map*; Black population in, 207; Black property ownership in, 14–15; Black slaveholders in, 34–35, 222n9; Bourbon Street, 14; Central Business District, 14; during Civil War, 33–34; commercial businesses of Black women in, 22; Congo Square, 4, 17; creole architectural style in, 25–26; decline in free Black population, 27; emancipation in, 5; emigres from Caribbean in, 28; entrepreneurship in, 22; French-African population in, 28; fugitive slave network in, 28–29; late antebellum era African American communities in, 4, 17–18; laws removing rights and privileges of free POC, 26; majority and near-majority Black populations in, 11–12, 13; as majority-Black city, 207; mixed-race people in, 66; Rampart Street, 17; rental properties, 16; slave revolt near, 11; as turn of nineteenth century majority/near-majority Black city, 4; Union occupation of, 34

New South: Black city-building process and, 6; Black population in, 208; Black press in, 89–90; Black property ownership in, 72, 76, 228n31; Black urban centers, 6, 68; cities of, 69–72; economy of, 95; forging of cities of, 68; founding new institutions, 77–87; Great Migration and, 68, 94, 95; housing in, 73–77; inequality, 68; internal conflict in, 93–95; Jim Crow system and, 68; new city politics, 87–93; politics in, 87–93; rhetoric about class and race relations, 6. *See also* Atlanta; Birmingham; Durham (NC)

newspapers. *See* Black press

New York (city): abolition of slavery in early nineteenth century, 5; benevolent societies, 131; Black businesses in, 125, 129–30; Black church movement in, 128–29, 234n18; Black city-building process in, 3*map*, 7, 124*map*, 131–36; Black communities in, 125; Black fugitives in, 133–34; Black homeownership, 125; Black population in, 135, 208; Blacks departing South Carolina with British military for, 31–32; British takeover of, 132; Colored Orphans Asylum, 131, 135–36; Colored Sailors Home, 131; Five Points neighborhood, 127, 132, 134; Fresh Water Pond, 7, 124, 125, 127, 131, 132; Fugitive Slave law and, 133–34; Manhattan Dock Ward community, 126; Manumission Society of, 134; mob violence in, 134, 135–36; percentages of Blacks in, 135; rental properties, 125, 135; riots of 1834, 134; Seneca Village, 4, 7, 127, 135; suburbanization of Black people, 209. *See also* Northeast

New York City riots of 1836, 135–36

New York riots of 1834, 134

Nicholas, Elva Moore, 186

Nieves, Angel David, 2–3

Norfolk Nine, 63

North: city-building process in, 7. *See also* Northeast

North Carolina: Mutual Life Insurance Company, 82. *See also* Durham (NC)

Northeast: Black city-building process in, 3*map*, 7, 123, 124*map*; Black property ownership in, 123, 234n16, 245n16; building Black cities in, 123–24, 144–45; building infrastructure in, 128–31; city-building under siege in, 131–36; establishing and shaping build environment in, 124–27; liberating the Black city in, 136–44; major centers of Black urban life in, 124*map*; schools in, 130. *See also* Boston; New York (city); Philadelphia

North Kenwood–Oakland community (Chicago), 209

North Richmond Colored Methodist Episcopal Church (NRCMEC), 194

North Richmond Missionary Baptist
Church (NRMBC), 194
North Side (Chicago), 7
North Side (Milwaukee), 7
North Side settlements (Philadelphia), 7
Northup, Solomon, 60

Oakland (CA), 190, 191, 204–5; Black
businesses in, 195–96
Obama, Barack, 211
Odd Fellows Hall, 84
Odingsells, Anthony, 35–36
Ohio Valley, 7, 147map. See also Cincin-
nati; Cleveland; Pittsburgh
oil industry, 97, 98
Oklahoma, 99, 115–16. See also Tulsa
Oklahoma Territory, 99
oppression. See Black oppression
Order of Odd Fellows, 50, 80, 81, 109
other-side-of-the-tracks places, 2, 101
Overton, Anthony, 161, 167
Overton, Spencer, 212
Overtown (Miami), 6
Oyster Woman (Mary Purvis), 22

Parker, Arthur H., 83
Parrish, Mary Elizabeth, 107
Pattillo, Mary, 208–9
Paul, Thomas, 128
Payne, Daniel Payne, 22
Peachtree Street neighborhood, 5
Pearl (schooner), 61–63
Pearson, William, 88, 89, 92
Peck, Fannie B., 168, 173
Peck, Nathaniel, 58
Peck, William, 173
Pendarvis, James, 34
Pennsylvania, 177. See also Philadelphia;
Pittsburgh
Pennsylvania Abolition Society, 130
Penny Savings and Loan Company, 83
Pentecostal churches, 109, 156, 194
Pettiford, William R., 83, 90–91
Pettis, F. H., 133
Pharoah, R. E., 83
Pharr, Kelsey, 108
Philadelphia: abolition of slavery in early
nineteenth century, 5; Black businesses
in, 125–26, 129, 129–30; Black churches
in, 127–28; Black city-building process
in, 3map, 7, 124map, 127, 129, 134; Black
communities in, 125; Black homeownership, 125–26; Black institutions, 127;
Black population in, 135; Black property
ownership in, 66; Cedar Street Corridor, 126; entrepreneurship in, 129, 130;
fraternal organizations, 130; Free African Society (FAS), 137; free Black
population in, 126; Manumission
Society of, 134; mixed-race people in,
66; mob violence in, 134; Mother Bethel
church in, 49–50, 77; North Side
settlements in, 7; percentages of Blacks
in, 135; rental properties, 125; riots of
1834, 134; schools in, 130; South Side
settlements in, 7; suburbanization of
Black people, 209. See also Northeast
Philadelphia riots of 1834, 134
Philips, Bruce, 16
Phillis Wheatley Association (PWA),
157–58
Pieters, Luycas, 132
Pin Hook neighborhood (Durham), 80
Pittsburgh: benevolent societies, 156; Black
businesses in, 162–63; Black city-build-
ing process in, 3map, 147map, 148;
Black communities in, 7, 151, 153–54,
154; Black population in, 148; CP
recruitment in, 169; entrepreneurship
in, 162–63; Great Migration and, 148;
Hill District, 151; HOPE VI and, 208;
Loendi Club, 156, 157fig.; Urban League
of Pittsburgh (ULP), 158; US Steel
Corporation, 70; voting in, 170. See also
Midwest
Place d'Armes, 17
Planter (Confederate), 33
Plymouth Congregational Church, 167
Pointe DuSable, Jean Baptiste, 162
police relations: community patrols, 204;
in Ferguson, 8; in Houston, 111
politics: Black candidates in Maryland, 45;
Black politics in Midwest, 172; Deep
South cities as political lever, 28–38; of
early Lower South cities, 12; effects of
racial and ethnic diversity on, 6; Great

politics *(continued)*
    Migration and, 95; during late nine-
        teenth century, 88–89, 147; liberation
        politics, 5; Midwestern Black politics,
        147; mobilization of Black community,
        54–55; Negro Republican Party, 88;
        New Negro Movement, 146–47; in
        New South, 87–93; of postbellum urban
        South, 68; racial and gendered, 239n9;
        Radical Republicans, 53, 114; shift in
        Detroit's, 173; in twentieth-century
        Midwest, 147, 172; West cities as politi-
        cal resource, 202–5. *See also* Democratic
        Party; Republican Party
Pope, Elizabeth, 74
Populist Party, 94
postindustrial age: Black metropolis
    in the twenty-first century, 8; color
    blind inequality of, 4; destructive
    impact of, 1; reflections on,
    207–12
postrevolutionary era: African American
    responses to challenges in Northeast
    during, 7; rise of Upper South in, 5. *See
    also* Upper South
Powell, Warren, 86
Powell, William, 131
Powers, Bernard, 16
Pratt, Lewis, 75
Pratt, Walker, 153, 154
Pratt Coal and Coke Company, 69–70
predatory inclusion, 210
preindustrial communities: Black popula-
    tion growth in, 47; in Midwest, 177–78;
    in urban Upper South, 5
Price, Thomas S., 58
Prince Hall Masonic order, 21, 50, 80, 81,
    93, 109, 138
Prohibition, 150
property ownership. *See* Black property
    ownership
Prosser, Gabriel, 54–55
Prosser family, 129
Protection Society of Maryland, 59
Protective Circle of Chicago, 146
Prout, John, 51, 56
Pruitt, Bernadette, 110
public housing projects, 8, 150, 208–9

public markets, 23
Purvis, Mary, 22

Quakers, 51, 58, 61, 125
Quarles, Frank, 81

race riots: Atlanta Race Riot of 1906, 77,
    85–87; Chicago riot of 1919, 149;
    Cincinnati riot of 1944, 149; Detroit
    riot of 1943, 149; Houston Race Riot of
    1917, 111; Philadelphia riots of 1834, 134;
    Race and Draft Riots of 1863, 131; Race
    Riot of 1906, 91; Tulsa Race Riot, 106,
    107, 111–13, 119
racial apartheid, 72, 104–5, 119, 205
racial capitalism, 1, 4
racial discrimination: CIO and, 176–77;
    Executive Order 8802, 176; in housing
    market, 8, 149, 245nn16,20; in Midwest,
    149–50; in New South, 75, 87–93. *See
    also* Jim Crow system
racial inequality: African American
    responses to challenges of, 7; impact of,
    1; in New South, 68; patterns of, 8;
    persistent forms of, 179; racial restric-
    tions, 6
railroad industry, 97, 98, 103
Rainey, Walter C., 170
Randolph, A. Philip, 168, 175–76
Rayfield, Wallace A., 83
Raynor, Daniel and Nellie, 158
Reeves, Henry, 108
Reider, J. H., 160
Reizne, Benjamin, 15
religious infrastructure, 4. *See also* churches
rental properties: in New South, 72, 76; in
    Northeast, 123, 125, 234n16; in South-
    east and Southwest, 104; in urban Deep
    South, 15–16; in urban Upper South,
    43–44; in West, 245n16
reparations, 11, 96, 123, 145, 147, 205; case
    for, 1, 8; demands for, 1, 211–12; in
    Evanston (IL), 8; patterns of inequality
    and, 8; rationale for, 1, 179; reparative
    justice programs, 1; Tulsa Race Riot
    and, 119
repatriation: Black church movement and,
    47; Liberia relocation program, 28,

Second African Baptist Church: in Richmond (VA), 48; in Savannah, 4, 19
segregation: assaults on, 77; in Midwest, 150, 152–55, 175; in military, 175; in New South, 72, 73, 74, 75; residential segregation, 44–45, 75, 104–5, 150, 152–55; in Southeast and Southwest, 100, 104–5; in southern churches, 19; in Upper South, 44–45
self-hiring, 26, 27
Seminole Nation, 100
Seneca Village (NYC), 4, 7, 127, 135
service sector, 12–13
Sewell, John, 116–17
Sharp Street Methodist Church, 49, 57, 64–65
Sheftall, Jackson B., 35–36
Shermantown, 74
Shiloh AME (Atlanta), 78
Shiloh Baptist Church (Birmingham), 78
shotgun-style houses, 75, 102–3, 104, 105
Simmons, LeRoy, 172
Simpson, Leah, 24
Singleton, Tabatha, 15
Sipkins, Thomas, 128
Sixteenth Street Baptist Church (Birmingham), 77, 78–79, 83, 95*fig.*
Sixth Avenue Baptist Church (Birmingham), 78
Slaughter, John L., 164
slaveholders: Black city-building process and, 15; Black slaveholders, 34–35, 220n62; in Houston, 99
slave patrols: in Deep South, 32; in Midwest, 177–78; in Upper South, 45, 46, 59
slavery/slave trade: African American responses to challenges of, 7; assaults on, 59–60; Black-owned businesses and, 24–25; Black slaveholders, 34, 220n62; Congressional Compromise of 1850, 62; destructive impact of, 1; reparations and, 8; social movements against, 4; transatlantic, 1; in urban Deep South, 12, 13, 66; in urban Upper South, 5, 40, 41, 59, 60, 66, 225n45. *See also* antislavery movement; manumission of slaves; reparations

Smalls, Robert and John, 33
Smallwood, Thomas, 55, 60–61
Smith, Abiel, 130
Smith, Harry C., 163
Smith, Hoke, 85–86
Smith, John, 174
Smith, Lucy, 156, 165
Smith, Notible B., 83
Smithfield (AL), 73, 76, 83, 228n29
Smith v. Allwright, 115
Smothers, Henry, 51
Sneed, Glenn Owen and Martha Emma, 103
Snow, Beverly, 46
Snow Riot, 46
Socialist Party, 169–70
social movements: armed struggles and, 31; Harlem and, 3; social justice movements, 4, 7; use of urban spaces and, 4. *See also* Black liberation movements
social welfare: Black organizations addressing, 21, 53–54, 218n26; in Midwest, 156–57
Society of Free Dark Men, 37, 218n26
solidarity, 6–7
SoRelle, James, 114–15
Soulié family, 14
South: Black city-building in, 3*map*; Black population in, 208; comparisons of experiences in urban, 6; development of Black life in, 4; rebuilding of African American communities in, 3. *See also* colonial era; Deep South; New South; Southeast; Southwest; Upper South
South Carolina: Black churches in, 77; Black-owned construction businesses in, 23–24, 25; Blacks departing with British military from, 31–32; during Civil War, 32–33, 35, 36; manumission limitations in, 26. *See also* Charleston (SC)
Southeast: African American quest for self-sufficiency in, 100; benevolent societies in, 109–10; Black city-building process in, 6, 97*map*, 98–99; building institutions in, 105–10; forms of solidarity in urban, 6–7; fraternal organizations in, 109–10; gaining ground in,

97–105; inter- and intra-racial conflict and politics in, 110–19; postbellum Black cities in, 96, 119; racial and ethnic diversity in urban, 6; rental properties, 105; residential segregation in, 104–5. *See also* Houston; Miami

Southern Claims Commission, 35

South Side (Chicago), 7, 149–50, 152, 163, 164, 171–72

South Side settlements (Philadelphia), 7

Southwest: African American quest for self-sufficiency in, 100; benevolent societies in, 109–10; Black city-building process in, 6, 97*map*, 98–99; building institutions in, 105–10; forms of solidarity in urban, 6–7; fraternal organizations in, 109–10; gaining ground in, 97–105; inter- and intra-racial conflict and politics in, 110–19; postbellum Black cities in, 96, 119; racial and ethnic diversity in urban, 6; rental properties, 105; residential segregation in, 104–5. *See also* Tulsa

space-making, 2–3, 11–12

Spanish colonization, 13

Spaulding, Charles C., 82

Standard Oil, 71, 98, 159

Star of the East Association, 50

St. Augustine Catholic Church (DC), 48

St. James Protestant Episcopal Church, 65

St. John AME church (Birmingham), 77

St. Joseph AME Zion Church (Durham), 78, 80, 82

St. Mark Episcopal Church (Birmingham), 77

St. Mark's AME church (Milwaukee), 156

St. Michael's Church (Charleston), 30

Stowe, Harriet Beecher, 51, 63

St. Paul's Methodist Episcopal church (Birmingham), 77

strikes, 33, 70, 71

St. Thomas Episcopal Church (Philadelphia), 128

St. Titus Chapel (Durham), 81

suburbanization of Black people, 8, 209–11

Sudduth, Horace, 160

suffrage, 34, 88, 171, 177

Sugar, Maurice, 173

sugar production, 13, 31

Sullivan, Mary, 43

Summer Hill, 74

Sunday Schools, 21–22

Sutter (San Francisco), 8

Sweet, Henry Ossian, 167

Takagi, Midori, 45

Tanner, Aletha, 51, 52

Tappan, Arthur, 134

Tappes, Shelton, 169

Tarry, Ellen, 76

Taylor, Henry Louis, 7

Taylor, Keeanga-Yamahtta, 210

Taylor, Richard, 43, 53

Taylor, Ula, 175

Texas, 99. *See also* Houston

textile production, 70

Third African Baptist Church (Richmond, VA), 48

Third African Baptist Church (Savannah), 19

Third Ward (Houston), 103, 104, 109

Thomas, Charles William, 87, 92

Thomas, Richard Walter, 154, 172

Thompson, Shirley E., 14

tobacco production, 40, 71

Toomey, Richard, 108

Torrey, Charles T., 60–61, 63

transportation sector, 12–13

Trinidad, 58

Trinity AME Church (Houston), 108, 117

Trinity Baptist Church (Smithfield), 83

Trinity College, 82

triple oppression, 175

Trotter, Joe William, Jr., 2

True Reformers, 80, 83

Trump, Donald J., 211

Tulsa: Black businesses in, 103, 106–7; Black city-building process in, 3*map*, 6; Black communities in, 101; Black land and homeownership in, 102–3, 104; Black population in, 99, 100; Black residential buildings in, 101; building institutions in, 105–7; enslaved people in, 99; Greenwood District, 6, 104, 105–7, 112; oil industry, 98; as Southwest city, 96, 97*map*. *See also* Oklahoma; Southwest

Tulsa Race Riot, 106, 107, 111–13, 119
Turner, Francis M., 43
Turner, Henry McNeil, 91
Turpin, William, 15
Tuttle, Julia, 98
Tyson, Elisha, 58, 59

UAW (United Automobile Workers)
    union, 169, 173
underground railroad, 61, 63
UNIA (Universal Negro Improvement
    Association), 118, 164, 174–75
Union Bethel AME Church (Durham), 78,
    80, 81
United Automobile Workers (UAW)
    union, 169, 173
United Civic League, 172
United Mine Workers of America, 72
Universal Negro Improvement Association
    (UNIA), 118, 164, 174–75
Upper South: Black city-building process
    in, 3map, 6, 39, 66–67; Black communi-
    ties in, 45; Black population during
    antebellum era in, 42, 47; Black popula-
    tion in, 208; Black property ownership
    in, 45, 65, 66; during Civil War, 39;
    comparisons to Deep South, 39; estab-
    lishing homes in, 40–47; freedom
    struggles in, 5, 54–66; institution
    building, 39, 48–54; mixed-race people
    in, 39; postrevolutionary era rise of, 5,
    39; preindustrial communities in, 5;
    public school systems in, 63–64. See also
    Baltimore; Richmond (VA); Washing-
    ton, DC
Urban League of Pittsburgh (ULP), 158
US Steel Corporation, 70, 71, 72

Vann, Robert L., 162–63, 170
Vashon, John B., 177
Vernon AME church, 105
Vesey, Denmark, 32
Vesey revolt of 1822, 19, 29, 31, 32
violence: in Deep South, 36; in Los Ange-
    les, 187; in Miami, 110; in Midwest,
    148–49, 167; mob violence, 6, 36–37, 62,
    94, 116, 117, 123, 144; in New South, 84,
    86–87, 90; in Northeast, 134–37; in

Southeast and Southwest, 110–19; in
    Washington, DC, 46. See also lynch-
    ings; race riots
Virginia: ACS in, 47; ban on slave manu-
    missions in, 42; Black city-building in,
    3map; early free Black property owners
    in, 42; enslaved people's farming in, 42;
    slavery/slave trade in, 5, 31, 62; state
    capital relocation, 41; as Upper South,
    40map; working for liberation in, 58.
    See also Richmond (VA); Upper South
Virginia Colonization Society, 47
Virginia Gazette, 32
voting issues: in Durham (NC), 85; fighting
    for the vote, 138–40; in Midwest, 169–
    70; in New South, 84–85; in Northeast,
    138–40; in Southeast and Southwest,
    115–16. See also disfranchisement;
    politics

Walker, C. J., 160
Walker, David, 138
Walker, Juliet E. K., 24, 53
Walker, T. W., 78, 91
Ward, Shaddie, 110–11
Warner, Nicholas, 52
War of 1812, 26
Washington, Booker T., 84, 86
Washington, DC: ACS in, 46–47, 55;
    antislavery movement in, 59–60, 63;
    Black church movement in, 48; Black
    population in, 208; Black property
    ownership in, 66; Compromise of 1850,
    225n45; enslaved people in, 39; estab-
    lishing homes in, 40–44, 46, 47; insti-
    tution building, 48, 50–52; K Street
    rule, 44; as nation's capital, 41; slave
    markets in, 60; as Upper South city, 5;
    working for liberation in, 58. See also
    District of Columbia; Upper South
Watkins, William, 55, 56, 58, 59, 64
Watson, Anthony, 35
Weaver, Robert C., 153
Webb, Matthew, 14
Webster Street (San Francisco), 8
We Shall Independent Be (Nieves and
    Alexander, eds.), 2–3
Wesley, Carter and Doris, 104

Wesleyan Metropolitan African Methodist Episcopal Zion Church (DC), 48

West: Black city-building process in, 3*map*, 7; Black Freedom Movement and, 7; Black population in, 181*map*; Black property ownership in, 181–91, 245n16; cities as political resource in, 202–5; constructing the Black city in, 180–81, 205; organizing institutions in, 191–202. *See also* Los Angeles; Oakland; San Francisco; Seattle

West, E. James, 163

West End (Boston), 7

West End (Cleveland), 151

Western Addition (San Francisco), 7

Weston, Anthony, 24–25

Weston family, 17

West Side (Chicago), 7, 151, 164

wheat production, 40, 125

Wheat Street Baptist Church, 77, 79

White, Horace, 167

White, Lulu B. and Julius, 104

White, Walter, 176

Whitefield, George, 18

Whitehead, John, 4, 127

white migration, 100

White Rock Baptist Church (Durham), 78, 80, 81

white supremacist system: assaults on, 4, 7; challenging of, 202–5; Ku Klux Klan, 117, 210; in Midwest, 146, 148; in New South, 68, 72, 84–86, 90, 95; post-emancipation, 68; in postindustrial age, 207; in Southeast and Southwest, 113, 116–17, 119; white-majority wards, 4. *See also* Jim Crow system; slavery/slave trade

Whitlow, Henry, 101

Whitted, James, 89

Wiese, Andrew, 209, 211

Will, J. Walter, 159

William, Ruby, 175

Williams, Andrew, 4, 127

Williams, Eugene, 149

Williams, F. A., 197

Williams, Guthrie John, 185

Williams, John, 14, 27, 34

Williams, John and Loula, 106, 112

Williams, Lacey Kirk, 167

Williams, Nathaniel, 34

Williams, Paul, 198

Williams, Peter, Jr., 128, 134, 144

Williams, Peter, Sr., 128

Williams, Rhonda Y., 2

Williams, Ruby, 175

Windham, Thomas C. and Benjamin L., 78*fig.*, 80, 83

Winthrop, John, 123–24

women: Black Freedom movement and, 141–43; Black-owned businesses of, 24; Black suburbanization and, 211; Black women's organizations, 50; clubs and auxiliaries, 81, 109–10; Communist Party (US) and, 175; entrepreneurship of Black women in Deep South, 22; entrepreneurship of Black women in Midwest, 160; entrepreneurship of Black women in Southeast and Southwest, 109–10; entrepreneurship of Black women in Upper South, 43; free women of color property owners, 15, 65; in Fulton Bag and Cotton company, 70; Garvey movement and, 174–75; House-wives League, 168; modern Black feminism, 175; Nation of Islam and, 175; pastorships of, 109, 117; push for equal rights, 37; role in religious/fraternal infrastructure of New South, 81

Woods, Jesse S., 156

Wood's Chapel AME (Atlanta), 78

Woodson, Lewis, 177

Woolfolk, Austin, 40, 41, 59

Wormley, William and James, 43, 46, 52–53

Wright, Edward H., 171

Wright, James, 32

Yamacraw neighborhood (Savannah), 15

Yates, John Henry "Jack," 108

Yesler Terrace neighborhood (Seattle), 184*fig.*

Young, Coleman, 169

Zion Lodge, 50

Zion Lutheran Church, 49

Founded in 1893,
UNIVERSITY OF CALIFORNIA PRESS
publishes bold, progressive books and journals
on topics in the arts, humanities, social sciences,
and natural sciences—with a focus on social
justice issues—that inspire thought and action
among readers worldwide.

The UC PRESS FOUNDATION
raises funds to uphold the press's vital role
as an independent, nonprofit publisher, and
receives philanthropic support from a wide
range of individuals and institutions—and from
committed readers like you. To learn more, visit
ucpress.edu/supportus.